AN APOSTLE OF FREEDOM:
LIFE AND TEACHINGS OF NICOLAS BERDYAEV

An Apostle of Freedom:

Life and Teachings of Nicolas Berdyaev

by

Michel Alexander Vallon

PHILOSOPHICAL LIBRARY   NEW YORK

Printed in the United States of America

ARGUMENT

The scope afforded by this dissertation is threefold. First, a chronological account of Berdyaev's life; second, a systematic presentation of his teachings; and third, a comparative study of his religious philosophy with that of Russian and Western thought on common subject-matters. It should be noted, however, that the range of agreement in each case does not preclude the existence of areas of disagreement elsewhere.

To my companions of the French Underground of the Vercors who fought and died for the cause of Freedom.

TABLE OF CONTENTS

PART II

MAGISTER DIXIT

AN APOSTLE OF FREEDOM:
LIFE AND TEACHINGS OF NICOLAS BERDYAEV

INTRODUCTION

THE RUSSIAN BACKGROUND:
THE BOUNDARY WHERE DIONYSUS AND CHRIST MEET

> Russia is not to be understood by
> intellectual processes.
> You cannot take her measurements
> with a common yardstick.
> She has a form and stature of her
> own:
> You can only believe in Russia.[1]
>
> —Tyutchev.

"No man is an island entire of himself;" wrote the poet John
Donne, "every man is a piece of the continent, a part of the main." [2]
What a man is depends to a large extent on the nature of his social
and geographical environment: he is the product of his country's
soil, mores, and institutions. Indeed, he shares both its failures
and achievements. He is an inherent part of its people; he embodies
its people's particularities. An Abraham Lincoln, for instance, could
hardly be imagined outside the Anglo-Saxon world; likewise a
Mahatma Gandhi would be possible nowhere else but within the
boundaries of India. Accordingly, the truth about a man becomes
more comprehensible when he is viewed in his true context, as a
member of a given generation, society, and time.

"Man is tied to his destiny, and has no power of renouncing it,"
stated Berdyaev in the line of Donne's thought. "It is what I experience of life, in the trials I suffer, and in my search for reality, that

1

my spirit is formed and moulded."[3] Now Berdyaev's destiny and experience, as he himself repeatedly stressed all through his life, were intimately interwoven with the experience and destiny of Russia. He was a son of the Russian land, nurtured by Russian life and culture. He lived, thought, and acted as a Russian. Truly to understand Berdyaev's religious and philosophical teachings one must have some general knowledge of Russia and the Russians—of their history, religion, and national characteristics.

Naturally it would be impossible by way of introduction to this study of Berdyaev's life and thought to provide a complete survey of Russian civilization. Nevertheless an attempt will be made at tracing the outline of one thousand years of the Russian *curriculum vitae*, from its beginning to the twentieth century. A special emphasis will be laid upon the geographical, historical, and religious factors which might account for the Russian psychological constitution.

Following a brief description of the topography and climate of the Russian homeland, there will be given a succinct analysis of the six periods of Russian history as they are acknowledged by the native historians, namely:

1. The Origins of the Russian People
2. The Russia of Kiev
3. The Russia of the Tartar Yoke
4. The Russia of Moscow
5. The Russia of St. Petersburg
6. Soviet Russia

From the Carpathian Mountains and the Baltic Sea to the Plateau of Pamir and the shore of the North Pacific, there stretches an immense, flat sweep of slightly undulating and, to the eye, never ending plain. This is Russia, the largest country in the world. Nearly three times the size of the United States and forty times that of France, it covers about one-sixth of the land surface of the earth. Its population was estimated in 1956 at 200,000,000 inhabitants,[4] of which three quarters are ethnically Russian, and the remainder consists of some one hundred diverse nationalities.[5]

This prodigious expanse of land is conventionally divided by the Ural Mountains into European Russia and Asiatic Russia. Actually

2

the conception of a two-part Russia corresponds to neither historical nor geographical reality. Far from separating the country, the small ridges of the Ural by their topographical and geological features have in fact bound the eastern and western parts of Russia into one continental land mass with definite characteristics of its own.[6] Some modern Russian geographers even call the country Eurasia. It is Eurasia not only because today Russia extends over Asia and Europe alike, but also because its landscape and climate make it one geographical unit distinct both from Europe and Asia.

The most important geographical characteristic of the whole area is its division in two main latitudinal strips very different one from another. Neglecting the two marginal and almost uninhabited bands, that of the tundra along the entire coast-line of the Arctic Ocean, and that of the Aral-Caspian and Mongolian deserts, the Russo-Siberian plain comprises, to the north, a zone of forests, and to the south a zone of steppes. Both zones are richly provided with ramified networks of rivers.

"The forest, the steppe, and the river," wrote the celebrated Russian historian Klyutchevsky, "are the fundamental elements of the Russian hinterland from the point of view of its historical importance." [7] Indeed, the absence of internal boundaries and the multitude of water-ways, diversely directed, determined one of the major factors of Russian history—a continuous eastward colonization.[8] In the process, the abundance of woods engendered a large lumber industry, the fertility of the steppe encouraged agriculture and cattle breeding, and the rivers fostered domestic and foreign trade. These favorable life conditions have for long centuries attracted incessant migrations, promoted rapid settlements, and favored an extraordinary growth of population. Moreover, they have stamped the Russian folkways with enthusiasm and broad sociability which constitute the charm of the *âme slave*.

But on the other hand—and this is a second major factor of Russian history—these huge open spaces have kept Russia in isolation from the rest of the world. Russia's coastlines and land frontiers are inhospitable and often inaccessible. The northern frontier is ice-bound all year round, and navigation is difficult. The southern borders are barred by impassable mountains and wild deserts. The unexplored and almost uncharted Stonovoi Range and the Sea of

3

Okhotsk make the eastern frontier forbidding and forlorn. The rest of the western frontier is formed by the Marshes of Pinsk and the Carpathians, both of which have but few suitable passages between Russia and Western Europe. The only two accessible sea outlets into the wider world are found in the west, and these are the half-closed Baltic and Black Seas the straits of which, however, have always escaped Russian hold. This lack of facile lines of communication with other countries has at all times condemned the Russian people to a geographical and cultural isolation without precedent in the comparative record of living civilizations.

The third major factor of Russian history follows, paradoxically, from this very isolation. While the exit from Eurasia is bristled with difficulties, the access to the Russo-Siberian plain is incredibly easy. For this reason the Russian hinterland has always attracted invaders alike from the west and the east: from the moment they succeeded in seizing control of the ways leading into it, there was no hindrance to arrest their penetration into its open, defenseless territory. Thus in the course of its entire history, Russia has regularly been the victim of hostile intruders who laid waste the country. As a result, the Russian temperament has been pervaded with a sense of the tragedy of life, individual insecurity, and suspicion of foreigners.

Contrary to the evenness of the hinterland, the seasons in Russia are strongly marked. Spring is generally sudden and short. The melting of the snows brings about the overflow of the rivers, the vast solitudes become swiftly covered with green grass, everything is on the move—the forest and the steppe return to life almost overnight. For the peasant, and the lumberman, this is the beginning of an extended period of hard work. Summer is hot, often visited with drought. Autumn lasts a few brief weeks and ends in rain and broken roads. Then follows the interminable, stern winter when no serious work can be done, and all life seems drawing to a standstill.

These extreme variations and abrupt changes in weather are the essential features of Russian climate. Together with the continuous uniformity of the landscape and the infinity of the wide open spaces, they have constantly influenced in a special way the psychology of the Russian people, their character, mentality, and even their beliefs.

The Russian cold affords, indeed, a stimulus for latent energies.

It galvanizes some sound and robust constitutions; but at the same time, it hatches under its white mantle inertia and sloth. On the other hand, the outbursts in summer of the most strenuous work are not sufficiently steady to induce creativity and instill perseverance; the exhausted body and spirit soon relapse into a long period of enforced inactivity leaving behind a permanent want of achievement. Moreover, the boundlessness of shimmering horizons calls forth vague yearnings, the longing for something else, the reverie and prostration which characterize so well the Russian, who is as violent in his anger as a snow flurry, as volatile and imprecise in his affections as moonlit night.

Thus more than in any other country geography and climate have played a decisive role in the formation and evolution of the individual and society alike. They have conditioned the unfolding of Russian history. Apart from his native environment the Russian cannot be understood. But when considered in the perspective of his immense homeland which extends from China to Norway, and from the Arctic Ocean to the Caspian Sea; when approached in the light of his stirring history and particular geography; finally, when viewed against the background of the native intemperate climate, then will become apparent the reasons why the Russian people have not yet achieved an integration of their contradictory elements, of force and weaknesses, of tenacity and laxity, of rudeness and humaneness, of insensibility and goodness, of lawfulness and anarchism, of orderliness and nihilism, of Dionysianism and Christianity. What a signal blessing will descend upon mankind the day Russia will finally attain some degree of inner stability, proportion, and self-control.

1. THE ORIGIN OF THE RUSSIAN PEOPLE

Eurasia has not always been inhabited by the Russians. For a long period of time peoples of all kind were attracted by its immensity and fertile livelihood. Some of them settled to an agricultural life; others continued their nomadic wanderings throughout the boundless steppes. For many centuries B.C. and A.D. the zone of forests in the north, on both sides of the Ural, was inhabited by

5

the Finnish tribes. (They were eventually assimilated as the Russians advanced into their territory, and, in turn, left their own indelible marks on the ethnic type of the Russian—the round face embossed with prominent cheek-bones—Lenin was typical in this regard—is a Finnish legacy.)

As to southern Russia, its first inhabitants of whom we have definite knowledge were the Scythians, an Iranian tribe, and the Greeks. The latter founded prosperous commercial colonies along the Black Sea coast and at the mouths of the rivers Danube, Dnieper, Bug, and Don. There even was formed in the fifth century B.C. a vast Helleno-Scythian empire ruled at one time by Greek sovereigns, and at another time by the Scythians. By the first years of the Christian era, the Scythians had given way to another Iranian people, the Sarmatians, and later to Roxalans and Alans. During the third century A.D. a Germanic tribe, the Goths, descended from Scandinavia and occupied the shores of the Black Sea and the surrounding regions. One century later, they too were forced out by another intruder from Asia, the Huns. Since that time and for almost a thousand years Asia continued to send into Europe its nomadic tribes through a series of uninterrupted invasions. Thus the Avars succeeded the Huns, the Ugrians and the Khazars dislocated the Avars, and in turn were superseded successively by the Petcheniegs, Polovtsies, and Tartars.

About the same time there lived in northwestern Russia, in the basins of the Western Dvina and Niemen rivers, several Baltic and Lithuanian tribes; and still farther to the northwest, in Scandinavia, the Norsemen or Varangians, as they were also called. All these peoples had, in time, advanced upon Eurasia and played an important part in Russian history.

Regarding the Russians proper, they belong to the ethnic group of the Slavs whose first known homeland in Europe was located on the northern versant of the Carpathian Mountains. The Slavs were known alike by the Romans, the Goths, and the Huns under the appellation Vnedes, Sklavens, or Antes.[9] Of the latter one clan was known as *Rukhs-As* (the magnificent Antes), and it was from this name that *Ros* or *Rus* (hence, Russia, Russians) is presumably derived.[10]

As early as the third and the fourth century A.D. a great movement of dispersion of the Slavs began under the pressure of the Teutonic invaders from the north. Some tribes went southward (the Balkan Slavs—Serbs, Slovens, Croats, and Bulgars); others moved westward (the Western Slavs—Czechs, Slovaks, Moravians, and Poles); others yet (the Russians) made their way into the forests and steppes stretching to the east. By the seventh century A.D., the Russians occupied the northern woodland and the river Dnieper to the Lake Oka and the upper river of the same name.

The Slavs were not nomads. They practiced agriculture and commerce from the start. Soon after their arrival in present Russia, they established numerous commercial centers which within a short period became thriving cities. The most important of them are still in existence, namely, Novgorod, Polotsk, Rostov, Smolensk, Kiev, and Tchernigov—all of which are located along water-ways.

The social and political organization of the ancient Russians was known as *obshtchina*, that is, community of property, and of economic and military interests. They possessed nothing of their own, but had everything in common under the general management of a Council of Elders (*vetche*). Thus Russia entered recorded history of the world with a social and political organization akin to her twentieth century communism.

The cities served as warehouses and meeting-places for merchants, both domestic and foreign. The majority of the foreign merchants were Varangians. Together with their Russian colleagues they would organize caravans of goods which were directed to the market places of the Khazars on the Volga and of the Greeks on the Black Sea and Danube. The trading caravans developed the habit of protecting themselves with armed companies which were provided either by the cities themselves (*druzhina*) or by private initiative of "men of courage" (*vitiaz*). In either case the companies were commanded by a chief, usually a Varangian, named *konung* (*könig* in German; *kniaz*, i.e., prince in Russian). Sometimes it happened that the *konungs* forsook their assigned duties and seized a city instead, thus imposing themselves as its undisputed masters. Since the city authority naturally claimed the surrounding areas, there came into being after this fashion a number of actual principalities, more or less extensive and powerful. Such a one was founded in 856 by Riurik, a Varangian adventurer and pirate who, strangely enough, resorted

7

to no stratagems, but was called upon by the inhabitants themselves of a region to come and rule over them. With Novgorod as his capital, Riurik initiated the official beginning of the Russian State.

The historical texture of Russian origins has left an ineffaceable imprint on the subsequent evolution of Russian events and institutions. When the group of Slavonic tribes which entered Eurasia was forced by the northern invaders to abandon their Carpathian homeland and draw their settlement away in the direction of the east, the destiny of the Russian people was sealed for centuries. Henceforth Russia was to remain separated from the rest of the European nations, and have but slight participation in the main current of thought and action of Western Europe. Instead of taking together with other peoples advantage of the great heritage of the Greco-Roman civilization, the Russians were doomed to find before them only savage tribes of Finns and Lithuanians or, worse yet, to confront the vast, unexplored expanses of rivers, steppes, and forests. They were never to know the European Upper Middle Ages, nor the Renaissance, nor the Reformation. Indeed they were never to belong wholly to Europe again.

In their eastward struggle against man-made and natural elements, the Russians of this period developed new traits of character which eventually became a constituent part of the national type—credulity and superstition fostered by the invisible, always possible enemies hidden in the ever-murmuring forest; but also nostalgia induced by the silent call of the steppe. And because the workaday existence in either landscape was strewn with hardships, they acquired a great physical strength and a taste for domineering.

While the forest and the steppe harbored a constant menace, the river, on the contrary, was the real ally of the Russians. It permitted them to undergo long forages into the unknown by easy and sure ways. It prevented them from losing direction and guaranteed a safe return. The proximity of the streams prompted them to cross the overland by portages: thus they discovered fresh land and established new relationships. The river aroused their interest in far-distant countries and stirred them to strive for "openings" to the seas and continents which lay beyond the blue horizons. Moreover, the river stimulated the innate disposition of the Russians for music, singing, and dancing among a congenial company. For this reason the river became the "beloved mother" of the Russian people. It became customary to bestow the appellation "mother" to any waterway of some importance; of all, the most celebrated has been the Volga—Volga-Mother River.

Life in the unfamiliar, often hostile, surroundings bred not only fear, but also inspired trust in the forces of the unseen whence protection against harm was expected. As a result, a profound sense of the divine presence gradually suffused the soul of the ancient Russian. He waxed a metaphysical optimist. Strong in his confidence in an ultimate, spiritual power the Russian became less prone to rationalization and logical ordering of thought: he just accepted life as it was "given" to him, and lived it accordingly. This attitude allowed him to share both the joys and the sorrows of others as his own, since all men, so he intuitively felt, were shaped by the same ineluctable fate. Hence, on the one hand, his inherent capacity of seeing unity underlying diversity, and on the other, a deep-rooted aversion to all closed systems of philosophy and religion. The Russian has experienced the impossibility for the mind to encompass the limitless. Consequently, he cultivated a tendency to contemplation and withdrawal into himself. In time this particularity of his temperament enabled the Russian to accept Christianity without much resistance, and in many instances led him to asceticism and mysticism. Moreover, the Russian inability of systematization has often caused intellectual nihilism, social anarchy, and emotional frenzy which in the long run paved the way for the irruption of Dionysian forces during the Bolshevik Revolution.

2. THE RUSSIA OF KIEV

Riurik's successor, Oleg, also a Scandinavian by birth, shifted his political and military interest to the south. He seized the city of Kiev with its huge adjacent territory and proclaimed himself its ruler. Thus a new state, the Russia of Kiev, came into being, and it might be considered as the foundation of modern Russia. The new state engaged in considerable commercial and cultural relations with its European neighbors of which Byzantium was the most influential. It was through Byzantine channels that the most sig-

9

nificant event or the whole of Russian history before the Bolshevik revolution occurred, namely, the conversion of the Russians to Greek Orthodox Christianity.

Oleg was succeeded by his nephew, Igor. Although a pagan, the new ruler looked upon the Christian infiltration into his domain with toleration. It is certain that in his day at least one church functioned in Kiev.[11] When his wife, Olga, became the dowager regent, she embraced Christianity officially in 950. It was, however, under Vladimir, the grandson of Olga, that the mass conversion of the Kievan state began. A contemporary account of this momentous step relates that Vladimir was visited by representatives of Islam, Judaism, Roman Catholicism, and Greek Christianity, each of whom sought to win him. It is further said that of the various missions the Greeks made the deepest impression on the prince and that he took the decisive step after a delegation commissioned by him to Constantinople reported the splendor of the Greek liturgy in the cathedral of Saint Sophia at which they had assisted. It is interesting to speculate on the possible course of history had Vladimir decided in favor of the Talmud, the Crescent, or the Vatican. Following his conversion in 987, Vladimir undertook actively the christianization of his people. He ordered the destruction of all pagan idols, and summoned the citizens of Kiev to betake themselves to the Dnieper river for mass baptism. He built churches, founded monasteries, and initiated a widespread missionary work. By the end of his rule (1015) there were in Russia two bishoprics and a Metropolitan see in Kiev.[12]

The introduction of Christianity in Russia was much more than a mere change in faith. From the outset Christianity became a state religion; its institutions, laws, and values evolved into a common inheritance of the nation. Its pervading influence profoundly affected all phases of Russian life and altered the Russian character.

To Christianity the Russians were indebted for the beginning of their cultural life. Monks introduced the alphabet and wrote the first literature in the form of translations of Church ritual and canon law. Original sermons, lives of saints, and chronicles were soon composed directly in Russian. The first schools for children were opened and for years only the clergy supplied teachers.[13] Under the influence of Byzantine art an ecclesiastical architecture and painting was developed; church music flourished, and popular religious poetry was created.

Another salutary effect of Christianity upon Russia was exercised in the realm of social and family ethics. Prior to conversion freemen and slaves were the only two social classes in Russia. The latter had no legal status. They were the absolute property of their owners who could with impunity dispose of their lives.[14] The preaching of Christian love and salvation of souls helped to improve the lot of the slaves and check the abuses of their masters. Moreover, the church itself did not indulge in thralldom and set free the slaves it received as donations. The example attracted followers: many a slave-owner on personal initiative emancipated his slaves. Also, the church successfully fought against the family pagan practices such as polygamy, ravishment and sale of women, ejection of wife by husband, the cruel treatment inflicted on women and children, etc.[15] The church paved the way for morals more humane and social relations more just.

The political structure of Russia likewise was greatly moulded by Christianity. The church followed closely the Greek ecclesiastical hierarchy. The state territory was divided into a number of dioceses, which varied in size, but used the same methods of administration. These again were subdivided into deaneries, and deaneries into parishes. The latter were dependent on their respective deans; these in turn were supervised by bishops; and the bishops for their part owed strict allegiance to the Metropolitan in Kiev. The government was encouraged by the clergy to imitate in matters of administration the church organization. Furthermore, the church aided Russian princes in realizing the dignity and responsibility pertaining to their office, and summoned the unruly subjects to show respect for, and obedience to, political authority. The church brought in the concept of the divine right of kings.[16] Finally, the clergy was instrumental in establishing civil and religious judiciary systems based on the laws imported from Byzantium. Thus the influence of the church extended over the whole range of social organization from the public activity of the ruling princes to the privacy of family life. And when in the process of time contentions for power and foreign occupations were plunging the nation into division and

11

trouble, the church alone succeeded in maintaining the continuity of inward unity and order of the Russian people.[17]

It was upon the Russian soul, however, that Orthodox Christianity imposed its ascendancy. The new faith gradually polarized and highly colored Russian patterns of thought and behavior. Truly, being a Russian became synonymous with professing Orthodox faith. Therefore a short exposition of Orthodox religious beliefs and outlook on life seems particularly pertinent at this point.

The faith of the Orthodox Church is summarized in the Nicene creed; it recognizes no other creeds, and it does not use any articles of faith.[18] The Nicene creed, however, while embodying essential dogmas necessary to faith, enunciates no theological doctrine obligatory for all. It gives rather expression to two great mysteries upon which rests the whole edifice of Christianity: the mystery of the Holy Trinity and the mystery of the Incarnation. But their exploration and interpretation remains forever open to further development. Orthodoxy, in these matters, applies Augustine's principle: *"In necessariis unitas, in dubiis libertas, in omnibus caritas."* [19]

It follows that the Church is not an institution founded on rigid dogmatic definitions. Its ecclesiastical hierarchy does not encroach on the believer's personal freedom. The Church for the orthodox Christian "is a new life with Christ and in Christ, guided by the Holy Spirit;" [20] or, in different words, "it is the power which attunes men to God's will, and makes them capable of working together with their Creator." [21] The visible Church is but the external manifestation of the real Church which is a spiritual certainty and a quality of life, and as such hidden in the consciousness of the faithful. "Thus the Church in its very being is an object of faith; it is known by faith;" and not only as a special, inward experience, "but also quantitatively: as an all-embracing unity, as a life unique and integral, as universality, after the pattern of the oneness of the three Persons of the Holy Trinity." The divine life of the Church comprehends the whole of mankind: "The life of each man enlarges itself infinitely into the life of others, the *'communio sanctorum,'* and each man *is* humanity." This strong sense of corporateness is extended by Orthodoxy alike to the living, the departed, and even the generations yet to be born. "In God and His Church, there is no difference between living and dead, and all are one in the love

12

of the Father." [22] But there is more to it: "The Church universal is not limited to humanity alone;" it also embraces "the whole of creation" which, indeed, "shares the destiny of man." The destiny of nature is connected to that of man; corrupted because of man, she yearns with him after healing. For, in the words of Paul, "All creation groaneth and travaileth together" (Romans 8:22-3). Both man and nature await being "transfigured in a 'new creation.' . . . In the Church man thus becomes a universal being; his life in God unites him to the life of all creation by the bonds of cosmic love." [23]

Consequently, salvation is not viewed by Orthodoxy in terms of the individual soul forgiven and accepted by its Maker; rather,

> it is visualised . . . as a gradual process of transfiguration of the whole cosmos, culminating in *theosis,* or the deification in Christ of the members of the Church as representatives and spokesmen of the entire creation. The East is clear that salvation for an individual means to become part of the redeemed community, and to share the gifts of the Holy Ghost given to the whole body. Man is saved, not from the world but with the world, because he is its guardian and master; he is saved, not apart from others, but with the rest of the Christian family, as one of its members.[24]

The concentration of piety on the Holy Trinity is so intense that, "in the liturgical life of Orthodoxy, . . . the name of the Holy Trinity predominates over the name of Jesus, which shows that the knowledge of Christ is inseparably connected with that of the Holy Trinity." [25] The world was created by the Holy Trinity, the One-in-Three. "The Father creates the world. . . . . The Son . . . created, in announcing it, the ideal existence of the world. But the Holy Spirit also furnishes, vivifies, gives to the world reality." [26] Man is the end of the Trinitarian creation and its master. Created after the image of God, man, in his personal consciousness "possesses the image of the union of the three hypostases: he is conscious of himself not only as *I*, but as *you* and as *we*." [27] In man the divine Trinity is achieved, manifested in creation.[28]

Original sin brought about general corruption of human nature. Man turned away from the life in God. His very freedom became an act of self-assertion, spiritual pride, and rebelliousness. Neverthe-

13

less all the disastrous consequences of the fall of man could not completely blot out God's image and freedom in man. For man, created in the divine image, was made to be like God. For this reason, and because of His love and goodness, God took upon Himself all humanity and became incarnate in the man Jesus.

The mystery of Incarnation is understood by Orthodoxy not in terms of a Christological doctrine, but rather as life itself—a new life in Christ, a "positive relation between God, who created man in His image, and man, lifted by the incarnation, to the possibility of deification." [29] This positive organic relation between God and man is expressed in the idea of the God-Man or Godmanhood. Jesus was the perfect embodiment of Godmanhood. For in him the two natures—divine and human—were united without division or confusion thus making him true God and true man, who came into the world for the salvation, i.e., deification of mankind.

The work of deification is the gift of grace. No human merit is ever deserving of it. But, on the other hand, it cannot be attained without a personal endeavor, for "deification is not a physical or magical act of *man*, but an interior action, a work of grace *in* man. This work is accomplished in man with the cooperation of human liberty and not without his will." [30] This idea is commensurable to neither the doctrine of salvation by faith alone nor the Catholic doctrine of merit. In a more profound sense, salvation is not an instantaneous act, although it has already been accomplished—or rather has been made possible—for us by God in Christ; it is a constant process of inner transformation and sanctification. It must be freely initiated and nurtured by each particular man; it must be active; it must include good works. "God realizes the objective aspect and lays the foundation for man's salvation, but man must realize the subjective side and choose salvation." [31] In this sense man is called upon to participate personally in his own salvation, and thus have a share in the common salvation both of mankind and of the whole creation, because he is no "island entire of himself," but "a part of the main." [32] He partakes of the life of the cosmos and, in turn, the cosmos lives in him and is sanctified through him.

Because of the special emphasis upon faith as life and not as doctrine, Orthodoxy has placed the cult in the very heart of religious experience. The Orthodox liturgy combines in the most harmonious way the element of beauty with prayer and edification. It is warm, elaborate, and pervaded with a spirit of genuine corporateness. The interior of Orthodox churches is covered with mural decorations and ornamented with ikons. The clergy, constantly in motion, is attired with splendid vestments and visibly follows the old-established, artistic service-patterns received by Russia from Byzantium. Together with a great number of colorful candle-lights, screens of incense smoke, continuous and deeply moving choral chanting, and the physical closeness of worshipers standing in prayerful attitudes (there are no pews in Orthodox churches)—all this is capable of evoking an atmosphere of spiritual and emotional exaltation which is unique in Christianity.

The whole service "is not only the commemoration, in artistic forms, of evangelical or other events concerning the Church. It is also the actualization of these facts, their re-enactment on the earth." [33] It is Life Divine present in the temple. The richness and complexity of the cult are only vehicles for deeper verities. "Beneath this heavy covering of gold there flows the living water, a faith sincere and simple, the knowledge of Christ, the light of the Resurrection." [34] And this faith precedes and prepares "the new creature, the transfiguration of all creation, 'the new earth and the new heaven.'" [35]

To the spiritual seeds implanted by Orthodoxy along the banks of the Dnieper the Russian culture was to owe its highest achievements, nay, its very substance. But, on the other hand, the Church bore the leaven of much evil that proved fatal to the future development of Russia. The reason for this lay in the clergy's endeavor from the outset to introduce in the Kievan state not only the Gospel, but also a new political ideal, that of Byzantium—the idea of power considered as a divine right and the principle of indispensable co-operation between the spiritual and the temporal. Thus the grounds were made ready for the subsequent rise of tsarist absolutism and ecclesiastical caesarism. The great schism (*Roskol*) of the seventeenth century which divided the Church into *Pravoslavnye* (True Believers) and *Starovery* (Old Believers) was one of the direct consequences of the Church hegemony. The other could be easily discerned in the revolutionary movements of the nineteenth and

15

twentieth centuries, and in the anti-religious rage of the Bolshevik Revolution.[36] For the time being, however, and until Peter the Great, the Orthodox Church remained the pivot and the stronghold of Russian life.

3. THE RUSSIA OF THE TARTAR YOKE (1240-1480)

In the thirteenth century the Mongolian invasion brought the existence of the state of Kiev to a close. Following a triumphant campaign against the Chinese (1215), Genghis Khan ("the heavenly emperor") turned his hosts to the west. He overran the Caucasus Mountains, ravaged the steppes of the Don River and the Black Sea, and crushed the Russian forces at the battle of Kalka in 1223. Another Tartar expedition headed by Batu, the grandson of Genghis Khan (who died suddenly in 1227) swept across the Volga into northwestern Russia capturing the old cities of Suzdal, Vladimir, and Moscow. In 1240, Kiev was seized and destroyed. Thus nearly all of Russia became tributary to the great empire of the Golden Horde which at that time extended from the Pacific Ocean to the Adriatic Sea.

The immediate and most disastrous effect of the Tartar yoke was Russia's seclusion both from the West and from Byzantium for more than two centuries. As a result, cultural and commercial ties with European countries were severed altogether. The spiritual life was deprived of all contacts with the Orthodox world outside Russian boundaries. The normal, organic course of growth of the Russian people was arrested. At the end of Mongol domination, Russia was to find itself culturally and politically lagging three hundred years behind Western civilization. It is still similarly retarded in spite (or rather because) of communist revolution.

During this period a process of intense asiatization, both psychological and administrative, gradually took place. Mixed marriages and customs evinced new traits in the Russian national type and folkways. A Russo-Mongolian aristocracy came into being which naturally had no taste for the European patterns of thought and life. The Mongolian concept of the authority of the ruler was of

16

a special consequence for the subsequent unfolding of Russian history. It was akin to the one already contained in germ in the Byzantine Church of the Kievan state. The power of the Khan was absolute. His subjects owed him an unqualified submission. Land and people belonged to him unreservedly. (This view and practice of political authority were adopted by the Grand Dukes of Moscow. When the Tartar yoke was eventually broken, they openly regarded themselves as absolute masters and proprietors of their realm.[37] In time the noun *samoderjavye* [autocracy] came to express the very essence of the Russian monarchy.)

The severity of the Mongolian rule and the prolonged suffering imposed upon the Russian people led to a general weakening of the native character. A once independent, freedom-loving citizen of democratic Kiev, the Russian now turned submissive and resigned. His moral sense shrank.[38] He became indolent and fatalistic. However, since there is no evil but some good should come out of it, the Tartar yoke brought about some beneficent results also. It greatly strengthened the Church and made it the focus of the Russian people's affections and loyalty.[39] As a rule, the Mongolian attitude toward the Church was tolerant and friendly. The Khans acted as patrons of Orthodoxy.[40] They granted full recognition to the civil rights of the clergy and exempted them from certain kinds of taxation.[41] In fact, the Church remained the only institution untouched by Mongolian interference. Consequently, it came to be looked upon not only as a source of religious solace in the uncertainties and dangers of the times, but also as the preserver of the national consciousness and unity. "Orthodox," "Christian," and "Russian" were considered as interchangeable, and Russia became "Holy Russia." [42]

Moreover, many sensitive souls answering to a secret call withdrew into forests and devoted themselves to a spiritual and ascetic life. Their example intensified the yearning for inner purity and piety. Religious life deepened across the breadth of Russia. Mysticism gained in scope and meaning. Monasteries multiplied and their influence spread widely. They became centers of spiritual edification, scholarship, and artistic creativity.[43] Around many of these monasteries settlements were established. Laymen were attracted by the sanctity of the place and wished to put themselves under its protection and advice. Through the monasteries, the missionary work was forwarded and the Russian language and culture progressively extended over new areas.[44]

4. THE RUSSIA OF MOSCOW (1480-1700)

During the second half of the thirteenth century and the beginning of the fourteenth there sprang into life, in the northeast of Russia, a principality which hitherto led an existence obscure and unobserved—the principality of Moscow. The name of Moscow is mentioned for the first time in the texts of 1147.[45] Its favorable location on the river Moskva (hence the name) which connects the city with the great network of the Volga basin, as well as a special solicitude on the part of both the Mongolian khanate and the Orthodox clergy contributed to the rapid growth of the future capital of Russia. The skillful policy of the Moscow princes accomplished the rest. They offered to collect taxes and tribute-money for the Khan, and were accepted in this capacity. Gradually they gained the fullest confidence of the Tartar government. And when, in the middle of the fourteenth century, internal dissensions began to disrupt the Golden Horde, Moscow grew stronger and finally revolted. In 1380, Dimitri, Grand Duke of Moscow, defeated a Tartar army at the battle of Kulikov Meadow on the upper reaches of the river Don. The victory achieved a tremendous psychological effect despite the fact that Mongolian domination was to continue for one whole century.

Henceforth the Moscow principality underwent a progressive expansion which, except for brief intervals, has not yet been checked —at least as far as the present-day Kremlin's intentions are concerned. The emergence of Moscow into the lime-light of Russian history secured the ultimate triumph of monarchical principles to the detriment of the democratic ideas and standard of life which were prevalent in the period of Kiev.

In the second half of the fifteenth century the Grand Duke of Moscow, Ivan III, enlarged his dominion over almost all the hitherto independent cities and principalities of northeastern Russia. He also turned his interest westward and succeeded in annexing large areas belonging to Lithuania. Moscow developed into a strong military and political power. It also became the official seat of the Metropolitan. The Russians began to regard the great city as the champion of national unity, and its Dukes as "the Gatherers of the Russian Land." [46] Eventually, Ivan III took advantage of the wrangles between the Tartar rulers and in 1480 broke the last threads of Mongolian subjection.

Prior to this, however, a political and religious event of far-reaching consequences had contributed to the rise of Moscow's power and prestige. When in 1453 Constantinople passed into the hands of the Turks, Moscow felt itself the successor of the Byzantine Empire and the chief center of Orthodoxy. Following his marriage to Sophia Paleologus, the niece of the last Emperor of Byzantium, Ivan III claimed to be the heir of the fallen Orthodox Byzantine Empire. He appropriated the Byzantine double-headed eagle for his coat of arms and started imitating the customs and practices of the former Court in Constantinople. He did not, however, assert his rights to the succession of the Christian rulers of Byzantium to the extent of assuming the imperial title. This step was taken by his grandson, Ivan IV (Ivan the Terrible, because of his brutal cruelties). At his coronation in 1547, he entitled himself Tsar, that is, Caesar—the heir of the Emperors of Rome and Constantinople. Some years later the Metropolitan of Moscow was raised to the rank of Patriarchate—an ecclesiastical dignity equal to that of the Byzantine Patriarchate. Thus originated in Russia the institution of tsardom.[47]

The significance of this political change found its expression in the conception of "Moscow, the third Rome." The idea was propounded in the sixteenth century by the monk Philotheous. The Russian Tsar, he wrote, "is the only Christian Tsar in the whole world. . . . In the God-bearing city of Moscow the Church . . . shines with light side by side with Rome and Constantinople."[48] The reason for this fictitious notion might be traced back to the battle of Kulikov Meadov. After almost one century and a half of indescribable suffering and humiliation, a Russian prince succeeded in achieving a smashing victory over the Mongolians. As a result, the

Russians awakened once more to the consciousness of their national unity and power. The subsequent political and military successes only confirmed them in the belief that they were a people chosen by God—"a new Jerusalem"—called upon to play a great role both among other Orthodox nations and in the world at large. The spiritual and political leadership, so they thought, which once was connected with ancient Rome, and later on passed over to Constantinople, the "second Rome," belonged now, after the fall of Byzantium, to Moscow, the "third Rome." "Make sure, O pious Tsar," wrote the monk Philotheous, "that all the Christian kingdoms be united under your power; two Romes are fallen; but the third shall endure forever; a fourth there cannot be." [49]

The idea of the "third Rome" became an "article of national faith and revealed to the Moskovites the universal significance of their national existence." [50] It also symbolized the ideal of national politics all through Russian history right down to its communist period. "It was taken as expressed in the Tsardom of Moscow and then in the Empire and in the end as the Third International. The Tsar was regarded as the viceregent of God upon earth." To him belonged "not only care for the interests of the State but also care for the salvation of souls." [51] Stalin's designation as "Father of the Peoples," was but the logical sequence to Ivan's "Tsar of Orthodoxy."

The seventeenth century marked the beginning of the so-called "Times of Trouble," during which the power of Moscow suffered a temporary setback. Contentions for the throne plunged the tsardom into social and political confusion. The Poles and the Swedes availed themselves of the situation and invaded the Russian land. Governments followed one after another. So did Tsars. Eventually the election in 1613 of Michael Romanov to the supreme office restored order and unity. With him began the reign of the Romanov dynasty which lasted until the February Revolution in 1917.

Relationships with the European countries which had been interrupted by the Tartar yoke were resumed. The Western influence rapidly extended in the urban centers. Foreign settlers, chiefly Germans, moved to Moscow in increasing numbers. At the end of the century the stage was set for the reforms promulgated by the most celebrated of the Romanovs, Peter the Great.

5. THE RUSSIA OF SAINT PETERSBURG (1701-1917)

The reign of Peter the Great opened a pivotal period in the history of Russia. The tsardom of Moscow broke away from Tartar tradition and entered the European sphere of influence. To indicate the new political and social orientation, and also to avoid the prevailing Asiatic tone of Moscow, Peter built for himself upon the swamp of the Neva River a new capital, "the open window to Europe," called after the name of its founder, the city of Peter, or Petersburg, later known as Saint Petersburg.

Peter's reforms effected not only a convulsion of political and social institutions, as was the case with the French and Bolshevik Revolutions, but produced a radical transformation of the Russian people. The Emperor imposed the abandon and repudiation of all ancestral traditions, and the acceptance of new ways of life ranging from religious beliefs and folkways to Western dress and shaving of beards. The Church and State administrations, the army, the judiciary, education, and social classes, were reorganized after European patterns. The industry and the trade of the country developed; schools for technical and scientific training were established.

Peter's most distinguished successors, Elizabeth (1741-1761) and Catherine the Great (1762-1796) carried on his work. The two Empresses directed their efforts toward founding universities and colleges, establishing libraries, building observatories, encouraging scientific societies, and devising a widespread system of elementary public education. The Russian mind, disengaged from narrow religious entanglements, gradually came into its own. The eighteenth century saw the rise of the first Russian scholar, Michael Lomonosov (1711-1765). He was a pioneer of Russian science and the first reformer of the Russian written language which he brought closer to the spoken language and purified of the influences of the Church Slavonic tongue. Moreover, he was a remarkable poet.

It was not before the nineteenth century, however, that the Petrine legacy produced its most vigorous and pathetic effect. After centuries of intellectual stagnation, there occurred in Russia a sudden, all but miraculous outburst of original creativity. The most prominent names amidst the great galaxy of splendid writers of that time are those of the poets Pushkin, Lermontov, Nekrasov, and

Tiutchev; of the critics Belinsky, Herzen, and Tchernyshevsky; of the novelists Gogol, Turgenyev, Dostoyevsky, and Tolstoy; of the play-writers Gryboedov, Ostrovsky, and Tchekov; of the philosophers Tchaadaev, Khomyakov, Kireyevsky, Mikhailovsky, and Solovyov. Special consideration should be given to three thinkers whose outlook exercised a deep and lasting influence on Nicolas Berdyaev. They are Khomyakov, Dostoyevsky, and Solovyov.

Aleksei Stepanovitch Khomyakov (1804-1860) was an extraordinarily well-educated, brilliant person, with many-sided gifts and interests. He studied theology, philosophy, history, literature, and could speak and write French, English, and German like a native.[52] He knew Latin, Greek and also Sanskrit so well that he even compiled a dictionary of Russian words akin to Sanskrit.[53] He was a self-taught doctor, a successful farmer, a capable engineer, and a specialist in horses and dogs; he invented a long range rifle and some sort of steam engine which he patented and exhibited in London.[54] He wrote poetry, tragedy, and philosophy of history. Above all he was the first original theologian of Russian Orthodoxy and an authentic spokesman of the Russian Church. "There was only one source of inspiration in his whole life, and that was his belief in the unique truth of Christianity. The greatest treasure for him was his membership in the Church."[55] He left no systematic treatise of his thought, only numerous articles and letters on political and religious-philosophical subjects; and also three volumes of an unfinished work called *Thoughts on Universal History*. Nevertheless, Khomyakov's philosophy constitutes a coherent whole, and might be described in the following outline.

Its basic point of departure is the doctrine of man. Khomyakov envisaged man as a finite being endowed with two inalienable attributes, reason and freedom. Reason discerns right from wrong; freedom determines the choice between the two; the result is a specific line of action. Thus knowledge and action are inseparable. To know is to act according to reason in the light of freedom. Knowledge, therefore, is not conceptual but existential. The living reality of both temporal and spiritual realms can be known only in so far as man actively participates in them and, in turn, is interpenetrated by them.

Khomyakov decisively repudiates individualism. Man cannot be segregated either from the cosmos or from mankind of which he is an organic part. A man is a human being only in relation to other men and the world as a whole. Indeed, all men are bound by an organic unity. "The isolated individual," Khomyakov wrote, "is marked by complete impotence and irreconcilable discord."[56] Isolation and self-sufficiency stand in opposition to the laws of creation. "Whosoever separates himself from people creates a desert around him. . . . Only in living communion with others can a man break out of the deadly loneliness of egotistic existence and gain the standing of a living organ in the great organism."[57] Outside the human fellowship no moral and intellectual growth is possible. "A man who wants to develop his latent creative forces must first sacrifice the selfish side of his personality and thus penetrate into the mystery of common life. He must be united with it by the ties of a living organic fellowship."[58] And again, "a single intellect segregated from living contact with others is barren; only from communion with life can it increase in power and creativeness."[59]

Inner and social integration, according to Khomyakov, cannot be achieved by man alone without help from above. The whole creation is in a state of sin. Egocentric existence, not cooperation, is the predominant factor of the human condition. Salvation is possible, however, because God came down to the creature and entered the historical process in Jesus Christ as the God-man. God in Christ brings man to the full realization of his sin, but at the same time He encompasses the sinful creature with a fatherly love. "He unites Himself to every creature that does not reject Him."[60]

This knowledge—"the living knowledge"—can be attained only by faith. Now faith, according to Khomyakov, stands in opposition not to reason, but to rational cognition. Faith itself is a function of reason. "What I call faith," he wrote, "is that faculty of reason which perceives actual (real) data and turns them over to the analysis and consciousness of rationality."[61] Faith in this sense is the ability of grasping the reality of things directly, beyond the symbols which represent or hide it. Like Bergson's intuition, Khomyakov's faith apprehends things from within, in their ultimate simplicity and absoluteness, and, thereby, allows an indefinite expansion to human thought in contact with experience. The knowledge of faith

23

is not *isolated* from experienced reality but permeated by it. . . . It beats with every pulse of life, accepting all of life's multiplicity, and penetrating it with its own understanding. It grasps the relation of experienced reality to the as-yet-unmanifested first principle. . . . It does not usurp the province of rationality, but itself furnishes rationality with all the data for independent activity, and in turn is enriched by the latter's wealth. It is a knowledge which is *living* in the highest degree, and in the highest degree irresistible.[62]

In other words, the "cognitive process . . . *begins* in faith and continues in the rational processes."[63] This living knowledge "requires the constant wholeness and unchanging harmony of man's soul."[64] Thus knowledge is also determined by the moral quality of life.

To comprehend the truth rationality itself must conform to all the laws of the spiritual world, . . . and be related to all the vital and moral forces of the spirit. Therefore, the deepest truths of thought are accessible only to a reason which is harmoniously organized internally and in full moral conformity with the omni-essential reason.[65]

It is clear that man's wholeness, according to Khomyakov, depends on his right relation with the Creator and his fellowmen. Further, no right relation can be established outside the Church. For it is in the Church and through the Church that men, if they so choose, can appropriate the redeeming grace of Christ which restores to harmony the sinful soul. "Only in the Church can man find himself, and establish right relations with the rest of creation, for within her fold his heart, mind, and will are regenerated and purified and his being made whole by the action of the Holy Spirit."[66]

The Church, for Khomyakov, was neither a doctrine nor an ecclesiastical institution, but a spiritual organism animated by the divine Spirit.[67] But God is love, and so is the nature of the Church. "Love is the crown and the glory of the Church."[68] Hence, knowledge itself depends on love. "The communion of love is indispensable for the understanding of truth; all true knowledge is based on love, and is unobtainable without it."[69] Love requires freedom; it can be neither given nor received without the full consent of one's con-

24

sciousness. The Church, therefore, is opposed to every form of con-
straint, oppression, and discord. It is equally opposed to authority.
"It is extremely unjust," wrote Khomyakov, "to assume that the
Church demands forced unity or forced obedience. On the contrary,
it *abhors* both the one and the other. Forced unity, in matters of
faith, is a lie—and forced obedience is death." [70] Accordingly, Khomyakov admitted no other head of the Church but Christ himself.

Khomyakov's doctrine of the freedom of the Church, however, is
in no wise to be understood as an assertion of individualism. Freedom belongs to the Church *as a whole*, rather than to each member
of the Church in particular. "Although the believer's freedom is not
subject to any external authority, it is justified by his oneness of
thought with the Church." [71] This Church, for Khomyakov, is invisible, or rather visible only to the eyes of faith. It is inner life
and significance. It is the spirit of God indwelling in the community
of believers. [72] "The Church is a prime-reality, and in union with
it the individual person discovers himself for the first time—not in
his contingent empirical manifestations, but in his true and profound principle." [73]

To describe the particular nature of the Church and its relation
to the individual members, Khomyakov laid special stress on the
word *sobornost*. This word, untranslatable, is derived from the verb
sobirat which means to reunite or bring together. In the Slavonic
text of the Nicene Creed it stands for "catholic." The Church is
catholic—it brings together and unites. *Sobornost* may also mean
harmony and unanimity. [74] The Church, according to Khomyakov,
is opposed both to authoritarianism and to individualism—it is
unanimity achieved in Christ and as a Body of Christ. In its fellowship all men are brought together in an organic whole the head of
which is the Lord—a togetherness based on freedom and unity in
love which results from the living presence of the Holy Spirit in
those who are baptized.

The Church is One: *Tserkov odna*—this is Khomyakov's climatic
profession. "The unity of the Church follows of necessity from the
unity of God; for the Church is not a multitude of people in their
separated individualities, but the oneness of Divine grace indwelling
in reasonable creatures who freely submit themselves thereto." [75]
Accordingly, salvation is never individual, but always corporate.

25

> We know that if one of us falls, he falls alone, but no one can be saved alone. Those who are saved are saved within the Church as her members in unity with all the rest. If anyone has faith, he shares a common faith; if he loves, he shares love; if he prays, he shares the prayer of all the rest.[76]

In speaking of the Church Khomyakov always meant the Orthodox Church. Catholicism and Protestantism, in his belief, have been untrue to Christian principles. Catholicism, according to him, was unity without freedom, and Protestantism freedom without unity. In either case, unity and freedom are not real, only external.[77] But Khomyakov, least of all, is to be suspected of sectional bigotry. The dictum *extra ecclesiam nulla salus* was unacceptable to him. God's Church, he maintained, has its secret ways with all of mankind.

> The mysterious bonds that unite the earthly Church with the rest of mankind are not revealed to us; therefore we have neither the right nor the inclination to suppose that all who remain outside the visible Church will be severely condemned especially as such a supposition would contradict the Divine mercy.[78]

Berdyaev retained many of Khomyakov's ideas, and above all his doctrine of the Church as *one* and *free* based upon the mutual love of its members and safeguarding the believer's total freedom.

Fyodor Mikhailovitch Dostoyevsky (1821-1881) stood in opposition to Khomyakov, who lived and moved in the sphere of Kievan and Moscovite traditions of Orthodoxy. Khomyakov's outlook remained unaffected by Western influences which entered Russia with Peter the Great's reforms. Indeed, he regarded them as pernicious to the national life, and proclaimed his belief in the vigor and originality of the native culture. Dostoyevsky, on the other hand, was the product of the Russia of Petersburg. He reflected the latent, painful crisis of the Russian soul which occurred precisely as a result of the impact upon the Russian soil of the Asian and European conceptions of life, and which was to lead the way to Bolshevism.[79] Dostoyevsky was not concerned with traditions, but with man; not with the past, but with the future. He disclosed the fatal predicament of the Russian people—and of man in general—and anticipated the Bolshevik Revolution.

Like all Russian thinkers Dostoyevsky was anthropocentric—the problem of man was his lifelong and only study. For him man is independent of nature, though at the same time a part of the order of nature, and subject to its laws. He envisaged man as a microcosm. "Man contains the enigma of the universe," wrote Berdyaev in his explanation of Dostoyevsky's ideas, "and to solve the problem of man is to solve the problem of God." [80] Hence the absolute value of the human being. But at the same time man is shown by Dostoyevsky as a creature floundering in perplexity and involved in contradiction. Dostoyevsky's heroes disclose to a high degree the power of self-assertion and destruction which is hidden in the "underground" of the human soul. They are capable of extreme corruption, vice, and crime. They actually kill—others or themselves. And yet they also reveal longings for goodness, justice, and truth. Dostoyevsky discovered that human nature constantly exhibits two opposite impulses—toward good and evil, hate and love, sin and salvation; and also that man is endowed with absolute freedom to make a choice between the powers of darkness and the powers of light, between God and Satan. Indeed, freedom, according to Dostoyevsky, is the true essence of man. [81]

The concept of human freedom stood in the very center of Dostoyevsky's anthropology. He discussed it in all his major novels. He illustrated its tragic dialectic. His conclusion was that freedom may conduct a man either to self-destruction or to the heights of spiritual transfiguration. The difference lies in whether man rejects or accepts God. Raskolnikov, for example, in *Crime and Punishment,* is driven to self-affirmation and godlessness. He wants to prove to himself that he is a superman, therefore exempt from moral law. "Everything is permissible," he utters and proceeds to an act of murder. The crime, however, did not make him the man-God he dreamed of, but sent him to Siberia instead. Through suffering and repentance in prison he learns selflessness and eventually loses his pride. Through love for his girl-friend Sonia, who followed him to Siberia, Raskolnikov began his regeneration.

Raskolnikov's experience awakened him to the realization that man is not God, and that without God he is not a man at all, but only a helpless puppet of his own self-destructive irrational forces. Not all of Dostoyevsky's heroes, however, achieve a return to life from the pit of self-love and will to power. Svidrigailov,[82] Stavrogin, Kirillov, Verkhovensky[83] resisted God to the very end and eventually incurred self-annihilation. In this respect, Kirillov exemplifies the final results of man's denial of God and self-affirmation: "There will be a new man, happy and proud," exclaims Kirillov in a conversation with Stavrogin, "who will conquer pain and fear and will himself be God. . . . Then there will be a new life; then there will be a new man; everything will be new. . . . He will bring the world to an end who bears the name of man-God." "God-man?" asks Stavrogin. "Man-God," answers Kirillov. "There is the difference." [84]

The way of the man-God leads, according to Dostoyevsky, to loss of freedom, crime, and suicide. Only the way of God-man is conducive to goodness, personality, and freedom. Man has to make his decision between these two ways. *The Legend of the Grand Inquisitor* in *The Brothers Karamazov* is, in this regard, of prime significance. Berdyaev mentioned it repeatedly. In fact, its conception of Christianity is absolutely basic to Berdyaev's own thought. Supposedly, the legend contains a terrible indictment against Christianity as viewed by the Grand Inquisitor. Actually it is one of the most subtle and most profound dialectics of spiritual freedom and slavery ever written in the literature of the world.

The old Inquisitor charges Christ, whom he has imprisoned, with the folly of choosing an illusory freedom instead of the fundamental values men live by—Bread, Authority, and Gregariousness. And this, he points out, in spite of earnest warnings conveyed by "the wise and mighty spirit" in the wilderness:

> Thou wast warned. . . . Thou hast no lack of admonitions and warnings, but Thou didst not listen to those warnings; Thou didst reject the only way by which men might be made happy. . . . The great spirit talked with Thee in the wilderness, and we are told in the books that he 'tempted' Thee. . . . Could anything truer be said than what he revealed to Thee in three questions and what thou didst reject?

The meaning of the first question, the Inquisitor explains, was this:

Thou wouldst go into the world, and art going with empty hands, with some promise of freedom which men in their simplicity and their unruliness cannot even understand, which they fear and dread—for nothing has ever been more insupportable for a man and a human society than freedom. But seest Thou these stones in this parched and barren wilderness? Turn them into bread, and mankind will run after Thee like a flock of sheep, grateful and obedient, though forever trembling, lest Thou withdraw Thy hand and deny them Thy bread. But Thou wouldst not deprive man of freedom and didst reject the offer, thinking what is that freedom worth, if obedience is bought with bread? Thou didst reply that man lives not by bread alone. But dost Thou know that for the sake of that earthly bread the spirit of the earth will rise up against Thee and will strive with Thee and overcome Thee, and all will follow him, crying, 'Who can compare with this beast? He has given us fire from heaven.' Dost Thou know that the ages will pass, and humanity will proclaim by the lips of their sages that there is no crime, and therefore no sin; there is only hunger? 'Feed men, and then ask of them virtue!' that's what they'll write on the banner, which they will raise against Thee, and with which they will destroy Thy temple. . . . We alone shall feed them in Thy name, declaring falsely that it is in Thy name. . . . In the end they will lay their freedom at our feet, and say to us, 'Make us your slaves, but feed us.'

The Grand Inquisitor then accuses Christ of lack of love and indifference for the weak and oppressed by imposing upon them the unbearable burden of freedom. For those who are capable of bearing the cross of freedom are but a few elect:

. . . only some thousands; and what of the rest? . . . What is to become of the millions and tens of thousands of millions of creatures who will not have the strength to forego the earthly bread for the sake of the heavenly? Or dost Thou care only for . . . the great and strong, while the millions . . . who are weak but love Thee, must exist only for the sake of the great and strong. . . . And how are . . . the weak ones to blame, because they could not endure what the strong have endured? How is the weak soul to blame that it is unable to receive such terrible gifts? Canst Thou have simply come to the elect and for the elect?

29

The coming of Christ, the Inquisitor continues, brought about only confusion and suffering because of moral demands impossible to fulfill:

> Thou didst desire man's free love, that he should follow Thee freely, enticed and taken captive by Thee. In place of the rigid ancient law, man must hereafter with free heart decide for himself what is good and what is evil, having only thy image before him as his guide. . . .Thou didst hope that man, following Thee, would cling to God and not ask for a miracle. But Thou didst not know that when man rejects miracle he rejects God too; for man seeks not so much God as the miraculous. . . . Thou didst not come down from the cross when they shouted to Thee, mocking and reviling Thee, 'Come down from the cross and we will believe that Thou art He.' Thou didst not come down, for again Thou wouldst not enslave man by a miracle, and didst crave faith given freely, not based on miracle. Thou didst crave for free love and not the base raptures of the slave before the might that has overawed him for ever. But Thou didst think too highly of men therein, for they are slaves, of course, though rebellious by nature.

The Grand Inquisitor's bitterest reproach, however, is directed at Christ's rejection of earthly power and authority:

> Why didst Thou reject that last gift? Hadst Thou accepted that last counsel of the mighty spirit, Thou wouldst have accomplished all that man seeks on earth—that is, some one to worship, some one to keep his conscience, and some means of uniting all in one unanimous and harmonious ant-heap, for the craving for universal unity is the third and last anguish of men. . . . Hadst Thou taken the world and Caesar's purple, Thou wouldst have founded the universal state and have given universal peace. For who can rule men if not he who holds their conscience and their bread in his hands?

The Grand Inquisitor boasts, in conclusion, that he and the Inquisition have done infinitely better than Christ—they destroyed freedom and thus made men happy:

> For now for the first time it has become possible to think of happiness of men. . . . We have corrected Thy work and have

founded it upon *miracle, mystery* and *authority*. And men rejoiced that they were again led like sheep, and that the terrible gift that had brought them such suffering, was, at last, lifted from their hearts. . . . We have taken the sword of Caesar, and in taking it, of course, have rejected Thee and followed *him*. . . . Thou art proud of Thine elect, but Thou hast only the elect, while we give rest to all. . . . With us all will be happy and will no more rebel nor destroy one another as under Thy freedom. . . . We shall allow them even sin, they are weak and helpless, and they will love us like children because we allow them to sin. We shall tell them that every sin will be expiated, if it is done with our permission, that we allow them to sin because we love them, and the punishment for these sins we take upon ourselves. . . . The most painful secrets of their conscience, all, all they will bring to us, and we shall have an answer for all. And they will be glad to believe our answer, for it will save them from the great anxiety and terrible agony they endure . . . in making a free decision for themselves. And all will be happy. . . . I repeat, tomorrow Thou shalt see that obedient flock who at a sign from me will hasten to heap up the hot cinders about the pile on which I shall burn Thee for coming to hinder us. For if any one has ever deserved our fires, it is Thou. Tomorrow I shall burn Thee. *Dixi!* [85]

The Legend of the Grand Inquisitor states Dostoyevsky's (and also Berdyaev's) fundamental theme—freedom. The Prelate decided in favor of miracle, mystery, and authority as the means of subjugating human will and consciousness and thus deprived man of his freedom of the spirit. He believed that happiness might be obtained only at the price of freedom. His is the embodiment of the evil spirit in the wilderness which Christ rejected to safeguard both freedom and man. This is the conception of Christ that underlies Berdyaev's Christian outlook. He summed it up in one phrase when he wrote: "The mystery of the Crucifix is the mystery of freedom." [86]

Vladimir Sergeyevitch Solovyov (1853-1900) opened in Russia the period of philosophical systems. Neither Khomyakov nor Dostoyevsky, nor any of the gifted thinkers of the nineteenth century prior to Solovyov, had left any separate theoretical constructions— they were too deeply immersed in the social and political wrangling of the time and devoted themselves to concrete problems of daily life rather than to abstract speculations. Solovyov was the first to create a complete system based upon the search for an exhaustive knowledge of reality as a whole—both physical and spiritual.

The primary intuition of Solovyov's life was his vision of creation as an all-embracing unity.[87] He viewed the universe as a living organism, originated in one source, animated by one spirit, moving toward one goal. The whole visible world, according to Solovyov, was not a collection of dead and dried things, but the interwoven body of living, creative, progressive unities in "continuous development and growth."[88]

Solovyov's metaphysics—expounded chiefly in his work *Lectures on Godmanhood*—starts with the intuition of the Absolute. The latter constitutes the *donnée immédiate* of all experience. It is not separate from the universe; it is everywhere present; it permeates all things. The Absolute is God; its existence cannot be rationally or empirically proved; it can be verified only by faith. As Solovyov put it in his great work, *Justification of the Good*: "In true religious experience the reality of that which is experienced is immediately given. . . . The reality of Deity is not a *deduction* from religious experience, but the *content* of it—*that which is experienced*."[89]

How did the visible world come into being? The Absolute, according to Solovyov—did not directly create the world, but first brought out of himself into existence another Absolute—His Other. God wanted His Other in order to express His love and manifest Himself in a spiritual reality which was not Himself. But the Other, upon his creation, revolted against God. At that very moment the Fall occurred: the Other separated himself from God and as a result of the Fall the visible world emerged into life:

> . . . Thus the world-soul separated its relative centre of being from the Absolute, asserting itself apart from God. But in so doing it lost its freedom with respect to creation, lost its power over it. The unity of the cosmos disintegrated, . . .the universal organism was transformed into a mechanical aggregate of atoms; the whole of creation was subjected to the vanity and slavery of decay . . . By a free act [the Other] . . . which had been united by [God], fell away from Deity and broke up into a multitude of warring elements.[90]

Thus the Other or the World-Soul, as Solovyov also called it, became immersed in Nature and consubstantial with the visible world. But since, on the other hand, the World-Soul by its very essence participates in Deity (in spite of the Fall for, in the ultimate analysis, "no being can have the ground of its existence outside of God, or have substantial being apart from the divine world"[91]), it follows that Nature, too, is not substantially different from Deity but forms only "another arrangement or permutation of . . . elements which have their substantial being in the divine world."[92]

The fall did not sever altogether the relation between God and the World-Soul. Even in a world that has fallen away from God, the Other (now Nature) kept longing for reunion with God. In turn, God's love continued seeking for His Other. Thus, following the Fall, there originated a convergent movement of God and the Other back toward total unity. The world's return to God is being accomplished through a long and laborious cosmological process in which the dualistic opposition of World and Absolute is gradually and painfully overcome. There are, according to Solovyov, five stages or kingdoms in the process toward oneness: "the *mineral kingdom* (or the non-organic), the *vegetable kingdom,* the *animal kingdom,* the *kingdom of man,* and the *kingdom of God.*"[93] The first three stages mark the evolution of nature; the fourth that of history; the fifth, the culmination of the ascension of being and re-establishment of unity. They correspond to five stages of existence necessary for the final achievement of the kingdom of God, that is, "the being must first of all *be,* then it must be *alive,* then *conscious,* then *rational,* and finally *perfect.*"[94]

Solovyov's doctrine of life-stages or evolution postulates that in the process something new is constantly created, something qualitatively different from the immediate causes and therefore unpredictable. Thus he wrote:

> The fact that higher forms and types are manifested or revealed following the inferior ones by no means proves that they are the product or creation of the inferior realm. . . . The evolution of inferior types of being cannot by itself alone create superior types, but it does create material conditions and offer the necessary milieu for the manifestation or revelation of the superior. Thus every manifestation of a new type of being is in a certain sense a *new creation,* but a creation which can least of all be designated as a creation out of nothing; for firstly, the natural basis for the birth of the new type

is offered by the former one; and secondly, the superior type's own positive content does not arise out of non-being, but exists from all times. It only enters (at a certain point of the process) into another sphere of phenomena. The conditions of the phenomenon depend on natural evolution; that which is revealed depends on God.[95]

Thus God is at work within the fallen world helping His Other to achieve the final return to Divine unity. How is God present in the world? Through his Sophia or the Divine Wisdom, is Solovyov's answer. Through Sophia God originated His Other in the first place. After the Fall, Sophia—the image of God in His Other—is continuing the work of unification and restoration. She struggles against the evil, chaotic forces of the Other—which are called into being by metaphysical freedom contained in the Other and, in turn, marked the Fall—and laboriously gropes toward unification and restoration.[96]

The emergence of man upon the earth occasioned a profound and essential change in the history of the world. In man, for the first time, the purely cosmic process is overcome and a link established between the realms of visible and invisible. The human being discloses the mystery of the World-Soul in the process of becoming. He is "the natural mediator between God and material being."[97] In this regard Solovyov wrote:

> In man nature grows beyond itself and enters (in consciousness) into the realm of absolute being. . . . Not only does man have the same essence of life—or total-unity—as God, but he is free to desire to have it as God does . . . [i.e. he can] assert himself apart from, and outside of, God.[98]

Man has done just that. He asserted himself in pride and selfishness against God. "Now, having asserted his selfhood, having shut his soul off from all things, he finds himself in an alien and hostile world, which no longer speaks to him in an intelligible language, and neither understands nor obeys him."[99]

In order to further the process of redemption from the Fall and help man to collaborate with God in restoring the original total-unity, the Divine Principle, in an act of love, descends into history as Logos incarnated in Jesus Christ. Thus Christ is the meeting

34

place between Sophia now working through man toward God, and Logos moving from God toward man. He is the God-man. "The whole of nature has striven and gravitated toward man; the whole history of mankind has been directed toward the God-man." [100] In Christ the God-man both the soul and physical nature—the whole creation—are redeemed; in Him also is opened "the path of humanity towards God-manhood, and towards the all-embracing unity, towards the Kingdom of God." [101]

Solovyov's doctrine of God-manhood is characteristic of Russian religious thought. Its origin and justification lay in the Orthodox interpretation of the historical event of the Incarnation. According to the Orthodox church, the doctrine means that "there exists a commensurability between God and man and on that account only is a revelation of God to man possible." [102] Such a commensurability is manifested in Jesus Christ, the God-man. In Him we behold one individual Person uniting two natures—that of God and that of man. The divine-human unity is not, however, the privilege of one individual; on the contrary, it is the prime principle, and the very essence of the evolutionary process whereby the fallen world might return to God. "The idea of God-manhood means the overcoming of the self-sufficiency of man in humanism and at the same time the affirmation of the activity of man, of his highest dignity, of the divine in man." [103] Indeed, it affords the possibility of the ultimate transfiguration not only of man but of the whole cosmos.

It should be noted that Solovyov, following in the footsteps of the Orthodox tradition, envisaged mankind as a single whole—"a collective organism," [104] although composed of separate individuals. "All human elements form an integral *organism,* which is at the same time universal and individual—a pan-human organism." [105] The salvation of the world, therefore, is not so much individual process of redemption as a common reintegration of mankind and the universe as a whole with the Absolute. Accordingly, each nation, like each individual, is called to a special mission in performing with God the salvation of all. The inter-relation of society and the individual is the logical conclusion to Solovyov's world outlook.

> Society is the completed individual, and the individual is concentrated society. . . . Each individual possesses as such the

35

potentiality of perfection, but by remaining isolated and limited an individual deprives himself of the real fulness of life, i.e. of perfection and infinity. . . . The Kingdom of God is both perfectly universal and perfectly individual. Each wants it for himself and for everyone, and is only able to obtain it together with others. . . . The purpose of moral progress is not to create solidarity between each and all, for it already exists, but to make each and all aware of this solidarity . . . so that each should fulfill the common work as if it were his own.[106]

Connected with the metaphysical theory of the "Absolute in the process of becoming" stands Solovyov's conception of love. He expounded it in his book *The Meaning of Love* which Berdyaev regarded as "the one and only original word which has been spoken on the subject of love as Eros in the history of Christian thought." [107] Love, according to Solovyov, has a much deeper significance than family and procreation; its aim and justification are the actual transformation of man and woman who love each other into one true person—the androgyne.

> The true human being in the fulness of its ideal personality, obviously cannot be merely a man or merely a woman, but must be a higher unity of the two. . . . To *create* the true human being as a free unity of the masculine and feminine elements, which preserve their formal separateness but overcome their essential disparity and disruption, is the direct *task* of love.[108]

Solovyov's vision of an all-embracing unity of the whole cosmos was particularly manifest in his work for the reunion of the Christian Churches. In the *Three Conversations,* he described Catholicism, Protestantism, and Orthodoxy as three equal branches of the one and the same Church. He expressed his idea of ecumenicity in these words:

> As long as we assert our religion, *first of all* in its denominational particularity, and only *after this* as ecumenical Christianity, we take away from religion not only its sane logic, but moreover its moral significance; we thus transform it into an obstacle on the path of man's spiritual regeneration.[109]

He conceived union between the Churches, not as the absorption of one Church by the other, but as a "combination, in which each

Church will preserve its formative principle and its particularities, dismissing only hostility and exclusiveness." [110] The Church, therefore, should strive to become truly One, Holy Ecumenical, and Apostolic in order to discharge the sacred mission which was bestowed upon her by God in Christ—the reconciliation of God and the world. [111]

This is in brief the Russian country, history, faith, and thought that moulded to a great extent Berdyaev's religious philosophy. His writings in form and character are thoroughly Russian. But at the same time his vigorous defense of personal freedom and the vantage point of his spiritual outlook afforded him enough detachment from national entanglement to raise his thought to mankind's proportion.

The final period in this outline of Russian history is of course that of the communist regime. Since it shall be described in many places in connection with Berdyaev's life under the Bolsheviks, we shall mention only briefly its main and immediate effects upon the historical evolution of Russia.

6. SOVIET RUSSIA (1917- ?)

The Bolshevik Revolution of 1917 brought to a close not only Russian tsardom, but also the period of Saint Petersburg, which lasted a little more than two hundred years. In 1918 the new government abandoned the capital of Peter the Great and moved back to Moscow. In 1923 the Soviets abolished the name of Russia which became a federative state designated by the initials U.S.S.R. (Union of Socialist Soviet Republics). The Union has been theoretically opened freely to any socialist state on earth, and practically has aimed at world domination.

The Revolution extended over all spheres of life. It was cultural as well as social and political. It annihilated not only the old regime but strove to alter mental habits and folkways of the Russian people in order to create a new kind of man, the *homo Sovieticus*. To what extent it has succeeded in its original undertaking is an interesting question to ask the specialist. One thing Soviet Russia did definitely achieve—the murder of Russian culture and freedom.

PART I

GROWTH AND STRUGGLE

CHAPTER I

FALLEN INTO AN ALIEN REALM:
SEARCH FOR THE MEANING OF LIFE

> For the spirit that comes
> from heaven birth is death.
> —Empedocles.

Empedocles' statement[1] uttered some five hundred years before Christ reflects Orphic and Pythagorean myths concerning the origin of the human soul,[2] as also the subsequent dualistic hypothesis that underlay the whole Gnostic theory of redemption.[3] These religious movements speak of a falling away of man's spirit from a higher, ethereal world of goodness and freedom into a lower, corrupted world of phenomena, subject to necessity and evil.

The trend of thought dominant with Gnosticism and the two predominant mystery religions is also significantly characteristic from the very beginning of Berdyaev's attitude toward the world.

> The first response to the world of a creature who is born into it is of immense significance. I cannot remember my first cry on encountering the world, but I know for certain that from the very beginning I was aware of having fallen into an alien realm. I felt this as much on the first day of my conscious life as I do at the present time. I have always been a pilgrim.[4]

Berdyaev began life as a stranger in the world and never managed (indeed, nor even tried) to achieve any other status. His own

41

family, to say nothing of friends and the people at large, were alien to him. He never was conscious of "belonging" to his parents, and carried the sentiment to the point of relegating all family ties to the order of "necessity,"—deeming the family itself as an "enemy and enslaver of personal freedom." [5] Berdyaev lived in the world and never merged with it. At no time did he feel comfortable in the earthly environment, thoroughly at home among men.

> My sense of uprootedness and disestablishment in the world, which later I came to express philosophically as objectification, is at the heart of my whole world outlook. From childhood I dwelt in a world unlike the one which surrounded me and only feigned implication in the world of my environment. I was on the defensive against the world and kept watch over my freedom.[6]

Although not of the world, Berdyaev lived, however, in the world, and was exposed to its impressions. One of the most indelible was engendered by his nurse, Anna Ivanovna Katamenkov. Her living memory never left him completely. A nurse to two generations of Berdyaevs, that of the father and the son, she was (although a serf), loved and respected as a member of the family. She was a simple, dignified and deeply religious woman, devoted to the Orthodox faith and to her duties. Anna taught young Nicolas the love of large gardens and dense woods which, in time, became in his eyes "nature's symbols of the primeval mystery of life." [7] Over years of intimate companionship he could likewise discern and appreciate in his *nyanya*[8] the high moral qualities of the Russian people, and the features of human worthiness which he praised and defended to the end of his life.

Nicolas Alexandrovitch Berdyaev was born of an aristocratic family in Kiev, on March 19 (March 6, old style), 1874. His family on both sides descended from military and landed nobility rooted back in the Middle Ages.

On his father's side he belonged to the old military gentry. Nicolas' grandfather, Mikhail Nicolaevitch Berdyaev, distinguished himself as a young lieutenant in the Napoleonic wars, at the battle of Kulmsk in 1814. He was awarded the Cross of St. George and the Iron Cross, the highest Russian and Prussian decorations, and later became the *ataman*[9] of the Don Cossacks. While holding this position he received orders from Tsar Nicolas I to abolish the traditional liberties of the Cossacks. The measure was a part of the government's policy for military and political centralization. During a military parade in Novotcherkask, the Tsar summoned the *ataman* to see to it that his order should be carried out. The latter refused: the Cossack's autonomy had always been a matter of great pride. Instead, he submitted his resignation, thus running the risk of immediate disgrace and exile. The Cossacks expected a violent reaction on the part of the Tsar. But impressed by the dauntless daring of the old general, the imperial autocrat embraced him publicly and countermanded his order. Indeed, the love of freedom was anything but new in Berdyaev's family tradition.

Complying with ancestral custom Nicolas's father, Alexander Mikhailovitch Berdyaev, became an officer in the Imperial Horse Guards—an exclusive, aristocratic regiment. But he did not display much taste for a military career. Soon he retired and went to live on his estate, Oboukhovo, a village in the district of Kiev, where he was made Marshal of the Nobility.[10] During the Turkish war he rejoined the army; but subsequently he became president of the regional Agrarian Bank and held the post for a quarter of a century. He was a man of great culture and distinction. He spoke several languages, relished traveling, and read widely. He had a fine library of philosophical and especially historical works. He cultivated a particular liking for Voltaire, which might explain his growing "liberalism," although never to the extent of militating for it. Since the days of Catherine the Great it had become fashionable with the Russian aristocracy to exhibit fondness for the French Enlightenment without necessarily any desire to reform the regime. A true disciple of the sage of Fernay, however, Alexander Berdyaev was not a religious man.

Nicolas' mother, Alina Sergeevna, was born Princess Kudashev. She was the daughter of the Countess Choiseul, and so half-French. At heart she remained more Gallic than Russian: she received her early education in Paris, wrote letters and spoke almost exclusively in French, and, though born an Orthodox, had a strong leaning toward Roman Catholicism. She always prayed from her mother's French breviary.

Both Nicolas' father and mother had access to the court circles of Tsar Alexander III. They were also related to the immensely rich Countess Maria Branicka of the Polish nobility. In his childhood Nicolas went often with his mother to stay at the Branickis' summer estate in Belaya Tserkov, a town which they owned. The dreamy boy enjoyed especially driving a gig and two ponies into surrounding woods, or riding a donkey about the park. Later on, even as a converted Marxist, he would spend weeks of quiet study at the Branickis' winter residence.

The cloister, along with the army, was another time-honored tradition in the Berdyaev family. Nicolas' paternal grandmother and great-grandmother were secret nuns.[11] His mother's grandmother, Princess Kudashev, actually entered a convent after the death of her husband. Thus the chivalrous spirit of Medieval Europe—knights for Christ, knights for the king—cultivated over generations in some quarters of the Russian gentry, had evolved as a constituent part of the Berdyaev family.

Noteworthy, also, were certain traits of character which seem to be hereditary in Nicolas' family. His father was a good-natured and kind man, but at the same time he was also vehement, willful and obstinate. He had many quarrels, vexations, and disappointments in life on this account. Nicolas' brother, Sergius, some fifteen years his senior, was endowed with remarkable, yet never developed (he died at an early age), talents for poetry and mathematics. But he, too, was neurotic, often overpowered by paroxysms of rage, nearly abnormal.[12] The family life was rather rifted by bitter disagreements and beclouded with outbursts of violence, hysteria, and emotional anarchy among its members.

Illness, moreover, was an ever-present reality in the home of the Berdyaevs. Alina Sergeevna suffered for years of a serious liver ailment. She had frequent attacks in the night, and her agonizing cries would arouse the household and blanch the children with quivering fright. Alexander Mikhailovitch was forever undergoing cures of some kind, in most cases for no reason at all. The little Nicolas himself was constantly treated for one complaint or another. Doctors and nurses were a customary sight in the daily round of family life. Later on, recalling the circumstances of his life, the

44

philosopher represented them as being reminiscent of the families described in Dostoyevsky's novels.[13]

Neurotic legacy and family illnesses profoundly affected Berdyaev's psycho-physical make-up. He was impulsive, self-willed, and inclined to fits of temper. Very early he developed a morbid fear of disease. He was also subject to a nervous tic from which he had suffered since childhood. As a young boy he used to fume in tantrums of anger. He even experienced genuine ecstasies of rage.[14] The privileged position of a nobleman and the habitual impunity which he enjoyed at home only stimulated the frequent display of his inflammable temper. Berdyaev remained irascible, quick-tempered, and aloof all his life. Despite an almost irresistible personal charm due to his exceptional qualities of heart, his gracious kindness and lavish generosity, there subsisted in his relations with others a certain loftiness and reserve reminiscent of the feudal patrician.

The life of young Berdyaev was associated with the ancient city of Kiev.[15] The family estate in Obukhovo was sold at the insistence of Alina Sergeevna when Nicolas was still a child, and in its place his father bought a mansion with a large garden in the exclusive suburb of Kiev known as Lipky.

Berdyaev seemed duty-bound by family tradition to follow in the footsteps of his military forebears. In accord with his father, however, he had no inclination to make a career of the army. He contemptuously disliked armed forces (except in war-time), and rebelled from childhood against regimentation. Nevertheless, he had to obey the hereditary custom and undergo military training. At the age of twelve the boy entered the Kiev Cadet Corps, an exclusive school intended to form future officers of the Guards regiment which enjoyed the Tsar's special protection.

The curriculum included, besides matters of strategy and tactics, a complete program of high-school education. No elective courses were allowed. The students were instructed in the humanities, history, divinity, and social and physical sciences. Considerable importance was attached to mathematics and modern languages. Sports and dancing were regularly practiced. The discipline was rigorous.

Due to his health and influential relations, Nicolas was granted a quite exceptional favor. Though following classes at the school, he lived at home. This signal advantage, however, in no degree altered his deep-rooted aversion to soldiery. Actually he loathed the military school, frankly disliked his fellow-cadets, and barely passed the examinations. Yet he tried hard to conform to the discipline of the Corps and prepare his class work. But he never was able to submit his mind to an institutional education. At no time was he able to memorize or even assimilate the substance of the courses conducted by his teachers. To him knowledge was a creative process: the object of knowledge was not to be apprehended from without, but re-discovered within as a subjective experience. Consequently, he regarded all knowledge as a conscious activity initiated in one's thought.

> I am incapable of retorting, echoing in a passive way: I instantly want to develop my own line of thought. . . . I have, likewise, never been able to submit my mind to external direction or to be instructed by others: I am self-taught and my methods are autodidactic. I have never acquired knowledge and truth by way of instruction and education, rather I struggled for them. I was, therefore, always obliged to draw up my own plan of enquiry.[16]

And he did it in a remarkable way. While obviously a failure at the school, Berdyaev began, in his personal way, to develop intellectually very early, and display an unusual interest for philosophy. At the age of fourteen he was reading Schopenhauer, Kant, and Hegel. All his life he remained an eager reader, and acknowledged his great indebtedness to practically every eminent figure in the fields of philosophy, literature, and theology—the Old Testament prophets and the book of Job; St. Augustine, Meister Eckhart, and Angelus Silesius; Plato, Plotinus, Pascal, Voltaire, Fichte, Schelling, Nietzsche, Vladimir Solovyov, Herzen, Bakunin, Leontyev, and Ibsen; the Greek tragedians, Cervantes, Shakespeare, Goethe, Byron, Lermontov, and Tyutchev; Hoffmann, Dickens, Balzac, and Baudelaire.[17] He particularly stressed the influence of Jacob Boehme, Immanuel Kant, Schopenhauer, Hegel, Karl Marx, Dostoyevsky, and Tolstoy. These great minds helped Berdyaev in his search for truth and meaning. Much of their thought underlies his philosophical attitude, particularly of those whose mode of thinking was congenial to him. But he never became their disciple. He never acknowledged any authority; nor did he comply with any philosophical tradition. The very idea of being identified with a particular system of philosophy was distasteful to him. He adhered to no "school of thought," and succeeded in continually preserving intellectual self-determination and freedom of inquisitive imagination.

> I was only stimulated by books: my thinking had another source and proceeded from some primal experience which cannot be acquired by means of study and reading. The reading of books provoked thought, but my reactions to what I read were often quite negative and unlike those apparently intended by the author. The key to the thought of others was my subjective insight. Thus it was that what I found and appreciated in their thought became an experience on my own spiritual and intellectual path.[18]

Reading did not supersede personal cogitation; on the contrary, it served to develop and strengthen his own thought. His hidden abilities awakened by books became consciously active and creative, and led him to the realization of his vocation as a philosopher.

Berdyaev's interest in philosophical problems arose in his very early years, and already as a boy he became aware of his philosophical calling.[19] Among the writers who sharpened his philosophical tendency, at that commencing stage of his intellectual orientation, none endowed him with penetrating insights into the truth concerning Russia and her destiny more than Tolstoy; nor, throughout his life, nourished his love for the freedom of the spirit and fostered his understanding of the truth about man and his situation in the world better than Dostoyevsky.

In Tolstoy's *War and Peace,* a brilliant panorama of Russian life in the Napoleonic Era, the character of the wealthy prince Andrey aroused in young Berdyaev particular admiration. The prince, an arrogant, conceited, somewhat cynical and cold man left his pregnant wife whom he despised, and went off to war for the purpose of escaping the bondage of domesticity. While lying wounded on the battle-field at Austerlitz, Andrey contemplated the deep, intense hue of clear sky stretched over him, and for the first time discovered how petty and insignificant his life had been in contrast with the sublime majesty of the blue. Then, casting his bitter thoughts upon the futile agitation of this world, he set the paltry vanity of a Napoleon against the unfathomable mystery of the boundless firmament and the terrible reality of death. A wide chasm, he felt, separated truth as recognized by social conventions from the actual, divine truth. Life as appearance and life as meaning afforded no identity. Berdyaev was never to forget Andrey's dramatic insight into the two worlds—temporal and spiritual, fictitious and real—and their uncompromising opposition each to the other as symbolically represented by the French Emperor and the infinite sky at Austerlitz.

Berdyaev received his most determining and lasting impression, however, from Dostoyevsky, especially in his *Legend of the Grand Inquisitor*. In the foreword of his study consecrated to the great Russian novelist, Berdyaev stated:

> Dostoyevsky has played a decisive part in my spiritual life. While I was still a youth, I received a grafting from him. Dostoyevsky shook my soul more than any other writer or philosopher has done. I have always divided people into Dostoyesky-ites and those to whom his spirit is foreign. The fact that my consciousness was, at a very early period, drawn by the problems of philosophy is certainly due to those "cursed questions" which Dostoyevsky had raised.[20]

Gradually these questions sharpened into a constant focus of Berdyaev's life-long inquiry and elucidation. Dostoyevsky's characteristic themes, deepened and expanded, became the groundwork of Berdyaev's philosophy—the Destiny of Man, God, Suffering and Evil, Love, Christ and Antichrist, Eternity, Universal Vocation of Russia, Socialism and Revolution; and most of all the idea of the Freedom of the Spirit which became fundamental in his perception of the world. Alexis Remisov's witty comment that "Dostoyevsky is Russia; without him there is no Russia,"[21] might with greater reason be *mutatis mutandi* applied to Berdyaev: without Dostoyevsky's formative impact Berdyaev would probably have never attained the profundity of intuitive insight which is the distinctive mark of his thought.

Berdyaev came to philosophy on personal initiative. "Nobody ever suggested that I should study philosophy: the impulse came entirely from within me." [22] The impulse, in turn, originated from an ingrained, twofold apprehension that typified Berdyaev his whole life long—that of solitude and anguish.

The everyday life Nicolas led at home effectually fostered his hereditary predispositions: it contained none of the habitual patterns of togetherness—religious, intellectual, or sentimental—which impart a feeling of coherence and unity to many a kinship. During his childhood the members of the family underwent a painful transition from the old-established social traditions to a more liberal way of life. Consequently, a poignant sense of distress and maladjustment afflicted their daily moods; an awareness of uprootedness, exposure, and insecurity distorted their mutual relations. No authority was acknowledged. Self-control and discipline were unknown. Later Berdyaev wrote: "I was never constrained or obliged to do anything in childhood." [23] It would be wrong, however, to infer that an attitude of hostility, affectional insensibility, or even indifference, was dominant in the family. Actually ties of genuine attachment existed, although of a peculiar vein. Nicolas, for his part, loved and esteemed his parents; not by virtue of any feeling of sonship, but rather out of a protective impulse. He cared for them and was tormented by the thought of their death.[24] This latent solicitude, shared alike by children and parents, did not, however, relieve the general atmosphere of separateness and abandon.

Left to himself, the boy naturally surrendered to the unquenchable claim to independence rising from the depths of his being. The reading of novels, plays, and poetry aside from the books of philosophy stimulated his imagination in constructing a world of his own peopled with fictional characters and situations. Yet, to him, this world was not deprived of substantial authenticity:

> Life in this world of mine did not, however, belong merely to the sphere of phantasy and make-believe. I never lacked a sense of reality and, in particular, of the reality of the afflicted world around me. My experience has been, indeed, not so

much of the unreality as of the alien character of the objective world.[25]

The earthly universe appeared to him as "untrue, devoid alike of primacy and ultimacy."[26] He moved in the world of his environment as an expatriate, lonely and forlorn, and saw the human condition as one of estrangement and thralldom. He envisioned man as being neither engendered by, nor adapted to, this world, but rather as fallen into and enslaved by it.[27]

Anguish was the other basic element of Berdyaev's psychological make-up. He suffered it like a permanent, painful reminder of the insignificance and transitoriness of the temporal world associated with the longing for the transcendent. Anguish pointed to a different, spiritual realm and, concomitantly, evinced the unfathomable abyss that separates the two. It awoke his awareness of the Other, "which reaches out beyond all boundaries and limitations and holds within itself the mystery of life."[28] It also deepened and extended his feeling of alienation to all social occurrences of his life.

Berdyaev's experience of uprootedness and estrangement did not, however, spell withdrawal and indifference. His solitude and anguish were of a metaphysical, not social, character. In actual living he was just the reverse of a secluded anchorite. He was sociable, had friends, and took active part in social affairs and political movements. He addressed meetings, engaged in propaganda, whiled nights away in heated argumentation, indulged in public disputes, published pungent articles, and delivered challenging lectures. Anytime and everywhere he seemed involved in some struggle, remonstration, criticism. He was always deeply and energetically committed. Indeed, his very thinking derived stimulation and intensity from antagonism and contention. He was a fighter by temperament:

> All my life I have been a rebel: I was a rebel even while making great efforts to humble myself. Rebellion marked not a phase in my intellectual development but an innate quality of my thinking and living. I was easily roused to revolt, and injustice and violence done to the dignity and freedom of man evoked angry protests in me.[29]

But fundamentally he was unable to reconcile himself with any state and course of things, conservative and revolutionary alike.

He could conform to no collective, indeed, to no patterns, habits, or conventional norms of human life. His rebelliousness sprang from an intense love of freedom—a freedom, however, not of this world, but opposed to it. His joining or repudiating of a course of action was motivated by the measure in which it promoted or hindered the attainment of his idea of freedom. In the last analysis, though, Berdyaev remained peripheral to the world, even in the midst of bitter dissensions, and dwelled in some unrelated, empyreal region.

During the cadet years Nicolas' feelings, apperceptions, and insights, forwarded by reading and meditation, underwent a rapid process of maturation. His mind gradually perceived a subjective world which he instinctively set against the world of his environment. This personal world was as yet hesitant and indeterminate. It lacked precision and assurance. It was attended with doubts. It also assumed a character of passivity. No impetus arose to break through the maze of irrational impulses and generate a unifying, creative dynamism. But in time a new understanding penetrated Berdyaev's subjective world and impressed it forever:

> Once, on the threshold of adolescence, I was shaken to the depths by the thought that, even though there may be no such thing as a meaning of life, the very search for meaning would render life significant and meaningful. It is to this that I desired passionately to dedicate my life. This insight marked a true inner revolution which changed my whole outlook.[30]

The experience was to him as a spiritual re-orientation. It brought a sense of inward stability and provided ground for purpose and direction of thought.

Subsequently Nicolas decided that he could no longer tolerate military training. After six years of distasteful schooling, he bid farewell to arms, left the Cadet Corps, and registered as a student in the department of natural sciences at the University of Kiev.

Henceforth Berdyaev will dedicate his whole life to the search for the meaning of life. A novel and arduous path opened out to his philosophical pilgrimage. And the first stage of the journey led him to Marxism.

51

CHAPTER II

BREAK WITH NATIVE ENVIRONMENT:
FROM MARXISM TO "IDEALISM"

> I looked around me and my soul was
> lacerated by the suffering of mankind.[1]
> —Radishchev

Berdyaev's encounter with Marxism occurred at the University in 1894.[2]

Russian universities in the second half of the 19th and the early 20th centuries had always been nurseries of socialist convictions and revolutionary movements. The milieu of higher education was seething with political agitation, emotional restlessness, intellectual effervescence. Athirst for knowledge and truth, young people drawn from every walk of life converged upon the great cities of culture and learning. They forgathered in a socially classless but a spiritually distinctive, liberty-conscious group—the Intelligentsia. They were painfully aware of the unbearable conditions in which the country lived, the indescribable physical misery and moral destitution of the Russian masses. The whole empire was groaning under the heavy oppression of political despotism. The Intelligentsia wanted to change the drab reality of the present. They were imbued with plans for the future, and ready to sacrifice their lives for the sake of freedom and social justice.

Two movements—Slavophil and Westernizing—rapidly developed within the Intelligentsia and brought its ranks into division. The

Slavophils strongly conceived the possibility of achieving the social revolution by some internal process. They insisted that Russia should follow her own way, independent from the European ideological outflow, and preserve unsullied her religious and cultural folkways. On the opposite side, the Westernizers contended earnestly that the exposure to the influences emanating from the welter of the progressive thought of the West could alone impart new creative impulse and save the country from a political and intellectual standstill. In spite of the differences as to the aims and means, the votaries of the Intelligentsia shared in common a complete disregard for their own well-being and a total devotion to the revolutionary cause. Eventually, however, the gulf between the two factions deepened into final break. The Slavophils formed the Populist Party, later known as the Social-Revolutionary Party; the Westerners, on the other hand, embraced the teachings of Karl Marx and constituted the Social-Democrat Party.

The cultured circles in Kiev, as elsewhere throughout Russia, resounded with passionate controversies as to the truth or falsehood of the current social philosophies. The theories of the Populists and Marxists alike were dissected, assailed, or defended in an atmosphere of urgency and tension. Pros and cons were vehemently exchanged. Sides were resolutely taken. In the course of time Marxism prevailed. Increasingly many intellectuals came under the sway of George V. Plekhanov, the chief exponent of Marx in Russia, and one of the founders of the Social-Democrat Party. Contrary to the sentimental, somewhat utopian socialism of the Populists, Marxism seemed to bring forth a realistic socialism, based on a thorough knowledge of history and economics. It also possessed a workable method of action, a sense of organization, and, above all, an articulate doctrine of social revolution.

During his first year at the University, Berdyaev became acquainted with David Logvinsky, a student attached to the department of natural sciences and an ardent spokesman for Karl Marx. Youthful Nicolas felt a strange attraction for the unusually tall, narrow-chested, and signally brilliant Jew. Bonds of genuine friendship were soon to tighten the relations between the two young men. Together they spent interminable hours in exploring social, political, and philosophical issues raised by the Marxist movement. As a result, Berdyaev's interest in the leading German social thinker and his followers quickly intensified and deepened. He applied himself to studying *Das Capital,* and accepted this critique of capitalism without reservation.[3]

Through Logvinsky he came into contact with a group of militant Marxists. Among them he met with Anatoly V. Lunatcharsky, the future first Commissar of Public Education after the Bolshevik Revolution. The glowing enthusiasm which animated the members of the group evoked in Berdyaev an attitude of active participation in social problems. Concurrently, his dislike of the nobility increased and turned into a bitter repulsion. He saw in it mostly arrogance, prebendary privileges, and class selectiveness.[4] He longed for a complete break with the life and traditions of his native environment. In accordance with this frame of mind, he left his home and moved into a down-town flat: at last he felt himself set free from the fetters of a *status quo* no longer sufferable. He joined the Social-Democrat Party, began addressing meetings and presiding over the sessions of the party Executive Committee, and before long was regarded as the ideological leader of the Marxists of Kiev.

What motivated the aristocrat Berdyaev to make, in preference to any other, common cause with Marxism? His passionate feeling for social justice? This consideration certainly played an important part in his association with the revolutionary Intelligentsia. Indeed, he could never come to terms with the existing condition of social stratification, and judged the privileges of his own class with utmost severity. He rebelled against the poverty, the helplessness, and the humiliation of the Russian *moujik.*[5] He loathed the unequitable distribution of labor, and poignantly grieved over shameless exploitation by the landowners and capitalists of the peasants and wage-earners. Consequently, he held the social demands of Marxism as just, and approved their goal of political and moral liberation of Russia.

It should also be noted that Berdyaev's socialist leanings had developed before he entered the University and joined the Marxist fold. Along with many intellectuals of his generation, young Nicolas came under the influence of the prominent Russian thinker of that time, N. K. Mikhailovsky (1842-1904). A sociologist of wide erudition, Mikhailovsky was the leading mind of the Revolutionary

Socialists and a staunch defender of individual rights and freedom. His concept of the dual unity "truth-justice"—a typically Russian idea of acknowledging truth in the sense of justice and vice versa[6] —appealed to the educated circles of the Intelligentsia and provided an ethical impetus to their struggle for the awakening of the social consciousness of the people.

It would be a mistake, nevertheless, to see in Berdyaev's intense social concern the decisive reason which won him to the Marxist camp. His association with the world of the revolutionaries stemmed from sources much deeper:

> My adherence to revolutionary ideas appears to me a very complex matter, and I do not think I merely followed the trail of the majority of the Russian Intelligentsia. What struck me above all was the prospect of a spiritual revolution: a rising of the spirit, of freedom and meaning against the deadly weight, the slavery and meaninglessness of the world. Actually I was not much of a political revolutionary. . . . The revolutionary impulse sprang from an innate inability to acquiesce in the world-order and to submit to its exigencies. It had, therefore, primarily a personal, not a social significance. I was concerned with the revolution of the human person rather than of the people or the masses.[7]

At this stage of Berdyaev's intellectual evolution, Karl Marx assumed the semblance of a controlling spirit of the times to come. Berdyaev acquiesced in Marx' assertion that bourgeois capitalism is the carrier of an inner process of dehumanization which makes man the slave of the products of his own creation, and turns him into a mere organ and function. He also believed that capitalism erected fetishes and independent entities out of the products of human toil—a pernicious illusion against which the proletariat was called upon to fight. He realized the significance of the insight that reality itself—not the human mind alone—reveals elements of contradiction. Along with the master, Berdyaev conceived ultimate truth not as a fixed, eternal, and immovable verity; he apprehended it instead as a dynamic, dialectical movement of the contraries impelled by the universal law of perpetual becoming. Above all, he felt, Marxism conjured up a new vision of life and the promise of a new world. It postulated in clear-cut reasonings what ought to be and what could be expected in the near future. It construed society in terms of a creative, progressive organism, and proclaimed an integrating view of man that united thought to action. Indeed, Marxism appeared to Berdyaev as a doctrine of man's victory over irrational forces of nature and society:

> The Marxist movement of the late 'nineties was born of a new vision: it brought with it . . . a purpose and a new conception of man. It had, furthermore, a distinctly higher intellectual and cultural standard than most of the preceding movements. Marxism, at that juncture, was in fact a signal for the spiritual as well as social liberation of man. What attracted me most of all was its characteristic appreciation of the moving forces below the surface of history, its consciousness of the historic hour, its broad historical perspectives and its universalism. . . . The fact that Marxim took root among the Russian Intelligentsia was evidence of a further Europeanization of Russia and of her readiness to share to the end the destiny of Europe. I myself felt very anti-nationalistic and was never tempted to assert Russia against the West.[8]

It was, then, in the name of the revolution of the spirit, not of the collective, that Berdyaev became a Marxist. He was much more concerned with man's individuality and his freedom than with political and social values. He desired to overthrow the imperial autocracy not in order to supersede the Tsardom by another political order, however revolutionary, but to emancipate, or at least unfasten the heart and mind of men from all political authority. Accordingly, he did not confine to the boundaries of Russia alone his solicitude for the liberation of man: he extended it to the whole world. For it was the world in its entirety that lamented in bondage to evil and oppression. Everywhere Prometheus was chained to a rock: the history of mankind bore witness to the tragedy of man's destiny.

> Even before I came to take a more active part in social life I was awakened to the realization of the boundless falsehood and evil which pervade and underlie the life of the world, society, and civilization. My reading of history only served to confirm this impression. History unfolded itself before my eyes as a progression of crimes and falsifications, even if I recognized that it is no mere pointless game but a process

endowed with some mysterious, if tragic, meaning. . . . I was apprehensive and sceptical of every form of the glorification of history, past or present, and felt that true, authentic life is not to be found within the precincts of history and civilization, with its dictates, conventions, customs, and conformities. But . . . I could never assume the posture of a spectator or judge *vis-à-vis* the world, and my sense of history made me identify myself with the historical destiny of man.[9]

At that time Berdyaev's identification with the historical situation of his country assumed the aspect of the Social-Democrat revolutionary movement. A fervor of exaltation took possession of the philosophy-minded student with the inevitable consequence that he threw himself into the struggle against the past order of things with all the daring and fire of youth.

For all that, Berdyaev never felt completely at home with the Marxists. From the very beginning he was disturbed by a sense of uneasiness and apprehension in regard to the lack of inner freedom among his revolutionary comrades. He looked askance at the low type of culture and a certain professionalism which seemed endemic with the revolutionaries. He also treated with disapproval and contempt the conspiracy aspect of the movement. The total effect, however, was not sufficiently powerful at the time to lead him out of this association.

At first, Russian Marxism was much less rigid than the later 'party-line' bolshevism of Lenin and Stalin. Some measure of freedom of opinion was current with the Social-Democrats; divergent viewpoints could be expressed. So it was that a differentiation took place within the Marxist Intelligentsia and soon divided them in two main groups: the Orthodox and the Criticists. The Orthodox insisted upon accepting the doctrine of Marx as a whole. They held dialectical materialism to be a complete and indisputable interpretation of life which provides an answer to all individual and social problems. They did not admit the reality of separate spheres of knowledge and action apart from Marxism. The world they envisioned was that of a strictly integrated, monolith-like cosmos; in it thought and action, theory and practice were organically welded. They were totalitarian in intellectual outlook, and authoritarian in political attitude. Consequently, they demanded an unreserved

57

subjugation of personal conscience and interest to the interest and conscience of the collective. They were well organized, disciplined, unfaltering in their allegiance to the Marxist creed, and extremely intolerant.[10]

The Criticists were at one with their opponents in considering the teaching of the German master as right in its evaluation of capitalism and valid as a method for social transformation; but, contrary to the Orthodox, they conceded the existence of other spheres of thought and action besides the political and the economic. They acknowledged the autonomy of religion, philosophy, art, and ethics, i.e., recognized the existence of spiritual values and creativeness independent from social conditioning. They promoted a critical revision of Marxism and tended to combine it with non-materialist philosophies. A critical Marxist could without inconsistency allow the social and economic truth of the system and at the same time reject its metaphysical implications. Accordingly, some of the revolutionaries—such as Peter Struve, Sergius Bulgakov, and S. L. Frank—turned from Marxist materialism and adopted the position of Idealism. They admitted the existence of moral and spiritual values which were not subject to matter, but independent of it. They assumed an attitude of more freedom toward the decisions, judgments, and behavior of the collective. The Criticists stressed the individual right to private opinion, shared in a liberal conception of the world, were tolerant, and shied away from the discipline of the group.[11]

Naturally, this was the position taken by Berdyaev from the start: was it not similar to that held by Kant? In fact, before his Marxist period, Berdyaev was nurtured by the philosophy of Kant, and felt a special affinity with its dualism. He accepted Kant's distinction between the realm of phenomena and the realm of 'things in themselves,' between the order of nature and the order of freedom. Thus he visualized an ideal world in opposition to the world of objects, and held the first as the actual source of moral values. On the basis of his irreformable idealism arose the ideological conflict between Berdyaev and the Orthodox Marxists. The conflict, latent at the beginning, turned into bitter controversy and open hostility especially with Lunatcharsky who represented the orthodox Marxian viewpoint. On this he commented as follows:

I maintained the existence of truth and goodness as idealist values which are independent of the class struggle, of social conditions and the rest; and I do not acquiesce in the final subjection of philosophy and ethics to the revolutionary class struggle. I believed in the existence of truth and justice as determining my revolutionary attitude to social reality, and not as determined by it. Lunatcharsky asserted that such a defense of disinterested truth, of the independence of the intellect and the right of personal judgment, contradicted Marxism, which subordinates the interpretation of truth and justice to the revolutionary class struggle. Plekhanov also used to tell me that it is impossible to remain a Marxist while holding my independent idealist philosophy.[12]

Plekhanov and Lunatcharsky were both right: one cannot remain loyal to Marx and at the same time defend the autonomy of truth and knowledge. Berdyaev knew it too, but he persisted in believing that a synthesis of Marxism and Idealism was still possible.

At this time a question might pertinently be asked: had Berdyaev ever shared in Marxist atheism? Not exactly, although at one time he denied God. His atheism, however,

> . . . was, in fact, an inverted religious conviction, an antitheism rather than atheism, implying a denial not of God but of the man-made image of God, of what I believed to be the traditional religious conceptions and travesties of him. I was not an atheist if atheism be taken to mean the denial of the supreme reality of spirit and absolute values independent of the material world. Neither was I a pantheist believing in some homogeneous primary matter extending through infinite space and identical with God. My intellectual position at that time (that is, during and after my university years) may most adequately be described as ethical Idealism as represented by Fichte. The God in whom I believed was the God of German Idealism, a God who is involved in the process of becoming.[13]

Berdyaev's independence of thought went hand in hand with the freedom of his social relations: he did not confine himself to the Marxist group exclusively, but kept in touch with other intellectuals. During this period he frequently met George Chelpanov, a University professor, who helped him to resist the possessive demands of his Marxist comrades and extricate himself from their intellectual medium. Later on he became acquainted with a young writer whose works on Dostoyevsky and Nietzsche were just beginning to appear. His name was Leo Shestov, and he was destined to become Berdyaev's intimate and life long friend, both in Russia and in exile abroad after the Bolshevik Revolution.

In 1898 Nicolas Alexandrovitch was arrested in connection with the discovery by the *Okhrana*[14] of the illegal printing press of the Social-Democrat Party in Kiev. This was a heavy blow to the revolutionaries, and a happy exploit to the imperial police. Kiev was one of the chief centers of the Russian Marxist movement at the time: through its publishing secret agency a considerable amount of anti-governmental and revolutionary literature was produced and disseminated throughout the empire. Berdyaev was arrested along with some hundred and fifty others, and interned in the Lukyanovsky prison on the outskirts of the city. Because the governor general of Kiev, Dragomirov, was a friend of his father, Nicolas was released within a month, but was forbidden to leave Kiev, and remained under constant police supervision.

Berdyaev's prevailing mood at the time of his arrest was typical of the Russian revolutionaries, and it is worth noting:

> My memories of this more serious occasion on which I was arrested are of a time of great excitement: at no other time have I known such a sense of a community of fate with my fellow-men. When I was arrested and cross-examined I did not feel cast-down or dejected: on the contrary, my mood was one of exhilaration, defiance and militancy. My subsequent arrests were accompanied by similar experiences. I must confess, however, that my own state of mind and that of many others at the time was altogether rather peculiar, and, as I see it now, there was something almost farcical about it. For we had no sense at all of any failure: on the contrary we were conscious of being victors; it seemed to us that a new era was beginning in the movement of liberation, that the news of our arrest would echo everywhere, even in Western Europe.[15]

In the meantime Berdyaev was expelled from the University. Thus his formal education came to an end: never again will he make any attempt to resume regularly his university studies. Awaiting trial (he was accused of conspiracy against the State), Berdyaev began to write. His first article "*F. A. Lange and Critical Philosophy in its Relation to Socialism*," was published in 1899 in *Neue Zeit* by

Karl Kautsky, the editor of the Marxist magazine, and himself a strong partisan of a revisionist type of Marxism. Berdyaev's interest was awakened by the fact that F. A. Lange adopted a position close to his own: he accepted materialism as a method of scientific research, but rejected its philosophical implications. Being also influenced by Kant, Lange conceived an ideal world transcending the sensible phenomena. The article drew the criticism of the extremists, and marked the beginning of an open conflict between its author and the revolutionary Intelligentsia. It spelled also a spiritual crisis and the first step toward his liberation from Marxism.

Berdyaev's friendship with Shestov, and most of all his intensive reading of Ibsen widened the issues which were tormenting him: how to combine materialism and idealism. Shestov brought him to a closer realization of the existence of the tragic in life to which Marxism has no satisfactory answer and in which it gives evidence of no interest. Ibsen, on the other hand, drew his attention to the tragic predicament of person, of creativity, and of spiritual freedom as they are posited within the immoral and binding setting of social conventions. All this naturally moved him farther away from Marxism: yet he did not abandon his socialist outlook.

In his first philosophic work, written immediately after the article on Lange, but published while in exile, *Subjectivism and Individualism in Social Philosophy*, Berdyaev effectuated a bold attempt to reconcile Marxism and Idealism.[16] In fact, however, the theme developed in the book appeared more as an apology for Idealism than an argument for its integration into Marxism. Again the author asserted vigorously his conviction of the independence of truth, goodness, and beauty from the social environment. Later, referring to this book, Berdyaev acknowledged that in it he

> endeavored to show the possibility of a synthesis of critical Marxism and the Idealistic philosophy of Kant and partly of Fichte. . . . The idea of the book sprang from a fundamental conviction concerning the ultimate independence of truth, goodness and beauty *vis-à-vis* the social environment or the revolutionary class-struggle, and from a belief in 'transcendental consciousness' as their source or origin. I held firmly to the Kantian *a priori*, which denotes a reality of the logical and ethical order. On the other hand, I maintained that, on the psychological level, consciousness is dependent on and deter-

mined by man's environment and the place he occupies as a member of a given class. There may be circumstances, I wrote, more or less favorable to the assimilation of truth and the approximation to justice, whilst truth and justice, in themselves, are rooted in transcendental consciousness. 'Class-truth,' in my view, was a wholly contradictory and meaningless expresssion. There can, however, be 'class-untruth,' such as the untruth which informs the bourgeois classes, implicated as they are in the evil of exploiting their fellow-men. This idea provided the basis for my theory of the messianic calling of the proletariat; for the proletariat is free from the sin of exploitation, and its social and psychological condition enables it to receive and bear witness to truth. I viewed the working-class as embodying, as it were, the proximity, or even the identity, of man's psychological condition with the transcendental consciousness. In my opinion this gave a much more adequate foundation for radical, revolutionary Marxism than the views of the other adherents of critical Marxism. I accepted the materialist interpretation of history over against the bourgeois illusion, according to which things in heaven are commodities relegated to another life because they are unobtainable by the workers, from whom they have been stolen by the representatives of a ruthless individualistic society; but I repudiated the metaphysical implications of materialism. I believed, above all, that truth cannot be imprisoned in any social net, socialist or capitalist, and that those who pursue the knowledge of truth step tiresomely and boldly out of neat prisons into worlds that have more to them than sociology or science could ever contain. My thought was thus left free to move in whatever direction it chose.[17]

In other words, Marxism was right in stating that society is the outcome of man's struggle for life: a social ground is therefore necessary for the spiritual and cultural growth of the individual. But, at the same time, man has also spiritual ends and a destiny independent of his social life. The destiny of the world and the destiny of the individual are not identical. And no social transformation of the former could bring about the alteration of the latter.

The publication of the work was differently received—with scorn by the Orthodox Marxists, with enthusiasm by the small group of the Critical Marxists. Berdyaev was hailed as the leader of the

Russian Revisionism to which one of its adherents, Sergius Bulgakov, gave the name "From Marxism to Idealism."

Nevertheless, the attempt to 'revision' Marxism by any idealistic approach was doomed to failure: for Marxism denied spiritual reality, while idealism made of it the very ground of its philosophy. The barrier between Berdyaev and the Marxist circles rapidly grew unsurmountable. Did our philosopher find at least a personal, intellectual satisfaction in his findings? Not even that. More than ever he seemed entangled in the inner contradictions of Marxism and of his own attempts at revising it. In fact, Berdyaev's problem at this time lay elsewhere: imperceptibly he was outgrowing his very idealism. As he wrote later,

> I became increasingly aware of the transcendent dimensions of life. I saw myself thrown into this world, and all around me were whirling the unknown, unseen forces of transcendence: I could not remain content within the closed circle of one-dimensional, flat, mundane existence.[18]

The affair of the illegal printing press dragged on for two years at the end of which Berdyaev was sentenced to two years of administrative exile in the district of Vologda, in northern Russia. Consequently, he removed from Kiev to the ancient city of Vologda; there he set up quarters at the inn the "Golden Anchor." The exile caused him no serious hardship. He moved undisturbed by the police and had relationship with the local society. But most of all, he enjoyed his independence in regard to his own party. He received without inconvenience correspondence, magazines, and books from his friends and relatives in Kiev. He could read and write at will. Vologda was at the time an important center of political deportation. Many fellow-exiles came to see Berdyaev at the inn. But the spirit of enthusiasm and friendship of the early days was gone. His reputation as a revisionist and idealist did not help his relations with the Social-Democrats. He enjoyed, however, his intercourse with the novelist Alexey Remizov, and continued to debate with Lunatcharsky, both of whom arrived shortly after him.

Two articles among others written in Vologda greatly contributed to the worsening of his relations with the Marxists. They were

The Struggle for Idealism and *The Ethical Problem in the Life of Philosophical Idealism.* The latter, published in the symposium *The Problems of Idealism,* was Berdyaev's first attempt to formulate the idea of personalism which came to be the backbone of his whole philosophical outlook. As a result, he provoked a wave of hostility against him. He was branded a "dangerous individualist"[19] and accused of idealistic aberration. Some went so far as to call him a traitor.

The Vologda period marked the beginning of a new stage in Berdyaev's spiritual evolution. In theory, he still belonged to the Social-Democrat party. He continued to regard the Marxist critique of bourgeois capitalism as essentially correct and corresponding to historical facts, although he did not accept the social and economic determinism. But his interest came to be focused more and more upon man's personality and individual destiny. He began to view the individual as a being unique and not interchangeable, who should not be subjugated to any power in general. Man alone was important, not society, and Marxism had neither esteem for the person nor love for human freedom. Years later, Berdyaev, summed up the sad conclusions he reached at the time in the following words:

> But I saw with grief that in that [Marxist] camp also there was no reverence for the dignity of personality, and the liberation of the people was too often associated with the enslavement of man and his conscience. At a very early stage I saw the results of this process. The revolutionaries had no love for freedom of the spirit; they denied the rights of human creativeness.[20]

With such a frame of mind, the actual break with Marxism could no longer be postponed. This came about with the publication in the magazine *Mir Bojii* (God's World) of his article *The Struggle for Idealism.* Of this he wrote:

> This article was the signal for a break with the traditional outlook of the Intelligentsia, and its worm's eye view of the world. I proclaimed the primacy of spiritual and esthetic values, smothered and suppressed by them. I had a strange sensation of the approaching spiritual upheaval in Russia which

marked the first decade of the twentieth century. The article in question also embodied an experience of the conflict between personality and society—an experience possibly more characteristic of me than of the other representatives of this upheaval.[21]

What actually happened to Berdyaev's infatuation with Marxism was simply this: his eyes gradually opened to the fact of the irreconcilable contradiction between the idealist and materialist sides of Marxism and the growing ascendancy of the latter over the former. The belief in a moving spirit as independent of the illusory and deceptive world of objectivity became barely mentioned in the discussions of the revolutionaries. Economic materialism took over instead, shaping the minds and dictating the course of action. Now since, according to Marx, economics determines the whole structure of society and of human life, it necessarily follows that all spiritual culture—religious beliefs, philosophy, moral values, literary and artistic creativeness—are but superstructure of an inevitable economic process, and mind but an epiphenomenon of matter. Accordingly, Marx placed the social class above man whose freedom, creativity, and deepest spiritual experiences he reduced to a class function. The tragic irony of Marxism, as Berdyaev saw it, basically consisted in the final denial of the personality of the individual in whose name Karl Marx revolted against capitalism. The living subjects thus became reduced to the status of means and objects. Marx reproached the bourgeoisie for turning relations of men into relations of things; but then he achieved the same ideological standing for the sake of materialism. The individual exploiter was replaced by the collective, and man subjugated to a self-created myth, that of the impersonal, infallible proletariat. Thus Marxism became much more than a science or politics—a new religion actuated by a diabolic will for power, and exclusive of person, of spirit, of God.[22]

In the last resort, the fatal error of Marxism was to confuse nature and spirit, and reduce thought to matter. But its capital sin resided in the rejection of God:

> In the ultimate analysis Marxism is a lie, because God exists, i.e., a supreme power which is the fount of all power—

65

a spiritual and not an economic power. It is true that social life is controlled by power, but neither economics nor class struggle is the supreme force; that can be found only in the spirit.[23]

At this point Berdyaev's break with the Revolutionary Intelligentsia became an accomplished fact. History is transient, classes are fugitive, economic goods are ephemeral: above and beyond them Berdyaev was henceforth to conduct his search in the direction of the only eternal reality within the temporal world, that of the human soul; and transcending it—that of the mystery of God.

CHAPTER III

THROUGH CULTURAL RENAISSANCE IN RUSSIA:
BEYOND IDEALISM

> The individual must never be sacrificed, he is sacred and inviolable, and all the efforts of our mind should be directed to following his destiny minutely, and establishing him at the point where he may triumph.[1]
>
> —Mikhailovsky

Berdyaev returned from the exile in 1901—a lonely figure. He was then twenty-seven years old. The social medium he found in Kiev was no longer favorable to him. The Social-Democrats overtly accused him of political disloyalty and flayed him with invectives in their publications. The liberals, on the other hand, treated with scorn his idealism and judged the man skeptically. The rest of the Intelligentsia merely ignored him. Nicolas Alexandrovitch felt deeply disturbed by the changing of circumstances. The break with his former socialist friends made him unhappy after all; and he had not yet established new associations. At heart he kept harboring his past leanings toward Marxism. But he also sensed that the relationships with revolutionaries had reached the point of no return: he could not backtrack on his present ideological position. For years he had believed a workable combination between philosophical idealism and dialectical materialism was possible. To this effect he had put forth his thought and action. He had dismissed as both unconvincing and hypocritical the arguments advanced by liberalism and individualism against socialism, and their defense of freedom as spurious. But during the long period of the Vologda confinement he came to the full realization of the impossibility of such a synthesis: Russian socialism, as he rightly saw it, was developing not in the direction of the emancipation of man, but rather that of the destruction of human freedom, thus leading to a totalitarian system of tyranny and despotism. He was deeply shattered by this realization. The most ambitious dream of his youth lay broken against the callousness of sordid actuality. Thus he had to relinquish a long-cherished undertaking. In turn, he felt forsaken. He bore his isolation with acute pain. Gradually the sheer drudgery of daily life became a weight on his energy: he all but stopped writing. The time arrived when weariness brought discouragement. The past expectations proved illusory—and who can live on the basis of past expectations alone?

Yet, significantly, Berdyaev at this time seemed more than ever assured in his idealistic position. He was repelled by the commonplace and ugly trend of the contemporary Russian political scene where the individual person was sacrificed on the altar of an impersonal collective. To the social he opposed the individual—the primary reality and significance of the individual as a free spirit. For all his attitude toward the communal, it would, however, be a mistake to fancy Berdyaev allured by the snares of philosophical egoism. Ostensibly he was close to it. But in fact, he never identified himself with individualism. How did he succeed in avoiding this pitfall? Simply in keeping the individual organically connected with his social environment; except that he envisaged him in terms of an independent, spiritual entity, and not as a sociological category.

Foregoing all public activities for the time being, Berdyaev sought contacts with new people. He wanted to check his ideas against those of others; he desired to gain new insights, to extend his knowledge, to sharpen his intuition of man and his destiny.

One of the first, and most consequential encounters he made upon his return to Kiev was that of Sergius Bulgakov, then a professor of political economy at the Polytechnic Institute of the city. The latter had a wide reputation as a public lecturer, and his articles on economics were appreciated throughout the country. A former socialist, Bulgakov knew intimately Karl Kautsky, August Bebel, and Wilhelm Liebknecht—all leaders of German social-democracy. In his youth he became, as so many of his contemporaries, enthusiastic over Marxism. He accepted dialectical materialism as a valid method of scientific inquiry and a positive ethical norm. After years of extensive studies, both in Russia and abroad, he had, among the first, reached the conclusion that Marx' doctrine was insufficient to account for all aspects of life as it pretended to do; and specifically in the field of land economy, it was even not justified by the history of agriculture.[2] Subsequently, his intellectual development followed a path similar to that trodden by Berdyaev: he freed himself from the fetters of economical materialism, and accepted the fundamental propositions of idealism. At the time of their meeting, Bulgakov seemed to have outgrown the last position as well. Thus, while Berdyaev was still soaring high on the wings of idealism, his friend was gradually making headway toward Christianity.

The encounter in fact marked the end of Berdyaev's purely philosophic and social activity; from this time on, and for the rest of his life, he became increasingly absorbed in religious phenomena. Never before had he been so seriously challenged as during his conversations with Bulgakov; these dwelt not on Kant and Marx alone, but also and above all on Christian theology. He discerned in Bulgakov the riches of a deep inner experience, that of faith, and his heart felt strangely kindled with a thirst which his professed idealism could satisfy no longer. Together the two seekers after truth spent many a night debating problems of religious belief. And Berdyaev discovered new horizons whose expanse stretched out to infinity. Shall he embrace Orthodoxy? Not yet. But the process of inner re-orientation was touched off. At this stage of his spiritual pilgrimage, Bulgakov was the guide who pointed out the way to Christ; at a later period, a mentor of a different vein, Dostoyevsky's *Great Inquisitor*, will usher him into the depths of the Christian experience—from henceforth to return no more.

Notwithstanding the newly aroused interest in religion, social problems did not cease to exercise his conscience and concern. It must also be noted that the beginning of the century appeared in no wise suitable for abstract speculations. Russia was ignited with revolutionary agitation. The atmosphere was tense and sinister. An impending doom moved its somber shadow over the vast empire.

The years 1901-1903 inaugurated a period of unprecedented economic and political crisis in the Tsardom of Nicolas II. The conflict between the Government and its countless subjects was rendered inevitable by the growing opposition of the former to the most elementary needs of the population. Toward the end of the 19th century the discontent of the masses found vent in numerous anti-government manifestations among the students in the universities, in labor disturbances, and strikes in the industrial centers. The Government counteracted severely. Reprisals were intensified and police control extended over all aspects of social life, the press included. But contrary to official expectation, the immediate result of this brutal policy was only to increase public resistance and prepare the way for new demonstrations. Meanwhile the demands of the working class, which for the past years had been strictly professional, assumed more and more a political character. They requested not merely higher wages and better living conditions, but also the granting of civil liberties and a constitutional government. In 1901 a general strike paralyzed the the huge military plant of Obukhovo. A bloody collision followed between the factory men and the tsarist troops sent to restore order. The survivors were treated with abject savagery. The strike was beaten down without mercy, but its repercussions were destined to exercise a far-reaching sway both over the world of industry and, for the first time, among the peasants. Soon after the Obukhovo affair, the walk-outs multiplied throughout the cities of Russia. Furthermore, the *moujiks* of the Volga region launched a vast campaign against the land holders, setting their residences on fire, and murdering the estate owners by the scores. Under the influence of the revolutionary action promoted by the workers and the peasants, the movement of opposition became more pronounced also among the students. From Vladivostok to Baku to Moscow and St. Petersburg the universities resounded with demands for a change in the regime. Even the army had been affected: subversive leaflets and newspapers made their appearance in the barracks and were avidly read by the service men. And everywhere, always, the increasing

70

demands for social justice and political freedom were met by the autocratic Government in the same way—with bullets, prison, deportation to Siberia. But the official attempt to forestall the social upheaval proved abortive. The revolution was irresistibly making headway.

The Russian predicament kept Berdyaev constantly anxious. More than ever did he sense the dawning of a new era over the country. He felt the underground rumbling of the approaching storm. He could not remain outside the conflict. He craved for an active participation in the general movement of liberation. With whom should he ally himself? Russian Orthodoxy offered no political platform for action. With the Social Revolutionaries he had always refused to have anything in common. The ranks of Social-Democracy at present were forbidden to him. And the liberals wanted unity and organization. After a period of inner struggle, Berdyaev reached the conclusion that a temporary change of political climate would, for the time being, offer the most salutary course of action. Accordingly, in 1903 he went to Germany. There he entered the University of Heidelberg and during the summer semester attended the lectures of Wilhelm Windelband, a celebrated historian and philosopher.

The year 1903 marked a turning-point in the history of Russian Marxism: the birth of Bolshevism. The signal event occurred at the Second Congress of the Social-Democrat Party held in London. At that time Lenin announced that the working class would be unable to effect any substantial reforms without the help of a well trained leadership of the "professional revolutionaries." [3] Consequently, he demanded the immediate building up of a strong party apparatus whose appointed goal would be the fight for the dictatorship of the proletariat. This was a flagrant departure from the orthodox Marxist theory of the inevitability of the revolution in view of the infallible process of economic determinism. Serious differences of opinion arose between the partisans of Lenin's program for a tight party organization and discipline and the supporters of Martov who spurned the idea of realizing a social revolution in Russia by violent means. The latter maintained that in order to achieve socialism a bourgeois democracy had to develop first which

71

would include all classes and not solely the proletariat. After long sessions of bitter polemic, Lenin's arguments won the vote of the majority. Thus, at the end of the Congress, the Russian Social-Democracy irremediably split into two factions: the members of Lenin's radical majority, subsequently known as Bolsheviks (*bolshinstvo*, majority), and the Martov's moderates which became known as Mensheviks (*menshinstvo*, minority).

In the same year, 1903, the Russian liberal groups organized, in turn, a political party named the League of Liberation under the leadership of Professor Paul Miliukov. Their program did not follow Marx and Western socialism, but was rather based upon the European and American ideals of democracy. They did not attempt to reach the masses of the people, but to influence the thought of the government and evoke thereby social reforms. Two years later, the League of Liberation became instrumental in the founding of the Constitutional-Democrat (Cadet) Party which, until the revolution, represented the most radical political body in the opposition to the tsarist regime.

In Heidelberg Berdyaev met with several members of the Liberal movement. He befriended them. He approved of their goals and believed he had found at last the political framework he was seeking in order to carry on the struggle for the release of Russia from the secular bondage of autocratic satrapy. He went to two of their conferences, held respectively in Schwarzwald and Schaffhausen, beside the Rhine falls. Yet, he actually never displayed any enthusiasm for the League. Indeed, he preferred the beauty of the surrounding country much more than the conferences. Socialist at heart, he remained always conscious of the gulf separating him from the Liberals—a gulf, as he put it, "deeper than that which divided me from the Social-Revolutionaries and Social-Democrats."[4] His interest in the League of Liberation was not political: within the newly constituted organization he saw the possibility of taking the good fight up again without compromising his spiritual searchings. On the other hand, Berdyaev never joined the Constitutional-Democratic Party precisely on account of its bourgeois leanings. Nevertheless, his feelings did not prevent him from being active and even representing the League in its dealings with other parties.

In the early summer of 1904 Berdyaev returned from Germany to Kiev. After his experience abroad, he felt only uneasiness and incongruity in the city of his birth. He was no longer prophet in his own quarter. In fact, the place—its life, interests, and pre-occupations— became totally alien to him. Besides, he had heard of a new cultural and spiritual movement which was about to spring into vigorous action in the metropolis of the North. Thus he planned to move to St. Petersburg.

That was the year of the Russian-Japanese War. Early in February, without any declaration of war, the fleet of Japan attacked Russian armed vessels in the outer harbor of Port Arthur. Soon they succeeded in blockading the port and landing on the mainland. After a series of severe setbacks, the Russian army suffered a complete defeat at Mukden. The fleet, sent under the command of Admiral Roshdestvensky from the Baltic Sea to the Far East around Africa, was destroyed by the Japanese in the battle of Tsushima.

In the midst of Russian military and naval defeat Von Plehve, the reactionary Minister of Interior, was assassinated; street demonstrations broke out against the unpopular war; public discontent waxed daily; violent riots embroiled country and city alike. Demands for reforms were voiced throughout the empire.

On Sunday, January 22, 1905, a crowd of several thousands of unarmed workmen, accompanied by their wives and children, carrying ikons and singing hymns, made their way to the Winter Palace in St. Petersburg to address a petition to the Tsar. The procession, led by the priest Gapon, was arranged by the Union of Russian Workers, an organization sponsored by the Government and loyal to the regime. The petition appealed for the Emperor's justice and protection against exploitation. It also requested the granting of civil liberties, the convocation of a Constituent Assembly, autonomy for urban and rural administration, and termination of war. Nicolas II refused to receive the delegation. Instead, the whole procession was dispersed by gunfire, as a result of which hundreds of people were killed or wounded. The massacre destroyed the last vestige of public faith in monarchy. "Bloody Sunday," as the day came to be called, produced world-wide indignation, shook the nation to its foundations, and opened the revolutionary crisis.[5] Indeed, the tsarist double-headed eagle had sealed its own fate.

That day marked the beginning of the first Russian Revolution. Strikes, demonstrations, insurrections gained momentum and spread from coast to coast. A series of assassinations of governmental officials was touched off by the terrorists. The Government retaliated with armed forces. In many cases the soldiers, affected by revolutionary propaganda, revolted against their officers. In June, 1905, the battleship *Potemkin* roused to mutiny in sympathy with the strikers in Odessa, and for a while flew the red flag of the revolutionaries. Finally, under duress and unwillingly, the Government decided upon concessions in the matter of political reforms. On August 19, 1905, Nicolas II signed a manifesto summoning a national assembly—the Imperial Duma—with advisory powers, but without legislative functions. This was, however, a half-measure which satisfied no one, serving only to fan the ardor of the people's passion for freedom. In the fall of 1905, following the termination of the Japanese war, the situation became critical. Late in October the All-Russian Railway Worker's Union called a general strike. In the cities electricity and water were cut off; the postal and telegraph service suspended; railroad transportation came to a standstill throughout the Empire. At the same time local Soviets—special councils composed of the leaders of the Socialist parties and representatives of the workers—were gaining authority in St. Petersburg, Moscow, Odessa, and elsewhere. The revolution was steadily progressing toward the overthrowing of absolutism. But before the Soviets achieved any important results, the Tsar, pressed by his advisors, issued a second manifesto, which amounted practically to capitulation by the Government. This decree granted to the Russian nation freedom of speech, conscience, and assembly, the right of labor to organize, a more liberal suffrage law, and the guarantee that no legislative proceedings could henceforth be concluded without the Duma's consent. The result was that the Manifesto succeeded in satisfying the majority of the people. In spite of subsequent strikes and an armed insurrection in Moscow instigated by the Bolsheviks—who resolved to fight the monarchy to the end—the first Russian revolution subsided. The

74

Government was enabled to retake control of the country. The local Soviets were disbanded; all further opposition suppressed by force.

The Russian defeats in the Far East were painfully felt by Berdyaev. He suffered for his motherland, and his patriotic pride was deeply hurt. Unlike the Bolsheviks, who regarded the capitulation of Port Arthur as the golden opportunity for a national uprising against absolutism, Berdyaev, who shared in their revolutionary expectations, questioned the adequacy of the moment and the decency of their method for such an attempt.

Of the revolution itself, Berdyaev stated that

> . . . it became a source of a real agony to me. The revolution, in my view, was quite inevitable; I welcomed it and disagreed with the Mensheviks who had given it half-hearted and lukewarm support. . . . Nevertheless, these were not 'days of freedom'; indeed, to me they brought a sense of moral and spiritual suffocation. The atmosphere of bloody slaughter seemed to hover over one's mind, and the massacre of many thousands of revolutionaries and workers seemed to kill the last remnants of hope not only in the Tzarist regime but in the revolution itself and in the possibility of any change on this basis.[6]

All was not gloom, however, in Berdyaev's life at that critical period of Russian history. A few months before the revolution, he met the girl who was to become his beloved, lifelong companion. Lydia Yudifovna Trushev, his future wife, and her sister Evgenia, were the daughters of a wealthy and celebrated lawyer. The two girls had just been released from prison where they served a term on account of their subversive activities. Lydia combined a deeply religious conviction with a strong revolutionary impulse. She was a poet and a mystic.[7] As a poet she was highly appreciated by Mikhail Gershenzon and Vyacheslav Ivanov, though she always refused to have her poems published during her own lifetime. Later on she became a Roman Catholic. Nicolas and Lydia married soon after their meeting and moved to St. Petersburg.

On arrival in the great northern metropolis, Nicolas Alexandrovitch entered a world of intellectual and cultural expanse hitherto unknown to him—the literary world of the Russian cultural renaissance. Of this admirable intellectual and spiritual adventure he wrote:

> At the beginning of the century there was in Russia a real cultural renaissance. Only those who themselves lived through that time know what a creative inspiration was experienced among us and how the breath of the spirit took possession of the Russian souls. Russia lived through a flowering of poetry and philosophy. Intense religious inquiry formed part of its experience, a mystical and occult frame of mind.[8]

The cultural revival was distinguished by a return to the traditions of the great Russian literature and religious-philosophical thought of the past. From Chernyshevsky and Plekhanov, the intellectuals turned to Dostoyevsky, Tolstoy, Vladimir Solovyov. The 19th century Russian thinkers, like Khomyakov, Leontyev, Fedorov, and Rozanov, who had fallen into half-oblivion or as yet but little known and appreciated, were re-assessed and received recognition. This was a time of creativeness—of an astonishing awakening of spirit and mind. There occurred within a certain stratum of the Intelligentsia a dramatic re-orientation from Marxism to Christianity, from materialism to spiritualism, from dull and dreary commonplace to the heights of inspiration in arts and literature. The merely social world outlook, which was traditional with the educated Russian milieu, became outworn and obsolete. Minds were set free from the purely materialistic values. The emphasis was focused upon man's spiritual nature, his creative freedom and his independence of social utilitarian determinism. This did not imply, however, that the social interest had been consigned to the attics of indifference. On the contrary, the current problems did not cease to preoccupy the men of the renaissance. What actually happened was a profound revaluation of the Russian social reality: it was no longer regarded exclusively as economic and political, but spiritual as well. It is true, however, that in the long run the spiritual concern took the upper hand over the temporal. The enlarged intellectual outlook eventually dimmed individual awareness of social truth among the Intelligentsia, slackened interest in social questions, and led to passivity and indifference. As a result, the emphasis was gradually shifted from practical problems to mere abstract polemics.

This cultural renaissance, it should be noted, was prevalent only within a comparatively restricted strata of the Intelligentsia, i.e., to a cultural *élite* which exerted little influence on the broader masses of the people, and none on the revolutionary forces surreptitiously shaping the destiny of the nation. The movement developed in isolation from the wider social currents of the time; it often attached insufficient value to the social ideals which informed the Left Intelligentsia and which clothed them with power. The promoters of the Russian revolution, on the other hand, were inspired by a world-view developed under the tutelage of nihilism and positivism and were completely indifferent to the traditional treasures of the 19th century national thought.

> This fact had a fatal effect on the character which the great Revolution in Russia assumed: it began by perpetrating a real pogrom against what was best in Russian culture. In fact, the intelligentsia committed cultural suicide. It may be said that in pre-revolutionary Russia two human generations grew up side by side. The blame for this state of affairs rested with both sides, that is to say, alike with the leaders of the revolution and with the promoters of the cultural renaissance, who were indifferent to social and moral problems.[9]

Furthermore, symptoms of unmistakable decadence and corruption tarnished the genuineness of intellectual and spiritual awakening and deprived it of strength. For many the great cultural intensification became merely a matter of fashion and imitation to conform themselves to the moods of the day. Ethical values were disparaged to the detriment of an unwholesome estheticism. There was too much ambiguity covered with cultural refinement. This often ensued in irretrievable confusion of right and wrong; and prevented forming a true estimate of the scope and depth of that remarkable period.

Despite the above reservations, the cultural renaissance had a pregnant bearing upon the intellectual and spiritual pursuits of the Russian mind at its best. This became manifest above all in philosophy and religion. An original school of thought made its appearance. Interest was quickened in traditional Orthodoxy. Poetry, too, sprang back into life. Art flourished afresh. French symbolists, German philosophers and mystics, great Russian novelists aroused enormous interest. After decades of religious apathy, there was initiated at that time an extensive movement toward Christianity. Concurrently one outstanding fact emerged—a radical change in the ideas of the most gifted men and women of the Intelligentsia; a decisive victory was achieved over the evils of materialism, positivism, utilitarianism; and a pathway was paved for the liberation of the spirit.

The formative stage for the Russian cultural renaissance was prepared, strange as it may seem, by Marxism—in its critical rather than authoritarian form. Indeed the introduction of Marxism in Russia in the 'nineties provoked an intellectual crisis in the consciousness of the Intelligentsia.[10] This ideology exposed the weaknesses of the then prevalent cultural tenor; it engendered the want for a change in the world-outlook and spiritual structure. The old historical and philosophical conceptions seemed outworn and no longer relevant. The socialism of the obsolete revolutionary *Narodnichestvo* had proved sentimental in doctrine and politically fallacious. The struggle for social truth and justice demanded a system reflecting historical reality more accurately and better grounded intellectually. At the same time a process of differentiation began to take place between the various fields of culture. Among the more educated members of the Intelligentsia there arose a firm conviction that religion, philosophy, and art should be detached from dialectical materialism; and that moral and spiritual life should be proclaimed free from subjection to revolutionary materialism. The main bulk of the Intelligentsia, however, insisted upon the theory that culture is wholly determined by social processes. Consequently, the latter embraced Marxism in its entirety; the former, while retaining the general Marxist outlook of history, went over to idealism and eventually to Christianity. Thus upon the soil of Marxism, and in response to its

78

challenge, there originated a prodigious intellectual and spiritual movement from which the renaissance issued. The movement was operating simultaneously in two directions; there was a high-soaring flight toward something original—new expressions and insights; but there was also a return both to the traditions of Russian thought of the 19th century and the prevalent currents of European culture.

The cultural renaissance in Russia had three immediate sources: literary, philosophic, and poetic.

The first source was literary, and the leading part here was played by Merezhkovsky and Rozanov. Both initiated a different approach to the Russian literature of the 19th century and broadened its understanding to an extent never reached before. While neither of them was morally profound, not even touched by spiritual earnestness, they stimulated a search for unknown or forgotten treasures of world literature. Merezhkovsky in particular lifted from the dust of oblivion the cultural values of Greek and Roman antiquity, of the Italian Renaissance, of French belle-lettres, of Nietzsche and Ibsen. His book on Tolstoy and Dostoyevsky contributed to a deeper appreciation of their writings, and led the way to their growing and decisive influence on Russian thought. Rosanov's literary activity, on the other hand, is connected with the view of rehabilitation of the flesh and of sex. He emphasized the sacred character of sex, which he considered as the "mysterious foundation" of life.[11] Besides, his freshness of style and mastery of expression produced a sensation among the literati and became the model for many essayists in Russian prose-writing.

The second source of the renaissance was the 19th century Russian religious philosophy. The names of Father Sergius Bulgakov and Paul Florensky, Leo Shestov, and Nicolas Berdyaev himself are perhaps the most outstanding in this connection. The new trends in philosophy were under the influence of the original heritage of Russian thought as expressed in the work of Alexis Khomyakov and Ivan Kireyevsky, Nicolas Feodorow and Vladimir Solovyov. All the named philosophers cherished the common goal to overcome the abstract rationalism and idealism of Western thought, and endeavored to formulate a philosophy of spiritual realism. At the same time there occurred a widening of the impact of Kant, Schopenhauer, Hegel and Schelling; even the German mysticism of Silesius, Boehme, and Eckhart crept into Russian consciousness and left its mark upon the religious thought.

Russian poetry formed the third current of the renaissance. This was the period of symbolism associated with Alexander Blok, Andrey Bely, and Vyacheslav Ivanov. They created a most remarkable poetry whose significance was esthetic and spiritual alike. The predominant influence here was that of Baudelaire, Nietzsche the mystic, and Solovyov the poet. The symbolists regarded things and events not as true in themselves, but only as tokens of some other, ultimate realities. They believed in the existence of a spiritual realm within and beyond the material. The visible, as Solovyov put it, was but the shadow of the invisible. The most distinctive characteristic of the Russian symbolists consisted in their being engaged less in building esthetic values than in searching for meanings of a spiritual order. They went beyond the boundaries of mere art and wended their way to Christianity and mysticism. Moreover, the poets' religious intuition took a prophetic character—they were filled and dominated by the forebodings of a dreadful fate which was moving over Russia. The atmosphere was one of expectation on the eve of some apocalypse. The symbolists expressed the feeling that the old Russia was coming to an end, and they anticipated the rise of a new, exalted Russia within a transfigured world.[12]

All three currents of the Russian cultural renaissance—literary, religious-philosophical, and poetical—shared in common a notable trait—a spiritual dimension. This was reflected in their tendency of transcending the limits of their respective spheres and turning their minds toward the kingdom of divine mystery. The men of the contemporary *élite* were the pioneers of a "new religious consciousness,"[13] indeed not typical of traditional Orthodoxy (and in the case of Rozanov and some others not even Christian)—the consciousness of a supranatural ground of existence. Their general outlook was revolutionary-mystical, nay, eschatological. Never before in the Russian cultural evolution had there occurred so intense an awareness of the illimitable unknown surrounding human life,

80

of the mystery of being, and the terror-breeding abyss with which man and history are faced. This was a time of intellectual unrest and inward tension, of profound religious challenges and secret longings; a time of almost ecstatic experiences; truly, an appointed time for the vision of new worlds—worlds of light, of creativity, of the spirit.

The community of ideals and perspectives begat the need for a *rapprochement* between the different sections of the renaissance Intelligentsia, and their mutual understanding. As a result there were organized in great cultural centers the Religious-Philosophical Societies which afforded a favorable opportunity for encounters and discussion. Berdyaev was very active in the Society of St. Petersburg which, it should be noted, was founded upon his initiative. These gatherings were attended also by representatives of the Orthodox Church, one of whom was Bishop Sergius, the future Patriarch of Russia under the Soviets. Renaissance periodicals served as channels for inter-communication and gave expression to the whole range of the prevalent cultural moods. One of the first was *Novy Put'* (The New Way), edited by Merezhkovsky and the group of which he was the center. For a time Berdyaev joined the editorial staff and published his articles in it. For various reasons, however, the publication had to be discontinued within a few months. It was succeeded by a new magazine, *Voprosy Zhizni* (Questions of Life), founded by Berdyaev and Bulgakov (who in the meantime had settled in St. Petersburg). Prose and verse contributions to the magazine were signed by the best authors of that period—Merezhkovsky, Rozanov, Anton Kartashov, Vyatcheslav Ivanov, Fyodor Sologub, Alexander Blok, Andrey Bely, Valery Bryusov, Aleksey Remisov, Chulkov, Gershenzon, Simeon Frank, Peter Struve, Prince Evgeny Trubetzkoy, Pavel Novgorodsev, Fyodor Zelinsky, Alexander Volynsky, Vladimir Ern, and, of course Bulgakov and Berdyaev. *Questions of Life* constituted the last attempt at representing a unified field of encounter to all current trends—political, intellectual, and religious—in a spirit of freedom and reciprocal esteem. This periodical, too, had to be suspended within a short time: the working conditions of those days of social unrest made it difficult to pursue its publication; besides, the dissensions which early arose among the contributors eventually led them to part company thus bringing to naught their common journalistic adventure.

Along with the Religious-Philosophical Societies and the literary periodicals, another featured highlight of the Russian renaissance was Vyacheslav Ivanov's so-called "Wednesdays." For several years on that afternoon the cultured *élite* of St. Petersburg would convene in Ivanov's large flat, known as "The Tower," on the top floor of a high building overlooking the Palace of the Duma in Taurida Park. The Tower was an established meeting ground of all the most remarkable men of letters, philosophers, scholars, artists, actors, and even politicians of that time. They attended in great number, and the debates were carried on through the night. They stated and discussed problems on a wide scale of interest—philosophy and art, history, culture, and politics; and always in a vein of searching eagerness and elevated inspiration. Yet, Berdyaev felt the incongruity of these assemblies. Later on he wrote in this connection, not without a sad irony:

> When recalling the 'Wednesdays,' I cannot help realizing that 'The Tower' was in the fullest sense of the word an ivory tower, where mystical conversations and literary reading took place, while below in the streets of Petersburg the revolution was raging and the tragic destiny of Russia took its course.[14]

Berdyaev's years in St. Petersburg, full of new intellectual and emotional experiences though they were, by no means proved satisfactory. He kept himself busy in writing, making speeches at political gatherings, and presiding over Ivanov's meetings. He learned a great deal about men and ideas; he acquired new insights into the problem of history and individual destiny; his understanding was considerably deepened; his mind was opened to new vistas; he was stimulated and inspired. But he did not discover the one thing that ultimately mattered: the motive and meaning of his life and thought. In the very midst of the storm-driven spiritual revival, the sense of loneliness never left him. He succeeded in keeping his critical faculties alert even when the world about him seemed to yield to irrational forces. Actually, the Russian cultural renaissance never had a really decisive impact on the manner and style of Berdyaev's thought: at heart he remained true to himself, to his inborn attitude of non-compliance to anything and anybody. Then, too, he was gradually moving away not only from Idealism, but from the milieu and outlook of the Intelligentsia as a whole. The articles published during this time, and later collected in a book entitled *Sub specie aeternitatis,* bear witness to the strengthening of his spiritual orientation. They disclose for the first time his frank shift from idealism to a religious ideology.[15] The new position was still colored with certain unconscious restiveness and vagueness, but it indicated an important step in Berdyaev's consciousness toward Christianity.

The failure of the First Revolution, and its disintegrating effect on certain sections of the Intelligentsia only increased Berdyaev's concern for the destiny of man; but at the same time the way of man brought him closer to the throne of God: the relation between the human and the divine—which escapes rational comprehension— postulated the need for religious faith, without which there can be no answer either to the problem of being or to the tragedy of life.

The revolutionary period of 1905-1906 failed to achieve a true parliamentary government. The expectations of the revolutionaries had not been fulfilled. Behind the fake constitutionalism of a powerless Duma—dissolved by the Government three times before its final end in the Revolution—the traditional autocracy resumed its oppressive absolutism. Berdyaev, contrary to many, was not dismayed by the tragic outcome. For him the true revolution lay elsewhere.

> To me this provided evidence for my own profound conviction that every political revolution is doomed and becomes stupefied by its own surfeit: the subject of true revolution must be man, rather than the masses or the body politic. . . . And the attempt to attain freedom by means of denying freedom to oneself or to others is doomed to failure. The failure of the 1905 revolution only served to intensify my longing for the revolution of the spirit.[16]

St. Petersburg circles provoked in him a growing irritation. He began to realize their egocentricity, nay, futility. On occasion he demonstratively rebelled against their demands and practices. He ended by reacting vigorously against all contemporary tendencies of the Intelligentsia. This coincided with his widening appreciation of the religious realm of existence. Eventually he decided to break all connections with the literary world and move away.

In 1907 he left Petersburg for Paris. He sought for a change in the world of men; what he found was the realm of God.

CHAPTER IV

ON THE EVE OF THE GREAT UPHEAVAL: CONVERSION TO CHRISTIANITY

> The essence of life is not man's separate being, but God contained in man. . . . The meaning of life is revealed when man recognizes his own divine essence.[1]
>
> —Leo Tolstoy

Nicolas Berdyaev was not brought up in the traditional atmosphere of Orthodoxy. His education at home was devoid of religious interest. His father was a free-thinker and a Voltairian.[2] His mother, a Roman Catholic convert, showed no taste for proselytism. Neither attempted to inculcate in the boy their respective convictions. As a child Nicolas was taken on state holidays to the church of Kiev's Governor General. But he was only annoyed at the ostentatious display of uniforms and decorations by the high-ranking bureaucracy attending the service merely because of social duty. He preferred the monasteries of Pechersk, although he felt oppressed by their gloomy precincts. Besides, he disliked monks. Contrary to a common trait of the Russian temperament, Berdyaev had never known any particular sentiment for the Orthodox liturgy; its elaborate ritual and profuse imagery left him quite unmoved. Moreover, he possessed no natural religious leanings.[3]

Berdyaev's gradual drift toward religion was prompted by motives other than either family upbringing or innate disposition. His orientation in respect to divinity had rather been determined by

> a consciousness, however dim and inarticulate, that reality is not and cannot be exhausted by this external world which forces itself on us; that we can exist only in the progress towards another world; that we are not fixed in a permanent position within a crude and self-sufficient universe; that we dwell in the midst of mystery.[4]

Religion appeared to him as the experience of man's hunger for God. The human soul, constrained by its earthly limitations, searches for a higher realm of life, for meaning and eternity. Marx' bitter contention is radically false: religion is not the opiate of the people, but rather the true source of their wholesomeness. Religion invests with sense everything it touches—philosophy, society, art. It is the realm of freedom and justice, of good and love. Religion is the answer to the deepest aspirations of the human heart, and as such, the major concern of men—albeit, often unawares.

All this is well and good, whines the echo of pain ridden humanity, but then why do men suffer? Is not the ever-present fact of evil in the world irrefutable argument against the existence of God? Berdyaev was not insensitive to evil; nay, he was rather excessively responsive to the depths of human misery and destitution. However, the problem of evil, which for many is a stumbling block on the roadway to belief, exercised just the opposite effect on Berdyaev—it adduced a decisive reason for his faith in God:

> My original religious impulse was bound up with a bitter feeling of discontent with and dissent from the world with its evil and corruption. And this was a first indication of my subsequent conviction that the existence of evil is not so much an obstacle to faith in God as a proof of God's existence, a challenge to turn towards that in which love triumphs over hatred, union over division, and eternal life over death.[5]

But this avowed religious idealism was as yet remote from Christianity: there was in it a want of the central Christian presupposi-

tion—the revelation of Christ. At this stage of his spiritual maturation Berdyaev did not engage in any specific profession of faith;
while the conventional Orthodox tradition supplied no lure to
his heart. He remained quite apprehensive of the Church's rigid
dogmas and ideals because they disclosed in his eyes a tangible
evidence of religious secularism and materialism. He conceived
of them as being agents of spiritual bondage—the Cains of the
freedom of the spirit. Despite the vagueness of his religious beliefs
at this time, Berdyaev's steps, nevertheless, were bending Cross-
ward: the tone of his religious experience already sent forth a
deeply Christian resonance:

> I see myself immersed in the depth of human existence and
> standing in face of the ineffable mystery of the world and of
> all that is. And in that situation I am made poignantly and
> burningly aware that the world cannot be self-sufficient, that
> there is hidden in some still greater depth, a mysterious, trans-
> cendent meaning. This meaning is God. Men have not been
> able to find a loftier name, although they have abused it to
> the extent of making it almost unutterable. God can be de-
> nied only on the surface: but he cannot be denied where
> human experience reaches down beneath the surface of flat,
> vapid, commonplace existence.[6]

As a result of this experience, Berdyaev was seized with an
earnest desire to deepen his comprehension of the Christian faith.
How could he best discover and determine the essence of Christianity? He resolved to undertake a thorough study of it. He embarked on an extensive program of reading theological works. He
also sought contacts with the representatives of Russian Orthodoxy.

Even before he moved to St. Petersburg Berdyaev's interest had
already been awakened by the Religious-Philosophical Societies in
which spokesmen of the cultural renaissance confronted their
ideological viewpoints with those entertained by the hierarchy of
the Orthodox Church. Berdyaev followed the arguments closely
for he felt that his own approach to Christianity was partly dependent on such confrontation.[7] The meetings would pass along
in an atmosphere of cooperation and genuine endeavor for mutual
understanding. The list of questions submitted to examination
was broad and diversified. Problems of culture and social life were

viewed along with subjects of art and creativity against a religious background. One of the main themes of discussion concerned the problem of the relation between sex and the Christian teaching. It revolved about the question whether Christianity is a religion of life-denial and asceticism, or whether it called for endorsement of the world and a program of mankind's weal. The theme was associated with the names of Vasily Rozanov and Dimitry Mereshkovsky.

Rozanov's religious and philosophical position was centered on sex taken as a religious concept. The latter for him was not primarily a function or an organ: he conceived of sex metaphysically and regarded the whole of man as its expression and development. "Sex is not the body," he once wrote, "the body merely whirls about it and out of it."[8] He was possessed by a vivid awareness of the mystery of sex. Birth is linked with sex; sex is life, nay, it is the triumph of life over death. The relation of sex to God is "stronger than the relation of intellect to God—stronger than the relation of conscience to God."[9] Since life and birth are holy, then sex, which is their source, must be sanctified also. In this matter the Christian attitude, according to Rozanov, entails an absurd contradiction. On the one hand, it abominates sex as a mortal sin; on the other, it recognizes the sexual union in order that life may continue. A great deal of Rozanov's intellectual keenness went into attacking what he termed the Christian hypocrisy in regard to sex. He divided religion into religion of birth and religion of death. He opposed to the religion of Golgatha— the religion of death—that of Bethlehem—the cult of marriage, family and childbearing. He believed in a religion of perpetual nativity, and considered the procreation of the human race as the only eternity. Eventually he ended in complete rejection of Christ in whom he saw a denier of life, the one who burdened the world with the shadow of his death and poisoned the joy of the generative process. He reverted to the Old Testament—the "religion of the Father,"[10] that is, the religion of Him who fecundates and begets—and adopted a position approximating the Hebrew and Canaanite cult of phallus.

Berdyaev was much in sympathy with Rozanov's exposure of the ambiguity of Christianity in the matter of sex. But he did not approve of his friend's glorification of the flesh. He decidedly opposed the Astarte-like worship of human fertility. He discerned in Rozanov's crude naturalism a complete disregard for personality and individual freedom. "Sex," he commented, "which is not integrated in and transfigured by spirit is always evidence of man's subjugation to the genus." [11] Berdyaev rejected any claim to the acceptance of the flesh as the supreme reality, and countered it with an emphatic assertion of the primacy of the spirit. He concluded, however, that spirituality does not of necessity stand in opposition to sexual life. Nor is flesh intrinsically evil: only the way in which flesh is used might be good or evil. Indeed, it is one thing to live in the flesh, and quite another to live according to the flesh. The second is Rozanov's ideological position; and it is wrong because it makes sex an end in itself. The spiritual life is not a mere running away from flesh: it is rather a life that is spiritual in all its wholeness—body and soul alike. And this is true asceticism: the transfiguration of the whole of man's being by the spirit. Furthermore, Berdyaev maintained—but this Rozanov had never been able to admit—that Resurrection, not Crucifixion, was the final word of Christianity. All the same, the great merit of Rozanov, according to Berdyaev, consisted in his stating the problem of sex in all its acuteness. He challenged Christianity to leave its traditional ambiguity toward sex, and come out with a decisive answer. His own solution was untrue. In the ultimate analysis his doctrine of deification of child-bearing meant a return to ancient paganism, and its far-reaching consequences led to the totalitarian supremacy of race over the individual. But he was with Weininger, Freud, and Lawrence among the pioneers who, at the end of the nineteenth and the beginning of the twentieth century, brought into the open the reality and importance of sex in human life. Rozanov had a profound influence on the religious and philosophic searchings of his generation. The influence is felt to a certain extent in Berdyaev's religious anthropology—in that for him the problem of God is not exclusive of the physiological aspect of life since all existence is grounded in the divine mystery.

Merezhkovsky's thought moved along similar lines of sharp opposition to historical Christianity, which he identified with asceticism. He advocated a new type of Christianity resulting from the synthesis of classical culture and the traditional dogmas, i.e., in his understanding, of paganism and Christianity. He required the rehabilitation of the flesh and sex by the Orthodox Church. "Henceforth," he once wrote, "the truth not only of the spirit but of the flesh, not only of heaven but of earth, must be revealed in universal history." [12] Christianity, he argued, should no longer be the religion of the isolated individual, but the religion of a "consecrated sociality," [13] which alone is the true Church. "Christianity is only a hope and prophecy of God-manhood and the Church; the Church itself will appear beyond the limits of Christianity." [14]

Merezhkovsky expected a new revelation within Christianity through the "mystical vision of the flesh." [15] Following Rozanov, he too held the conviction that there is a mystery of the flesh which still awaited its final disclosure. But unlike the startling yet profound formulas with which Rozanov clothed his religious thought, Merezhkovsky's statements often sounded much more like brilliant wordiness than thoughtful propositions. He was very fond of stylistic constructions. His ideas moved in antitheses—Christ and Antichrist, Flesh and Spirit, Chaos and Abyss, Earth and Heaven, etc.—which had actually become mere verbal symbols, turning one into another interchangeably. He lacked a real sense of human destiny. The distinction between good and evil was blurred under his pen. Even in his search for God he remained a man of letters rather than of spirit.

Berdyaev detected all this and challenged him many times to a showdown in specific terms of his religious outlook. The attempts proved futile since Merezhkovsky would each time screen himself behind a luxuriant but empty phraseology. Berdyaev repudiated the latter's antitheses and maintained that the confusion of ideas they created stemmed from the fact that they were artificial, not real antinomies. He affirmed that, for instance, the antithesis of "flesh" and "spirit" was erroneous and misleading: the real opposition lay rather between freedom and necessity. He also objected, as he did in the case of Rozanov, to Merezhkovsky's worship of the flesh; but neither did he go along with the Orthodox asceticism. Both the apotheosis of the flesh and its extreme denial,

90

in Berdyaev's judgment, spelled the enslavement of man. "Freedom," he wrote, "is attained neither through ascetic denial nor through naturalistic glorification of the flesh, but through inwardness, whereby no part of man's nature is external to him." [16] But the main reason of Berdyaev's disagreement with Merezhkovsky arose from the latter's deliberate confusion of his claim for the rehabilitation of the flesh and the Christian idea of incarnation. As for himself, Berdyaev contended that the history of Christianity has been only too long immersed in the sensuousness of the "flesh" at the expense of the spirit. Should not a true Christianity—that of the spirit of Christ—at last come into its own in a historic embodiment?

Despite this criticism, Berdyaev was at one with Merezhkovsky in his opposition to traditional ascetic Christianity. He, too, wanted to combine elements of the Greco-Roman culture with the Byzantine and indigenous riches of Russian Orthodoxy. Together with many other intellectuals devoted to religious searchings, Berdyaev insisted that historical Christianity had revealed only a half-truth, that of flesh-denying, otherworldly salvation of the individual soul; the other half had been incorporated in secularism—in scientific, economic, political, and artistic developments of social life. The Church in the past "understood heaven as the rejection of the flesh." This unwarranted schism has

> poisoned life, has turned the world into total sinfulness. And the life of the world goes on its own way, justifying itself with sanctity that is not Christian. The sexual life, the social life, all the brilliance of the world of culture, of art and science, have hanged themselves at the opposite pole, having repudiated the religious interpretation of historic Christianity.[17]

"The time has come," wrote a contemporary religious thinker, "to reveal the hidden Christian truth of the *earth* . . . , social salvation in Christ and the religious mission of secular power." [18] Berdyaev agreed, and posited that the antinomy of Christianity and secularism must be surmounted in a synthesis of "religious sanctification of life, of universal culture, a new holy love, sanctified social life, holy 'flesh,' transformed 'earth.'" He concluded:

91

"It appears that it is not only possible to love heaven and earth at the same time; it is not possible, according to Christ's teachings, to love them separately." [19]

The earnestness and wide range of religious preoccupation in which Berdyaev found himself involved at the time did not, however, make him a Christian. The travel to Paris only increased the feeling of dissatisfaction with his spiritual attainments. "Religious problems," he commented, "pressed in upon me, and I felt that I must face these issues in order to extricate myself from the half-truths and half-realities which dominated the scene of my life in Petersburg." [20] Yet, the insights gained over the discussion of these "half-truths and half-realities" opened new vistas into the depths of his perennial quest for meaning. Indeed, the very reactions against Rozanov and Merezhkovsky proved a creative stimulus towards accepting Orthodox Christianity. But this came later. For the time being, after whiling away a few months in Paris to no purpose, and ever so tired of Petersburg, he returned to Russia and settled in Moscow.

Back home Berdyaev joined the Moscow Religious-Philosophical Society of which the most active and outstanding members were his old acquaintances Bulgakov, Prince Evgeny Trubetzkoy, Vladimir Ern, Georgy Rachinsky and Vyacheslav Ivanov. The group seemed distinctly traditionalist after St. Petersburg. Bulgakov had by that time arrived at traditional Orthodoxy. In comparison, Berdyaev was regarded as a "left-winger" and a "modernist," although he read a great deal of Patristic literature and expressed an intense desire of rapprochement with the Orthodox faith.

The Moscow Society, like that of St. Petersburg and Kiev, devoted much time to the discussion of social, political, and cultural problems in relation to Christianity. Here the influence of Khomyakov, Dostoyevsky, and Vladimir Solovyov was strongly felt. During this period Berdyaev avidly studied the works of Origen, Gregory of Nyssa, and Isaac the Syrian. He took a special interest in the theology of Victor Nesmelov, then professor at the Kazan Theological Academy. His theology was anthropocentric with an urgent stress in the centrality of man's spiritual experience. "Nesmelov," wrote Berdyaev, "is particularly insistent upon the fact that human personality is inexplicable in terms of the natural world, that it rises above it and demands a higher order of being than that of the world." [21] At the same time, Berdyaev learned from Kierkegaard, Marcion, and the Gnostics. Was he aware of his imperceptibly becoming a Christian? Without any doubt, although no event in his life, as he acknowledged in his autobiography, could be described as a conversion in the Western sense of the word. Yet, he admitted,

> there must have been a moment when I became conscious of myself as a Christian, even if I am not able to relate it to any particular day in my life. I remember one experience when some strange knowledge and light were communicated to me: it happened one summer in the country; at a moment of great anxiety and depression. I went into the garden at twilight. Heavy clouds hung overhead, and the shadows were falling, when suddenly a burning light flared up in my soul. But I do not call this experience a sudden conversion, although it happened at a time of intense spiritual conflict, because before it I was neither a sceptic, nor a materialist, nor an agnostic; and because thereafter the conflicts within me did not vanish. I knew no time of enduring inner peace and went on laboring under the pressure of tormenting problems. [22]

Berdyaev did finally arrive at Christianity, but not the traditional Christianity of the Russian Orthodox Church. Indeed, as he put it, "historical Orthodoxy and all exclusive claims to Orthodoxy struck me as smelling strongly of heresy, i.e., of sectarianism, and as devoid of the spirit of universality." [23] This should not be surprising: ever since the reforms introduced by Peter the Great in order to give Russia a Western outlook, the Church had been coerced into subjection to the imperial government. Prior to Peter the relations between the Church and the State were not clearly defined, although there existed a close coordination of their respective policies. [24] The Tsar was recognized as the supreme protector of the Church and took a hand in ecclesiastical affairs. In turn, the Patriarch was often called upon for advice and actual participation in the administration of the state. With the accession to the throne of Peter, however, the traditional church-state relations underwent a radical change.

Following the death of the patriarch in 1700, Peter refused to allow the election of a successor. The office was not formally discontinued, but remained vacant. Only a guardian for the patriarchal seat was appointed. Greatly influenced by the Protestant principle, *cujus regio, ejus religio*,[25] Peter—who was rather tolerant in matters of faith—endorsed it as meaning that the Church should be subordinated to the civil power. Accordingly, twenty years later the dignity of Patriarch was abolished for ever. Instead of an individual, a body, a clerical *collegium,* later named the Holy Synod, composed of clergy and laymen, assumed charge of the Church. The new organization was headed by a Procurator appointed by the Crown. He represented the Tsar and was accorded the right to veto. Peter reserved for himself a large and active control over the affairs of the Church in keeping with the general line of his reformatory policy. From that time on the Russian Church became distinctly subordinate to the state—more a cog-wheel in the machinery of government than a religious body divinely established. Consequently, the Church was called upon to cooperate in and support without grumbling whatever political activity the whim and good pleasure of the autocratic monarchs would dictate.

All this was as true under Nicolas II as it was during the reign of Peter the Great, and even more so—owing, on the one hand, to the experience accumulated over two centuries by the Russian government in handling ecclesiastical affairs and, on the other, to the long habit of Church subserviency to the State. The Church grew into just another social institution ruled by political and liturgical practice—the living spirit was no longer present in it.

Berdyaev's understanding of Christianity was imparted to him by the lonely figure of Christ in Dostoyevsky's *Legend of the Grand Inquisitor.* As he himself acknowledged:

> It might be said that taking my stand as a Christian I accepted the picture of Christ in the Legend of the Grand Inquisitor; I turned to Him, and in my Christianity I was opposed to everything which could be ascribed to the spirit of the Grand Inquisitor. But I saw this spirit of the Grand Inquisitor displayed both from the right and from the left, in authoritarian religion and statecraft as well as in authoritarian revolutionary socialism.[26]

In the name of that Christ, he fiercely protested against the state-ridden ecclesiasticism. He denounced the Church hierarchy as merely a tool of the government for the promotion of a totalitarian policy of religious discrimination and anti-Semitic pogroms. He openly attacked the Holy Synod's campaign against political and cultural liberalism. He demanded a change in the antiquated curriculum of the theological schools. Above all, he exposed the bond between the clergy and the absolute monarchy as the source of the Church's worldliness and its scandalous aloofness from matters spiritual.

As one might have expected, Berdyaev's attitude aroused a wave of self-righteous indignation among the officials of both government and Holy Synod. At one time he was even charged with blasphemy—an offense punishable by lifelong banishment to Siberia.[27] Only the outbreak of war with Germany saved him from a fateful trial. Despite the growing reaction of the authorities, Berdyaev did not stop his criticism of the Church. His bitter judgment upon the deplorable state of religious affairs was eloquently summed up in an article written in 1907 on the occasion of the death of the ultra-reactionary Procurator Constantin Pobyedonostsev in whom he saw the personification of the pre-revolutionary Church:

> A nihilistic attitude toward humanity and the world, growing from religious attitude toward God—that is the pathos of Pobyedonostsev, shared by Russian statism, and grounded in the historic Orthodoxy. Pobyedonostsev was a religious personality: he prayed to his God, he engaged in 'saving his soul'; but toward life, toward humanity, toward the world process, his attitude was nonreligious, atheistic. He saw nothing divine in life, no reflection of the divine in man. Only a terrible, yawning abyss of emptiness opened itself before him in the world. The world was not God's creation for him; he never sensed the divinity of the world soul. . . . He was of the number of those who are hypnotized by the Fall, for whom being is hidden, who are cut off from the mystery of God's creation. The devil rules the world and determines the course of universal life; he penetrates to the very roots of man's nature. The good, the divine, has no objective power; one cannot build his life upon its foundations; with the power of good no historic

95

perspectives are bound. . . . Pobyedonostsev looked upon human society as a mechanism.

Pobyedonostsev is a tragic type—one of those for whom Christianity has killed Christ and the Church has obscured God. Christ made God infinitely near to man, made man a son of the Heavenly Father; the spirit of Pobyedonostsev makes God infinitely distant from man, and turns the son into a slave.[28]

But the mere unmasking of the evils besetting historical Orthodoxy was not enough. Berdyaev felt the need for a more constructive course of action. Russia's situation, both cultural and political, was at this time extremely critical. Notwithstanding the grim warning sounded by the First Revolution, the court circles of Tsar Nicolas II and the nobility continued to view with hostility the attempts at reforming the political and social *status quo* of the Empire. They insisted upon the necessity of maintaining a strong autocracy, and repudiated all claims for a representative government. Paying no heed to the ineluctable unfolding of historical process, these reactionary circles were concentrating their forces to prevent realization of the promises made by the Crown in the Manifesto of October 17, 1905. As a result, the country settled down to a convulsive political struggle, both overt and underground, which beclouded the workaday life with a sense of apprehension and insecurity.

Simultaneously with the internal political tension, the educated *élite* was passing through a disintegrating crisis of its own. The cultural renaissance so exceptionally pregnant with life and creativity during the first years of the century was now breathless with exhaustion. True, they were still longing for the spiritual release of the individual from the bondage of autocracy and economic determinism, but for many the original flame was gone. What was to be done in order to rekindle the hearts against the growing apathy and atheism? and thus to meet the challenge of the oncoming revolution? Berdyaev felt that a religious revival alone could, before too late, save the cultural and spiritual values of Russia and thus preserve their creative and transforming potentialities. This did not imply a turning away from his inherent burning concern for daily bread: he kept believing that socialism supplied the logical answer to the problem of food and of man's exploitation by man. Moreover, socialism, according to Berdyaev, holds a profound ethical insight, which is also religious, that of work as the sole justification of the right to existence. Accordingly, only he who works is in all justice worthy of the daily bread. A society must of necessity be concerned about labor—or it is not deserving of the name.

But there is another type of socialism which is antagonistic not only to the bread of the spirit, but to that of wheat as well—namely, Bolshevism. This kind of socialism poses as a new religion, and as such is exacting from its devotees the sacrifice of their persons at the altar of social utilitarianism. It was against Bolshevism and its devastating consequences that Berdyaev made a vehement stand in the fight for spiritual and economic freedom. And it was in the name of freedom that he raised a hue and cry to awake the consciousness of the Intelligentsia in preparation for the impending social catastrophe.

These ideas were shared by many of the Moscow Religious-Philosophical group. Eventually they were expounded in a remarkable symposium published in 1909 under the title *Vyekhy* (Milestones). This joint intellectual undertaking proclaimed the fallacy of all positivistic systems of thought exclusive of the life of the spirit, and made a dramatic call on the Intelligentsia to regain the religious awareness of their role and vocation. In the article he contributed to the book, Berdyaev wrote:

> Only the consciousness of the guilt of our mind and will may lead us toward a new life. We shall be outwardly free when we unbind ourselves from slavery within, that is when we realize our own responsibility and cease to shift always the blame on the external forces. Only then a new soul will be restored to the Intelligentsia.[29]

In a similar vein of self-conviction and characterization he brought into the open the transgressions of the Russian upper class:

> The historic Government committed great crimes: it worshiped the idol of imperialism and served the instincts of the ruling classes; with a few exceptions it was not of the people. The Russian educated society lost the feeling of being Russian citizens and saw their dignity and worth in alienation. The *people,* until now, remained a puzzle. The edu-

cated Russian has felt himself a citizen of the planet Mars, in no way a citizen of Russia. . . . In his wholly isolated society, the educated Russian has become accustomed to profess the most extreme socialistic and anarchistic ideals, totally abstract, devoid of historical flesh and blood. An obligatory break with his ancestry, with the whole past, with history, has become the life norm for the educated Russian. The Russian Intelligentsia have been alienated, not only in relation to the Government—in that respect they were right—but in relation to Russian literature, Russian philosophical thought, the faith of the people, the feeling of nationality—in which respects they were wrong. Much has been written and spoken among us on the theme of the break between the educated classes and the people, but the writers and speakers have viewed the theme exclusively from the sociological point of view. From that point of view nothing can be understood or solved. The theme goes immeasurably deeper.

For a country we have been nurturing negative consciousness, strengthening atheistic and nihilistic ideas. The latest conclusions of European culture have been reflected in Russia in their most extreme, radical form. When a Russian became a socialist, he was no mere Western socialist, but the most extreme, fanatical socialist; his socialism was outside time and space; it was his religion. When a Russian became an anarchist, he was the most radical anarchist, plotting against the very first principles of being. When a Russian became a materialist, then for him materialism became theology; when an atheist, his atheism became religion; when a decadent, then he disintegrated into his component parts. Radicalism is our national characteristic, and that characteristic gave birth to much that is bad; but it may also become the source of the greatest good, for it prevents us from being merely bourgeois.[30]

On the other hand, it is an error to strive for a Christian government—such a government, declares Berdyaev, is not possible. The Church hierarchs in their association with the State are guilty of nurturing an enterprise which is basically anti-Christian. Is not the Russian caesaropapism, introduced by Peter, the very antithesis of the Kingdom of Christ? Is not theocratic absolutism just the opposite of the freedom of conscience inherent in the Christian faith? How then can the Church justify its approval of outward force and compulsion in matters of faith and conscience? With this in mind Berdyaev wrote:

A Christian theocratic government is a lie, because Christian theocracy is a rule of grace, but the State is a rule of law, a pagan rule. Saint Augustine founded the theocracy of the Middle Ages by confusing law with grace. Humanity in the development of its self-consciousness has sensed the lie of a Christian government, the religious falsity of absolutistic papalism and theocratic absolutism, and has become aware of the confusion, which was the great offense of Christian history, one of the temptations of the devil which had been overcome by Christ in the wilderness. The Reformation, and later the progressive disintegration of Christianity and religion in general, were the results of the great collapse of the effort to establish a Christian government, to organize a religious rule over the world. . . . Humanism became victorious over the antihumanistic pseudo-theocracy, papal and imperial. In place of the human self-assertion and will-to-power which cloaked themselves in the pretense of divine rule and gained the aura of religious authority, humanism openly and honorably affirmed man and purely human rule. The truth in this instance was on the side of humanism; but only a relative, not an absolute, truth. And even this truth is at present transforming itself into a lie, into a new deceit.

Unbelief has more and more increased, but the false bond between the Church and the Government has remained as if untouched. This relation has continued to poison the sources of religious life increasingly. Society has become atheistic, and for the greatest part does not know any more who Christ was. In the soul of the nation, the religious sense of the holy has died. The conventional and forcibly imposed lie of the official, governmental religion continues to corrupt human souls. Religion has become a utilitarian tool for the rule of the world.

All forcible support of the Church and faith by the Government is the result of unbelief in the power of Christ. His faith shall revive only when it again is persecuted, not when it persecutes. . . .The Holy Spirit has never been on the side of the persecutors and of force—but the Spirit of the Great Inquisitor has been![31]

Finally, as if summing up his burning faith and hope, Berdyaev, in a pathetic appeal, pointed out the direction of redemption:

Only Jesus can command the unclean spirit to depart from the body of Russia! Only Christ can be the Redeemer! But for that it is necessary that there be an inner return to Christ,

99

seeking him for the assuaging of our thirst and for the ending of our tortures. . . . And the unclean spirit shall depart to its proper dwelling place, into the herd of swine.[32]

In order to add a fresh impetus to his struggle for a return of the Intelligentsia to the sources of the Christian faith, Berdyaev and his friends founded a printing house, *Put* (The Way), which edited works of theology and philosophy, and especially the writings of the 19th century Russian thinkers. But despite *Milestones* and a good many similar books and articles published over the years preceding the First World War, the spiritual movement initiated by the Moscow Religious-Philosophical Society was not followed. The religious crusade failed to bring about a change in the consciousness of the State-Church hierarchy, and left the Intelligentsia as a whole untouched. The times were in no wise suited for the labors of the spirit. It was too late—Russia was irresistibly drifting to her Bolshevik doom.

Although Berdyaev's staunch polemic conveyed the impression of an unshakable Christian conviction, he remained restless and inwardly insecure. He kept searching for more spiritual perception and guidance. Accordingly, he sought communion with the Orthodox fundamentalists and with the *startsy*[33] in their monastic hermitages. He attended a course of lectures in anthroposophy given by Rudolf Steiner in Helsingfors. He took interest in theosophy and other forms of occultism. In a Moscow inn called *Yama* (The Pit) he frequented the assemblies of the "wandering Russia" —a vast variety of mystical sects, such as *Bessmertniki* (Immortals), *Dukhobors* (Wrestlers for the Spirit), *Khlysti* (Flagellants), Tolstoyans and others. Most of all he came increasingly under the influence of the German mystics—Jakob Boehme, Angelus Silesius, John Tauler, and Franz von Baader.

In the light of the new encounters and further studies, Berdyaev's philosophical orientation gained in depth and precision. A fresh tenor of thought was felt in his book *Philosophy of Freedom* published in 1911. Toward the end of his life, Berdyaev set little value on this work owing to its ontological presuppositions.[34] Actually, the book was an important propounding of existential philosophy which was to remain basic to his lifelong teaching.

"The idea of existence," he wrote, "is first intuition and not the result of the discursive thought." [35] Man's inner experience alone can discover meaning and content in the problems of life. Reason, Berdyaev declared, should become again a function of existence, and philosophy, in turn, a function of religious life. Another book, *The Meaning of the Creative Act,* written partly in Italy in 1912 and published during the war, enlarged upon the previous ideas and posited one of the central themes of his thought, namely, the concept of man as a creator in his own right and his responsibility for the transformation of the world. Defending, as he always did, the position taken in this work, Berdyaev commented later:

> It is fruitless and absurd to ask whether creativity is justifiable from the point of view of the religion of redemption, because, though man be degraded and defiled by sin, there can be no redemption and no salvation without man's response to God. Redemption and salvation are therefore, also acts of divine-human creativity. Similarly, the ultimate fulfilment of redemption and the coming of God's Kingdom comprises a creative act on the part of man. [36]

As could be expected, these ideas provoked hostile criticism on the part of Orthodox circles of all shades. His very friends looked askance on him. Consequently, Berdyaev broke with the Religious-Philosophical Society and no longer attended their meetings. He also severed his contacts with other religious groups, and ceased to work in the publishing house *Put.* He was still active in defending his ideas and denouncing the misuses of the governmental and ecclesiastical authority. But he also began more than ever appreciating solitude.

The impending global catastrophe of which he was prophetically aware, did not obstruct his vision of a Christian renaissance of the world—a renaissance in which man, beyond Marxism and Humanism, will discover, in the grace of Christ, his fulfillment in a creative act which God expects from him. Man's vocation is God's anticipation.

On June 28, 1914, the Archduke Ferdinand was assassinated in a Bosnian town, Sarajevo. One month later the First World War broke out . . .

CHAPTER V

FROM WAR TO REVOLUTION:
UNDIVIDED THROUGH DIVISION

> O my Russia, fraught with sublime
> forebodings,
> What thought absorbeth thee at the
> present?
> To which Orient wilt thou belong,
> To that of Xerxes or of Christ? [1]
>
> —*Vladimir Solovyov*

In a letter written to Maxim Gorky in 1913 Lenin made this statement: "War between Austria and Russia would be very useful to the cause of the revolution in western Europe. But it is hard to believe that Franz Joseph and Nicolas will grant us this pleasure." [2] A year later they did.

Approximately a month after the murder of Sarajevo on July 23, Austria issued an ultimatum to Serbia, impelled by the idea that the plot against the Archduke Ferdinand was instigated by the Serbian Government. Serbia's reply was a practical submission to the demands of Vienna. Nevertheless, the Austrian minister in Belgrade pronounced the Serbian answer unsatisfactory, and on July 28 Austria declared war against Serbia.

Russia mobilized her army on July 30 avowedly to prevent the annihilation of the Serbs. On August 1 Germany declared war on Russia, and on August 3 the German troops crossed into French

102

territory. Within two more days armed hostilities broke out between Austria and Russia. Next, following the German invasion of Belgium, Great Britain declared war on Germany. In the course of time, the countries of all five continents one after another entered the infernal round of death. Thus commenced the first global war the world had known since the dawn of its recorded history.

Germany's declaration of war aroused in the Russian people enthusiastic feelings of patriotism and national unity. In the main cities of Russia spontaneous mass meetings took place as a token of agreement with the policy of Slavonic emancipation declared by the Government. The long-lasting struggle against the regime seemed to subside altogether. The general mood of the country was one of trust in the cause of Panslavism and conviction of the victorious end—and this lasted for some time. Despite the bitter defeat and heavy losses suffered at the battle of Tannenberg on August 31, 1914, the Russian military effort went on unthwarted during the whole of the first year of the war. Soon, however, things began to take a quite different turn. In order to alleviate the extreme pressure of the new German divisions transferred from the Western front, a general retreat of the armed forces was ordered by the Russian supreme military command during the summer of 1915. This resulted not only in the abandonment of all enemy territory occupied from the Carpathians to the Baltic, but also of Poland, Lithuania, and Courland, and a vast expanse of Ukrainian and White Russian provinces.

As a result, a surging tide of harsh criticism and discontentment swept across the nation. The former grievances against the Tsarist autocracy, stowed away at the outset of the war, sprang back into the Russian consciousness with the impetuosity of a repressed mechanism.

The failures of 1915 exposed and amplified the weak spots both in the conduct of war and in the approach to domestic affairs. The transportation system was plagued with serious disruptions. The country's industrial plant was badly equipped and raw material insufficient. In addition there was a shortage of labor. Agricultural output decreased, while the agrarian question (the transfer to the peasants of the ownership of the land) loomed ominously in the background of current events.

On the front line the crisis in the supply of munitions was fatal. By fall of 1915 a third of the Russian soldiers were sent into battle without guns to support them. The number of killed and wounded was staggering. This tragic state of affairs was attributed to the shortsightedness of the Government and the General Staff. Public opinion increasingly demanded a thorough shake-down of military and civil authority, and the appointment of men whom it could trust. Once more a wide gap opened between the people and the rulers, but this time it was unbridgeable.

As a solution to the menacing internal political conflict, the Tsar announced his decision, in opposition to the unanimous opinion of the Government and the military headquarters, to assume personally the Supreme Command of the Russian Army. That was a great mistake: Nicolas was no strategist, and he would incur directly the popular blame for all further failures.

The decision was received with indignation both on the battle fields and in the interior of the homeland. Gradually, the Emperor found himself forsaken by his most intelligent advisors, and politically isolated. He began relying more and more on the counsel of his wife, Alexandra Feodorovna. The Empress, in turn, was known to be under the hypnotic sway of Rasputin, an uneducated and disreputable monk whom she regarded as a saint.

A profound disgust for the monarchy crept through the rank and file of tired and demoralized Russian divisions. The entire nation was overwhelmed by repugnance and exasperation. The murder of Rasputin on December 29, 1916, did not bring any change in the policy of the Tsar. Fomented by the Bolsheviks there was a growth of defeatism and insubordination. Large sections of educated classes demanded the immediate suspension of hostilities and the opening of peace negotiations. At the same time the economic situation was becoming worse each day. The cities had difficulty in securing food supplies. In addition, soaring prices, heavy taxes, and expanding inflation rendered civic life quite unbearable. By March, 1917, things were moving rapidly. Food riots in Petrograd [3] soon waxed into a mutinous insurrection. Industrial workers went on strike. Huge street demonstrations prevented practically all normal activity. The troops sent by the Government to check the rebellion joined the crowds instead. On March 12, the capital of the

Empire passed into the control of the insurgents. A Provisional Government of Russia was appointed by a Duma Committee with Prince Lvov as prime minister, later succeeded by Kerensky. Simultaneously, there was organized a Soviet of Workers and Soldiers' Deputies. On March 15 the Tsar abdicated. Thus the three hundred year rule of the Romanovs came to an end.

Before long there were formed in every Russian city Soviets after the type of that in Petrograd; they shared the authority with the representatives of the Provisional Government. In fact, Russia had two governments from the very beginning of the revolution: the Provisional and the Soviet, embodying respectively the political and the social revolutions. Soon a vehement political rivalry opposed to each other the two revolutionary forces. The nation was torn apart by new dissensions. This state of affairs elicited immediate repercussions on the front line. The Russian Army fell into dissolution. In many places the soldiers laid down their arms and fraternized with the enemy. Finally, on November 7, 1917, the Bolsheviks seized the power by a *coup d'état*. And the Empire collapsed.

Neither the leaders of the Duma nor the Bolsheviks had instigated the riots in Petrograd which led to the downfall of Tsardom. The Revolution was the inevitable outcome of the Tsarist regime itself. As Bernard Pares rightly put it:

> No one made the Russian Revolution, unless it was the autocracy itself. . . . It was elemental, and for that reason all the more conclusive. It was a direct result of the utter bankruptcy of the autocracy, and for that reason it was irrevocable.[4]

Berdyaev had for a long time held that the revolution in Russia was inevitable and amply deserved. Moreover, in an article published in 1907, he foresaw that the approaching social upheaval would eventually turn Bolshevik. But he did not believe, like so many others, that the change in the Russian political status would necessarily spell the triumph of liberty. In fact he expressed his conviction that the Revolution would "entail a supreme and terrible sacrifice of man's freedom. Such was to be the tragedy of the historical destiny of Russia."[5]

Berdyaev's attitude during the years of war had been one of confidence in the Russian destiny and her redemptive role within the Slavonic race; a confidence tempered, however, by warnings of a corrupting disease lodged in the depths of the Russian soul, and which he detected beneath the surface of the prevalent events. When the Revolution befell Russia, he welcomed it. He regarded it as a just and inescapable process of dissolving false historical symbols, and wished it as a means of moral purification. But at the same time, he looked upon it with distrust.

The storm of the March Revolution reached Berdyaev in his Moscow flat working at his desk as usual. In the midst of the rending whirlwind, he remained sober and calm. He continued writing even when the fighting was being waged in the streets of the city and the bombs were bursting near his home. However, he did not keep himself aloof from events, and on occasion displayed his attitude otherwise than through publishing related articles. One day, for instance, he joined the revolutionary crowd which was moving toward a Moscow downtown square. Eventually, they were blocked by a detachment of soldiers loyal to the Tsarist Government and standing ready to shoot. The urgent summons dispatched by the commanding officer exerted no effect on the demonstrators. The threatening crowd moved on in a closed ring nearer and nearer to the center of the square. The fusillade was expected at any moment. Realizing the frightful predicament, Berdyaev pushed his way through the crowd, went up to the soldiers and pleaded with them not to fire on the unarmed people. The shooting did not take place.

After the proclamation of the new Russian Republic, Berdyaev was for a short time elected a member of the National Soviet (pre-Parliament). But repelled by the vulgar and impassioned atmosphere of this body, he soon submitted his resignation. The November Revolution provided him with additional impetus for activity. He initiated an extensive program for public education, and in order to afford it with an adequate intellectual platform, he founded the Free Academy of Spiritual Culture. He gave public lectures, conducted seminars, presided over debates on controversial subjects, and wrote prolifically. He also participated in

106

the administration of the All-Russian Union of Writers, the only organization of its kind supported by the Government.

Despite Berdyaev's accurate anticipation of the Revolution and the presentiment of its destructive nature, he could not humanly gauge the actual proportions of the national disaster. But now things were taking a diabolic turn. Countless innocent people were herded into jails already overloaded with victims seized earlier. Tens of thousands were summarily liquidated. Fires set by the revolutionaries were consuming innumerable estates throughout the vast stretches of the Russian homeland. As they extended the radius of their control, the Bolsheviks were transforming the country into a slaughter house. The horrors of the revolutionary aftermath were rising to the height of undescribable tragedy. Indeed, Russia was literally murdered. But even more that the physical annihilation, Berdyaev passionately resented the systematic undermining of the spiritual foundations of the Russian people.

In a series of "letters" written in 1918 and published only five years later in Germany under the title *The Philosophy of Inequality*, Berdyaev vehemently denounced the destroyers of Russian culture—both the Bolsheviks and the Intelligentsia whose weaknesses and irresponsibility had consigned to doom the Russian culture and life. His violent indignation is expressed in every word he wrote at that time:

> To you who have poisoned the soul of the Russian people with a terrible poison, to you who are destroying Russia, I dedicate these letters. . . . At first your oppression was spiritual, for you ruled the weak souls of the Russian intellectuals; but now you have become persecutors of all higher, spiritual life, and have boycotted all who believe in higher spiritual realities and values, who acknowledge a religious goal of life. . . . You have established an unheard-of tyranny, threatening at last to destroy the human image. You have always hated freedom, have always been extinguishers of the divine in man. You have ever bartered the human birthright for a mess of pottage of ephemeral well-being and of passing interests. You are destroyers of the eternal: you would pluck out of the human heart the sense of the eternal and the longing for the eternal. . . . I have long fought you to the extent of my strength. Now, even those who were formerly seduced

by your spirit, all those enlighteners, progressives, and humanists who were content with the superficialities of life, who recognized no evil, who possessed the souls of aesthetes, innocently dreaming of the good of the people and happiness on earth—even they are beginning to know you. We long ago fore-warned them, and pointed out whither the paths taken by the educated Russian society would lead, into which they have also enticed the Russian people. We have exhorted them about the awful responsibility that is incumbent upon the 'haves' of the ruling class; for they were doing almost nothing of a creative nature to prevent Russia and the Russian people from falling into the fateful abyss.[6]

He then fiercely exposed the Bolshevik fostering and exploiting the new type of Russian which the war had produced, a type inclined to authority and cruelty, indifferent to justice or sympathy. He wrote:

You, Bolsheviks, you have no face, you are the mediums of faceless powers; in you speak alien voices. These voices are deprived of human quality, one can only hear the din and the roaring of elemental forces. It is in vain that you, of the Revolution, bethink yourselves as new souls, that in you a new man is being born. You are old souls, with you the old man draws to an end, with his ancient sins and weaknesses. All you negative feelings—anger, envy, vengeance—enchain you to the old life and make you prisoners of the past. You are the passive reflex released by the evil of long ago. You are but a reaction against the past. There is no creative breath in you. . . . You are filled up with the memory of the past evil, you are unable to set yourself free from it. But you are in want of the memory of the past goodness, and of the imperishable truth and beauty which it contains.[7]

Time and again Berdyaev vehemently insisted upon the dignity and worth of the human person. The Bolsheviks, he insisted, brought about only death and destruction. This was due to the very nature of their movement which repudiated the truth of the spirit. Only the spirit is endowed with transforming power; the real revolution is spiritual.

The revolution of the spirit has nothing in common with your external, material, political, and social revolutions. Marx never was a revolutionary of the spirit. Nietzsche was. But what has he in common with your external revolutions? He despised them as uprisings of plebeians. Dostoyevsky was a revolutionary of the spirit. But you have ever regarded him a conservative and a reactionary. And what have you to do with the prophetic Vladimir Solovyov, or what has he to do with you? All that was spiritually significant in the history of Russian thought and of the Russian creativeness in the nineteenth century is not on your side but is against you. The greatest representative of Russian culture, Pushkin, is not yours. You have abused and denounced him, opposed to him a stove pot and boots. Neither has Leo Tolstoy loved you; on the contrary, he has condemned your doings. Only second- or third-rate men are with you; not a single genius has been born, or has risen among you.[8]

Above all, he attacked the establishment of the collectivist system, the indiscriminate social leveling which destroys human personality and other moral realities alike:

You reject and destroy personality, all you heralds of the materialistic revolution. . . . You would like to convert men into atoms, and the human society into an atomic mechanism, into a collective of impersonal atoms. But in truth, man is not an atom, but an individuum, and individual, a differentiated being. Every man possesses a unique, individual lot in this life and in the life beyond, in eternity.

Your human collective, that anthill of the future, the terrible leviathan, shall finally destroy personality as well as other reality. . . . Your collective is a pseudo reality which will supersede all true realities after destroying them—the realities of personality, nation, government, Church, humanity, cosmos as well as God. For every reality is a personality and possesses a living soul—man, nation, humanity, cosmos, Church, and God.[9]

Berdyaev's passionate outbursts against the revolutionary principles and methods sounded like glowing utterances of a Hebrew prophet arisen in defense of man and his spiritual rights and truth; and although he was aware that no revolution is ever morally pure or socially just, this very fact only adduced one more reason for continuing the moral struggle.

But during the five years of Berdyaev's life under the Soviet

109

regime, he gradually came to a deeper understanding of the Revolution, a more Christian estimate of its inner meaning. The Postscript Berdyaev wrote in 1923 to his *Philosophy of Inequality* offers his altered outlook and reads like an eloquent confession. No longer are there words of bitterness and violence; no merciless accusations. All resentment is gone. A profound Christian humility breathes through the lines instead. The Berdyaev of the Postscript is the philosopher known in the West, the outstanding Christian cleansed by suffering and matured under trials and ordeals. The importance of this text of classical majesty for the study of Berdyaev is such that it is indispensable to quote extensively.

The *Philosophy of Inequality,* he informs us, was written during the summer of 1918,

> in an atmosphere of painful spiritual revolt against the victorious Communist Revolution. In it are reflected, perhaps too strongly, negative emotions which at present no longer dominate me. At that time I as yet had not experienced spiritual catharsis; I had not yet felt the spiritual experience of the Revolution in its very depths; I had not thought it out to the end in the light of religion. Even now, in 1923, I accept the distinctions among the basic hierarchical social-philosophical ideas that I made in 1918; but my attitude is much more cleansed and liberated from the dominance of negative feelings, from all hate, even though those feelings were aroused on behalf of true ideas and the right faith. Revolution—atheistic and demonic by its nature—must be experienced with deepened spirituality and luminous religion. He who has brought away only the feeling of wrath and hatred, only a desire for restoration, has not experienced the Revolution spiritually and religiously. . . . Nor has he experienced the Revolution spiritually who has experienced it greedily. The landed proprietor or factory owner who desires above all else the return of his confiscated lands or factories, and vengeance upon those who took the property away from him, has not experienced the Revolution spiritually. The politician who is wroth above all else because his political party and his political ideology have not won, and bides his time to seize the rule and repay those who have been victorious in the Revolution, has not experienced the Revolution spiritually. The ideologist and thinker who is full of wrath because his ideas are persecuted, and is ready

to join any power capable of revenging him for his non-recognition and the crushing of his ideas, has not experienced the Revolution spiritually. The citizen who sees in the Revolution only the harm done to his interests and to his accustomed style of life, has not experienced the Revolution spiritually. He alone has experienced spiritually who has seen in it his own and his nation's unhappy share, who has discerned in it punishment for past sins, who has repented of not only the Revolutionary but the pre-Revolutionary falsehoods, who has acknowledged the necessity for enlightenment and transformation of life. Such a person becomes not only a Revolutionary or a pre-Revolutionary, but a post-Revolutionary individual, a man of a new era. Our counter-revolution should become post-Revolutionary, not pre-Revolutionary; and it should profess principles unlike those dominant during the Revolution, or those of the pre-Revolutionary period which brought about the Revolution. A spiritual experience of the Revolution cannot lead to a desire for restoration, i.e., the re-establishment of the old regime which has brought about the falsehood of the Revolution; a return to it would be senseless, and would condemn the people in an endless circuit. It is imperative that we abandon the endless circuit of revolution and reaction for a new kind of life— the life of creativity. We cannot oppose the "bourgeois" truth to the anti-Christian Communist falsehood, for there is no more Christ in the bourgeois type of life than in Communism, and one atheism gives birth to another. Communism is but the atheistic falsehood of the bourgeois world consistently carried out to its end.

To me, revolution is not an external event; it is a reflex of something happening within me and with me, of my guilt, of my spiritual malady. If I, and every other I, had been spiritually sufficiently strong and had had genuine power of faith, the Revolution would not have occurred, but instead of it, enlightenment and transformation of life would have taken place. It matters not if I be called "reactionary," for I am in reaction—a profound, spiritual reaction against falsehood and lie, against the inhuman and godless character of revolution. But one must understand the meaning of such "reaction." My "reaction" is not pre-Revolutionary, but post-Revolutionary. . . . It does not lead to a restoration of the pre-Revolutionary style of life, a pre-Revolutionary spiritual state. The Revolution has taken place, and it was as ugly as every other revolution. But one must go on to what is possible after it, and not back to what has come before it.

111

For the antecendent conditions brought it about. We shall aim
at creating conditions that shall not lead to a revolution
again. Revolution must run its course and terminate itself,
for it cannot be terminated externally.

All these ideas have followed each other during the three
years, and I thought it necessary to formulate them in this
Postscript so that the ideas expressed in this book could be
understood in their true light. No one should utilize them for
a nefarious goal. . . . A spiritual understanding of the events
that have transpired in the world during the few last years
confirms the truth of historical pessimism which has a firm
basis in Christian prophecies, and which I have long professed. That strict historical pessimism liberates from all
earthly utopias and mirages of a perfect social organization.
But it does not liberate us from the duty of realizing Christ's
truth as far as our strength allows. It is not easy to vanquish
the radical evil of human nature and of the nature of the
world; the final victory over evil consists of the transformation of the world, a 'new heaven' and a 'new earth.' But it
does not, therefore, follow that we should consent to the rule
of evil and to evil rule; that our wills should not be directed
toward the maximum of truth in life.[10]

In the course of his life in Western Europe, Berdyaev returned
a number of times to the problem of communism and the Russian
Revolution. He was tormented by the stirring social and political
event which came to have such a far-reaching influence on the life
of Russia as well as of the whole of mankind. His original conviction as to the essential character of the Revolution remained
unchanged. He regarded it as a historical calamity. He also believed that it was foredoomed to failure like all the rest of them.
But he was no longer intent on attributing exclusively to the
Bolsheviks all moral and material crimes of the Revolution.

The Russian émigrés used to have frequent discussions of the
question of responsibility for the Revolution. Berdyaev dismissed
it as irrelevant and futile. He contended that every revolution
is the fatal upshot of disturbances and grievances which have
gathered momentum during the preceding generations; although
it is also an irruption of demonic, irrational forces set in motion
by a specific, latter-day event. The Russian Revolution, he insisted, had been prepared over the whole of the 19th century by
the Intelligentsia; it had behind it a heroic tradition of sacrificial

and implacable struggle against oppression, and its motivation was recognizable throughout the age-long yearning for freedom and social righteousness and equality. If the Revolution exhibited negative attitudes it was because these had always belonged to the radical Intelligentsia—sectarian intolerance, hostility to the cultural and spiritual values, a religious devotion to materialism.[11] Certainly, the immediate impetus to the eventual outbreak of the Revolution was given by the war. But the Bolsheviks did not so much engineer the Revolution as take advantage of the moment and assure its final success. Revolutions, Berdyaev interpreted, are instances of divine judgment upon nations and men. They are permitted by God. And it behooves us to bear them "with dignity, the same dignity with which we should bear an illness or the death of a friend." [12] And also to learn from them.

The Revolution, therefore, belongs to everyone. As such it is not only an external event, but an inward occurrence as well.

> The revolution must not be considered only externally, as though one saw in it simply an empirical fact without any relation to *my* spiritual life and to *my* destiny. . . . The revolution did not take place only outside and beyond me, an event having no common measure with my own life and so without any meaning for me; it was also as it were an interior happening within me. Bolshevism has been embodied in Russia and triumphed here because *I* am what I *am*, because there was no real spiritual power in me, none of the strength of faith that can move mountains; it is my sin, and an affliction that is visited on me. The suffering that it has caused me is a satisfaction for my failure and for my iniquity, for our common failure and our common iniquity: all are responsible for all. This way of living and of understanding a revolution is the only one which religion can inspire, the only one that brings any light to the soul. The Russian revolution is the destiny of the Russian people—and my destiny; the ransom and reparation due from the people—and thus from me.[13]

Thus, according to Berdyaev, it is puerile and vain to impute blame for the Revolution to any particular man or movement: all Russians are responsible for it. The root of evil is not outside ourselves; on the contrary, it is planted deep within our own being.

Every Russian ought to take his share of moral responsibility for what happened in his country. Bolshevism, wrote Berdyaev,

> is inherent in the Russian people, a serious moral disease, their organic defect. . . ; it is a reflection of the tendency to wickedness that there is in all of us. . . . Bolshevism corresponds to the moral condition of us Russians and displays outwardly our inward crises, our loss of faith, our religion in danger, the hideous weakening of our moral life.[14]

But this is not at all equivalent to saying that other nations of the world are immune to Bolshevism. The process of moral corruption and spiritual disintegration is equally an ever-present menace to the whole of mankind. Moreover, the destiny of Russia is inseparable from the destiny of other nations. The 20th century events have demonstrated the proof of this.

> Nobody is bound to have an optimistic outlook on the future. . . . The world is moving towards a tragic duality and a struggle between opposite spiritual forces. But it is a matter of immense importance that illusions should be dispelled and man come face to face with positive realities.[15]

The positive realities are, for Berdyaev, spiritual. The problem of Bolshevism cannot be solved by outward devices: it is primarily moral and religious. Regeneration must be worked from within.

> Bolshevism cannot be disposed of by a well-organized army, however large. . . . . Bolshevism must first of all be overcome from within, spiritually, and only afterwards by politics. A new spiritual principle for the organization of authority and culture must be found. . . . The truth that spirit and morality must always take precedence of politics needs to be recognized more than ever nowadays.[16]

The Christians are not excluded from criticism:

> Christians, who condemn the communists for their godlessness and anti-religious persecutions, cannot lay the whole blame solely upon these godless communists; they must assign part of the blame to themselves, and that a considerable part. They must be not only accusers and judges; they must

also be penitents. Have Christians done very much for the realization of Christian justice in social life? Have they striven to realize the brotherhood of man without that hatred and violence of which they accuse the communists? The sins of Christians, the sins of historical churches, have been very great, and these sins bring with them their just punishment.[17]

Accordingly, Berdyaev launched a pathetic appeal to Christians all over the world for more religious earnestness and the realization of the Christian way of life in order to save the freedom of human spirit:

> Are Christians willing to take Christianity seriously, to order their will towards its realization? Unless they submit themselves to a sublime tension of the spirit, unless they put forth their utmost activity toward the realization of the Christian way, the atheistic Communism shall conquer the world. But the free spirit, the spirit of deliverance must act independently of whatever forces are dominant and triumphant. Christianity is returning to the pre-Constantinian status and must once more undertake the conquest of the world.[18]

After the seizure of power by the Bolsheviks, one of the first measures introduced by the new regime was concerned with the requisition of private property. On this score, however, Berdyaev had no complaint to make. Notwithstanding his evident opposition to the Soviet order, and his vigorous defense of the Christian world view, he was not deprived of his apartment (including the portraits of his military ancestors displaying tsarist decorations!). His library was left untouched, and he was permitted to continue his writing. He was even made the recipient of a special food allowance which was granted by the Government to a few outstanding writers, irrespective of their ideological position (amidst the prevalent food shortages, they were wittily nicknamed "the immortals"). Nevertheless, when the decree regarding labor conscription was promulgated, Berdyaev was forced to join the working squads and assigned the task of clearing the streets of snow or digging outside the city. But despite the unaccustomed strain of the hard labor, the humiliation of marching for miles in columns surrounded by soldiers, the severe cold, and the perpetual hunger, Berdyaev did not feel crushed and miserable; he confronted the predicament with the sense of sharing in the common expiation of the Intelligentsia's guilt and responsibility for the horrors of the Revolution.[19]

During all the time of his life in Soviet Russia, Berdyaev managed to keep the fire of a true devotion to intellectual creativity and human dignity burning on the altar of freedom when the rough winds of social upheaval were threatening to blow it out. For five years, every Tuesday evening, he presided in his living room over the gatherings of the freedom-loving remnant. They included representatives of varied trends of thought united in a common recognition of the independence and primacy of spiritual values. As usual, papers were read, lectures given, discussions promoted. Opinions differed, also as usual, but all present were earnestly awakened to their moral obligation of letting no adversary power abrogate the last vestiges of the Russian cultural life.

Berdyaev's reputation as an orator and outspoken enemy of the regime's policy against freedom developed in proportion as the Soviet order was being worked out into a totalitarian system. Such huge crowds converged upon the halls where he was scheduled to occupy the rostrum that many, for want of seats, stood outside. His debates on Christianity excited an impassioned interest and attracted even the Communists. Indeed, the intellectual and spiritual yearning were as yet not all gone.

In order to avoid the slightest ambiguity concerning his ideological attitude, Berdyaev severed his relations with a number of his old friends—among others with Vyacheslav Ivanov and Mikhail Gershenzon—because of their conciliatory manner toward communism. He reproached them with accepting the patronage of Lunatcharsky, the new commissar of education, who most obligingly bartered means of subsistence for the writers' submissiveness to the Government. Berdyaev repudiated all close association with the Soviet officials as capable of enslaving the last stronghold of public freedom—that of expression—in exchange for alluring promises.

Despite Berdyaev's aggressive profession of the Christian faith, he abstained from any cooperation with the Church, although he was not impassive to her predicament. The Bolsheviks saw their most dangerous enemy in religion and, from the first days of the Revolution, directed a bitter campaign against the Church. She was deprived of her traditional privileges. Her land was confiscated. Religion was excluded from the schools, and the law forbade the teaching of Christianity to persons under eighteen in groups of more than four. Numbers of priests suffered violent deaths or were put in prison. But with all this, Berdyaev sensed that the deepest need of the Church was not in recoupment of material losses but rather in a spiritual awakening to her divine apostolate. However, the Church hierarchs seemed to be exclusively concerned with their historical disaster. They did not acknowledge their culpability in the ushering in of the Revolution; and experienced no desire of inward reformation. They looked back at the past with regret and secretly hoped for a speedy restoration.

Berdyaev attended several meetings of the Moscow Patriarchate which was re-established under Kerensky. In 1918 he even took part in a vast demonstration headed by the Patriarch Tikhon in protest against the Government's anti-Church policy. This performance, however, remained exceptional. He kept aloof from ecclesiastical affairs knowing through personal experience that light sometimes breaks only at the end of one's tether: suffering could at least purify and strengthen the Church.

During this period Berdyaev wrote extensively. A seminar he conducted on the problems of the philosophy of history was later published under the title *The Meaning of History*. The same may be said of his book about Dostoyevsky which was originally delivered as a course on the social and religious implications of the *Legend of the Grand Inquisitor*. An extemporaneous harangue in defense of Christianity delivered at a meeting sponsored by the anarchists was later expounded in the pamphlet *On the Worth of Christianity and the Unworthiness of Christians*. Other studies carried on at the same time were later reworked for publication, namely, *The Destiny of Russia*, and *Constantin Leontyev*, besides the *Philosophy of Inequality* previously mentioned.

In 1920, surprisingly enough, Berdyaev was offered the chair of philosophy at the University of Moscow. For one year he gave lectures in which he openly criticized Marxism. But everything has its appointed time. One night of that year twelve Tchekists

117

(members of the security police) entered his apartment and ransacked his study. With restrained indignation Berdyaev observed: "You are searching in vain. The truth is simple. I am an opponent of Bolshevism because I am a Christian. You will find nothing in my private papers that I have not openly declared in my lectures and meetings." [20] The Tchekists, however, continued their search till dawn. Of course, they did not find anything, and confined their report to the declaration made by the defendant. Thereupon Berdyaev was arrested and imprisoned at the Lubianka, the dreadful headquarters of the Tcheka.

One night he was taken out of his cell and brought for an examination before the redoubtable head of the secret police Dzerzhinsky. The meeting was also attended by Kamenev and Menzhinsky, the vice-president of the Tcheka. Far from recoiling in dismay at the presence of the man stigmatized as the Robespierre of the Russian Revolution, Berdyaev immediately decided to take the offensive rather than defend himself with justifications. When permitted to speak, he launched into an eloquent exposition of his views. In a forty-five minute tirade, he summed up the religious, philosophical, and moral reasons for his opposition to Bolshevism, but stressed that he was not concerned with the political aspect of the regime. He denounced dialectical materialism as destructive of human freedom and dignity, and contrasted it with the Christian vision of life. From time to time Dzerzhinsky would interpose a short remark. Once, for instance, he commented: "It it possible to be a materialist in theory and an idealist in life, or on the contrary, an idealist in theory and a materialist in life." [21] In the end, visibly impressed by the sincerity and honesty of a genuine Christian thinker, Dzerzhinsky brushed away the charges against the prisoner and set him free, but forbade him to leave Moscow without authorization. Indeed, the notorious chief of the Bolshevik secret police inquired for a car to take Berdyaev home— but since no car was available, a Red Guard transported our philosopher to freedom on a motorcycle.

For some subsequent months Berdyaev continued his habitual speaking and writing activity relatively undisturbed. The situation began to change suddenly in the spring of 1922, when religious persecutions were sternly intensified by the newly organized anti-

118

religious front. The Church was accused of conspiracy against the Government in association with Western powers. The places of worship were confiscated and closed. The trials against the Christians multiplied. Berdyaev was arrested for the second time. He was incarcerated once more in the Lubianka. After eight days of detention he was notified of his banishment from the Soviet Union, with his family. The grounds for expulsion were stated in one sentence: ideological adversary of communism. In addition, he was informed that should he attempt to return, he would be shot. To make sure of his clear understanding of the decision, they made him sign a paper to that effect.[22] Then, he was released.

Two months later, in September 1922, a group of twenty-five exiles and their families left Petrograd for Stettin on a German steamer. The loss of his library weighed heavily on Berdyaev. He did not even succeed in carrying along his numerous manuscripts. However, he entrusted them to the German Embassy; later they reached him in Berlin by diplomatic service.

But more than anything else, Berdyaev was overcome with grief and bitterness at being forced to leave his beloved country. Years later reconsidering the experience of the banishment, he made this statement:

> It is not easy for me to speak of the experiences and emotions which stirred me when the moment came to take leave of my country, of all the things and all the people that had become the inmost part of my life. The experience was, indeed, more agonizing than I would myself ever have thought it possible. But, though at the moment life in exile appeared to me as a mysterious and unwelcome Unknown, it proved in fact intensely significant for me and full of creative possibilities. And, maybe, I would not have fulfilled my calling without the providential displacement.[23]

Before his departure, an educated Communist, the president of the Academy of Arts, of which Berdyaev was a member, told him, "They hope in the Kremlin that when you find yourself in Western Europe you will understand on which side justice lies." In his autobiography Berdyaev pointed out that the Kremlin's hopes were futile: "I have remained an enemy of totalitarianism, in whatever form it paraded, in Russia and in the West alike." And he added by way of hard-learned wisdom:

> If I were to summarize the lesson I have learned throughout this time of trials and ordeals in revolutionary and post-revolutionary Russia, I would say that it has imbued me with a bitter feeling for the verdicts of history. At times the historical stage is dominated by those who call out
>
> > *Away from the shouts and the snickers,*
> > > *the hands that are slimy with blood,*
> > *Away, to the camp of the outlawed*
> > > *who struggle and perish for love.*
>
> And they go down into history as men and women who have made supreme sacrifices and surrendered their lives for a great cause. But then the hour strikes for them and their cause to triumph and be victorious: and lo, they too are quick to turn into those who shout and sneer and whose hands are slimy with blood. New generations follow and are impelled by a desire to join the camp of the outlawed. Thus the tragi-comedy of history goes on forever in unremitting, perpetual recurrence. The Kingdom of God alone transcends and overcomes this spell-bound course.[24]

The parting proved irrevocable: Berdyaev was never to see his native land again.

CHAPTER VI

FROM MOSCOW TO PARIS:
THE END OF AN EPOCH

> The flood waxes and bears us on
> To a dark immensity
> There where we sail, all around us
> The flaming abyss.[1]
>
> —Tyutchev

On their arrival in Berlin, the group of exiles was greeted with courtesy and kindness by representatives of several German organizations. They were offered immediate hospitality and assisted in finding accommodations despite acute post-war shortage of houses in Germany. No Russian *émigrés* came to welcome them.

During the first years of the Bolshevik Revolution, the scheme of executions carried out by Red Terror and the defeat of the White armies gave rise to a surging tide of mass emigration. Multitudes of panic-stricken refugees spread over the neighboring countries from China and Japan to the shores of the Atlantic. Germany at that time counted some half a million fugitives. The majority of them anticipated with conviction an impending fall of the Soviet regime and kept ready to return.

The *émigrés* who lived in Berlin looked upon their fellow countrymen recently landed from Russia with suspicion and hostility. Rumors began to circulate that the newcomers were not deportees at all but Bolshevik emissaries sent by the Soviet Government on the mission of undermining and disorganizing the Russian emigra-

121

tion. Nevertheless, soon after their arrival the exiles met with the leaders of the *émigrés* belonging to the White Movement. At its head was Berdyaev's former associate, Peter Struve. The Movement strongly advocated the idea that only an intervention of the Western powers could bring about the end of Bolshevism. Berdyaev, on the other hand, had always been utterly opposed to any foreign interference in the affairs of Russia. He was convinced that an epoch came to a close and that no return was either possible or commendable. The meeting which took place in Berdyaev's apartment ended in a real storm. Years later Berdyaev wrote in connection with the incident:

> Plans to overthrow Bolshevism by means of military intervention, which became a kind of daydream among the *émigrés,* were for me a monstrosity, or, rather a monstrous farce, and I realized that it was hopeless to expect from them the slightest understanding of the real situation. I had no faith in or sympathy with the White Movement: it belonged to an irretrievable past; it was irrelevant—just 'sound and fury signifying nothing', but, at times, something very pernicious. For my part, I envisaged a wholly different way of saving Russia from the perils of Bolshevism: I believed in her regeneration from within, through a painful process of inner purification. . . . I was conscious that Russia in her revolutionary experience, and through her the whole world, was on the threshold of a new historical epoch, and that, as a result of that experience she would come to learn her true vocation.[2]

Accordingly, Berdyaev avoided political contacts with the *émigrés*. He engaged in cultural activity instead, and devoted more time to study and writing.

At a suggestion made by the exiles, a number of whom were university professors and reputed scholars, there was established in Berlin, with the financial help of the German Government, the Russian Institute of Sciences. Berdyaev served in it as dean of the department of philosophy and taught the history of Russian thought. Moreover, he took the initiative of organizing the Religious-Philosophical Academy in the tradition of similar institutions which he had promoted in Russia.

In his autobiography, Berdyaev gratefully acknowledges the assistance in the foundation of the Academy afforded by the International Y.M.C.A. He highly praises the deep interest and sympathy for the spiritual and intellectual life of the Russian emigrants of men such as the Americans, Donald A. Lowry and Paul B. Anderson, and the Swiss, Gustav Kullman. In fact, the International Y.M.C.A., under the leadership of John R. Mott contributed vitally to the maintenance and development of the Russian religious and secular creativity. They organized centers of education for the Russian youth, sponsored the publication of newspapers and periodicals, and provided printing facilities for the Russian intellectuals. Particularly, the major works in philosophy and theology of well-nigh all leading Russian thinkers—Berdyaev included—have been published by the Y.M.C.A. Press.

Berdyaev lived in Berlin for two years. During this time a far-reaching transition occurred in his philosophical development: he ceased being solely a Russian thinker and turned into a European philosopher. This does not imply that he had altered his native mental habits or that the main lines of his spiritual quest had been changed. Indeed, he insisted upon the fact that if he loved Europe as his own it was precisely by virtue of being a Russian. He felt at one with Dostoyevsky who believed universalism is a distinctive Russian characteristic.[3] However, the profound intelligence and seriousness of his approach to continental problems and the penetrating sense of the Western destiny acquired him a reputation of being a European thinker. Also, Berdyaev's intellectual interests which hitherto had been envisaged from a prevailingly Russian viewpoint, although covering the whole possible area of philosophical inquiry, had increasingly extended their domain to cosmic proportions.

In Berlin Berdyaev became acquainted with a number of outstanding German thinkers, among them Max Scheler, Oswald Spengler and Count Hermann Keyserling. The last helped him in publishing a German translation of *The Meaning of History* with a personal introductory preface (1923). A year later Berdyaev published *The New Middle Ages*. The book achieved an immediate and lasting success. It was translated into fourteen languages and threw the author at once into the limelight of the European intellectual stage. He was discussed and quoted in many intellectual circles. Some even began designating him as a prophet of the new

123

times. The work is an attempt at philosophical interpretation of the ultimate meaning of modern history. The theme already dealt with in the *Meaning of History* was subsequently developed in *The Bourgeois Mind* (1934), and the *Fate of Man in the Modern World* (1934), besides the already mentioned *The New Middle Ages;* it was once more touched upon in *Toward a New Epoch* (1948).

What is this New Middle Ages heralded by Berdyaev? Does it imply a return to the period between the sunset of Antiquity and the dawn of Renaissance? No and yes. No, because an actual restoration of a former *status quo* in history is literally impossible—time is irreversible. Yes, on condition of grasping correctly the inner significance of that long-distance past.

The Middle Ages, according to Berdyaev, should no longer be interpreted in terms of "medieval darkness," i.e., of a period in which all culture had been blotted out by the torrent of Barbarian forces. True, classical civilization of Greece and Rome broke down at that time. Moreover, negative and hauntingly dark aspects unfurled a merciless display over several centuries: brutality, violence, cruelty, widespread ignorance, and religious superstition connected with the fear of hell-fire. But in a deeper ontological sense, the Middle Ages was a period of spiritual and intellectual incubation, during which new creative forces appeared and were disciplined. The soul-stirring crisis which had been opened by the shattering of the ancient historical order seized the European man with the awareness of the mysterious ground of life. A movement originated toward the depths of inner experience. The need arose for fresh symbols expressing the profundity of the newly acquired insights into the nature of ultimate reality.

The Middle Ages was not a time of void and darkness, but a period of night in the sense of the "dark night of the soul" as described by St. John of the Cross—wherein spiritual desolation, loneliness, and frustration which ensued after the fall of Rome gradually engendered not an irremediable despair, but a poignant yearning for God and an extended vision of man. The Middle Ages was also, and foremost, the period in which human personality came to be fully acknowledged in the light of the Christian revelation. Christianity affirmed the spiritual primacy of human

124

nature. It denied its origin in the realm of matter alone. It associated man directly with the divine existence and creation; and thus emancipated him from the ancient bondage to nature.

As a result, a surge of untried spiritual forces overtook medieval man. Scholasticism and Monasticism which came into being at that time bear witness to both the powerful awakening and the stern discipline of man's spiritual life in the Middle Ages. The same epoch, on the other hand, was marked by a vivid realization of sensual potentialities of the human body and the aesthetic promises of the world of nature. These found their expression in feudal chivalry and the knightly cult of feminine beauty. Both the ideals of monk and of knight helped, by spiritual and physical discipline, to concentrate and preserve the outflow of inner forces within a strong, integrated medieval soul. In the fulness of time the two underground, formative currents—ascetic and sensuous—culminated in Humanism. The latter, in turn, blossomed into the Renaissance.

The Renaissance, therefore, was neither a mere imitation nor a rebirth of antiquity, as is commonly supposed. It represented a new type of culture, based on a humanistic spirit of self-assertion, and having its own integrated world-view and character. The recourse to the classical forms of Greek and Latin art was meant strictly as an instrument of expression for its own autonomous spirit nurtured by ten centuries of Christianity. The Renaissance was in no way the final issue of ancient history, but the departing point of modern times.

At first, the Renaissance was primarily Christian. The ascetic side of the medieval soul kept the upper hand over its sensuous counterpart. The organic bonds with Christian sources remained unspoiled. This was made manifest by a brilliant flowering of saintliness and artistic creativity of the Italian *trecento* which Berdyaev regarded as the highest point of the Western culture.[4] The Christian Renaissance inspired Gothic cathedrals and Scholastic philosophy; to it belonged the mysticism of St. Francis of Assisi and the prophecies of Joachim of Flora; it found its highest expression in the genius of Dante and the artistry of Giotto. But the Christian Renaissance could not for very long carry on its majestic achievements. The anti-Christian element which it contained from the beginning gradually superseded the Christian influence and drifted away toward secularism in a process of transition from the depth to the surface of life. As Berdyaev explained it,

> This divorce from the spiritual depths, in which man's forces had been stored and to which they had been inwardly bound, is accompanied not only by their liberation, but by their passage from the depths to the periphery and the surface of human life, from the medieval religious to secular culture; and it implies the transference of the centre of gravity from the divine depths to purely human creation.[5]

The quattrocento witnessed already a time of division. It was then that the pagan element of the Middle Ages—sensuousness, which looked upon man as a part of nature and not of spirit—came into its own and clashed with the element of asceticism. The dualism of this period of the Renaissance, according to Berdyaev, is evidenced in Botticelli's paintings. His beautiful Madonnas are more the images of the terrestrial existences than the reflections of heavenly perfection.

The clash laid bare the tragic contradiction of Humanism—that of the immanent and transcendent principles of human nature—a dualism which has affected history ever since. Should we then draw the conclusion that the immanent principle of human life is destructive by virtue of some inner evil? In no wise, protests Berdyaev, only when it moves away from the Christian faith. And that is exactly what happened to the Renaissance: man's liberation under God turned into man's self-assertion without God. In a penetrating analysis of the problem, Berdyaev wrote:

> Humanism, as its name implies, denotes the elevation and setting up of man in the centre of the universe. It signifies his rebellion, affirmation and discovery. This is one of its aspects. It has been said that humanism discovered the human individuality and gave it full play, freeing it from its medieval subjection and directing it upon free paths of self-affirmation and creation. But humanism also contained a diametrically opposed principle, that of man's abasement, and of the exhaustion of his creative powers and of his general enfeeblement. For humanism, by regarding man as part of nature, transferred the centre to the periphery. It divorced the natural

from the spiritual man. It divorced him from the interior significance and the divine centre of life, from the deepest foundations of man's very nature; and it then gave him the freedom of creative development. In fact, humanism denied that man was the image and likeness of God; that he was the reflection of the Divine Being. In its dominant form humanism affirmed that man was a natural being, the child of the world and of nature, created by natural necessity, the flesh and blood of the natural world; and that he therefore shared all its limitations, diseases and defects. Thus humanism not only affirmed man's self-confidence and exalted him, but it also debased him by ceasing to regard him as a being of a higher and divine origin. . . . The result of man's self-affirmation, once he had ceased to be conscious of his tie with the highest Divine and Absolute nature and with the highest source of his life, was to bring about his own perdition.[6]

The process of the humanist morbid self-destruction which had been disclosed in the quattrocento gained acceleration in proportion to its gradual recession from the Middle Ages. The farther it departed from its medieval sources, the more it denied the living waters of the Christian faith, the sooner it drained to exhaustion its creative powers, thus exposing man to dehumanization.

The next stage in the unfolding of Humanism after the Renaissance was occupied by the Reformation. It was the contribution of the German people and brought into European history a different spirit—a striving after freedom of consciousness, a renewal of faith, and religious purity. The Italian Renaissance did not take the form of a revolt against the Catholic Church; it was merely a display of man's creative powers. Indeed, it enjoyed the Vatican's support and blessing. But corruption had infected the Roman ecclesiastical hierarchy; and it was against this that Luther took his stand. The Reformation assumed the character of a revolt and remained religiously unproductive. Its main task was that of spiritual liberation. But, while setting man positively free from papal autocracy, the Reformation, at the same time, asserted man's total dependence on God. In doing this, the Reformation deprived man of his newly won freedom to an extent the Roman Catholic Church had never achieved. Berdyaev's own argumentation on this point is noteworthy:

The Catholic Christian consciousness had affirmed the existence of two principles, the divine and the human. It had also affirmed man's independence before God and recognized both the interrelation of these two principles and their independent origin. The Protestant Lutheran consciousness, on the other hand, affirmed the existence uniquely of God and the Divine Nature, denying the independence of human nature . . . , and the ontological foundations of human liberty. Luther affirmed the freedom of the religious consciousness. . . , but he denied the primal foundations of man's freedom. . . . The unique divine principle is revealed within man, but the latter's independent nature and freedom before the divine principle is denied.[7]

The Eighteenth-Century Enlightenment, which formed the next stage in the evolution of the humanist movement, according to Berdyaev, was already showing deep-drawn signs of the beginning of the end. Reason divorced from the last vestiges of the divine life slipped into delusion and self-contradiction. In the absence of all mystery, which they relegated to the attic of fanciful superstition, the thinkers of the Enlightenment tried to prove that everything in the world moved according to the necessity of unchangeable and predictable physical laws. They cherished the naive dream that all problems were soluble by the discovery of objective answers, which, once found, would be all-evident and valid forever. Following in the footsteps of Descartes' rationalism and Locke's empiricism, the humanist self-assertion eventually converted philosophy into a natural science, reason into a mechanical function, and reduced man to an appendage of nature.

That the fountain of the Renaissance creative spirit was dried up was further illustrated by the speculative philosophy of Kant. Berdyaev always spoke with deep appreciation of the master-head of Königsberg. Was it not Kant who had established the reality of the noumenal realm and thus provided the basic presupposition for the philosophy of existentialism? Yet Kant's questioning of man's power of knowledge and his endeavors after epistemological justification stood in contradiction to the humanist unconditional trust in man and his possibilities of cognition. The philosophy of Kant indicated that the thirst for knowledge of the Renaissance had withered away.[8]

The French Revolution was the last distinguishing feature of the humanist spirit in modern times. Berdyaev's discerning assessment of this epoch-making event deserves an extensive quotation:

> Those elements which had been confined to the sphere of art and science in the Renaissance, to that of religion in the Reformation, and to that of reason in the age of enlightenment, were now applied to the sphere of communal and collective action. Thus man's faith in his ability as a natural being to change absolutely freely and independently human society and the direction of history; his belief in his perfect freedom from control and in his right to proclaim and fulfill this freedom; all these now manifest themselves in communal and collective action. In this sphere, then, the French Revolution realized one of the greatest of humanist experiments. It was an experiment which served to verify the interior contradictions, problems and consequences of a humanism divorced from its spiritual foundations. But the French Revolution was powerless to solve its own problems: it could realize neither man's rights nor the freedom of human life. It suffered a defeat. It succeeded only in realizing tyranny and abusing man. The Renaissance had been a great manifestation of man's creative powers, but it had failed to achieve the perfection of terrestrial forms. The Reformation had put forward the temptation of freedom only to reveal its religious impotence and to assume negative and not creative forms. And now the Revolution was attended with a still greater failure.
> . . . . For the Revolution which, in 1789, had been animated by the ideal of the Rights of Man, of the citizen and of freedom, arrives by 1793, at the negation of all rights and of all freedom. It consumes itself, thus revealing that it possessed at the foundations no ontological principle to justify the rights of man. It becomes apparent then that the rights of the man, who forgets those of God, tend to exterminate themselves without liberating him.[9]

Finally the nineteenth century precipitated the crisis of Humanism and hastened the end of the Renaissance spirit. It demonstrated beyond all doubt the truth that the humanist dialectic is necessarily self-destructive, *"for the putting up of man without God and against God, the denial of the divine image and likeness in himself, lead to his own negation and destruction."* [10]

129

With Karl Marx and Friedrich Nietzsche Humanism reached the limits of its expanse, and passed over into anti-humanism. These two thinkers, although at opposite cultural poles from one another, both presented, after sustained, independent cogitation, a distorted representation of man. They obliterated the likeness of God in the human being, and acknowledged no higher principles of life than those contained in the domain of nature. The result was man's complete disintegration—the denial of the human image.

In Marx, whose philosophical origins were humanist, the denial of the human image took the form of the social collective. He refused to place man above society, and subordinated the individual to the class, i.e., to an impersonal social category conditioned by the economic processes of a deterministic world. Marx denied the reality of human personality. The goal of dialectical materialism is mankind, not the individual. The human being is without spiritual content; he is just another function of the collective, paving the way for the advent of an ideal society which alone will possess real existence and creativity.

Nietzsche, too, arrived at similar conclusions, but his denial of the human image assumed the form of the individual, not of the collective. Indeed for him the collective—mankind—does not even exist—it is an abstraction; all that exists is a servile herd of homunculi. Moreover, man is a shame and a disgrace, the most contemptible thing. The goal of life is higher than either man or mankind, and man serves only as the means toward its attainment. What is that goal? The creation of a Superman. "God is dead!" [11] proclaimed Nietzsche, and man is only a transient, the mere trifle of a creature, whose only role at the present is in mediating the establishment of the reign of the Superman. Man is "a rope stretched between the animal and the Superman." [12] Nietzsche contemplated the rise of a race of divine human beings—beyond good and evil—the least among whom would still be infinitely greater than the greatest of men whom Zarathustra found only all-too-human.

This is then the assigned task for men: to surpass themselves. But how? Nietzsche supplied no satisfactory answer. Berdyaev agreed that Nietzsche was right in his emphasis upon man's power to create new values. But this power, he maintained, was not un-limited. "A man cannot create living beings; he can only beget them; he cannot create even a flea and there is a profound meaning in this. A creature created by man would have no living image; it would be a mechanism." [13] With Nietzsche the actual man dis-appeared in a hypothetical Superman, and life was left with no other references than the silent grave of God. The Superman was unrealizable, and this effected the tragic bankruptcy of Nietzsche's humanism—he wanted to create God out of nothing and into nothing he reduced man instead.

After Marx and Nietzsche, Humanism was no longer possible; nor the Renaissance of which it was the spiritual foundation. These two great thinkers laid bare all the mutually annihilating contradictions of Humanism. The way of boundless self-affirmation and presumptuous pride, of indifference to divine sanctions, and of exclusive reliance upon man's own will was doomed to bring about the inner ruin of the human being.

The end of Humanism and the Renaissance provoked the crisis of humanity. Modern civilization, both bourgeois and collectivist, lay in the throes of its death agony. Shaken to his very roots by the process of dehumanization and depersonalization, man emerges from contemporary history not only deeply disillusioned, inwardly divided, with a consciousness disintegrated and a heart seized by anxiety, but also creatively exhausted. Can he still be called a man? "We are witnessing the process of dehumanization in all phases of cultural and social life. . . . Man has ceased to be the supreme value: he has ceased to have any value at all." [14] This is conclu-sively evidenced by modern religious and philosophical thought, by politics and economics alike.

In the sphere of social life, Capitalism, according to Berdyaev, affords a tragic example of the humanist *dénouement* and spiritual decadence. Although spiritually a product of the Renaissance, which emancipated man from Church theocracy, and liberated his creative faculties, Capitalism has finally turned into mere economic materialism. The spiritual principle and motivation of economic activity was superseded by the principle of capitalistic profit. The person, which is a spiritual entity, was sacrificed for the sake of the individual, which is a biological entity, and the individual dedicated to the exclusive service of mammon instead of God. As a result, the spirit ceased to control man's mental and physical life; the relationship with the eternal was lost, and the social life thrown off balance. "Modern capitalist civilization is essentially atheistic and hostile to the idea of God. The crime of killing God must be laid at its door. . . ." It is "the spiritual phenomenon of the annihilation of spirituality."[15] True, Capitalism, according to Berdyaev, did not altogether repudiate religion; but its pragmatic and utilitarian approach to spiritual values was a real source of modern atheism. "The useful and practically effective God of Capitalism cannot be the true God."[16] There is nothing ontological left in him.

This does not imply that economic life is evil as such. On the contrary,

> it has real and divine roots in life; for man has both a duty and impulse to develop himself economically. But the divorce of economy from life, the exaltation of economics as the high principle of life, the technical interpretation of life, and the fundamental capitalist principle of profit transform man's economic life into a fiction. The capitalist system is sowing the seeds of its own destruction by sapping the spiritual foundation of man's economic life. Labor loses all spiritual purpose and justification and, as a result, brings an indictment against the whole system.[17]

In Berdyaev's belief, the penalty Capitalism has paid for its de-personalization and de-spiritualization of man was Communism, Fascism, and Nazism. All three are the children of Capitalism—the fatal scions of its inner dialectic. They arose in answer to a deep-felt need, both spiritual and economic, engendered by the illusions of capitalist liberalism. For the formal capitalist freedom, when unattended with respect for human person and dignity, must inevitably end, on the one hand, in economic destitution—that is, want of work, food, clothing and shelter; and on the other, in spiritual emptiness—that is, skepticism, cynicism, and moral indifference. In opposition to the capitalist disintegrating *laissez-faire*, the totalitarian systems offered man both economic security and a sense of inward, even though collective, worth.

Berdyaev acknowledged, however, that in practice the modern dictatorships have disclosed the spurious character of their ideologies and methods. Instead of the promised social protection, they brought into life new forms of social enslavement. And the collective worth, which was supposed to fill the living personality of the worker with pride and contentment, entailed instead the subjugation of his whole being to the social organism. For the totalitarian world is moved, after the fashion of Capitalism, by other values than those of man and human personality. To be sure, profit is no longer here the motivating end as it is with Capitalism. But the supreme values of Communism, Fascism, and Nazism—class, state, and race—are no less pernicious.

Fascism is based upon the myth of state, which it considers as the central value. The person is dissolved in it. Moreover, the fascist deification of the state marks an obvious return to paganism. Fascism, however, despite its mystical worship of the state, is less repulsive than Nazism, which is the mystical worship of the Aryan blood. Nazism replaces the spiritual concept of man by race—a "zoological category." [18] The very idea is pathological, "something which demands a psychoanalysis of the whole people which has fallen into a state of collective insanity and demonic possession." [19] As to Communism, its votaries idolize a social class—proletariat. It likewise deprives man of personality and originality by submitting him to a stern party line and nurturing him with a false philosophy of life.

The processes of dehumanization which are presently at work in history have been, according to Berdyaev, greatly facilitated by the nineteenth century's Industrial Revolution. In turn, both capitalism and collectivism have effected the triumph of the machine in the world. This turned into a fatal and inevitable vicious circle wherein "man as a whole being . . . disappears; he ceases to be a being with a spiritual centre, retaining his inner continuity and his unity. . . ." Instead of the image of man, there are left of him but "non-human and natural elements." [20] The phenomenal progress of modern technics brought about not only the mechanization of life in general, but a "break-up of organic unity which the machine entails on everything." [21] Mechanism took the place of organism and superseded organic life. *"But human powers that escape from a state of organism inevitably become enslaved to mechanization."* [22] This is a tragic misfortune because

> The organic structure of life is hierarchical, that is, cosmic, and in the cosmic organism the parts submit to the whole and all depend on the centre. The centre is the last end, the object, of the life of the parts. If the parts of an organism break away from the whole and cease to look to their centre they insensibly come under the control of a lower kind of nature. [23]

This is the predicament of the modern man: his organic unity is dismembered into mechanism, and his spiritual center is lost under the debris of the broken parts. In addition, who can tell where, if ever, scientific inventiveness will stop discovering the terrific means of human destruction? Physical sciences have already drawn the curtains aside on the catastrophic potentialities of nature uncontrolled by spirit. "The discovery of entropy, of radioactivity and the splitting of atoms in matter, finally of the principle of relativity, is like an apocalypse of modern physics." [24] The aftermath of the World War is most significant in this respect, and stands as a signal warning against the possibility of future global conflagrations. The warning reads: "Man, desiring no longer to be the image of God, becomes the image of the machine." [25]—and as such he is destroying himself. For experience teaches that *"where there is no God there is no man."* [26]

The process of dehumanization is also evidenced in modern religious and philosophical thought. To be sure, the process is not recent; it has been disclosed all the way from Luther to Karl Barth, and from Descartes to Heidegger and Sartre. Actually, a great deal of present-day thought is in reaction to the distortions of philosophical world-views of past centuries. But with all that, modern thought has failed to restore an integral image of man. For Heidegger and Sartre, for instance, man is a creature of nothingness without reason for existing. He is free, of course, or rather doomed to freedom, which is just a means of discovering his own meaninglessness. As long as man lives, his personality, his inner being, is lost behind anxiety which forever accompanies the exercise of his freedom of choice. Indeed, he has no actual reality at all, only a short, transient span of useless becoming between the

134

néant of birth and the *néant* of death. At the moment of his death, man is simply and irretrievably reduced to nothing. This type of philosophy is symptomatic of our times with its prevailing moods of pessimism, despair, and a sense of the absurdity of existence.

Not less characteristic of the same process of dehumanization in Western culture is the wide-spread influence exerted over the Christian world by the theology of Karl Barth. According to Barth, neither nature nor man reflect, or even could reflect God because he is "Wholly Other." The gulf which Barth finds between man and God is occasioned by man's sin. As a result, man is in no position of knowing God, unless God has graciously condescended to make himself known to man. Man is nothing; God is everything. Man's search for God is vain: he never finds God. God must come to man first, on God's own initiative. Karl Barth's theology "is the dehumanization of Christianity." In a world full of creative forces, all that Barth discovers is "sin and powerlessness. There remains a fervent faith in God, but in a God absolutely transcendent, separated by an abyss from the world and from man." [27] Karl Barth's world is, like that of Sartre and Heidegger, a godless world, even though God exists, Barth shares in their anti-humanist reaction and comes out in Christianity with a similarly distorted vision of man which results "in a degradation or even denial of man." [28]

To sum up, Berdyaev's judgment on all forms of social, political, economic, and cultural forms of modern life is a spiritual judgment. He denounced the secularist, anti-personalist, materialist trends of our epoch exclusively from the point of view of the spirit. His rejection of Capitalism, Fascism, Nazism, and Communism alike was motivated by their acceptance as controlling ideals other values than the personality of man, that is respectively—profit, state, race, and class. For the same reason he condemns modern philosophy, art, and religion, which likewise disfigures man by either separating him from God or reducing him to nothingness—thus bringing about "the emptiness of a superficial and unoriented existence." [29] They have all denied the sources of man's life and made a wilderness of his soul. How could he continue to exist? For,

135

cut off from his spiritual nature, he becomes a prey to illusions and his life is made up of phantasms. It must be recognized that man in his limited and relative earthly life is capable of bringing about the beautiful and the valuable only when he believes in another life, unlimited, absolute, eternal. This is a law of his being. A contact with this mortal life exclusive of any other ends in a wearing-away of effective energy and a self-satisfaction that makes one useless and superficial. Only the spiritual man, striking his roots deep in infinite and eternal life, can be a true creator.

But modern history

denied the spiritual man, handed over the eternal to the temporal, and took its stand by the natural man within the limited confines of the earth; and this creature who wanted to rely on himself alone now finds himself defenceless amidst unbridled elements and menacing natural forces. The likeness of man cannot be kept inviolate by the powers of natural man: it postulates spiritual man.[30]

Berdyaev was convinced that a whole period of history was coming to an end, that the world was entering the night of a new Middle Ages the outline of which was still not clearly defined. Consequently, he took his philosophical stand resolutely in the future, and thus shut the door to all possible criticisms of his contemporaries. In a short but aggressive apology *pro domo sua,* Berdyaev stated his case as follows:

My ideas are often misinterpreted and I know that people draw the most wrong conclusions from them. The explanation is that my thought is criticized according to current views, and attempt is made to bring it into line with such and such a direction of modern thought: this is an essentially wrong way of considering it. *The very substance of my philosophy is to have nothing at all to do with the thought of times which, so far as I am concerned, are over and done with. I look to the thought of a world which is to begin, the world of the new Middle Ages.* Contemporary spiritual principles and forces are used up, the rationalist day of a past history declines: its sun sets and the night is upon us. The means of research which are adequate to the sun-lit day cannot be of any use for the examination and disentangling of events and phenomena in this eveningtide of history. . . . All the signs and proofs show, that we have passed from an era of light to an era of darkness.[31]

What will the new Middle Age look like? Of course, Berdyaev did not pretend to describe the future after the fashion of a crystal-gazer. The outline he traced of its chief characteristics is based, on the one hand, on his intuition of the rhythm of history and the forces which move within it; and, on the other, on his insight into human nature and destiny.

The new Middle Ages, according to Berdyaev, is by no means a relapse into the state of some previous period in history—for the memory of the past does not disappear. The experience of modern times prevents forever a simple return to the old Middle Ages. The benefits acquired during the six centuries of the Renaissance and Humanism—both positive and negative—will be carried on into the new epoch. For strictly speaking nothing passes away; every-thing is only superseded. It is rather man's inner tenor that makes the difference:

> The Middle Ages safeguarded human powers and prepared the way for the splendor of the Renaissance. Man came to this flowering with medieval experience, medieval prepara-tion, and all that was authentically great in the Renaissance had a bond with the Christian Middle Ages. Today man is going toward an unknown future with the experience of modern history and what led to it behind him; he is not full of creative enthusiasm, as at the beginning of the Renaissance, but exhausted, weak, without faith, empty. All that gives us something to think about.[32]

The new Middle Ages, then, will be above all an epoch of re-covery of faith: man will find God once more. It will be a religious epoch; one in which the human being will undergo a spiritual revolution—a complete renewal of his consciousness. Man will re-ceive an initiation into the mysteries of Being and thus restore the spiritual centre of his life. The future society will assume the char-acter of a religious collectivity "in which opposing forces and principles will be defined and everything which is concealed in the underground or subconsciousness of modern history will be laid

137

bare."[33] This does not imply that the new Middle Ages will initiate a peaceful, warless times. The struggle may come, but it will be no longer political or economic, but rather religious and spiritual:

> I do not mean that the religion of the one God, the faith of Jesus Christ, is going to triumph absolutely and in the order of quantity, but that all aspects of life will be engaged in a religious struggle, grouped under opposed religious principles. This age of deadly warfare between Christianity and Antichristianity will then not be secular but sacred, and in it the religion of Satan and the spirit of Antichrist must needs dominate quantitatively.[34]

Moreover, the new Middle Ages in no way announces the revival of an ecclesiastical hierarchy dominating the State; nor the remaking of the State on a secular basis. Both the Church and the State will have their foundations laid *in* God and *for* God. "God must again be the centre of our whole life—our thought, our feeling, our only dream, our only desire, our only hope."[35]

The Church of the future will be identified with no particular Church of modern history. "The spiritual centre in the near future will not be, as in the Middle Ages, the Church alone."[36] At least not in the sense of a historical Church. For the true Church is not, and cannot be circumscribed within any official, external boundaries: the Church is universal and her life is developing along unseen, mysterious lines known only to the Spirit who breatheth where he will. Indeed, the Church has no other limits than those of the universe:

> The Church is cosmic by her nature and contains within herself the fulness of Being; she is the universe baptized. This ought to be a living and practical truth instead of just a theoretical and abstract doctrine; and the Church must pass from the period in which the sanctuary has predominated to a period of transfiguration of the cosmic fulness of life. Modern religion has become merely a department of culture, with a special place reserved for it—a very small one. It must again become *all,* the force which transfigures and irradiates the whole of life from within: its spiritual energy must be set free to renew the face of the earth.[37]

138

In outlining the possible positive traits of the future City of God, Berdyaev was far, however, from deluding himself with gratuitous illusions of a golden utopia. He was not unaware of the fact that an outbreak of the forces of evil might be expected at any time and thus make havoc of the life of the world. He warned that man, by virtue of the power of freedom innate in him, has always before him the possibility of a double future—either that of Christ or that of Antichrist. Actually, he foresaw the two possibilities alike, but not without launching first a dramatic appeal to Christians to make the right choice:

> The powers of wickedness will grow and take on new forms wherewith to plague us in new ways. But freedom of spirit, liberty to choose his path, has been given to man. Christians must will the creation of a Christian society and culture, putting before all things the search for the Kingdom of God and his justice. A very great deal depends on our liberty, that is, on man's creative efforts. . . . The night is coming and we must take up spiritual weapons for the fight against evil, we must make more sensitive our power for its discernment, we must build up a new knighthood.[38]

In 1924 Berdyaev left Berlin and moved to Paris. Ever since his first travels abroad as a boy, he had always had a liking for the capital of France (and who doesn't!). There at last he found a great city whose comprehensive patterns of intellectual life and freedom of expression offered him a congenial atmosphere of inspiration and creativity. Paris by that time had superseded Berlin as the centre of the Russian emigration: owing to the increasing post-war economic difficulties in Germany, a great number of Russian refugees settled in France where chances for work and shelter appeared more encouraging. The Religious-Philosophical Academy was likewise transferred to Paris, where its activities expanded and intensified. Berdyaev's lectures, always sparkling with original and challenging ideas, formed as usual the point of general attraction.

In 1926 he founded, with the help of the International Y.M.C.A., the monthly review *Put* (The Way), which he edited for fourteen years, until 1939, when the outbreak of the Second World War brought to a stop its publication. Most of the intellectual forces among the Russian *émigrés* sent their written contributions to *Put*.

The periodical was representative of no particular ideology, but rather of a number of Russian theologians and philosophers of various views and trends of thought who undertook the task of carrying on the cultural tradition of their native country. To Berdyaev it afforded the long-hoped-for occasion of defending and maintaining in a consistent manner his pivotal philosophical position, namely freedom. In its columns, as he put it, "I waged a war for freedom, for the freedom of spirit, for the freedom of conscience, for the freedom of thought. I did not miss a single opportunity of coming against those who quenched the spirit and violated thought and conscience." [39] In these ways he came to be known as the leading "left-winger" and a "revolutionary" of the Russian emigration, although, as he observed, "such designations have for me a spiritual rather than a political connotation." [40] In addition, his name acquired a solid reputation in the academic circles of Western Europe as the foremost Russian religious philosopher.

The year of his arrival in Paris Berdyaev took the initiative in organizing interconfessional meetings of Russian Orthodox, French Catholics, and Protestants under the auspices of the Russian Religious-Philosophical Academy, of which he was the president. The undertaking proved the first of its kind since the separation of Greek and Latin churches, and the Protestant Reformation. The meetings were conducted in a prevailing tone of goodwill and fellowship. Berdyaev's description renders excellently the spirit of genuine ecumenicity which animated them, and at the same time, sets a workable pattern for all similar gatherings:

> It was significant, perhaps, that . . . these gatherings provided the first opportunity for French Catholics and Protestants to come together for the purpose of discussing religious matters. It also proved an occasion for Catholic Modernists and Thomists to meet across the barrier of ecclesiastical sanctions. Orthodoxy provided a meeting-point between the various sections of a divided Christendom, uninhibited as it is by the weight of historical memories which impede mutual understanding between the various Western Churches. . . . The meetings were extremely alive and interesting; there was even a danger of their becoming something of a fashion. There was a feeling that the members of the respective confessions were brought face to face with completely new worlds, unknown

and yet unexpectedly akin to each other. We were all conscious of forming a Christian oasis in a desert of irreligion and hostility towards Christianity; and yet there was a complete absence of presumption and sectarian self-assertiveness. We discovered our fundamental unity in Christ and, at the same time, differences which we knew how to respect and understand.[41]

The most active participants among the Roman Catholics were Father Gillet, of the Institute Catholique, and subsequently General of the Dominican Order; Abbé Laberthonnière, the spokesman for Catholic modernism; and Jacques Maritain, the well-known exponent of Neo-Thomism, whom Berdyaev jestingly called the most Russian of the French intellectuals. Protestants were represented by Pastor Marc Boegner, President of the Federation of Protestant Churches of France; Professor Auguste Lecerf, an orthodox Calvinist; and Pastor Wilfred Monod, one of the leaders of the liberal social movement in Protestantism. In time the ecumenical group, within which philosophical problems gradually gained precedence over religious, was joined by other outstanding figures of contemporary French Catholicism. Among them were the writer Charles du Bos, the Christian existentialist Gabriel Marcel, the eminent specialist of the Middle Ages Etienne Gilson, the distinguished expert on Mohammedan mysticism Massignon, and Emmanuel Mounier, later editor of the monthly review *Esprit*. The writers Paul Nizan and André Malraux also participated in the discussions. Russian Orthodox representatives were headed by Father Sergius Bulgakov, the dean of the Russiaan Theological Institute of Paris.

Apart from these meetings, Berdyaev attended and spoke at many international conferences. He visited England, Germany, Austria, Switzerland, Holland, Belgium, Hungary, Czechoslovakia, Poland, and several other countries. In Bonn, Karl Barth asked him at the end of a lecture: "How do you know this?" The whole difference between their respective theological positions is evidenced in the question. For Barth knows nothing of God outside the Bible; while Berdyaev asserts his independence of the Scriptures and claims to penetrate the divine realm by intuition. He also took part at the annual *Décades* at Pontigny, held each August in a former monastery founded by St. Bernard. These cultural encounters attended by a great number of intellectuals from France and abroad were devoted to philosophical, literary, social, and political discussions. It was there that he became acquainted with André Gide, George Curtius, Fernandez, Groethusen, Martin Buber, Buonalotti, Léon Brunschwig, and many others. Besides the *Décades* at Pontigny, Berdyaev was also active with two more groups of French intellectuals, *Union pour la Verité*, a distinctly left-wing movement, and above all with the Personalists associated with the periodical *Esprit*.

In many of these activities the position held by Berdyaev was rather ambiguous and, therefore, a source of embarrassment for him: he was expected to speak in the name of official Orthodoxy—indeed he was regarded as the voice of Orthodoxy itself—while actually he could express no other convictions but his own. He did his best to dispel this misunderstanding, yet it kept recurring. Berdyaev can hardly be regarded as the mouthpiece of the Orthodox Church both because there is no "official" Orthodox theology and because of his philosophical position—at no time has he represented anybody or anything but himself. In this respect, Berdyaev was a free, individual Christian philosopher. On the other hand, he was deeply steeped in the spirit of Russian Orthodoxy. This was made possible by the very nature of the Orthodox Church, which remains open in matters of doctrine to new developments and formulations especially along the lines of theological teaching.[42] Accordingly, Berdyaev's heterodoxy despite its aggressive and uncompromising disposition could still be acknowledged as not altogether outside the circle of traditional Orthodoxy. Of this Berdyaev was particularly aware in confessing that his purpose was "not to introduce heresy of any kind nor to promote fresh schism. I am moving in the sphere of Christian problematics which demands creative efforts of thought and where the most divergent opinions are naturally allowable."[43] Berdyaev continued to live until his last day in communion with the Holy Orthodox Church. His creative thought and life experiences were both nurtured and colored by Orthodoxy, however bitter were his criticisms of Russian historical ecclesiasticism.

The Paris period proved to be Berdyaev's most active and fruit-

142

ful. He wrote extensively, gave numerous lectures, and carried on his regular schedule at the Academy. In 1927 he published *Freedom and the Spirit*. In this work Berdyaev made an attempt at a large-scale exposition of his religious views, although he recognized that "there is something essential which I cannot put into words, and that I cannot adequately develop my inmost thoughts. It is very difficult to find a form of expression which exactly suits the essential idea as it appears to oneself." [44] The book received the French Academy prize in moral and religious sciences.

It was followed in 1931 by a wide-ranging study, *The Destiny of Man,* which he defined as an essay on "paradoxical ethics." In it Berdyaev deals with the problem of man and his freedom from the point of view of moral life. The general trend of the work can be discerned in this statement: "Freedom is the essential condition of moral life—freedom in evil as well as in good. There can be no moral life without freedom in evil, and this renders moral life a tragedy and makes ethics a philosophy of tragedy." [45]

The Fate of Man in the Modern World (1934) returns to the theme previously expounded in *The Meaning of History,* which was published in Germany. Berdyaev's important concepts of objectification and God-manhood are respectively dealt with in *Solitude and Society* (1934) and *Spirit and Reality* (1937). The same year he published *The Origin of Russian Communism,* which analyzes the specifically Russian origins of Bolshevism. Berdyaev's metaphysical views were set forth in his *The Beginning and The End* published in 1947 (although it was written in 1941, in the midst of war). *Slavery and Freedom* published in 1939 and *The Divine and the Human* written ten years later gave in concentrated form the summary of all Berdyaev's philosophical and theological ideas. His last book, *The Realm of Spirit and the Realm of Caesar* was published in 1952. A special mention must be given to his spiritual autobiography, *Dream and Reality.* The book was written, for the greatest part, in 1940, and brought up to 1947. It is not only a valuable source of the main events of Berdyaev's life, but also an indispensable tool for an adequate understanding of his teaching.

The dreadful years of the Second World War did not effect any considerable change in Berdyaev's personal workaday existence, although he suffered much on account of the international bloodshed. Under the stress of the German occupation of France—and the same was true of all of Europe—with its interminable series of massacres, deportations, and starvation which culminated in an undescribable moral and physical destitution of the whole continent, Berdyaev sometimes questioned the goodness and lovingness of God, even though he never doubted God's existence.

> Nevertheless, this revolt against God took place within me in behalf of God, in the name of a higher understanding of God. Just the same, I experienced a sense of God forsakenness, of the loss of grace. To experience a sense of being forsaken of God does not signify the rejection of the existence of God: in fact, it presupposes God's existence.[46]

When Germany invaded Russia, the German Gestapo undertook a mass arrest of the Russian *émigrés* living in France. Berdyaev's friends urged him to seek refuge in some neutral nation or even to emigrate to the United States. But he refused to leave France. Moreover, he openly proclaimed his sympathy with the Soviet Army, and kept on denouncing Nazism. Despite his hostile attitude to the Germans he was not maltreated: the protective care of an unknown admirer among the ranking members of the German secret police saved him from being deported to a concentration camp.[47]

In September, 1945, Berdyaev suffered a terrible loss—his lifelong companion and beloved wife, Lydia, died. "This was one of the most torturing as well as the most significant events in my life . . . a capital experience. . . . I cannot resign myself to the death of a being so dear. . . . I cannot consent to the end of life . . ."[48] More than ever before Berdyaev became absorbed in meditations on death and life hereafter. "I cannot be reconciled to death and the tragic finality of human existence; and my whole being resists the notion . . . of death as the ultimate reality. There can be no life unless it restores all those we love to itself." The innermost value of death is love triumphant in eternal life.

> Life must be lost before it can be fully won. Love and death are inseparable, but love is stronger than death. . . . Death is an event in time and a token of the power of time over man;

but it is also an event bringing him face to face with and issuing in eternity, in which love and kinship are victorious over estrangement and disunion.[49]

With the end of the war, Berdyaev's reputation achieved new heights. His thought was better understood. His influence was increasingly expanded. This was especially true of England where he met with genuine sympathy and comprehension. People from all over the world came to see him. His opinion on Russian and European affairs was sought and heeded. He maintained a voluminous correspondence. His works were known in Europe, America, Asia, and Australia. But what about Russia which he loved so dearly? Shall he follow the path of so many of his compatriots who, responding to Stalin's appeal, were returning to their native land? During the war Berdyaev felt at one with the Russian soldiers, and his heart was filled with patriotic pride on account of their heroic exploits. Accordingly, he had even contemplated the possibility of ending his exile and going back to Russia. But in the end he renounced the idea. What could a religious philosopher do in a country which is the declared foe of religion and philosophy alike, except dialectical materialism? Besides, he followed with growing disappointment and suffering the reverting to the pitiless "general line" of the Soviet Government subsequent to the war. "Freedom is again in danger." [50] To be sure, the Orthodox Church seemed to enjoy more freedom than ever before since the Revolution. But the brand of religion as practiced and encouraged by the Soviet Government was but private soul-saving conservatism stripped of all creative thought. Time and again Berdyaev felt torn by the agonizing dilemma of the human personality free and undetermined by any external agent and its implications in the process of history,

> which does not admit of a return to the past and demands a constant revision of one's attitude to Russia in the light of the far-reaching revolution that has taken place and is still continuing there. I can endeavor to unite these two facets within myself, but can their unity be achieved on the open stage of history? [51]

Berdyaev died suddenly, and without answering his own last question, on March 24, 1948. A heart attack took him while he was working at *The Realm of Spirit and the Realm of Caesar*. On his desk, marking the steps of time, three things witnessed a great mind's human-divine encounter—a half-consumed, still smoking cigar, Reinhold Niebuhr's article "God's Order and the World's Disorder" published in *Christianisme social,* and an open Bible. And the clock on the wall indicated fifteen past four in the afternoon.

A year previous to his death, Berdyaev received from the University of Cambridge the degree of Doctor of Divinity *honoris causa.* The presentation made on this occasion by the Public Orator is indicative of the judgment bestowed upon Berdyaev by his contemporaries:

> Here is the second Socrates, an immovable soul, who, even though often at grips with hardships, has never departed from the pursuit and quest for truth. He was banished into exile by the tyrants who governed his fatherland, because of his relationships with men who, after the manner of the first Christians, wanted to share everything in common and apportion wealth according to each one's needs. The same men having in turn laid hold of power, he soon realized that the Kingdom of God shall not be founded that way. For they obeyed only some of the words of Christ, while despising others. Indeed, what was this to them "Man lives not by bread alone," or this, "It is the Spirit who gives life"? Therefore, departing a second time into exile, he put to practice a genuinely Christian spirit; he wrote, meditated, and taught others the rules of philosophy, in order that what is good in the present hour in the life and the government of his country might serve for the salvation of all men, and that which is wicked be uprooted and removed. The fact is that he holds it for certain it is not in vain nor perchance that we have been created, but by the will of a God Omnipotent; that we are destined to freedom not to servitude; that we are inspired and animated by the divine breath. It is with good reason, in truth, that the ancients used to say wisdom is the source of duty. Better yet, and simpler, the Guarantor of our Faith said: "You shall know the truth, and the truth shall make you free." It is therefore as a very agreeable guest that this man has come to us who cultivates truth, this philosopher of the free spirit whom now I invite you to honor, Nicolas Alexandrovitch Berdyaev.[52]

146

PART II

MAGISTER DIXIT

CHAPTER I

THE DIVINE MYSTERY:
FROM NO-THING TO ALL THINGS

> ... This wild Abyss,
> The womb of nature
>   and perhaps her grave,
> Of neither sea, nor shore,
>   nor air, nor fire,
> But all these in their
>   pregnant causes mixed
> Confusedly, and which
>   thus must ever fight.[1]
>
>   —John Milton

At the foundation of Berdyaev's religious philosophy lay not an intellectual concept but a mystical intuition—the intuition of the Divine Nothing or the *Ungrund*. What is this? No language of theology and metaphysics, in Berdyaev's view, is ever capable of describing the *Ungrund*. No rational explanation is ever possible of the Divine Nothing. The only thing that can be uttered about it is neither an explanation nor a description, but a statement of its ineffable mystery. Accordingly, the *Ungrund* might be acknowledged as the infinite mystery underlying all that is, visible and invisible—the fathomless abyss of the indeterminate. It is beyond cognition. It cannot be rationally comprehended. No predicate can be applied to it. The *Ungrund* is not this and not that or anything that we can say or think. To define it is to limit it. In accordance with negative theology, Berdyaev asserts that of the

149

Divine Nothing we can tell not what it is, but solely what it is not. The *Ungrund* is unseen, inapprehensible, uninferable, unthinkable, and indescribable. It cannot be thought of positively, it admits of negative characteristics only.

Berdyaev's initial mystical approach to life was greatly influenced by German speculative mysticism, especially that of Boehme whom he deemed as the greatest mystic of all time.[2]

Jacob Boehme (1575-1624) held that back of the whole universe, both spiritual and physical, there is the primal "groundlessness"— the *Ungrund* or the Absolute. Active in it is only an inchoate and subjective will which Boehme called the "Unmanifested Abysmal Will." Boehme's *Ungrund* goes deeper than God. It is the Godhead preceding God. It is the undetermined, the unconditioned basis of God and the world alike. More precisely, the *Ungrund* is nothingness longing to become something. It is, in Boehme's words, "the uncausable and uncaused . . . an eternal nothingness, and the cause of an eternal beginning, a craving for something."[3] One is reminded of the Brahman of the *Upanishads,* the "Divine Nothing" of Dionysius the Areopagite, the *"Gottheit"* of Meister Eckhart, the *"Identität"* of Schelling, and the absolute God of the mystics of the *Via Negativa.*

The "Abysmal Will," according to Boehme, prompted by Desire, manifested itself through a dynamic dialectic which resulted in a threefold process. First, a theogenic process which, in opposition to Aristotle's "Unmoved Mover," produced a dynamic God—God the Trinity. Second, a metaphysical process which out of One generated the variegated world of eternal ideas after the Platonic pattern. And finally, a cosmogonic process, i.e., a process of exteriorization similar to Schopenhauer's "objectification of the will" whereby the world of nature came into being.[4]

Thus, in contrast to Greek philosophy and Western scholasticism, but in agreement with other great German mystics—Eckhart, Tauler, and Angelus Silesius—Boehme posited the irrational and voluntaristic principle, the mystery of the *Ungrund,* as the primary basis of existence. Furthermore by drawing the distinction between the Godhead—the Divine Nothing—and God-the-Creator he formulated two far-reaching affirmations. On the one hand, the belief that the Godhead has no creative power since it is beyond causality and correlative to no worldly category of thought or being. The Godhead remains the *Mysterium Magnum*, the eternally transcendent and forever hidden. On the other, the view that God-the-Creator is correlative to the world and the creature, and therefore he is not Absolute. He is the God revealed in the Bible, the God of I-Thou relationship, the God of the Suffering Servant.

Berdyaev's own exposition of this intricate mystical insight follows along the Boehmian pathway—with one notable difference, however, among some others of lesser importance. In Boehme's view freedom is rooted in the triune God who creates it. To Berdyaev, on the contrary, freedom is "groundless" and lies outside God. In other words, freedom is uncreated. As a result Berdyaev postulates the actuality of two distinct processes. First from the bottomless abyss, from the *Ungrund,* both a triune God and Freedom are realized in eternity. And secondly, God, the triune God creates the world.[5]

It must be reiterated, however, that the *Ungrund* cannot be grasped conceptually, for it transcends the boundaries of discursive reason. The distinction between Godhead, God-the-Creator, and Freedom is not metaphysical or ontological. It is an original intuition—a vision. More specifically, it is Berdyaev's own vision which cannot be clearly understood unless one has gained a similar experience. In his words, it "can only express itself in terms of spiritual life and experience and not in the categories of a rigid ontology. As rigid ontology this truth can easily degenerate into a heresy." [6]

Berdyaev is careful to stress this point lest he should be suspected of ontological dualism which he repudiates no less than ontological monism.

> To avoid misunderstandings I was always anxious to emphasize that the idea of "groundless freedom" does not imply a kind of ontological dualism, which affirms the existence of two spheres of being, viz. God and freedom. Such affirmations are precisely evidence of rationalization, no less conspicuous than the affirmations of monism, which reduces everything to a single sphere of being, be it divine or human.[7]

Finally, in order to brush away the faintest doubt as to the nature of his fundamental presuppositions—the *Ungrund,* God-the-Creator, and uncreated Freedom—Berdyaev declares with unerring precision that "the opposition between God-the-Creator and freedom is secondary: in the primeval mystery of the Divine Nothing this opposition is transcended." [8]

Thus to Berdyaev the ultimate truths concerning the depths of the Divine Mystery—the *Ungrund*—are "truths of spiritual experience, living truths, not metaphysical categories nor ontological substances." [9] Indeed, they are the content of mystical experiences. For this reason they admit of a symbolic and mythological approach only. In the final analysis, the *Ungrund,* as well as the triune God and the uncreated Freedom are symbols. This is equally true in speaking of spiritual experience itself. Although it is "the greatest reality in human life," [10]—in which alone the divine is manifested —it cannot be demonstrated. All things in connection with the divine and the spiritual "are given to us in the experience of life; they reveal themselves but they cannot be established by ratiocination." [11] Therefore, writes Berdyaev in conclusion, "spiritual life is a symbolic life." [12]

To Berdyaev symbol and myth are not illusions or make-beliefs, which are radically opposed to reality. On the contrary, they give, he thinks, expression to events in the spiritual world which, otherwise, escape all attempts at comprehension by human mind. Rational knowledge is unable to advance beyond the threshold of mystery—it might be applied solely to the finite world of nature. Myth alone penetrates into the mystery of the original reality of the spirit. "Myth always represents a reality, but its reality is symbolic." [13]

Berdyaev's thought on this subject is similar to that of Paul Tillich and Reinhold Niebuhr who likewise hold that conceptional explanations of the divine mystery are impossible. In Tillich's view, "the content of every religion, the basis of every religious experience" [14] is expressed exclusively in symbols. Each symbol, according to these theologians, points to some reality beyond itself and at the same time participates in it. "Only symbolic thinking," writes Berdyaev, "can do justice to the facts of the spiritual world, and to the ineffable and original quality of its life." [15] For symbols, in Tillich's words, "are directed toward the infinite which they symbolize *and* toward the finite through which they symbolize it. They force the infinite down to finitude and the finite up to infinity. They open the divine for the human and the human for the divine."[16]

Symbols, then, introduce to our minds and experience levels of spiritual realities which in any other way remain inaccessible. In the same sense they are means both of representation and communication. For this reason they are, as Niebuhr puts it, "perennially valid."[17]

To summarize Berdyaev's argument for his initial presupposition, it might be said that the *Ungrund* or the Divine Nothing is a symbolic description of a reality which does not lend itself to logical definition. It points not to nothingness, i.e., absence of existence or *néant*; rather it conveys the idea of something which is not nothing but no-thing—beyond and above all things. It is the primeval, undifferentiated, "groundless" ground of life. It is the Divine Mystery underlying the temporal and the eternal alike, There is no rational, conceptional way of interpreting the *Ungrund:* it allows exclusively of a symbolic knowledge attained in the depth of spiritual experience.

The *Ungrund* is above all dynamism, movement, energy. It is pregnant with potentialities craving for actualization. Thus it is that out of its abysmal womb are born, but not created, the triune God and Freedom. The two are not, however, distinct beings. They are not beings at all. They are prior to being. The antithesis between God and Freedom is descriptive, not dualistic in any ontological sense. For it is, as has already been stated, transcended in the Divine Mystery. Upon the realization of God and Freedom out of the *Ungrund*, the former creates the world. Creation, therefore, is a secondary act. Such is Berdyaev's vision of the *Ungrund*.

Keeping in mind Berdyaev's understanding of the *Ungrund*, we will now examine the theological implications of this fundamental presupposition in the following order:

1. The Nature of God
2. The Nature of Freedom
3. Creation and the Fall

1. THE NATURE OF GOD

Is there any reality corresponding to the idea of God? And if so, how is it known? To Berdyaev the two questions are but one. The existence of God and the knowledge of God are, he believes, the content of one and the same experience—the spiritual experience. God is known in the spiritual experience. Conversely, the spiritual experience is the reality corresponding to the idea of God. Spiritual experience reveals the existence of the spiritual world and the possibility of spiritual life. But this world and life have nothing in common with the natural world. Spirit and nature are utterly incommensurable with one another. The natural world is objective. Spirit is not: still less it is something merely subjective. Both objectivity and subjectivity, according to Berdyaev, belong to the world of nature. Spirit belongs to an altogether different order of reality. Spirit is life as known in a concrete spiritual experience. It is known, however, not as an object. In Berdyaev's words,

> In the knowledge of spirit subject and object are not opposed to one another. Spirit as the knowing subject is at the same time the known object. Spiritual life is not an object of knowledge, it is knowledge itself of spiritual life. Life is only open to life. Knowledge of life is life itself. The life of the spirit is not set over against knowledge as an objective thing, such as nature. Everything that transpires in the life of the spirit and in its own knowledge of itself lies within the unfathomable depths of spirit. Everything that takes place in the spiritual world takes place in me.[18]

Spiritual life, therefore, is, according to Berdyaev, the most real and true kind of life—indeed, it is reality itself. As he puts it,

> The spiritual experience of the saints, mystics, and those who possess a higher type of spirituality, is reality itself, the appearance and manifestation of the Spirit of God. Spirit is real existence, and spiritual life does in fact appear and manifest itself. It is a basic fact which can be undeniably established but which cannot be proved. Spiritual experience is the greatest reality in human life. The divine is manifested in it, but its existence cannot be demonstrated. God and His divinity,

154

spirit and the spiritual, are given to us in the experience of life; they reveal themselves but they cannot be established by ratiocination.[19]

For this reason Berdyaev rejects all the traditional proofs of God's existence whether cosmological, teleological, ontological, or any other. He regards them as naive and even harmful because they conceive of God as an objective reality in the same sense as the natural world. But God has no objective reality, He is not being:

> A real, not verbal, proof of the being of God is in any case impossible because God is not being, because being is a term which belongs to naturalism, whereas the reality of God is a reality of spirit, of the spiritual sphere which is outside what belongs to being or to supra-being. God cannot in any sense whatever be conceived as an object, not even as the very highest object. God is not to be found in the world of objects.[20]

To Berdyaev the only proof of the existence of God is to be found in the spiritual experience alone. An objection can be raised at this point to the effect that the spiritual experience might indicate nothing else but the subjective life of the soul, and for that very reason unconvincing. To this Berdyaev would reply that he does not pretend to substantiate the actuality of the spiritual experience for those who know nothing of it. The man whose life is turned exclusively toward the world of objects as well as the man who denies God or shows no interest in Him cannot demand to have the reality of spiritual life demonstrated. For spiritual life is not a reality of the same order as physical or psychical; it is an extra-objective reality undetermined by time, space, or matter. "It is the reality of the 'initial' life."[21]

There is no guarantee that spirit exists: man can always doubt and deny. In doing so, however, man deprives himself of realizing in his life the qualities which are needed for the marshalling of the spiritual experience. Berdyaev admits the probability of the fact that the majority of mankind have never had a genuinely spiritual experience. Hence the wide-spread assertion that God is either non-existent or impossible. But, Berdyaev maintains,

> The fact that the consciousness of a particular man is limited gives him no right to suppose that the limitation applies to

all other human beings. If X or Y have never had any mystical experience that only proves that their experience is limited, but it does not give them the justification in any shape or form for denying it in the case of other people. . . . If in the experience of my life a particular thing is not revealed, I may not conclude that it will not be revealed to others.[22]

Berdyaev's final inference from the above discussion is, in his words, that "if there had only been a few men in history in whom a higher spiritual life had been kindled and in whom a thirst for the divine had been aroused, it would have been sufficient proof of the reality of spirit and of God, and the natural world would have been raised above itself."[23] In fact, the history of the Christian Church has been in no want for precisely such men from its very inception. Berdyaev regarded himself as one of the chosen. And such he was. His own spiritual life breathed depth and genuineness. The divine reality was manifest in his religious experience. There he discovered the existence of God and spoke of Him with fervor and exaltation. And the God he found in the very heart of his spirit was the God of Abraham, Isaac and Jacob, not of philosophers and savants, as Pascal had already learned some three centuries before Berdyaev.

This is not an abstraction, but a living God. As such Berdyaev experiences Him—not as being, but as existence. To him God is not being, God is Spirit. He precedes being. God is existence. Berdyaev dismisses altogether ontology, or the science of being, as corresponding to nothing at all, "except certain figments of the human brain."[24] "Being," he states, "is secondary, not primary."[25] Thus he breaks with the long-standing philosophical tradition, which goes back to Parmenides, Plato, Aristotle, Thomas Aquinas, John Calvin, and continues in many trends of modern thought as, for example in those of Karl Barth and Jacques Maritain.

Berdyaev follows Vladimir Solovyov's distinction between the existent and being. The existent is the subject of being; being is the predicate of the existent. Being is essence and therefore, merely an abstraction. All this is far different from Hegel's Absolute Idea, the rational Being in process of self-realization from a state of unconscious potentiality into a state of conscious actuality. To Hegel God is the absolute essence, and as such the basis

156

of existence.[26] Berdyaev, on the contrary, contends that the only thing real is not being in general, "but that to which and to whom being belongs, that is, the existent, that which exists."[27] At this point our philosopher joins Kierkegaard who attacks the essentialist trend of modern philosophy and posits to the contrary that abstraction from existence—essence—does not express the whole of human nature. He too stresses the pervasive factor of existence, which is "irreducible to a concept," and corresponds solely to "the individual thing."[28] In this line of thought Berdyaev writes

> It is not true to say that being is: only the existent is, only that which exists. What being tells of a thing is that something is, it does not speak about *what* is. The subject of existence confers being. The concept of being is logically and grammatically ambiguous, two meanings are confused in it. Being means that something is, and it also means that which is. This second meaning of "being" ought to have been discarded. Being appears as both a subject and a predicate, in the grammatical sense of these words. In point of fact, being is a predicate only. Being is the common, the universal. But the common has no existence and the universal is only within that which exists, in the subject of existence, not in the object.[29]

Thus Berdyaev sides with existential philosophers against essentialism. Confronted with the distinction between *essentia* and *existentia* thinkers as Jaspers, Sartre, Gabriel Marcel, and Jean Wahl have stressed the emphasis on existence, and asserted its priority over essence. Sartre, for example, holds that "existence precedes essence."[30] And according to Jaspers, existence is that which is the most immediate, the most personal, the most intimate in man's experience—that in which "I am rooted in the most profound manner."[31]

God, then, is not being but existence. As Augustine declared, "He is."[32] Indeed this is what He said of Himself, "I am what I am."[33] But what kind of God is He? What is His nature? His attributes? His relationship with creation?

God, according to Berdyaev, is not the Absolute in the Aristotelian sense of *actus purus*, the "immovable mover," an abstract and lifeless object. The Christian God is not static—He can be understood only dynamically. He is the God of the Bible endowed with an active and dramatic inner life. And of this life the main feature is suffering. God is the crucified One, the Eternal sufferer. It is true that man has made God in his own image bestowing upon Him the traits and psychology of human nature. Berdyaev has nothing but scorn for the anthropomorphic representation of God, not because it ascribes to God the human attributes at their best—love, sympathy, humaneness—but because it invests the divine with traits of inhumanity, cruelty, and lust for power.

Berdyaev denies that God is Master, that He has any power at all. The worship of God as Omnipotent, he believes, is sheeı idolatry. Human thought at a low level has interpreted the Christian God as a despotic monarch after an earthly pattern who exacts obedience and placation lest His wrath should be kindled to punishment and destruction. The element of cruelty in the interpretation of Christianity is found by Berdyaev in asceticism, monasticism, Augustinianism, Calvinism, and Roman Catholicism; it affects also Lutheranism and the Eastern Orthodoxy. But God is not an oriental tyrant. He is the God of love and freedom, of light and truth. God is life. God is spirit. Man's servile reverence of God is not worship at all—it is idolatry. In Berdyaev's words:

> The relations between master and slave, taken from social life, have been transferred to the relations between God and man. But . . . the base human category of domination is not applicable to God. God is not a master and He does not dominate. No power is inherent in God. The will to power is not a property of His, He does not demand the slavish reverence of an unwilling man. God is . . . the liberator, not the master. God bestows the feeling of freedom and not of subjection. God is Spirit and Spirit knows nothing of the relation of domination and slavery. God is not to be thought of in the analogy of what takes place in nature. We cannot think in deterministic terms in relation to God. He determines nothing. Nor can we think in terms of causality. He is not the cause of anything.[34]

Berdyaev stands in opposition to sociomorphic and cosmomorphic categories which traditional Christian theology has applied to God. "God is Mystery," he asserts, "a Mystery towards which man transcends and with which he enters into communion." [35] This mystery experienced mystically reveals not a God reigning over man and the world—understood as an objective being with all the properties of the natural world—but a subjective God who is at the center of consciousness; a God who is in man, not over against him—a God of love and freedom, in whom we move and live and have our being. Causality, determinism, and domination are connected with natural and social phenomena. These are rational concepts which cannot be applied to the divine mystery. To be sure, with God all things are possible,[36] although not by the *fiat* of His will or the exercise of authority. They are realizable only in direct communion with God whereby to His expectation man responds in love and creativity.

Berdyaev's Christian viewpoint stands forth in sharp contrast to Calvin's doctrine of God. To the latter God is the absolute, self-sufficient, omnipotent sovereign of the universe. "God," he declared, "governs heaven and earth by His providence, and regulates all things in such a manner that nothing happens but according to his counsel."[37] By God's providence Calvin meant that all things—past, present, and future—are overruled by Deity, so that not even a sparrow falls to the ground apart from His will. As the result of the belief that nothing can be out of the control of God, Calvin asserted what is often called double predestination. This teaching posits that God has from all eternity chosen some to salvation and others to damnation—election and reprobation. In Calvin's words, "by an eternal and immutable counsel, God has once and for all determined, both whom he would admit to salvation, and whom he would condemn to destruction."[38] The reconciliation of God's goodness with His choosing some for eternal damnation does not seem to have constituted a serious problem for Calvin. He warded off all objections on the Paulinian ground— "O man, who art thou that repliest against God?"[39]—that God's reasons are not to be measured by human standards, or comprehended by the limited human mind. He held it to be a mystery and, following Augustine, declared that "we should [not] scrutinize those things which the Lord has left concealed."[40]

Berdyaev regards Calvin's double predestination as a "horrible doctrine"[41] whose only merit was a *reductio ad absurdum*. He qualifies his statement, however, in saying that Calvin himself was but the logical outcome of the traditional doctrines of theology which turn the creation of the world and the Fall "into a divine comedy, a play that God plays with Himself." [42] According to these doctrines, Berdyaev observes, God foresaw everything forever, down to the everlasting damnation of many; and yet He consented to create man and the world and thus made Himself responsible for suffering and evil. Such a conception of God, affirms Berdyaev, is sheer rationalization, and therefore inadmissible. Mystical negative theology comes much closer to the unveiling of the divine character. Against Calvin's "whom God passes by . . . He reprobates," [43] Berdyaev comes forth with Pascal's "I would not have sought Thee hadst Thou not first found me." [44]

The moral implications of Calvinism (as the most contrasting theology to that of Berdyaev) will be mentioned later on in discussing Berdyaev's ethics as they emerge from his own understanding of God. For the time being suffice it to say that our religious philosopher denies that God should be held responsible for evil. The latter is the child of the uncreated freedom over which He has no power whatsoever. God's true nature is that of suffering love. The Divine inner life spells tragedy. As Berdyaev writes,

> God is a God who suffers with the world and with man. He is crucified Love; He is the Liberator. The Liberator appears not as power but as Crucifixion. The Redeemer is the Liberator, and that not as settling accounts with God for crimes that have been committed. God reveals Himself as Humanity. Humanity is the chief property of God, not almightiness, not omniscience and the rest, but humanity, freedom, love, sacrifice. It is necessary to free the idea of God from distorting degrading blasphemous sociomorphism. It is man, man most horribly dehumanized, who distorts his own image. But God is humane and demands humanity. Humanity is the image of God in man. Theology must be freed from a sociology which reflects the fall of the world and of man . . . purified and divested of false sociomorphism, from human inhumanity, objectivised and transferred to the sphere of the transcendent. . . . The problem of theodicy, the most tormenting problem of the human consciousness and conscience, is the problem of the slavery of man and of the whole creation. [45]

According to Berdyaev the doctrine of the "suffering God" undergirds the whole of the biblical revelation. Reinhold Niebuhr ex-

160

presses a similar belief when he writes: "The idea that God suffers in history is implicit in the whole Hebraic-prophetic idea that God is engaged and involved in history, and is not some unmoved mover, dwelling in eternal equanimity."[46] There is, however, a significant difference between the two theologians. To Niebuhr God's suffering is endured in history, that is, within the world of men in time and space. Not so for Berdyaev. He holds that God suffers in eternity, in a realm totally distinct from the objectified world: historical events on earth are but symbolic reflections of what is going on in the realm of the spirit. As he puts it:

> All historical events which are taking place in the natural objective world are but symbolic realities and reflections of the spiritual world. The life of Alexander of Macedon and of Napoleon, the emigration of peoples, and the French Revolution are only symbolic realities and merely possess the character of reflections.[47]

Berdyaev's position is to be interpreted in the light of his understanding of the Trinity. To him the Trinity is the symbolic revelation of the inner life in God—the tragic conflict of love and freedom. He interprets the three divine persons in mystical, not metaphysical, terms. God-the-Father longs for his Son. "He wants him to answer the call to enter the fulness of the divine life and participate in God's creative work."[48] Berdyaev believes that the Second Person of the Trinity is represented not only in the perfected humanity of Christ but in all mankind—at least potentially. The spiritual bond between the Father and the Son is maintained by the Holy Spirit. Accordingly—and this explains Berdyaev's contention that the natural life is but the symbol of the spiritual—the ultimate reality is the spiritual reality: the actual happenings are occurring within the inner life of the Trinity. "The perception of God as a Trinity is the perception of the inner esoteric movement within God which has quite clearly no analogy with that which transpires in our natural world."[49]

> The fact that God longs for His other self, for the free response to His love, shows not that there is any insufficiency or absence of fulness in the Divine Being, but precisely the super-abundance of His plenitude and perfection. We cannot

161

regard absolute fulness and perfection from the static and abstract point of view, for they can only be thought of in terms of a concrete dynamism, as life and not a substance.[50]

Berdyaev is critical of the traditional conception of God which ascribes to Him self-satisfaction, self-sufficiency, and immobility. To him God is, first and foremost, the God of sacrificial love who longs for "His other"—that is humanity—in a tragic movement toward reunion. He boldly asserts the divine nature of Man and, conversely, the human nature of God. Accordingly, God is the inmost center of man, the eternal, immortal, divine self. Indeed, every man is potentially one with God. This is obviously the language of mysticism. Berdyaev envisions not the communion with God which is the traditional emphasis of the rational theology, but the reunion with God which is the longing of all mystics. This, however, should not be understood in terms of mystical monism. Contrary to Eckhart, Berdyaev does not hold that eventually human nature simply dissolves within divinity. To him "there are two natures, the divine and the human which are not to be identified. But both these natures are in the divine Trinity."[51] The eternal Humanity is God's eternal Other, the Second Person of the Trinity, that is, of the Godhead. The two are bound by the Third Person, the Holy Spirit, in a dialectic of human and the divine. "The interior life of God is realized by man and by the world. The interior life of man and of the world is realized by God."[52] How does this realization take place? This shall be seen by studying Berdyaev's understanding of freedom and creation.

2. THE NATURE OF FREEDOM

It has already been pointed out that to Berdyaev freedom is uncreated. It derives from the *Ungrund* which is the common source of God and freedom alike. Freedom is not being: it precedes all being. For this reason no rational category can be applied to it. Freedom has no foundation. Indeed, it "is rooted in nothing, in baselessness, in non-being."[53] It is sometimes completely unfathomable. Berdyaev designates freedom as meonic precisely because

162

it is "nothing." Plato used the term *to me on* to define a particular kind of "nothing"—the one possessing a potentiality of being, a desire for realization.[54] The Greek philosopher distinguished it from *to ouk on* which conveys the opposite idea of a nothing deprived of any possibility for actualization.[55]

What is the nature of this meonic freedom? It is spiritual, answers Berdyaev. It is "the spiritual element in man . . . the inner, creative energy of man." [56] Accordingly, it might be discovered solely in the depth of the spiritual life. "Freedom is life which can only be grasped in the experience of life, for in its inner mystery it eludes the categoriers of reason." [57] Like Bergson,[58] although in a totally different way, Berdyaev is aware of the impossibility of elucidating the mystery of freedom with the help of rational philosophy. The latter inevitably leads to the insoluble dilemma of determinism versus free-will.

Freedom, Berdyaev maintains, is connected not with the will but with the spirit. It engages the efforts and attitudes of man's whole conscious being, not only of his will power. On the other hand, free-will is related but to the psychological aspect of freedom: it involves the will alone; its scope is confined to the utilitarian problem of man's moral responsibility. For this reason, Berdyaev rejects as false the antithesis between grace and freedom which has been the bone of contention for centuries in the Christian West. He does not think that the two should be placed in contrast with the other. This way of treating the relationship between freedom and grace issues from an objectified concept of grace which is understood as the transcendent divine potency acting from without. "But what is called grace acts within human freedom, as its interior illumination." [59] Moreover, freedom is envisaged by this doctrine only in terms of a limited possibility—that of receiving grace.

Berdyaev differs strongly from Augustine, Luther, and Calvin all three of whom denied freedom in favor of grace. They asserted the absoluteness of God without qualification. They posited, says he, an abstract God above experience, and then deduced logically His omnipotence from so-called divine eternal decrees—and therefrom explained individual experience. Thomas Aquinas also rejected freedom as standing between man's imperfection and God's

163

saving grace. He stressed above all the necessity for love of God. But, objects Berdyaev, "human freedom is not only freedom in God, but also freedom in relation to God."[60] The denial of freedom by the traditional Catholic and Protestant doctrines have, so Berdyaev thinks, had fatal results in religious and social life. They have defaced man and reduced him to an impotent puppet in the hands of an arbitrary God. Worse yet, they rendered God responsible for the existence of evil since in the final analysis everything hinges on His exclusive power and decree. To Berdyaev grace is not opposed to freedom: grace is active within freedom. The correct proposition, in Berdyaev's opinion, is to establish that both grace and freedom are opposed to nature and necessity. Against this background, he distinguishes two kinds of freedom; the irrational and the rational.

Irrational freedom is prior to good and evil and determines their choice. This is precisely the meonic, uncreated freedom which might be regarded as "a starting point and a means to an end."[61] It is related to the inner, unfathomable mystery of the spirit. In this sense it can be defined as "self-determination in the inmost depths of being and is opposed to every kind of external determination which constitutes a compulsion in itself."[62]

On the other hand, rational freedom consists in overcoming one's lower nature and ascending to a higher level of truth and goodness. This is freedom within reason as recognized by Socrates, Aristotle, and the Stoics. The same kind of freedom, as Berdyaev sees it, is referred to in the teachings of John: "You shall know the truth, and the truth shall make you free."[63]

The two kinds of freedom, according to Berdyaev, are respectively human and divine. They are not mutually independent. They are conditioned by each other. In order to obtain the divine freedom which is given in the knowledge of truth, one must recognize and choose the truth in the first place; and this is possible only in reference to the irrational human freedom. Hence the tragic character of their reciprocal relationship: taken separately, independently one from another, the two freedoms lead to self-destruction. If we admit only the irrational freedom which is prior to good and evil, and reject the rational freedom of truth and goodness, we pave the way for a world of moral chaos, where

164

ethical principles have no reality that can be depended upon, where the holiest yearnings of men may never find satisfaction. Unchecked by truth and reason the meonic freedom "precipitates man into the world of division and egoistical affirmation," and places him "under the domination of the laws of natural necessity." [64] History, as well as our own experience, witnesses to the destructive effects of social anarchy and individual passions born of man's irrational freedom. This kind of freedom is the fountainhead of unfathomable latent forces both for good and evil. It can, therefore, at any time plunge the world in the tragedy of disunion and death.

On the other hand, if we acknowledge exclusively the rational freedom, that is, the truth in the Johannine sense which has its source in God, and disregard the meonic freedom of choice we are inevitably impelled toward religious and social tyranny, since in this case we are not in a position to accept the good freely. In Berdyaev's words,

> If the first kind of freedom spells anarchy which ends by annihilating liberty, the second gives rise to an arbitrary organization of life, whether theocratic or communistic, in which the freedom of the spirit and of conscience is entirely destroyed. . . . The first kind of liberty means division and disunion. The second strives to subject this division and disunion to the control of organized truth and goodness and by this means to reduce the world to order and to a series of arbitrary and mechanical relationships; in a word its object is to create necessitarian freedom in and through necessity.[65]

To this tragic problem there appears to be no solution save in Christ, the God-man in whom is realized the union of the two natures, and who can reconcile the meonic and rational freedoms. "In Christ there is revealed to us a third kind of liberty which is a reconciliation of the other two kinds." [66] This freedom is that of grace which "proceeds not only from the divine nature of Christ, but also from the human, and from His heavenly humanity." [67] This grace exerts no outward restraint or coercion over irrational freedom; it acts upon it as the inner illumination instead. "The truth of Christ which makes men free constrains no one." [68] In Him grace and freedom are not opposed, but work in collaboration.

The grace of Christ triumphs over the forces of evil dormant within the irrational freedom and thus opens access to the divine freedom of truth.

3. CREATION AND THE FALL

The question of creation[69] is answered by Berdyaev in familiar terms: God created the world out of "nothing." This nothing, however, as it has been mentioned previously, is not the Biblical *ex nihilo* but the meonic or potential freedom born in the *Ungrund*. "Meonic freedom consented to God's act of creation; non-being freely accepted being." [70] Like Solovyov, although with a different orientation, Berdyaev asserts that "God desired another self and a reciprocal answer to His love," [71] and hence created the world. But this creation occurred within the realm of spirit not in the order of nature. The world of nature is the outcome of the Fall not of creation. As he puts it,

> The Fall could not have taken place in the natural world, because this world is itself the result of the Fall. The Fall is an event in the spiritual world, and in this sense it is anterior to the world, for it took place before time and, in fact, produced time as we know it.[72]

Berdyaev is naturally critical of the traditional theological understanding of creation which regards "the mysteries of the spiritual life as events in the natural order." [73] To him the only meaning of the natural world is that of a symbol pointing to the actual reality, that of the spirit. "The symbolic conception of the world is the only profound one . . . . The whole of our natural life here below is devoid of meaning save when there lies upon it a symbolic sanctity." [74]

Berdyaev's interpretation of creation should likewise be understood symbolically. He maintains that what God actually created in the beginning was not the "world," that is the cosmos of the common understanding, but His Other Self—the spiritual manhood of the first Adam.[75] The original state was one of paradisaical bliss and contentment. There was no knowledge of good and evil, no pain and suffering, no distinctions and evaluations. In that state "the cosmos was in man, and man was in God." [76] Now the newly created Adam was made out of meonic stuff which contained forces for both good and evil. God had neither responsibility for, nor control over, the uncreated meonic freedom. Eventually Adam chose the evil: his pride impelled him to an act of self-assertion against God.[77] Thus occurred the Fall which Berdyaev holds to mean "that man fell away from God, and the cosmos fell away from man." [78] Consequently, the first Adam or Manhood became divided and separated in as many individual consciousnesses as there are men born on earth.[79]

Berdyaev pictures the garden of Eden as a state of innocence and ignorance where Adam lived in a vegetative, unconscious bliss. In this realm of instinct, he was nurtured by the tree of life, not by that of knowledge. God was merely a protecting, sustaining Father. The paradise was static. At this point Berdyaev approaches Hegel's conception of the pre-fallen life. In Hegel's words,

> The state of innocence, the paradisaical condition . . . is a park, where only brutes, not men, can remain. For the brute is one of God only implicitly, not consciously. . . . The Fall is therefore the eternal Mythus of Man—in fact, the very transition by which he becomes man.[80]

Compare with this Berdyaev's statement that "the myth of the lost paradise symbolizes the genesis of consciousness in the development of the spirit." [81] The Fall marked the birth of consciousness. With it came the knowledge of good and evil and the experience of suffering.[82] Man began to make distinctions and valuations. He established the division between subject and object. But at the same time, haunted by the memory of the lost paradise—the Golden Age—man conceived dreams of regaining the Kingdom of Heaven. Are not the everlasting Utopias of an earthly paradise the perverted expressions of the one and same mysterious human longing?

Should then the knowledge of good and evil be construed as sinful? This is, according to Berdyaev, only one aspect of it. The Bible seems to indicate clearly that knowledge, that is, the attempt to know good and evil, did lead to the loss of paradise and therefore is a sin. As Berdyaev puts it, "plucking the fruit of the tree of knowledge indicates an evil and godless experience of life . . . a refusal to give a creative answer to God's call and resistance to the act of creation." [83] But on the other hand, knowledge might be considered as good since it signifies the discovery of meaning. In this sense knowledge is "a manifestation of the principle of wisdom in man, a transition to a higher consciousness and a higher state of existence." [84] The two aspects of the original knowledge are paradoxical and, in Berdyaev's opinion, illustrate once more that rational categories are inapplicable to the mystery which lies beyond the state of being.

Berdyaev has another word for the Fall, or rather the effects of the Fall: objectification. This can be better understood in terms of Kant's doctrine of the two worlds—noumenal and phenomenal. The noumenal world, in his opinion, is the real world, the world of things-in-themselves. This is the world of freedom. Applied to Berdyaev's view of the Fall, it might be said that objectification is the passage of "the freedom of noumena into the necessity of phenomena." [85] The two worlds stand to each other as reality to appearance. As Berdyaev puts it, "appearance is the objectified world, the natural and social world of necessity, servitude, enmity, and dominance; whereas the noumenal world is spirit, freedom and creative power; it is the world of love and sympathy." [86] Objectification then is man's projection into the external world of objects. It is the spiritual imprisoned in the matter. The objectified world is the fallen world in which the object is alienated from the subject and the uniquely individual and personal is absorbed in what is impersonally universal and generally commonplace. This is the realm of necessity, external determination, and socialization of thought and liberty. For this reason the objective world is not the true world. "Objectification is not true realization, it is merely a process of symbolizing; it presents us with signs but not with realities." [87]

A question comes to mind at the closing of this chapter. If this world is a world fallen away from its spiritual source, is there any hope for salvation or is the separation irreconcilable? Berdyaev's answer is positive: the hope of the world is wholly justified. But not as a return to a previous paradisaical bliss: rather as an achievement of an infinitely higher status of mutual relations between God and Manhood. Indeed, he distinguishes three stages in the development of the spirit. First, the original wholeness, already mentioned, prior to the Fall—a state void of consciousness, reason, valuation, choice, good, and evil. Second, the objectified world in which rules division, reflection, valuation, freedom of choice, pain, and suffering. And finally, the superconscious wholeness, beyond good and evil, that of the Kingdom of Heaven. The latter is the far-distant beacon guiding mankind through the darkness of time and space in its laborious ascension. As Berdyaev writes:

> Paradise is not completely lost. Its reflections and memories still linger in us. Through dividedness, pain and suffering man ascends to wholeness, unattainable for consciousness, to regeneration and bliss in God. Through the experience of evil he reaches the highest good.[88]

To sum up, God in Berdyaev's view is not a being but a spirit, not *essentia* but *existentia*. He belongs to the realm of existential, not to the world of objects. He is always a subject, and may be known only in the experience of spiritual communion rather than of intellectual apprehension. In that experience He reveals Himself as love, not as power. Indeed, God has no power whatsoever. Because He is love. He yearns for His "Other"—the unbegotten Second Person of the Trinity—the Son or Manhood. At first, the Other answers to the call of God. This is "creation" which takes place in the spiritual realm only. But subsequently he rebels against God and falls away from Him. As a result of the Fall the world of nature comes into being. Both the answer to, and the withdrawal from, God's eternal expectation is prompted by the uncreated freedom which contains possibilities of good and evil alike. God continuously longs for the return of the prodigal. But He cannot compel the estranged against his will: the latter ought to respond freely to God's appeal through inner transfiguration which will eventually lead to final reconciliation between God and Man. This language, of course, is symbolic, and the very experience mystical.

CHAPTER II

THE ETERNAL ADAM:
"IN THE IMAGE OF GOD HE CREATED HIM"

What is man?
—Psalm 8:5

The psalmist's probing question has continued to be a provocative challenge to men and women of thought in the whole course of Western civilization. In our own time it has evoked a congenial echo in Reinhold Niebuhr's following statement: "Man has always been his own most vexing problem. How shall he think of himself?" [1] The answers are many and various. Noteworthy because of their enduring incisiveness are the classical "Man is by nature a political animal" (Aristotle), "Man is a reasoning animal" (Seneca), "Man is a reed, but he is a thinking reed" (Pascal),[2] "Man is by his constitution a religious animal" (Edmund Burke), and "Man is a tool-making animal" (Benjamin Franklin).[3]

All the foregoing attempts at defining man have one character trait in common—they link man to nature, but with important qualifications. If these minds maintain that man is only an animal and he should not pretend to be more, they also admit that he is a unique animal which is subject to such pretensions. And also, they imply that should man insist upon a distinctive place within the framework of the world, his affirmation would, as Niebuhr put it, bear an "anxious note" which "betrays his unconscious sense of kinship with brutes." [4]

170

To Berdyaev also "man is a profound riddle to himself." [5] Indeed, "he is a riddle in the world, and it may be, the greatest riddle." [6] Man is a riddle both to himself and the world precisely because though a fallen creature and as such in subjection to the laws and limitations of nature, he is conscious also of the other-worldly, divine principle in him which transcends natural barriers and is subject to no law. On this point Berdyaev is in complete agreement with Niebuhr who writes:

> The obvious fact is that man is a child of nature, subject to its vicissitudes, compelled by its necessities, driven by its impulses, and confined within the brevity of the years which nature permits its varied organic forms, allowing them some, but not too much, latitude. The other less obvious fact is that man is a spirit who stands outside of nature, life, himself, his reason and the world. [7]

Berdyaev shares in the opinion that a great part of the confusion in the understanding of man is due to the fact of intermingling two originally different views of human nature: that of the classical Greco-Roman world and that depicted in the Bible. Roman Catholic thought in the Medieval period brought these views together in an intricate synthesis, but the merger was sundered under the intellectual pressure of the Renaissance and Reformation. The modern views of man, compounded of elements derived from the disrupted Medieval anthropology together with distinctively modern motifs are involved in many areas of difficulty and confusion. Modern man is uncertain whether to understand himself primarily from the standpoint of his reason or his affinities with nature; whether to regard himself as the social product of the given historical life situation or as an entity of individual freedom independent of economic and racial structures; whether he is a being basically good though often inclined to commit evil, or totally corrupt possessing but velleities for good.

The anthropological speculations of Plato, Aristotle, and the Stoics form the basis of the classical view of man. Although varying emphases exist among these philosophic schools, and especially between Aristotelian and Platonic dualism and Stoic monist and pantheistic concepts of life, they are in full agreement that

171

man is to be understood essentially in terms of his reason. In Plato and Aristotle, this rationalism tends to identify rational man with the divine and thus create a dualism which evaluates the body as evil and the spirit or mind as good. The Greek world outlook finds no defect in man: it is an optimistic view which stresses the basic wholesomeness, at least as a potentiality, of human nature.

On the other hand, the classical view is not as cheerful as the modern liberal view regarding the possibility of all men realizing happiness and a virtuous life. This is evidenced by melancholic and cynical statements in the writings of Greek philosophers, the pessimism of Greek tragedy, and the fact that classical historical thought found little meaning in history. The keynote of the common mood of the Greek daily reality from Homer to the Hellenistic age is set by the former in the *Iliad*. He makes Zeus declare that "there is nothing, methinks, more piteous than a man, of all things that creep and breathe upon the earth."[8] (True, there were in ancient Greece speculations in connection with human nature which achieved a different understanding of man from the classical view. Modern vitalism and romanticism can be traced back to the Dionysian theme in Greek religion and tragedy and Heraclitus' vision of ultimate reality as Flux and Fire. Orphism and Pythagoreanism contained the seeds of subsequent mysticism. Democritus and Epicurus, who interpreted man as wholly a part of nature, might be said to have paved the way to the nineteenth and twentieth century Marxism and materialism.)[9]

In taking up the Christian conception of man, Berdyaev stresses the differences which exist between the Catholic, Protestant, and Orthodox points of view. According to the Catholic church, he notes, man has been created as a natural being, for the exclusive glory of God. The Creator endowed man with no supernatural gifts which would give him access to the contemplation of God and communion with Him; the supernatural gifts were bestowed upon him by a special act of grace. The Fall destroyed the latter, but left the natural being comparatively undamaged. Such a view, in Berdyaev's opinion, does not do justice to the *imago dei* in man and may lead, as in the teaching of Thomas Aquinas, to a rather naturalistic interpretation of human nature.[10]

172

According to the classical Protestant conception, Berdyaev observes further, the Fall has completely ruined and distorted human nature. Man is totally corrupted. There is nothing good left in him—his reason is darkened, his freedom lost, he is subject to the most miserable necessity. His only salvation rests in the grace of God. This view, Berdyaev believes, deprives man of all possibility of transfiguration and sanctity, and likewise results in the victory of naturalism.[11]

In distinction from the foregoing Catholic and Protestant views of man, Berdyaev avowedly sides himself with the Orthodox view whose central doctrine is that man was created as a spiritual being. According to this doctrine the spiritual nature of man was not destroyed but merely damaged by the Fall, and the image of God in man only dimmed. In Christ, the God-Man, man is given a new way toward overcoming the sin of his falling away from God and thus reaching unfathomable heights of redemption and restoration.[12]

Obviously, Berdyaev is principally on guard against all naturalism in the doctrine of man: he senses it as un-Biblical and un-Christian. Naturalism, which regards man as merely a product of evolution, that is, explains him in terms of cosmic evolution, in fact achieves nothing at all: it envisages the human being at most as a transitory phenomenon, a perfected animal.[13] The sociological conception of man is equally insufficient, although, Berdyaev concedes, man is doubtlessly a social animal. As to the modern psycho-pathology which seems to regard man as first and foremost a sick creature, Berdyaev evidently has not much respect for it either. This does not mean that he discards all these theories completely. On the contrary, he acknowledges that the naturalistic, sociological, and psycho-pathological concepts of man contain elements of truth. He writes: "man is a rational being and a bearer of values, he is an evolving being, a being suffering from the conflict between consciousness and the subconscious."[14] However, Berdyaev thinks, none of these theories expresses the essence of man as a whole. Moreover, they may lead to a fatal misconception of human nature as is shown by the three major trends in the modern social and intellectual life, namely, scientific humanism, historical materialism, and intellectual nihilism.

Scientific humanism holds the possibility of a perpetual extension of knowledge through reason and, accordingly, that of man's reign over the world within a process of endless progress. It views man as the actual master of creation, fit to penetrate the deepest secrets of nature, capable also of provoking stupendous changes and commotions. God, according to this theory, is non-existent and unnecessary. Indeed, He is but the name of human ignorance. The more we know reality, the less God is needed. Time will come when the very idea of God will be absorbed by the exhaustive knowledge of the structure and laws of nature.

Within a different philosophical context historical materialism, likewise, glorifies man in a world of nature and history which it experiences as self-sufficient. Man, so the theory goes, is the outcome of the economic forms of ownership and production. He is purely a material being. Eternity does not exist. Human nature is but a myth. Progress in history is genuine, but it is uniquely due to the fact that man makes it himself. His power is in action. Through human action the conditions of life might be altered at will: this in turn automatically effects corresponding changes in man's psychological make-up. The belief in spiritual experience— the very existence of religion—stands in opposition to the action of changing the world because it alienates man from his natural active role. Furthermore, because of its messianic expectation (Judaism) and the belief in a Kingdom of God beyond and above history (Christianity) the Biblical faith carries man away from the interest he should exclusively attach to the kingdom of this world. Thus religion weakens man's capacity for struggling against social injustice and the asperities of nature. Therefore, religion is the opiate of people. To Marx, for instance, the believer, especially the Christian believer, is one who has escaped from life, a dangerous being leading astray others from the great task of managing the world.

Intellectual nihilism so prominently typified by the philosophy of Jean-Paul Sartre, teaches an unlimited pessimism based upon its awareness of the contingency and absurdity of existence. For Sartre man is but *une passion inutile* to whom existence has been given for nothing.[15] Man is doomed to freedom, a freedom which is merely a means of knowing one's own nothingness. Grace has no room in such a philosophy. The Biblical faith which gives a sense to the universe and a meaning to the personal existence and destiny of every human being is looked upon by intellectual nihilism as a childlike explanation for that which affords no explanation at all. God, therefore, is but subterfuge for *néant*. The courage to be consists in squarely facing the absurdity of ultimate references rather than disguising them with the label "God."

All these systems have at least three major character traits in common: they are naturalistic, deterministic, and atheistic. They reject God and thus abandon man to himself, to his "glory" and destitution. Whether optimistic or pessimistic, the humanism of these doctrines is always and solely anthropocentric. God is crossed out of their world outlook in order, so they believe, to set man free and exalt the world of matter.

Obviously, Berdyaev rejects the above-mentioned modern trends of thought, and opposes to them the Biblical and Christian understanding of man. This, in his opinion, "alone deals with the whole man, with his origin and destination." [16]

As Berdyaev sees it, Christian anthropology is founded upon four main ideas, namely, (1) man is spirit, soul, and body; (2) man was created in the "image and likeness" of God; (3) man is a person, and (4) God became man, the Son of God manifested Himself as the God-Man. Discussing the first three ideas will occupy the remainder of this chapter. The fourth idea will be considered in the following chapter.

1. SPIRIT, SOUL, AND BODY

Berdyaev postulates that the distinction traditionally made between spirit and matter, or what is called the "psychical" and the "physical" is not ultimate. Moreover, the identification of "spirit" with "soul" is Biblically unwarranted. Berdyaev posits as more accurate the antithesis between spirit and nature. To the latter he ascribes both soul and body. As to the former, he asserts that it belongs to an altogether different reality. Thus he writes:

> Soul belongs to nature and its reality is of the natural order, for it is not less natural than body. Yet soul is not the same

entity as body and matter. On the other hand, however, spirit cannot be opposed to body and to matter, as though it were a reality of the same order as that of body and of the material world. It is from within, from the depths, that spirit absorbs into itself body, matter, and likewise soul, but spirit belongs to another order or reality and to a different scheme of things. Nature is not denied but rather illuminated by spirit. Spirit unites itself inwardly to soul and transfigures it. The distinction between spirit and soul does not imply their separation.[17]

In order to understand Berdyaev's distinctions in their proper, that is, Biblical perspective, it is indispensable to make an analysis of their grounds in the Old and New Testaments, as he comprehends them.

There are in the Old Testament three terms which outline Hebrew anthropology. They are: (a) *basar* or "flesh"; (b) *nephesh* or "soul"; and (c) *ruach* or "spirit." Let us examine their respective meaning.

(a) *Basar* or flesh. According to Gen. 2:7 the basic component in human nature is expressed by the idea of flesh: ". . . God formed man of dust from the ground." *Basar* or flesh, however, does not correspond exactly to the English word body or the Greek *sarx,* though it was often used interchangeably.[18] Flesh here designates that element in man's organic constitution which distinguishes him from the incorporeal world.[19] It describes the side of man's nature which makes him an integral part of living creation and subject to time and sense; and contrasts him sharply with the ever-living Yahweh, who is spirit.[20] *Basar,* therefore, as conceived by the Hebrews, was not a mere inert matter: it included within it the principle of a creature which is actually alive.[21] It was the product of "the dust of the ground" into which God breathed "the breath of life." [22]

In his bodily nature man is, according to the Old Testament view, related to the natural order. *Basar,* then is not something that belongs to the human species alone. It is shared with the animal creation.[23] The expression "all flesh" is descriptive of all living things, men and animals.[24] It could designate either mankind or the animal world or both. The range of the term varies considerably from one situation to another. The important thing to retain is that *basar* points to the common raw material from which is made both the human race and all created living things.[25]

The Hebrew thought drew however a distinction between man and beasts even from the point of view of *basar*. According to the Old Testament, the *basar* of animals springs from the ground, "like plants from the earth," in the course of the process of creation, "as a consequence of the divine word of power,"[26] whereas the *basar* of man is brought forth into existence by a special creative act. As a result, the substance of the animal may be described in the sense of *anima*—a vital element that permeates the living flesh, but whose functions are performed unconsciously or involuntarily. The substance of man, on the contrary, may be envisaged in the sense of *animus*—a living entity which is both sensuous and mentally and morally conscious.[27] As such, and in contrast to animals, man's *basar* is susceptible to all the features of human life—sin, suffering, trust, joy, pride, satisfaction, evil, mischief, etc.[28] It follows that the distinction between flesh and soul, for the Hebrew thought, is not in kind but merely in degree.[29] The flesh or *basar* is actually a manifestation of the soul. The two are inseparable. When flesh and soul are contrasted in the Old Testament, reference is not made to a dichotomy after the pattern devised by Plato and Aristotle, but to a comparison as between that which is weak—flesh—and that which is strong—the soul.[30] *Basar*, then, might be conclusively characterized as conveying the idea of man's whole being in terms of a fleshly soul—in opposition to the divine soul which is not flesh. It should be noted, however, that if the Hebrews conceived God as a being made of no flesh, it was in the sense that He possessed by compensation more soul which meant strength.[31]

(b) *Nephesh* or soul. Closely connected with *basar* is the concept of soul or *nephesh*. The soul, it has been observed, is not distinct from the body as in the Greek anthropological speculation, but constitutes a "totality with a peculiar stamp."[32] This concept is predicated upon the Hebraic interpretation of perception. The various media of sensation were not clearly distinguished by the ancient Israelite. He did not recognize the difference between objective—theoretical, inactive reasoning—and subjective, active thinking. Because of such an absence of discrimination in perception,

177

all sensations received are consolidated to form a single mental image. When the Hebrew confronts a fellow man, therefore, he will instinctively and immediately sense the various characteristics of the man—his physical and psychological features—yet they must all be related to the whole background and context of the individual, and this totality is the soul or *nephesh*.[33]

Now the "peculiar stamp" represented by *nephesh* may signify at least three things: the life-principle actualized, the human being personalized, and the totality of consciousness.

At the lowest stratum of meaning *nephesh* designates the life-principle in action. As such it was identified with a "breathlike substance, a rarified form of matter."[35] When a person died, it was said that the soul departed or was taken away from him.[36] When a dead individual regained life, it was said that his soul returned back again.[37] The connection between life and breath was evident. When a man's breath stopped, his life stopped also. Thus breath was naturally identified with the principle of life.

Secondly, *nephesh* may also mean "self" and as such stand for man's personality and individuality,[38] as shown in his behavior, name, and fortune. Abraham's household on its way to Canaan was made of the souls he had gotten.[39] The number of persons of the house of Jacob that migrated into Egypt was seventy *nephesh*.[40] Obviously, in these instances *nephesh* stands for personal pronouns. It is also a common term for person. When the Biblical text speaks of "all nephesh" it means "all men";[41] it can be equally said of a number of persons[42] or of a specific individual.[43]

Lastly, *nephesh* has a psychical connotation: it represents the totality of the consciousness. At this level it was thought of— though not exclusively—as "the seat of the conscious and personal life."[44] Accordingly, it denoted alike intellect, emotion, and will.[45] The lower functions of life as well as its spiritual lofty aspirations are ascribed to *nephesh*. As in the case of *basar*, soul or *nephesh* is, then, likewise "a whole that acts through all the details."[46] No clear-cut distinction is made between soul and body in their respective functions. At times the spiritual activities are assigned to *basar* and the impulse of senses are attributed to *nephesh*. Soul and body are but two modalities of the one and same reality. To-

178

gether they come into life, together they grow, and cease to live at the same time. The Hebrew knows nothing of the pre-existence of soul. This Greek doctrine "did not gain access into Hebrew thought until the postcanonical period." [47]

(c) *Ruach* or spirit. This term does not denote a new element in human nature, distinct from *basar* or *nephesh*. Like each of the other two, it designates man in his totality but "as a distinctive essence." [48] The distinctive essence is rooted in the belief that, unlike *basar* and *nephesh*, *ruach* is the attribute of both *Yahweh* and man. It evinces "a certain affinity . . . between the human and the divine." [49] *Ruach*, comments Berdyaev, "is . . . Divine breath, a Divine gift of life. Life depends on God, without Whom man has no life of his own. The human soul descends into the grave while *ruach* returns to God." [50] Through his *ruach* man has a special point of contact with God whereby man's inner nature is brought into relation with the life of God. This leads the way to the idea of a spirit in man which, on the one hand, he shares with God, and on the other, "is the God-given principle of man's life, physical, mental, and spiritual." [51]

When we turn from the Old to the New Testament we find therein at least two fruitful lines of development of the idea of man: (a) as expressed in the synoptic Gospels; and (b) as manifested in the experience of Paul.

(a) *The Synoptic Gospels.* Jesus built his ministry on foundations deeply laid in the thought and life of his Testament legacy.[52] There is nothing in his teaching for which the Old Testament does not supply a reference. The conception of one God, a personal God, creator of heaven and earth, who hates sin and loves righteousness, was as much Jesus' belief as it was that of Jeremiah, Isaiah, and the contemporary Synagogue. But with all that, the ideas of the past have been transformed and redirected by the personality of Jesus; thereafter they were never the same.

Jesus taught that man is from God. As such he is of supreme value in the eyes of his creator.[53] Man is of more worth than the sacred institution of Sabbath and even more than any other tenants of the world.[54] Jesus emphasized the inner side of human life, that of the spirit, not in opposition to the body, but because

179

the spirit of man is the realm of divine activity.[55] The fact that men are made in the image of God means that they may have fellowship with Him. The proper relation between God and Man is that of Fatherhood and Sonship respectively. Love is the law of life. Indeed, God is love.[56] Men should love even their enemies.[57] In all circumstances they should let themselves be guided by the spirit of justice, mercy, fidelity, and love.[58] Only such a life—a life molded upon the pattern of God's character—is creative and vibrant with power.[59] For it is not happiness in terms of earthly possessions, of power, or knowledge, which constitutes the chief aim of human life, but the blessedness of fellowship with God. This fellowship can be realized only through purity of heart and self-surrender to the will of God. The very suffering is a way to it. All these thoughts are summed up in Jesus' saying: "Seek first his kingdom and his righteousness, and all these things shall be yours as well." [60]

Jesus spoke, in Berdyaev's opinion, little of sin in general. He presupposed it as a matter of fact and held it to be universally present. Hence his call to repentance to all men,[61] for all are sinners.[62] However, Jesus was far from the subsequent doctrine of man's total depravity occasioned by the Fall. He saw much good in man[63] and in his possibilities for perfection.[64] He was in sympathy with human nature rather than contemptible of it.[65] Sin, for Jesus, was not original, but rather an ever present potentiality: man is always responsible for its actualization. Sin lies in the act of will and quite independently of its outer fulfillment.[66] It flows from man's heart where dispositions and attitudes are initiated.[67] Sin is disobedience and lawlessness.[68] Hence Jesus' stress on man's moral standing and the quality of his spirit rather than on external activities: these are but the fruits of the inner life.[69] In opposition to man's capacity to sin, Jesus proclaimed the gospel of forgiveness and reconciliation.[70] And he offered himself to the world as the mediator to whom "all things have been delivered." [71]

(b) *The experience of Paul.* Berdyaev holds that for all his Hellenistic education, Paul's view of man is essentially Hebrew. The Greek terms he uses to describe human nature are practically identical with those of the Old Testament.[72] Thus *basar, nephesh,* and *ruach* are respectively designated by Paul as *sarx, psyche,* and *pneuma.* These, likewise, do not spell various components of human nature, but rather as many ways of expressing man's totality as a living being. With Paul, however, the antinomy between flesh *(sarx)* and spirit *(pneuma)* is so widened as to break into an impassable chasm. To live "according to the flesh" is "fixing the mind on the things of the flesh"—that is to rebel against God.[73] This is sin—source of pride[74] and self dividedness[75] conducive to death.[76] To Paul, sin is no longer an individual matter, as it is with Jesus, but belongs to mankind as a whole: through Adam's transgression sin and death entered the world as dominant powers.[77] "The scripture," writes Paul, "consigned all things to sin."[78] He asserts that the power of sin forces all men into slavery: "for all have sinned."[79] Sin is king and lord over men[80] until it gives them death as wages,[81] the poisoned death of slaves of sin.[82] Thus with Paul human nature is comprehended primarily in terms of sin which to him is both original and universal.

In summing up, Berdyaev maintains that despite differences in emphasis, both the Old and New Testaments view man in a similar way as (a) an organic and functional unity, (b) created by God in His image, (c) endowed with moral freedom, and, consequently, with personal responsibility, (d) a sinner through disobedience, yet (e) made to achieve reunion with God.

Admittedly, Berdyaev's anthropology is rooted in the Biblical tradition—with an emphasis of his own. The emphasis lay upon spirit, which in his thinking, is more than a God-given principle *(ruach)* whereby he enters in relation with his creator; more than the human mind or self or even than a particle, so to speak, of the divine Spirit *(pneuma)*; to him spirit is actually the ultimate reality, "the appearance and manifestation of the Spirit of God."[83] Body and soul, thinks Berdyaev, are but symbolic representations of the spirit. They reflect in space, time, and matter, the inner, boundless life of the spirit. The former are transitory, the latter is eternal. In this sense Berdyaev's position is similar to Paul's in I Corinthians: "What is sown is perishable, what is raised is imperishable. . . . It is sown a physical body, it is raised a spiritual body."[84]

2. THE IMAGE AND LIKENESS OF GOD

The Biblical doctrine that man was made in the image of God and after His likeness has given the occasion for much erudite and theological speculation as to its precise psychological meaning. In this respect some of the conclusions of modern Biblical scholarship are very illuminating. To Oehler, for instance, the divine image is that quality of human nature whereby it is differentiated from that of animals. The divine image, he believes, should be "referred to the whole dignity of man."[85] Oehler's conclusion is ethical: "Man as a free being is set over nature, and designed to hold communion with God, and to be his representative on earth."[86] Schultz is of the opinion that the image of God "is the stamp left by a living spiritual being upon an inferior sensuous substance."[87] By virtue of this seal, says Schultz, man, who is essentially flesh, possesses personality, spirituality, and moral freedom. Piepenbring argues that in Hebrew thought the resemblance of man to God meant precisely two things: first, "the ability to rule like God"; and second, the bodily likeness: "man resembled God, and God man, both corporeally and spiritually."[88] The Catholic Paul Heinisch expresses the official Roman teaching which views the divine image in terms of man's "reasoning soul."[89] Knudson suggests that none of the forestated propositions is wholly representative of the Hebrew thought, and that the image of God should be associated instead with "man's participation in the higher personal or spiritual life of God."[90] Finally, to cite just one more, Eichrodt understands the divine image as "a unique connexion of the incomprehensible and mysterious Creator with his creature,"[91] which becomes real in the experience of human-divine encounter. Through it and because of it, man is a self-conscious, self-determined personality with power of dominion over nature. The image of God, then makes for sonship: it affords the possibility of knowing God and entering into fellowship with him.

In the realm of Christian theology, it was Augustine who, as Niebuhr rightly points out,[92] first developed a comprehensive doctrine of the image of God in man. Apparently he defines the image of God in terms of pure rationalism after the pattern of neo-Platonism. The image of God is to be sought in the immortality of the rational soul. It is the image of God, because man can use it, that is, his reason and intellect, to understand God. In Augustine's words: "For not in the body but in the mind was man made in the image of God. In his own similitude let us seek God; in his own image recognize the Creator." And again: "It is in the soul of man, that is, in his rational or intellectual soul, that we must find the image of the Creator which is immortally implanted in its immortality." [93] A closer analysis of the context, however, discloses that by "the rational and intellectual soul" Augustine actually means not so much the mental powers concerned with forming concepts and drawing conclusions, but rather the capacity of self-transcendence of the human spirit. This capacity to him is symbolized by the human memory. He writes:

> . . . I enter the fields and roomy chambers of memory, where are the treasures of countless images. . . . When I am in this storehouse, I demand that what I wish should be brought forth, and some things immediately appear; others require to be longer sought after, and are dragged, as it were, out of some hidden receptacle. . . . Other things suggest themselves without effort, and in continuous order. . . . Even while I live in darkness and silence, I can bring out colors in memory if I wish. . . . And though my tongue be at rest . . . yet can I sing as much as I will. . . . I discern the scent of lilies from that of violets while smelling nothing. . . . These things I do within, in that vast chamber of my memory. . . . There also do I meet myself, and recall myself—what, when, or where I did a thing, and how I was affected when I did. . . . Out of the same supply do I myself with the past construct now this, now that likeness of things, which either I have experienced, or, from having experienced, have believed; and thence again future actions, events, and hopes, and upon all these again do I meditate as if they were present. 'I will do this or that,' I say to myself in that vast womb of my mind, filled with the images of things so many and so great, 'and this or that shall follow upon it.' [94]

Like Pascal who is seized with awe before the view of the infinitude of the starry heaven, Augustine is confounded with amazement at the self-transcending power of memory: "Great is the force of memory, exceeding great, O my God—an inner chamber large and boundless! Who has plumbed its depths? Yet it is a power of mine, and appertains unto my nature; nor do I myself grasp all that I am. Therefore is the mind too narrow to contain itself." [95] The conclusion at which Augustine arrives in praising memory is that God Himself is accessible through this faculty: "I will soar, then, beyond this power of my nature also, ascending by degrees unto Him who made me." [96] Reason, then, is not the image of God: it cannot achieve the knowledge of the Divine. God is known only through revelation, that is, the disclosure which points to a life patterned on the divine will. "Insofar as concerns the nature of man there is in him nothing better than the mind or reason. But he who would live blessedly ought not to live according to them; for then he would live according to man, whereas he ought to live according to God." [97]

Standing in the line of Augustinian tradition, Calvin likewise interprets the image of God in terms of the rational faculties of the soul, but including among these an original and now lost perfection of character. He writes,

> . . . There is no doubt that the proper seat of [God's] image is in the soul. . . . Though the soul . . . is not the whole man, yet there is no absurdity in calling him the image of God with relation to the soul; although I retain the principle . . . that the image of God . . . denotes the integrity which Adam possessed, when he was endued with a right understanding, when he had affections regulated by reason, and all his senses governed in proper order, and when, in the excellency of his nature, he truly resembled the excellency of his Creator.[98]

Calvin's analysis of the soul reveals the same capacities of self-determination and self-transcendence which Augustine has described. The reformer sees the human soul as composed of two elements—understanding and will. The former, which he calls "the guide and governor of the soul," [99] has priority and authority over the latter. He writes,

> God has furnished the soul of man . . . with a mind capable of discerning good from evil, and just from unjust; and of discovering, by the light of reason, what ought to be pursued or avoided. . . . To this he has annexed the will, on which

depends the choice. The primitive condition of man was ennobled with those eminent faculties; he possessed reason, understanding, prudence, and judgment, not only for the government of his life on earth, but to enable him to ascend even to God and eternal felicity.[100]

Contrary to Augustine, however, Calvin maintains that the image of God was so badly corrupted, almost obliterated by the Fall, "that nothing remains from the ruin but what is confused, mutilated, and defiled." [101] This is also the position which Luther defends as he writes,

> Wherefore when we now attempt to speak of the image we speak of a thing unknown, an image which we have not only not experienced, but the contrary to which we have experienced all our lives and experience still. Of this image therefore all we now possess are the mere words 'image of God.' . . . But there was in Adam an illumined reason, a true knowledge of God and a will the most upright to love both God and his neighbor.[102]

Concerned as he is to stress man's miserable state of sin, Luther adds no new insight to a positive definition of the image of God. Luther's utterances in connection with the image of God may, as Niebuhr puts it, "be regarded rather as evidence of a partial corruption of the paradox that Christianity measures the stature of man more highly and his virtue more severely than any alternative view." [103]

To Berdyaev the problem of the image of God appears more complicated, but also more hopeful, than for the Catholic and Protestant traditional theologies. Whereas for the latter man's nature became divided and damaged by the Fall in contrast to a state of original perfection, in Berdyaev's view "the coexistence of opposite principles in man is due not to the Fall, as it is often supposed, but to the original duality of human nature and origin." [104] This duality stems from the fact that man is the child both of God and of the uncreated freedom. The Fall brought man's enslavement to nature and society. Man lost his spiritual independence. He began to be determined not from within but

185

from without. He became entangled with a nature lower than his original, spiritual one. Indeed, he became a sinner: separated from God and the spiritual world.

Now the conception of man's double origin leads to a remarkable consequence. The traditional theology which posits only one original source for man's existence holds that God, through the organized action of grace, helps man to overcome sin and thus recover from the Fall. Berdyaev, on the contrary, affirms that God is powerless in the face of man's freedom. Consequently, He bestows no gracious help upon man, but expects from him a free response to His appeal—a response which manifests itself only in a creative act. Creativity, according to Berdyaev, is that essential attribute which is common to God and man alike, indeed, it is the very image of God in man: "As the image and likeness of the Creator, man is a creator too and is called to creative co-operation in the work of God." [105] In extreme contrast to Augustine, Calvin, and Luther, Berdyaev asserts that sin is not the ultimate characteristic of human nature. Furthermore, he refuses to consider man exclusively in terms of reason as Aristotle and Stoics have it, or sociability as Seneca suggests. Nor is he willing to accept Darwin's conclusion according to which man is a product of selective evolution. As to Dostoyevsky and Kierkegaard who see man as a being torn by tragic inner conflicts, Berdyaev does not adopt their view either, despite his great admiration for their insights. It is true, Berdyaev concedes, man is partially what these thinkers propose him to be. However, "man is not merely a sinful being expiating his sin, is not merely a rational, developing and social being, not merely a being sick with the conflict between his consciousness and the unconscious, but, first and foremost, *he is a creative being.*" [106] Man, therefore, works out his own salvation in the freedom of rightly using the creative potentialities which he possesses within the image of God in him. Does this not leave too wide and dangerous latitude for an arbitrary appraisal of the nature of creativity? No, answers Berdyaev: "Man's creative action . . . is not arbitrary in character nor is it a revolt; rather it is the submission and surrender to God of all the forces of his spirit." [107] A surrender which must, of course, be voluntary. Hence man's great responsibility: but also his worth and glory.

186

3. PERSONALITY

If man is essentially a creative spirit, it is because he is first of all a personality. In order to understand what personality is, according to Berdyaev, it is important to establish the difference between personality and the individual. Personality is a spiritual category, while individuality is a biological one. An individual is part of the species: it is born and it dies within the confines of the biological generic process. But personality is not generated: it springs up in eternity. Biological, psychological, and sociological terms are not applicable to it. Personality is spiritual, and as such is the highest hierarchical value in the world. In Berdyaev's words,

> The entire world is nothing in comparison with human personality, with the unique person of a man, with his unique destiny. Man . . . wants to know who he is, where he comes from and whither he is going. . . . Personality in man is like nothing else with which it can be compared, nothing which can be placed on a level with it. . . . Personality finds no place in the continuous complex process of world life, it cannot be a moment or an element in the evolution of the world. The experience of personality presupposes interruption; it is inexplicable by any sort of uninterruption; it is inexplicable by any sort of uninterrupted continuity.[108]

By nature man is merely individual, or in Leibniz's word, a monad. But personality is not a monad for it subordinates nothing and it is not subordinated by anything. Personality is a microcosm—a whole universe in an individual form. It cannot be rationalized, or systematized, or analyzed, or divided. For personality is not an object as regarded by the anthropological sciences, but a subject which can be comprehended exclusively within personal experience. Nor is it a part of the universe; it is in itself a primary whole. As Berdyaev writes,

> To whatever extent empirical man enters as a part into any sort of natural or social whole, it is not as personality that he does so, and his personality is left outside this subordination of the part to the whole. According to Leibniz, and Renouvier as well, the monad is simple substance entering into a complex organization. The monad is closed, shut up, it has neither windows nor doors. For personality, however, infinity opens

187

out, it enters into infinity, and admits infinity into itself; in its self-revelation it is directed towards an infinite content. . . . Personality is not a part of the universe, the universe is a part of personality, it is its quality.[109]

Personality, then, is quality, inner value. As such it is likely to be developed, enriched, perfected. It is not a static, unproductive condition, but a creative self-determination. The development, however, concerns one and the same abiding subject. Personality is the fulfillment of something already existing—something which is of the other-worldly origin, absolutely autonomous, self-constructive and integral, unrepeatable and indestructible, without beginning and without end. Personality is the answer to the question of human destiny, it is the ideal existential center of a man. It is its own end. In a move for self-disclosure Berdyaev writes:

> As the result of a long spiritual and intellectual journey I have arrived at a particularly keen awareness of the fact that every human personality, the personality of the least significant of men, bearing as it does within itself the image to the highest existence, cannot be a means to any end whatever.[110]

The journey, indeed, has been a long one. It had started in remote times long before Berdyaev's own generation. In fact, the spiritual and intellectual quest for the person began in Greek antiquity. To be sure, in the centuries of Homer and Hesiod man was still entirely immersed in the life of his city and family, and subject to a blind fate, nameless and impersonal, against which even the gods remained powerless. Slavery was an institution well established and generally accepted by the rank-and-file and the most enlightened minds of the country alike. Greek formal thought—that of an Anaximander, Heraclitus, Parmenides, Democritus, Pythagoras, Zeno, and the rest—was mainly interested in intellectual abstractions and the establishment of general laws controlling the cosmos. The singular, the unique and unrepeatable was as yet unrecorded. Plato himself usually construed the individual soul in terms of participation both in the life of nature and that of the city. To him, as well as to Socrates, individual immortality belongs more to a wishful thinking and, at its best, is but a beautiful hypothesis. It is true that Aristotle asserts the individual as the only real. This constitutes his most funda-

188

mental disagreement with Plato: whereas Plato seeks to explain particulars in terms of universals which they manifest, Aristotle insists upon starting investigation with particulars, as we actually experience them. But Aristotle's god is incompatible with individual will, choice, and love: his immovable mover looks more as a dead abstraction rather than a living experience.

At the same time, however, the Greeks display an unmistakable sense of the worthiness of the individual. This is evidenced in their cordial hospitality, the urbanity of communal life, and the cult of the dead. Also there are attempts in Sophocles' tragedies at replacing blind fate by a discerning divine justice and stressing man's moral responsibility. Socrates' "Know Thyself" is, as Mounier observes, *"la première grande révolution personnaliste connue."* [111] It was Christianity, however, which first viewed each man as a free, responsible selfhood related to a personal and ethical God. In the light of the New Testament man emerges as a person—"an immortal being, endowed with capacity for moral living and divine fellowship . . . possessing in personality the supreme value, having separate status and individual rights of his own, and gifted alike with the privilege of sonship to God and the responsibility of an eternal destiny." [112]

The Christian view of personality, according to Berdyaev, involves several important implications:

(1) Personality presupposes capacity for joy and suffering. No collective realities, valuable as they might be, such as society, nation, state, church, and family can be recognized as personality: they are not capable of experiencing either suffering or joy. The so-called "sufferings of the masses of the people" actually refers to the sufferings of the separate personalities that constitute the masses of the people. Furthermore, in a certain sense personality to Berdyaev *is* suffering: "The struggle to achieve personality and its consolidation is a painful process." [113] The self-realization of personality requires an element of opposition and resistance on the part of the world. Hence, the existence of pain. "Pain in the human world is the birth of personality, its fight for its own nature." [114]

(2) Personality spells memory. Human sensations and experiences acquire significance only if memory holds them together and

presents them to the mind and imagination for interpretation. Memory reveals the triumphs of the spiritual principle in man that is, "not the subordination of man to the universe, but the revelation of the universe in personality." [115]

(3) Personality means self-transcendence. According to Berdyaev, there are two different ways man is able to move out of his closed circle of subjectivity; objectivization and transcension. The former lures man into the slavery of natural determinism, social necessity, individual egocentrism, socialistic utopianism, and eroticism. The latter alone is conducive to spiritual liberation of man, and victory over fear and death. In transcension " there takes place the existential meeting with God, with other people, with the interior existence of the world. It is the path not of objective communication but of existential communion." [116] This communion, not only with other men but with God as well, is personal in character. "The super-personal does not crush personality." [117]

(4) Personality posits the existence of suprapersonal values. There is no personality without reference to a higher world of the spirit. This reference, however, should not be understood as a relation between personality and a reality that stands above men. Time and again Berdyaev insists that the universal "does not lie in an ideal suprapersonal sphere, but in personality, which belongs to the existential plane." [118] The universal, therefore, is not objective but subjective in the same way in which humanity is not the numeric totality of the inhabitants on earth but "the value of all human unity in the human world." [119] It is not outside man; personality alone can experience humanity: mankind cannot. Accordingly, "the universal, embodied in the individual, overcomes the antithesis between the universal and the individual." [120]

Personality cannot rise and develop unless God exists. Indeed, man is personality precisely because God is personality, for God is the end of human personality. This does not mean, however, that the relation between man and God is that between a means and its end. As was noted before, Berdyaev regards personality as an end in itself. The relation between man and God is rather a correlation. It is a meeting and a communion, from equal to equal, not from the slave to the master for the greater glorification of the latter. The emphasis upon the centrality of personality should not

190

be taken, however, as a patent token of human pride and egoism. On the contrary, egoism and pride are, in Berdyaev's view, symptomatic of personality's illness or even destruction. "Personality presupposes a going out from self to an other and to others, it lacks air and is suffocated when left shut up in itself." [121] Personality cannot be defined by its relation to one's own ego, but exclusively in terms of I and Thou encounter, that is, the encounter with another personality—be it human or divine or both.

(5) Personality is connected with character. "A strong personality is an expressed character." [122] Character is the result of the victory of the spiritual principle in man over both slavery to one's ego and the natural and social environment. Character must be distinguished from temperament. "Temperament is a natural gift; character is conquest and attainment; it presupposes freedom." [123] Character indicates that a man has made his choice in the scale of ethical values, that he has established differences and enacted commitments. It means that he is not indifferent to the world, but is consciously involved in, and responsible for, specific life situations. Character, in a word, is personal freedom in concrete action.

(6) Personality is tied up with the consciousness of vocation. Every man, according to Berdyaev, has a vocation whatever the extent and the quality of his gifts. "It is a vocation in an individually unrepeatable form to give an answer to the call of God and to put one's gifts to creative use." [124] Every man might become aware of his vocation if he listens not to the sounds of the world but to the inward voice which challenges him to creative self-fulfillment.

(7) Personality is linked with love. "Love is the path to the realization of personality." [125] Berdyaev distinguishes two types of love—one which ascends (*eros*) and one which descends (*agape*). Both the ascending and the descending types are inherent in personality and necessary for its realization. *Eros* is construed by Berdyaev not in terms of sensual frenzy after the fashion of Greek tragedies and mysteries; he understands it rather in the Platonic sense of an upward flight above sensuality and rationality, toward beauty, supreme good, divine perfection, and immortality.[126] This is love cleansed of its original demonic and sexual traits and sublimated in mysticism. Berdyaev's definition of *eros* approximates

that of Plotinus for whom it is "the urge of the soul away from the world of sense and reason toward the Above and Beyond, past all frontiers towards the point where love and the beloved come together and are one." [127] Contrary to *eros* which at its highest means man's ascending love of the divine, Berdyaev sets *agape*—the descending love of God for men. It is the caritative, the compassionate love "directed towards the whole suffering world." [128] The two types of love are not exclusive of each other, but complementary: personality is both their meeting and the result of the encounter.

(8) Finally, personality presupposes other personalities and their intercommunion. This constitutes *sobornost* or the fellowship of personalities whereby the spiritual life is "manifested in a real and concrete form in the spiritual experience of humanity." [129] *Sobornost* does not mean collectivism. The latter is not a communion, but simply *sbornost* or being together. Berdyaev emphasizes the truth that whereas collectivism is a means for domination and will to power, *sobornost*, on the contrary, is the spiritual quality of men, and as such recognizes freedom and the value of the person. Personality's spiritual experience is not individual and isolated: in the spiritual life there is an intimate and vital relation with the divine reality in which all personalities meet. Evidence for this, according to Berdyaev, is adduced in "the lives of the saints, the great creative efforts of the pioneers of religion, and the great thinkers and artists which constitute the monuments of man's spiritual life." [130]

In summary, Berdyaev's view of man is based upon Biblical anthropology which he interprets mainly in terms of body-soul-spirit unity, image of God, and personality. To him body and soul pertain to the world of nature and as such are perishable. The spirit, on the contrary, is born in eternity and is immortal. The image of God in man is his aptitude to creativity whereby every human being is called to creative cooperation in the work of God. Being a creative spirit also means that man is a personality. The implications of this mean that personality is related to joy and suffering, memory, self-transcendence, God and suprapersonal values, character, consciousness of vocation, love, and *sobornost* or intercommunion between personalities.

CHAPTER III

THE GOD-MAN:

"AND THE WORD BECAME FLESH"

> God was in Christ reconciling the
> world to himself.
> —II Corinthians 5:19

"Both philosophy and theology," writes Berdyaev, "should start neither with God nor with man . . . but rather with God-Man."[1] This statement contains the core of his thought. Everything he has to say is a leading up to, or an inference from, the doctrine of God-Manhood. Berdyaev's central theme is not God or man, but *both* God and man as they appear to him interrelated in the Divine-Humanity of man and the Human-Divinity of God. Without bearing this in mind it is hardly possible to grasp the complex thread of his teaching. In his words, "the basic and original phenomenon of religious life is the meeting and mutual interaction between God and man, the movement of God towards man and of man towards God."[2]

Traditional theology, in Berdyaev's opinion, has seldom been able to realize the fundamental fact of religious experience, namely, the continuity-discontinuity of God. On the one hand, God is, as Barth truly holds, the "Wholly Other." He is transcendent and completely beyond the world and man. God's existence and activity cannot be comprehended in their essential nature simply in terms of history and the cosmos. On the other hand, God reveals Him-

193

self to man, penetrates his being and becomes the inmost content of man's very existence. How can God be at the same time immanent and transcendent? Logically this is impossible, agrees Berdyaev. For this reason some have accepted the formula—God-in-the-world and man; others have preferred the proposition—God-beyond-the-world and man. Both points of view, declares Berdyaev, are powerless to conceive the divine-human mystery. They rationalize God and make of Him an abstract, lifeless absolute. In their attempt to respect the elements of logic they misapprehend the living correlation of man and an immanent-transcendent God. Yet logical contradiction is no evidence of existential impossibility. Is life logical? Is it not rather strewn with contradictions? But all these contradictions, according to Berdyaev, point to the mystery of God-manhood, to the mystery of *coincidentia oppositorum* (to use the language of St. Augustine and Nicolas of Cusa)—the encounter and mutual infusion of God and man whereby transcendence and immanence are unified.

The concept God-manhood, in Berdyaev's intention, should not be understood as a metaphysical doctrine. It is rather, as in the case of the *Ungrund*, an attempt to describe that which is unfathomable, irrational, and inexpressible—a mystery of which a man can become aware only in the depths of his existence, not by means of reason, but by intuition. Like the *Ungrund*, it is a myth which can be expressed only in terms of spiritual experience, not rational categories. "The meeting of God and man is a mythological representation and not a philosophical proposition."[3] Berdyaev affirms that this meeting has found powerful historical expression in the Hebrew prophets; the Greek philosophers knew nothing of it. The basic mysteries of life have been revealed not by the votaries of discursive reason, but by the prophets and mystics, apostles and saints of the Church. "They spoke . . . of their spiritual experiences and their intercourse with God, which are the fundamental verities of the religious life."[4]

What, then, is the content of the myth of God-manhood? Berdyaev describes it as the "drama of love and freedom between God and man, the birth of God in man and the birth of man in God."[5] Spiritual experience discloses the fact that God longs for man, and that man longs for God. They need each other. "Man needs

God, and God needs man."[6] Their reciprocal relationship is dramatic, that is, dynamic: there exist between God and man two irresistible movements toward each other. This truth finds its fullest and most concrete expression in Christ. "The coming of Christ, the God-Man, is a perfect union of these two movements, the realization of unity in duality and of the divine-human mystery."[7]

The fact that the Word could become Flesh, that God was in Christ, shows that the distinction between the divine nature and the human nature is not absolute. It must be borne in mind that to Berdyaev human nature is construed neither in terms of the body nor of the soul but only as spirit. Now the spirit of God and the spirit of man are akin to each other. Otherwise, Berdyaev maintains, the Incarnation would have been impossible. True human nature, "true human-ness is likeness to God; it is the divine in man. . . . In this lies the paradox of the relations between the human and the divine. In order to be completely like man it is necessary to be like God."[8] Does man actually realize in himself the image of God? Alas, he is far from it! Much more often he realizes in himself the image of a beast instead. "Man as we know him is to but a small extent human; he is even inhuman. It is not man who is human but God. It is God who requires of man that he should be human; man on his part makes very little demand for it."[9] In the rare occasions, however, when man does realize the image of God in himself, then, by the same token "he realizes the human image, and in realizing in himself the human image he realizes the divine image. In this lies the mystery of God-manhood, the greatest mystery of human life."[10]

The idea of God-manhood, then, is related especially to the event of the Incarnation, which is historically continued and completed in the Church. Accordingly, we will treat first Berdyaev's view of Christ, and then of the Church.

1. CHRIST, THE GOD-MAN

Berdyaev professes the Christological dogma of the dual nature as it is understood by Orthodoxy, although he interprets it not only in relation to the Person of Christ, but also in reference to every human being. Thus he writes,

> Theologians will reply in alarm that Jesus Christ alone was God-man, and that man is a created being and cannot be God-man. But this way of arguing remains within the confines of theological rationalism. Granted that man is not God-man in the sense in which Christ is God-man, the Unique One; yet there is a divine element in man. There are, so to speak, two natures in him. There is within him the intersection of two worlds. He bears within himself the image which is both the image of man and the image of God, and is the image of man in so far as the image of God is actualized.[11]

Despite the fact that Berdyaev is apparently not interested in evoking the Christological controversies that have vexed the Church for centuries, it is significant to note that his view is reminiscent of that expressed by Apollinarius who was condemned at a synod at Alexandria in A.D. 362, and by synods at Rome and Constantinople in A.D. 381. Following the Hebrew tradition, as does Berdyaev, the Bishop of Laodicea taught that human nature is made up of these three elements—body, soul, and spirit. Body and soul pertain to the world of nature; they are shared in common by all men. The spirit or mind is individual and stamps each person with a unique, unrepeatable personality; it is the special characteristic of man. Christ, according to Apollinarius, like other men, consists of three parts with one notable exception, however, Christ's spirit or mind is not human but divine. In Him the Logos takes the place of the human mind. Berdyaev goes much further than Apollinarius and asserts that although the essential features of human nature in distinction from God are body and soul, in spirit, nevertheless, man is akin with divinity. Consequently, he maintains that in God there is a human element and, in reverse, that in man there is a divine element. It follows that the Word of God assumes the human form—in Christ actually, in other men potentially—thus revealing the final truth about God and man united in the spiritual category of God-manhood. In his words,

> In Christian revelation the truth about man's divine nature is really only the reverse side of the medal of the truth about

196

Christ's human nature. The Christology of man is inseparable from that of the Son of God: Christ's self-consciousness is inseparable from that of Man. The Christological revelation is also an anthropological revelation. . . . Christology is the only true anthropology. Christ, the Absolute Man, appeared on earth and in humanity and hence forever confirmed a central significance in the universe for man and for earth. . . . Only the Christology of man, the reverse side of the anthropology of Christ, reveals in man the genuine image and likeness of God.[12]

What then is the difference between Christ and other men, if any? To Berdyaev the difference consists in the fact that men are fallen, sinful beings, whereas Christ is not. Yet His perfection is not the result of the virgin birth or celestial parenthood: it is rather the perfection which comes out of effort, struggle, and resistance to temptation. It is the sinlessness which is displayed in the Garden of Gethsemane—which unreservedly places itself in obedience to the will of God.

Berdyaev seems to stand closer to the truth of revelation as it appears in the gospels than the celebrated formula of Chalcedon. By recognizing the concept of two different natures—divine and human—united in Christ "without confusion, without change, without division, without separation," the Council of Chalcedon (A.D. 451) beclouded the relationship of man to Christ and of Christ to God by presupposing an irreconcilable metaphysical dichotomy between human and divine, or natural and supernatural. How can Christ be the Mediator since, as George Seaver rightly observes,[13] the alleged synthesis of natural and supernatural in his Person is denied to the rest of mankind? In fact the Chalcedonian definition has remained a dead letter, a fate indeed which has befallen all abstract dogmas trying to rationalize a mystery. Moreover, in what does the supernatural consist? How do we experience it? Is it more than an intellectual abstraction without real content? Berdyaev rejects the distinction between natural and supernatural because, in his view, there is not and cannot be anything superior to the human-divine entity as experienced within the spiritual depths of a person. Berdyaev's theology, like that of Tillich, is altogether anti-supernaturalistic.

In making Christ no different in kind, but only in degree, Berd-

197

yaev brings Him closer to mankind and more accessible to all men. In Christ, then, the Word of God is shown to be not foreign to the spirit of man. And faith in Christ becomes no longer a Christological doctrine, but life itself, that is, participation in Christ's ministry, suffering, death, and glory of resurrection. Only in close fellowship with Christ may that inner transformation occur which makes men aware of being really the children of God and co-heirs with His Son. As Paul put it: "It is the Spirit himself bearing witness with our spirit that we are children of God, and if children, then heirs, heirs of God and fellow heirs with Christ, provided we suffer with him in order that we may also be glorified with him." [14]

What is the meaning of the Incarnation? Berdyaev seems to understand it according to the patristic literature of the East in its early form which, according to him, had preserved the Platonic tradition of the spirit and the spiritual life. On this point Berdyaev's interpretation of Plato is significant. He writes,

> In Platonism the earth is only the symbol of the heavenly and the spiritual. Man is at once an earthly and heavenly, a natural and . . . spiritual being; in him two worlds meet. Spirituality and the spiritual life are inherent in human nature in so far as it is the image of the divine. Spiritual life and spirit are immanent in man and not transcendent. [15]

It is well known that to Plato the world, both animate and inanimate, is moved by a self-moving universal soul. In Book X of the *Laws* Plato describes this soul as the source of motion in all things. It follows that the soul of the world is prior to the world of matter and that, as is shown in *Parmenides*, it participates in the life of the cosmos. The participation is realized by means of Ideas, that is, a system of universal forms, principles, and relations after the pattern of which all things are made. More precisely, Ideas are the spiritual originals or archetypes—perfect and eternal —of earthly things and beings—imperfect and transitory. Man himself, according to Plato, is but the imperfect embodiment of the perfect Idea of man. To avoid all misrepresentation, it should be noted that Plato's Ideas are not to be confused with the modern

198

common word "idea," meaning any thought or content of experience. Understood in the Platonian sense, Ideas are actual realities, indeed the only existent realities; they can be known by reason and expressed in rational formulas.

Now knowledge of ideas signifies much more than a mere intellectual contemplation of them, as it is sometimes understood by the interpreters of Plato. Actually, such a knowledge presupposes a perennial intercommunication between the originals and the copies, that is, between the realm of super-sensible and the world presented to the senses. But how is this possible? The answer is that human nature is endowed with a remarkable mental faculty. Before we were born on earth, Plato maintains, we have, in an anterior life, known at least a part of the eternal Ideas. We have kept ever since a latent memory of them. For this reason we are able to recall them. Knowledge, therefore, is but reminiscence. Accordingly, Ideas are not only outside of us: they are also within ourselves. If we know them intellectually, it is because we possess them existentially. And we really know only that which we contain already in the deep recesses of our being.

Plato's system of Ideas is a hierarchy. Hence, the variety in the domain of things and experiences. At the bottom of the scale there are things vile and evil; at the top, Divine Goodness. Obviously, the aim of life should be directed toward the realization of the supreme Good which Plato identifies with God. Translated in the Christian vernacular this means that man should continuously strive to realize God within himself in order to realize himself as man. But is this not merely an abstraction or wishful thinking? In the light of Plato's doctrine of Ideas, the answer to the question is negative. For man, he declares, contains in himself already the Idea of God. True, it is only in a potential state, but he has the power to bring it forth into actualization by means of "reminiscing," that is, in the sphere of ethics, to recognize the things in life that matter most and uphold his conduct on the highest moral level. Then he will reach the knowledge of God, or again in Christian terminology, God will reveal Himself to man.

In his treatment of the Incarnation, Berdyaev owes much to Plato. Thus he writes,

The incarnation of God, the coming of the Son of God into the external order of this world, shows that the physical world is not a closed system incapable of being influenced from without. It demonstrates rather the power of the infinite to enter the finite, the penetration of the spiritual world into the natural world, the divine manifestation of the bond which unites the two, the victory of grace over the intractability of the spell which holds it in bondage.[16]

The meaning of this is rather clear. As the Platonic Idea impinges upon the world and marks it with its stamp, so also God enters the life of men through His Son "in order that it may be illuminated and transfigured."[17] Berdyaev, like Plato, envisions human life as a process of continual growing into the "stature and wisdom" of the divine likeness. Both see it as already existing within, latent and to be elicited by the practice of cardinal virtues —wisdom, courage, temperance, and justice, for Plato;—faith, hope, and love, for Berdyaev. The former are the prerequisite of all possible reminiscence or knowledge and, eventually, of the ultimate unification with the Supreme Good. The latter being equally a condition *sine qua non* for the reception of the revelation wrought in the Incarnation.

Revelation, therefore, is a spiritual process from within, not from without. Here again Berdyaev follows in Plato's footsteps, although probably unawares. As was noted, Plato conceives knowledge strictly in reference to the content of Ideas already retained by consciousness from an existence preceding the earthly birth. Truth must be first recognized subjectively before it can be identified objectively. In the same manner Berdyaev affirms that the Word of God must be known within the spiritual experience before He can be recognized objectively as an historical event manifested in the person of Jesus of Nazareth. In his words,

> The Christ must be revealed in the interior life of the spirit before He is revealed in the exterior world of nature and history. Without the inward and spiritual acceptance of Christ, the truths set out in the Gospel remain unintelligible facts of the empirical, exterior world.
> But the Christian mystery of the spirit is objectified and exteriorized in the natural world and is symbolized in history. Christ is born, He dies and rises again, not only in the depths

of the spirit but in the natural, historical world. . . . But the reality of the truth which happened in history, in space and time, is the same in this case as in that of all reality in the natural world, that is to say, it is a symbolic reality reflecting the happenings of the spiritual world.[18]

Berdyaev does not, of course, reject the Jesus of history as He has been rediscovered by the historico-critical movement of the late nineteenth and early twentieth centuries. His emphasis on our Lord's humanity excludes all compromise. He rejects all docetic and monophysite attempts at explaining away the human character of Jesus' life, and gives a full and unreserved recognition of His human nature as essentially the same as our own. He accepts as a historical truth that Jesus was limited by the conditions of human nature in the world. Perfect manhood, it is true, was affirmed of Jesus by the Chalcedonian creed; but as long as self-consciousness and selfhood were not included in His human nature it is evident that his manhood was a mere abstraction. Berdyaev, however, thinks of Jesus as having had a personal human ego. He maintains that Jesus' knowledge was essentially the limited knowledge of a man. His moral and religious life had a human character. His very sinlessness, as it was noted, stemmed not from any signal divine favor but rather from His struggle against sin and temptations. At this point Berdyaev joins William Temple who likewise believes that Jesus overcame His temptations "exactly as every man who does so has overcome temptations— by the constancy of the will."[19] Was this not the understanding also of the writer of the Epistle to the Hebrews?

But at the same time, Berdyaev regards as impossible a complete reconstruction of the historical human figure of Jesus. His approach to the study of the Gospels approximates the pattern established by the historical method called *Formgeschichte*, or Form Criticism. Fundamental to the form critic's method is the idea that the gospel material first circulated in small independent stories, sayings, and expressions. There was no complete, full gospel narrative in the earliest days of the Church. Accordingly, the welding of originally separated sections of oral tradition reveal much more the editor's judgment and interest rather than the actual sequence of events in Jesus' life or the successive development in Jesus' thought. In order to understand the formation of the gospel tradition, according to Form Criticism, one must reconstruct the social situation —*Sitz im Leben*, or the setting in life—in which the evangelical material was used and preserved. Thus this method shifts its inquisitive focus from the individual career of the tradition to the group life of the primitive Church. But this inevitably involves the transferring of interest from the Jesus of history to the Christ of faith. "A historical biography of Jesus," writes Berdyaev, "cannot in actual fact be written," because "the Gospels cannot be acknowledged as historical documents."[20] To him, as to the *Formgeschichte* school, the choice of data for the writing of the Gospels was governed not by any historical consideration, but rather by the usage and needs of the first Christian believers. It was a reconstruction of faith within the personal and corporate experience of the first century Christians, and not a factual rehabilitation of the events concerning the life of Jesus. For this reason, Berdyaev goes on to say, "the life of Jesus Christ entirely refuses to lend itself to historical objectivation. It abides within the realm of Christian experience and that not individual only but also corporate, as the experience of the community."[21]

Berdyaev's position on the subject also reflects a common trend of modern Protestant theology. A few names in this field will suffice to illustrate the point. Despite the disagreements as to their respective Christological conclusions, Berdyaev's *point d'appui* here is the same as that which is held, for example, by Emil Brunner, Karl Barth, and Rudolf Bultmann. Thus to the first, "in faith we are not concerned with the Jesus of history as historical science sees Him, but with the Jesus Christ of personal testimony."[22] This, he observes, as Luther did before him, was the only intention of the four Gospel editors. And he adds, "the Christian faith does not arise out of the picture of the historical Jesus, but out of the testimony to Christ."[23]

Karl Barth equally rejects the deification of Jesus or even the wide-spread Protestant tendency of turning Jesus into a religious hero. Christian faith, according to Barth, is by no means based on the impression made by the personality of Jesus. The New Testament shows no interest in it. Moreover, the attempt to write the life of Jesus or reconstruct His personality has, in Barth's view, no relevance whatsoever to faith in Christ. He goes so far as to assert that behind the New Testament picture of Jesus there is nothing very God-revealing, but only the Rabbi of Nazareth, rather a commonplace figure alongside many of his fellow teachers. In his own words,

> Even in that function that is most surely His own, the teaching of the people, the training of His disciples, He does not achieve any aims, indeed He does not appear to have so much as striven for any definite aims. . . . Even in personality He does not appear to have had anything like so convincing and winning an effect as an amiable Christian journalism and rhetoric in recent days delight to represent.[24]

The historical skepticism connected with Jesus' earthly life reaches its heights when we consider the position of Rudolf Bultmann. He holds, in effect, that the living Word of God is never a word of human wisdom but a historical event. That God has acted in Jesus Christ is, however, not a fact of past history which can be proved by the objective investigation of the historian. Christ must not be understood in the context of world history. Rather, He must be viewed the way the New Testament sees Him—always in relation to the faith of the Church. In support of his thesis, Bultmann sets forth the example of Paul whose thinking, he holds, shows almost no interest in the historical Jesus, but only in the Christ of faith, that is, in the salvation-occurrence as recognized and experienced in the life of the Christian within the framework of the Church:

> All that is important for him in the story of Jesus is the fact that Jesus was born a Jew and lived under the Law (Gal. 4:4) and that he had been crucified (Gal. 3:1; I Cor. 2:2; Phil. 2:5ff., etc.). When he refers to Christ as an example, he is thinking not of the historical but of the pre-existent Jesus (Phil. 2:5ff.; II Cor. 8:9; Rom. 15:3).[25]

Of his own position on the subject, Bultmann writes as follows:

> *Interest in the personality of Jesus* is excluded, and not merely because, in the absence of information, I am making a virtue of necessity. I do indeed think that we can now know

203

almost nothing concerning the life and personality of Jesus, since the early Christian sources show no interest in either, and are, moreover, fragmentary and often legendary, and other sources about Jesus do not exist. . . . I am personally of the opinion that Jesus did not believe Himself to be the Messiah, but I do not imagine that this opinion gives me a clearer picture of His personality. I have in this book not dealt with the question at all—not so much because nothing can be said about it with certainty as because I consider it of secondary importance.[26]

In a similar vein of thought, Tillich rarely refers to "Jesus" or to "the Christ" but usually to "the New Testament picture of Jesus as the Christ." This picture is rather a symbol in the sense that the Biblical Jesus points beyond Himself to the Christ. "Jesus of Nazareth," Tillich writes, "is the medium of the final revelation because he sacrifices himself completely to Jesus as Christ."[27] But it is this only for those who receive Him in faith as the Messiah.

All this affords corroboration of Berdyaev's own belief that no scripture, dogma, or tradition can reveal Christ to us. Not even the record of the Gospels. The revelation of Christ is quite independent of our knowledge of the Jesus of history, and is made possible only in the depths of faith. True, the knowledge of the historical Jesus might confirm and deepen that revelation, but its very validity stands upon our prior comprehension of the Christ of religious experience.

For this reason, Berdyaev is critical of the traditional theology which represents revelation as a communication from an objective God to the knowing subject, that is, as something objective to consciousness. In his words,

> There can be revealed to us only that which is revealed *in* us, for only that which happens within can have any meaning for us. . . . In order to be received it requires a favourable medium to which the divine element is not alien; for a nature which had nothing divine about it could not receive it. . . . The revelation of God is not a transcendent event taking place on the objective and natural plane of reality, nor is it an illumination from without. It is on the contrary something which transpires within us, a light springing up in our inmost depths, a fact of the spiritual life which has

no connection with exterior realities. . . . Where revelation is concerned there is no distinction between that which comes from within, between that which emanates from the object and that which proceeds from the knowing subject, for everything is contained in the innermost depths of being and can only be symbolized externally. Revelation cannot be regarded either as entirely transcendent or as entirely immanent for it is both, or rather, neither, for the distinction between transcendence and immanence is a purely secondary one.[28]

It is, then, within the human soul that revelation occurs, and not as a consequence of an external disclosure. God's revelation to men as it is recorded in the Bible, from Moses to Jesus, should not be, according to Berdyaev, construed in terms of an actual "Thus saith the Lord." The voice of God is always an inner voice, though it might seem to come from inscrutable distance. He goes on to say that there is no sharp separation between the immanent and the transcendent, the two being only different dimensions of one and the same reality, that of the spirit. Pure transcendence, as also pure immanence, involve a complete separation between the divine and the human and make impossible any real encounter of the two. Only a transcendence which is at the same time immanent, and an immanence which is at the same time transcendent render the "I-Thou" relationship possible.

The transcendent is only part of the immanent, and incident in the course of spiritual development, a separation of spirit from spirit, constituting an antithesis to itself. In the process of this antithetical division of the spirit revelation appears to possess a transcendent and objective character, but actually in its inner nature revelation is entirely immanent in the spirit within which it occurs.[29]

In other words, in revelation the transcendent becomes immanent, and the impenetrable, meaningful. This is, according to Berdyaev, the nature of revelation—the disclosure of meaning. "Revelation," he states, "is always a revelation of meaning and does not consist of outward events in themselves apart from a spiritual interpretation."[30] As such, no revelation is to be considered as "special." True revelation is universal. Christ is not the representative of the Hebrew people: He is the perfect image of mankind. He is the universal man, though at the same time a concrete individual man, Jesus of Nazareth, who can be located in time and space. And for this very reason the revelation wrought in Christianity embraces the entire world. In Berdyaev's words,

> The traditional distinction between revealed and natural religion is exoteric and not very profound. Every religion in which we can see a measure of divine illumination is a revealed religion. Where the divine is manifested, there is revelation. The divine is revealed in pagan religions as well as in Christianity, and it is manifested through nature in natural religions.[31]

Berdyaev claims that everything in other faiths which is akin to the teachings of Christ *ipso facto* participates in Christianity. In other words, Christianity might be latent in all religions. Christ, therefore, is universal. He exists not only for those who consciously believe in Him, "Christ exists for those also who do not believe In Him."[32] And not only since Crucifixion and Resurrection. Christ was prefigured in all ancient religions as well. At no time has God left life and history without revealing Himself in some way which is always open to the whole of mankind. Berdyaev's position here stands close to that of William Temple. The Anglican Archbishop also saw in each particular revelation an event of universal significance. He wrote,

> Only if God is revealed in the rising of the sun in the sky can He be revealed in the rising of a son of man from the dead; only if He is revealed in the history of Syrians and Philistines can He be revealed in the history of Israel; only if He chooses all men for His own can He choose any at all; only if nothing is profane can anything be sacred.[33]

This may be compared with the theory of a continuous revelation and creation asserted by Origen. To the theologian of Alexandria Christ is eternally generated of the Father, that is, produced from the nature of God. He is co-eternal with God and perpetually God's revealing Son. "Let him," Origen says, "who assigns a beginning to the Logos of God or the Wisdom of God take care, that he be not guilty of impiety against the unbegotten Father himself, since he denies that he was always a Father."[34] Moreover, not only

206

the Son, but also the universe is, according to Origen, eternal. For the very nature of God is to exercise his creative powers through the agency of Christ. God cannot exist without creating; therefore the universe is co-eternal with God.

The fullness of Godhead is manifested in Christ. In Him humanity itself is ultimately fulfilled. Christ and the rest of mankind are alike the children of the same God. But, Origen maintains, while the former is the unfallen Son of God, the eternal spirits of men, which likewise pre-exist eternally, being free, chose the path of rebellion instead of obedience, and thus fell away from communion with God to the material bodies of a physical universe where they are subjected to discipline until, through bitter experience, they learn the worthlessness of "the things of this world," and so turn their steps again to their "Father's home." Similar ideas are reflected in the following quotation by Berdyaev, although with a strong emphasis of his own.

It is the Son, born from all eternity, equal in dignity to the Father, Who responds to the divine aspiration of the loving object. It is the divine, absolute, the God-Man and that, not only on earth in our natural historic world, but also in heaven in the divine reality of the Trinity. It is thus that nature, not indeed our sinful fallen nature, but spiritual human nature (which is pure and heavenly) succeeds in reaching the very heart of the divine Trinity. In the Son, in the divine Man, in the God-Man is comprised the whole human race, mankind in all its multiplicity and in every shape and form. . . . Through the birth of the Son in eternity the whole spiritual race and the whole universe comprised in man, in fact the whole cosmos, responds to the appeal of divine love. . . . Creation took place in eternity as an interior act of the divine mystery of life. The biblical conception of creation is only the reflection of this interior act in the consciousness of primitive man. Man after falling into a lower natural sphere is cast forth from divine Reality, but the Christian revelation re-establishes man at its heart. Through Him a new race of human beings begins, the race of Christ, born and regenerated in the Spirit. Christ is in man and man is in Christ. He is the Vine and we are the branches. The whole regenerated human race dwells in Christ the God-Man. In the spiritual man is included the cosmos and all creation. But the cosmos was violently separated from fallen man so that it became something external to him to which he was enslaved. Nevertheless the cosmos returns to regenerate man. In the spiritual world the cosmos dwells in man and man dwells in God. . . . Through Christ, the Logos, not only the human race but the whole universe turns to God and responds to the divine appeal and to the divine need of love.[35]

The whole of mankind participated through Christ in the work of salvation and in the deliverance of the world. The whole human race offers in Christ a free response to God. We belong to the same race as Christ and through His humanity we are associated with His human freedom. Through Christ we have our part in the Second Hypostasis, in the divine mystery which transpires within the inmost depths of the Holy Trinity.[36]

This is obviously the language of philosophical mysticism, not of dogmatic theology. It is not a rationalization of some trinitarian idea grounded in the Bible. Nor can it be accounted for in the doctrines of the Trinity as they are formulated along the lines of the Niceano-Constantinopolitan and Athanasian Creeds. It is not an exoteric communication delivered from an object to a subject. Berdyaev's statement is rather an intricate verbal way of expressing an ineffable revelation inwardly apprehended. The hypostatic character of Christ is viewed by him not *ab extra* as a redemptive power whereby the alienating enslavement of sin is overcome, but *ab intra* as an eternal inner drama within the Godhead whereby the Son both discloses the divine nature of man and the human nature of God and in Whom the Father suffers for the return of His prodigal Other. Thus understood, the second Person of the Trinity is no longer describable in terms of a concept, but exclusively as an intuition: the Trinity of the dogma is transmuted by Berdyaev in the Trinity of experience.

The experience does not unveil the whole mystery. Indeed, Christ hides as much as He reveals: mystery, Berdyaev holds, is a part of the very revelation. But through Christ this experience is made possible for all men. For in Him the individual man and the whole of mankind are spiritually united. "The absolute Heavenly Man is both the unique Man and the whole of *soborny* humanity."[37] And the nature of this experience is freedom. Christ's whole revelation symbolized by the Cross points to it. "The mystery of the Cross," writes Berdyaev, "is the mystery of freedom." [38] At this point he reverts once again to Dostoyevsky, that great dialectician of freedom. For it was this Russian genius who, in his Legend of the Great Inquisitor, gave Berdyaev the clue to the significance of Christ for human nature and destiny.

Christ came into the world not to constrain but to set free: "He does not force recognition of Himself upon anyone." [39] His authority is not of this world, and the kingdom he proclaimed pertains to a different sphere from that of the earthly life. This is the fundamental secret of Christ—the secret of freedom. To recognize Him for what He is requires a "truly heroic act on the part of the spirit" [40] which can be achieved only in freedom. Indeed, it requires a prodigious intensity of faith and quality of freedom, a spontaneous identification of things invisible, to apprehend the presence of God in a crucified Jewish rabbi condemned by His own people for blasphemy and extravagant claims. Peter's answer to Jesus, "You are the Christ, the Son of the living God," [41] was, in Berdyaev's belief, a great act of freedom on the apostle's part. Ever since, these words have shattered the world and determined the course of human history. To become a Christian, Berdyaev asserts, is to recognize in the figure of the Crucified the expected Messiah, and then, in the depths of one's consciousness, repeat Peter's confession of faith. The Cross of Calvary has remained "a stumbling-block to Jews and folly to Gentiles," [42] precisely because of the basic misunderstanding of Christ. According to the former, the true Messiah must appear with all the splendor and glory of Solomon, and by restoring Israel to her past national independence and power, end the existence of suffering and evil. To the latter, the whole idea of messiahship and suffering God was totally inacceptable. They too wanted authority not humiliation.

Ever since the days of Annas and Caiaphas numbers of the followers of Christ have expected from Him the fulfillment of things He Himself rejected in the Temptation in the Wilderness. These are: a) material security—protection from illness, failure, economic and social setbacks; b) miraculous intervention with a view to offsetting tragedy and pain; and c) authority in order to remove injustice and necessity. (All three instances must be understood with regard to the mode of divine intervention, rather than to its purpose.) Christ rejected all three temptations because, on Berdyaev's and Dostoyevsky's terms, He apprehended the true religion as the religion of the freedom of the spirit. Christ is not crowned with glory and power. He has no authority for compulsion. His only way with men is that of love. Now love and compulsion are mutually repellent. Love requires love, and this cannot be realized except in freedom. In the ultimate analysis, as Berdyaev sees it, love is the only correct interpretation of, and response to, Christ. "Freedom," he concludes, "must bring us to love, love must make us free." [43]

2. THE CHURCH OF CHRIST

Berdyaev's estimation of the Church is grounded in Paul's definition of it as the mystical Body of Christ.[44] Therefore, the Church and Christ are correlative. Christ has become embodied in the Church; in turn, the Church exists in and through Christ. Speaking of Christ is at the same time asserting the existence of the Church. For where Christ is, there is the Church; and conversely, where the Church is, there is Christ. Paulinian analogy —*soma Christou*, the body or organism of Christ—depicts both the mystery of Christian existence and the profound religious experience of the Primitive Church. The expression is not to be understood merely as a figure of speech: it is rather indicative of the organic oneness of Christ and the Church. It emphasizes the intimate union of the believers with the Lord in a living experience of faith. To belong to the Church is to be a part of Christ's body, that is "a cell within it, an organ of this mystical organism." [45]

Berdyaev accepts in general the traditional doctrine of the Church common to most of Christendom. In his interpretation of it, however, he naturally espouses the Orthodox view. Thus he takes Paul's words to mean that "the true reality of the Church . . . is inward and mystical. . . . Its nature is spiritual, for it belongs to the spiritual rather than to the natural world." [46] It follows that its true origin is not historic, but mystical. "It is lost in the unfathomable and the infinite."[47] The spiritual Church is a part of the spiritual life of Christ, the eternally begotten Son of God. For this reason no ecclesiastical organization, no parochial activity, no temples built in stone are ever able to convey the true idea of what the Church really is. "The Church," writes Berdyaev, "can only be understood by those who live within it. Its life must actually be experienced, for it is not a reality of the external kind." [48] Its reality, as that of God, belongs to the realm of invisible things and can be apprehended only by faith.

This does not mean, he goes on to say, that the Church is extrinsic to the world of nature and history. It does not remain invisible. Historically it can be seen in the life of Christ, in the lives of the saints, in the sacraments, and in its active corporateness. But the visible Church does not constitute its total depth and fulness. "The visible Church," Berdyaev states, "is only the partial actualization of the invisible Church; it is only an incomplete form of its substance and of the life of humanity and of the world." [49] Both the visible and the invisible Church are rooted in Christ. The latter rests in Him unconditionally. Not so the former, Berdyaev thinks. The historical, that is, visible Church would have been impossible, he argues, without a human element of chastity and purity due to which Incarnation was realized. This element was provided by the Virgin Mary whose innocent and crystal-like nature allowed her to receive God into herself. With Christ, therefore, she is the co-founder of the Church. In Berdyaev's words, "the church does not rest only on Christ, on divine grace, but also on the Virgin Mary, the Mother of God . . . which, having achieved purity and chastity, conceived in the spirit instead of through sinful nature." [50]

In making the Virgin Mary the co-founder of the Church, Berdyaev apparently oversteps the teaching of Orthodoxy, although the same idea is implicitly cherished by the divines of the Eastern Church. They hold in effect that Mary "is not merely the instrument, but the direct and positive *condition* of the Incarnation, its human aspect." [51] Without her free consent, the Word could not have become flesh and dwelt among men. Contrary to the Roman Catholic dogma of the Immaculate Conception, the Orthodox do not claim that the mother of Jesus was exempted from original sin. This would separate her from mankind, and make her unable to transmit to her Son a human soul and body. Moreover, the

211

Incarnation cannot be the result of God's exclusive initiative in making Mary chaste and pure. Innocence, as in the case of the Virgin, should be freely acquired.

When we turn from the origin of the Christian Church to its nature, Berdyaev's considerations have a more familiar ring. Here his language is near that of many modern Protestant theologians. It can be followed without difficulty. He asserts that the Church is *Soborny*, Universal, and One.

a) *The Church is "Soborny."* It has already been said that the Russian noun *sobornost* might be translated as qualitative togetherness. In this particular instance it can also be understood as *koinonia*—a fellowship of sharing and participation created by the power of the Holy Spirit. That the Church is *soborny* means, according to Berdyaev, it is neither a lofty ideal nor a mere aggregation of individuals, but rather a living community gathered around the Messiah. The Church is experienced when the believer begins to overcome his natural limitations and isolation and enters with other believers into the unity of the spiritual world. "The experience of the Church," Berdyaev writes, "is *soborny*, for *sobornost* is one of its ontological qualities. In this experience I am not alone, for I am one with all my brethren in the spirit." [52]

Christianity, on Berdyaev's terms, from the very beginning existed as a corporate reality, as a community. To be Christian meant precisely to belong to the community. An isolated Christian was inconceivable. The first believers felt that they were united not only among themselves, but first of all in Christ. Indeed, it was their communion with Christ which made the *koinonia* of men possible. Moreover, Christ Himself, so they believed, belonged to their community, as its Head. Consequently, the first Christians had all things in common. They shared alike in spiritual blessings of joy and love and in material goods of bread and shelter.

This character of the Church, Berdyaev insists, has not changed. The true Church remains a community of those who abide and dwell in Christ, and in whom the Son of God is abiding and dwelling by the Spirit. In contact with Christ all men are drawn near to each other in a new, redeemed life which transcends their individualities. In the fellowship of Christ the believers are lifted up above all earthly things into the eternal reality of the Kingdom

212

of God. Berdyaev's view at this point approximates that held by Nels F. S. Ferré, the modern proponent of the Church as a spiritual fellowship. Thus Ferré writes:

> Christ's death released a redemptive force in history which is peculiarly perpetuated by God's Holy Spirit through the redemptive fellowship which is the Church—a fellowship of grace, a fellowship of forgiveness, wherein by worship and by trust in a personal Savior man is able to alter his ways and even to become a channel of God's grace into history. No one can *live* orthodox Christianity without creating around him a Christian fellowship. Christianity is the redemptive spirit of Christ flowing through history.[53]

This redemptive spirit of Christ denotes, according to Berdyaev, a New Reality, that of the New Adam. In it men partake of Christ's mind, His love, and His freedom whereby they are able to apprehend that which is beyond their own intelligence. This is likewise the judgment of Gustaf Aulén who asserts that the Church is different from a mere human organization, but that it is a "fellowship created by the Holy Spirit," which is apprehended "only [through] the eye of faith." [54] For the Swedish theologian the *koinonia* of the Church means the dawn of a new Age, the age of grace and of *regnum Christi*. "It is the messianic fellowship," he writes, "the true Israel, the new covenant, *Kyrios-Christus* united with his own in the world." To be of the Church means "to participate in *regnum Christi*, [that is] to live in that new age which because of the victory of Christ is the new age of life." [55]

As a good Orthodox, however, Berdyaev explicitly holds that the Christian *koinonia* is not limited to the living. The *sobornost* of the Church encompasses "all the generations which have gone before." [56] Indeed, it contains even the unborn ones. For in Christ are brought together all the living spirits, whether present, or departed, or yet to come.

b) *The Church is Universal.* The New Reality in Christ or *ecclesia* as it is translated in the New Testament was conceived at the beginning as a specially elected group of God, "a chosen race, a royal priesthood, a holy nation, God's own people." [57] They were the direct heirs of the Chosen Remnant of the Old Testament. In Romans and Galatians the Apostle expounds in detail this theme with the inference that a clear-cut differentiation is being made between the elect and those passed by. The Pauline conception of *ecclesia* was taken up and variously commented on by the theologians of all Christian denominations. Berdyaev, for his part, and in agreement with Origen, posits the universal character of the Church without even discussing any opposing view.

To him the Church is not a reality existing alongside others; it is not a part of a whole. It is itself the whole. "The Church," he writes, "is all; it constitutes the whole plenitude of being, of the life of humanity, and of the world in a state of Christianization." [58] Indeed, to a Christ of Cosmic proportion—Berdyaev's Christ—only a cosmic Church can rightly correspond. It follows that the Church is virtually present everywhere. "It possesses a cosmic nature. . . . It is in the Church that the grass grows and the flowers blossom, for the Church is nothing less than the cosmos Christianized. Christ entered the cosmos . . . and thereby all things were made new." [59]

A similar view of the Church is held by Tillich, though he does not include nature in its domain. He, too, affirms that, visibly or latently, the Church is present in all living faiths and cultures. True, this presence, in Tillich's view, is often forgotten, neglected, even denied. But all the same, it is there. In his words, "Church and society are one in their essential nature; for the substance of culture is religion and the form of religion is culture." [60] The latent Church which is essentially of a preparatory character, is present in every ethical and spiritual endeavor, in every creative activity. The reason for this, as Tillich sees it, is that any authentic culture is a finite and conditioned expression of that which is infinite and unconditioned. To Tillich Christ—the Logos as *Kairos* or New Being—is not only the center of the Church but also of history. Nothing, therefore, can be outside Christ. Moreover, history itself should, in his opinion, be understood exclusively in terms of the Church. For the New Being transcends all cultural, religious, and social categories of all nations: in Christ it is man as such who is apprehended, whether Christian or not. Christ is related to the whole of mankind. Through the New Being in Christ, the Church affords the right perspective of the inexhaustible depth and meaning of culture and life alike.

214

Universality, however, does not spell identity. Both Berdyaev and Tillich voice warnings against any possible confusion of the Church with the Kingdom of God, still less identification with it. Tillich believes that the Kingdom transcends the Church not only in perfection, but also in universality. To him the Church is not an end in itself, but rather the bridge between the eternal and the historical situation. Berdyaev holds that the Church only points towards the realization of the Kingdom, while the realization itself "remains an eschatological and not a historical idea." [61]

Until the final consummation, however, the historic Church, in Berdyaev's estimation, leads a divided, even sinful existence. He is very critical of the Orthodox Church, and for that matter also of the Catholic and Protestant Churches. He exposes their frequent rigidity, self-righteousness, parochialism, and falsehood. He denounces their propensities for political power and worldly authority. The divided Church, as he sees it, has seldom realized the Truth of God because, having lost sight of its eschatological destiny, it hardly attempted to translate Christianity into life. Rather it has yielded to the temptations of the Wilderness: instead of bearing testimony to Christ, it often served the spirit of Anti-Christ.

It is interesting to compare Berdyaev's judgment on the historic Church with an almost identical criticism expressed by Reinhold Niebuhr, who writes as follows: "The Church is always in danger of becoming Anti-Christ because it is not sufficiently eschatological. It lives too little by faith and hope and too much by the pretensions of its righteousness." [62] The church, Niebuhr points out, has not yet worked out a restatement of its religious affirmations so as to make them consistent with the picture of the world as presented by modern science. It also seems unable to make ethical and social resources of Christianity available for the solution of the moral problems of our time. What is more, he declares, the Church has the tendency to give the semblance of finality to the relativity of history, and the odor of sanctity to the particular situations under the cover of religious ethical prestige. As a result, the decline of religion in modern civilization is an observable historical fact. The Church is poisoned with skepticism. On his terms, "A psychology of defeat . . . has gripped the forces of religion." [63]

Such also is the language of Berdyaev. This is a salutary criticism, not a sign of defeatism. The two theologians are far from showing any despair about the Church. On the contrary, they firmly believe in its imperishable foundations. If they expose sometimes with utter bitterness the claims and pretensions of the historic Church, it is solely in order to restore the vision of its primarily spiritual and eschatological nature.

c) *The Church is One.* Despite all external divisions, dissensions, and particularisms, the Church is one. "The Church," writes Berdyaev, "is by nature one; it is like personality a unique reality."[64] It is so not because of any external unity of organization; nor because it escapes all geographical or ethnographical determinations; nor yet because it is neither Western nor Eastern. The unity of the Church, according to Berdyaev, is qualitative, not quantitative. It is unity in Christ. Through His life and teaching, His proclamation of the coming of the Kingdom of God, His suffering and His death, His resurrection and exaltation in the glory of the Father, and by His sending of the Holy Spirit into the life of men forever, Christ accomplishes His work of reconciliation between God and the world. Ontologically, then, the Church is not and cannot be divided. Christ is the head of the Church, and His perennial presence within it gives to Christendom unity, cohesion, and continuity.

To be sure, this unity is not externally visible. As it appears to the eye, there is no external unity in the Church. The Christian churches are divided, and their divisions often are saturated with contention and mutual distrust. However, Berdyaev observes, "it is not the Church which lacks unity, but the kingdom of this world. . . . The division has taken place in the kingdom of Caesar, for the kingdom of God can only be one."[65] One in Christ, yet divided—this is the present status of Christianity in the world. The Church is united because of Christ, but it is divided because of the world. And just for this reason the divisions of Christendom are sinful: for sin is of the world, not of God in Christ.

Therefore, even if we are one in Christ and do not need to create that unity which is a gift of God, yet we must desire earnestly a reunion of all Christian Churches; only thus shall Christianity as a whole witness outwardly its inner unity; only a genuine

216

unity of all Christian denominations will bring to a close the scandal of tensions and disputes between various churches. How does Berdyaev envisage the future ecumenicity? Not as a state of interconfessionalism. There is no room in his thinking for any inter-church organization or authority; nor for any compromise in the matters of belief. He rejects all attempts at unity on that basis. "There is no creative religious force," he declares, "in the interconfessional spirit."[66] What he suggests instead, is to remain within one's own denomination and undertake the task of exploring the depths of its spiritual, ethical and social implications. In his words, "It is only by remaining in one's confession, and by deepening and broadening it, that one can work towards universalism or supra-confessionalism. This means that one must go deeper and higher rather than attempt to move on the surface of things."[67] For this reason, he goes on to say, the unity of the Christian world should be approached not through meetings and assemblies, all of which are external, but from within. Treatises and mutual conventions will achieve nothing in this regard. Indeed, "in order to achieve a real union of the churches it may even be necessary to avoid having union as our objective."[68]

This does not imply, however, that Christians must do nothing outside their respective religious bodies. On the contrary, they can do much to improve their mutual relations. But this is in no wise an affair of program and action: it is rather a matter of attitude. The union of Christians all over the planet will come, as he puts it, "through an attitude animated by love which permits of mutual recognition of other confessions as also living in the same spiritual world."[69] Beyond dogma and organization, Christians must reach to a spiritual union, the only groundwork of an ecumenical Christianity. "Above all we must try to change the mutual relationships between Orthodox, Catholics, and Protestants rather than those of their churches."[70] In a movement to reinforce his point, Berdyaev writes,

> Beyond the diversities of Christian confession the one universal Church is in process of affirmation, and of this fact we may become aware even while we still remain faithful to our own confessions. . . . The soul of the Church is one, and to it there belong, not only the members of the different churches,

but even those who are outside the visible Church altogether. There is a great spiritual brotherhood composed of Christians to which not only the Churches of the East and West belong, but also those whose wills are directed towards God and the divine, all in fact who aspire to some form of spiritual elevation.[71]

If Berdyaev emphasizes love as central to the Christian unity, it is because to him the Church "is the order of love and freedom, and represents their union."[72] Here he joins many of the major modern Protestant theologians who, whatever their differences elsewhere, are all agreed upon the centrality of love in the life and fellowship of the Christian Church. But it is perhaps to the position held by Ferré that Berdyaev comes closest. Ferré also professes that the Church is one in Christ, though divided by human sinfulness. He, too, rejects the literalistic, the liberal, and the sacramentarian approaches to ecumenical Christianity. Likewise, he believes that no historic Church can fully incarnate Christianity. It is only Christian love—Agape—that is normative for Christianity and is able to provide the common ground for a new catholicity of the Church. God has revealed Himself in Christ as redemptive love. It is as love, therefore, that Christ is present in the world to the end of time. For this reason, the Christian Church, as he puts it, "in spite of the imperfections on its human side," is "the embodiment of the Church Catholic,"[73] for love "acts out of complete concern not only for all, in all dimensions of life, and the conditions which sustain, promote and enhance life, but also for ever new life and new conditions of life."[74]

To sum up, Berdyaev's central theological teaching is neither that of God nor of man, but of God-Man. This is a myth which can be grasped not by means of discursive reason, but solely in the depth of the spiritual experience. The myth of God-manhood is described by Berdyaev as the "drama of love and freedom between God and man, the birth of God in man and the birth of man in God."[75] Between God and man there is an irresistible movement toward each other. Their mutual relationship finds its fullest and most concrete expression in Christ. His revelation concerns not only God but also man and the kinship of the two.

218

It is precisely because the divine and human natures are not alien to each other that the Incarnation was made possible at all. However, the meaning of the Incarnation—the God-manhood—cannot be known in the Jesus of history but only in the Christ of faith. The knowledge of the historical Jesus only confirms and deepens the revelation of Christ.

Now revelation is always a revelation of meaning. For this reason no revelation is "special." True revelation is universal. Christ therefore is not only the representative of a nation who can be located in time and space: He is also the universal man. He exists for both believers and unbelievers. His way with men is that of freedom. He came not to constrain, but to set free. He is love, and love requires love, not compulsion.

The Church was founded by Christ and the Virgin Mary whose free acceptance of God's will permitted the fulfillment of the Incarnation. The Church is *soborny*, that is, a *koinonia* of sharing and participation in Christ through the Holy Spirit; it is also universal, that is, actually or virtually, all-embracing: to it belong both Christians and non-Christians in different degrees, and also the living, the dead, and the unborn. Finally, the Church is one: it has a unique reality in Christ, although it is at the same time historically divided. The divisions within the historic Church are sinful. For this reason Christians must desire earnestly a reunion of all Christian Churches. Ecumenicity, however, cannot be achieved through external organization or authority; nor through inter-confessional compromise. It is only by remaining in one's own denomination, and by deepening and broadening it, that one can work toward a spiritual union of Christendom which is the real groundwork of ecumenical Christianity.

CHAPTER IV

ON THIS SIDE AND THE FAR SIDE OF GOOD AND EVIL: FROM HERE TO ETERNITY

> God creates!
> His essence is his creativity. This is the gist of a sound theology.
> God made man in his own image. God wills therefore that man, too, should be a creator!
> This is the gist of a sound anthropology . . . the key to ethics.
> Hereon hang all the law and the prophets![1]
> —Robert Elliot Fitch

It has already been noted that Berdyaev holds human personality to be the supreme value in a universe of values. To discover the meaning and worth of these values, and in particular to understand what is meant by good and evil, becomes necessarily a quest of prime importance for human destiny and conduct. For this reason the study of morality occupies a prominent part in Berdyaev's teaching. In his words,

> Ethics occupies a central place in philosophy because it is concerned with sin, with the origin of good and evil and with moral valuations. And since these problems have a universal significance, the sphere of ethics is wider than is generally supposed. It deals with meaning and value and its province is the world in which the distinction between good and evil is drawn, valuations are made and meaning is sought.[2]

In opposition to Kant, however, Berdyaev denies the utility of abstract *a priori* ethical systems. The basis of true ethics, he believes, is moral experience, and not an intellectual principle. This implies that ethics should not be normative for it is not concerned with impotent moral regulations, "but with real moral forces and qualities which have power." [3] Certainly, ethics has a scientific aspect due to its mutual relationships with other branches of scientific study. It uses for its own purposes the material provided by such disciplines as anthropology, sociology, psychology, mental pathology, comparative study of history and religion. But it is first of all a spiritual discipline and as such related to human freedom. "Ethics," states Berdyaev, "is knowledge of the spirit and not of nature, and is concerned with manifestations of spiritual freedom and not of natural necessity." [4] Now the knowledge of the spirit, that is, of the realm of values, he maintains, evolves from the depths of individual experience; therefore, ethics is personal. Moreover, since it calls for the moral reformation of man and a revaluation of accepted values, ethics is also prophetic.

Berdyaev begins his prophetic and personal system of ethics with the problem of the origin and distinction of good and evil. It has already been pointed out that he attributes the origin of good and evil to uncreated meonic freedom. But the criterion of distinction between the two, according to him, is based on personal spiritual experience. God cannot be held responsible for freedom which is the source of both good and evil. Man, however, remains accountable for his moral valuations. Consequently, the highest value—God, who is perfect love—lies beyond good and evil. "Ethics," Berdyaev writes, "is entirely on this side of good and evil," [5] the side of men. It is not concerned with the other side, the side of God.

Having established his basic ethical presupposition, Berdyaev then proceeds with the discussion of the moral valuations as expressed by the adjectives good and evil, moral and immoral, high and low, etc. He denies the reality of these distinctions, and regards them only as symbolic. As he puts it,

'Good' and 'evil,' the 'moral' and the 'immoral,' the 'high' and the 'low' do not express any real existent, but are merely

221

symbols—not arbitrary or conventional symbols, however, but reasonable and inevitable. In its inmost being reality is neither good nor evil, neither moral nor immoral, but it is symbolized in this way in accordance with the categories of this world. . . . In reality there is neither 'high' nor 'low,' but the symbol of 'height' does give us some insight into the nature of reality. . . . Our ethics is symbolic and so are all its distinctions and valuations.[6]

At this point one must be reminded that to Berdyaev this whole world is nothing else but a symbol of the spiritual, invisible world which constitutes the only reality. Every thing in connection with this world, therefore, necessarily assumes a symbolic character. Berdyaev declares, however, that this symbolism is neither artificial nor wrong. "It tells us," he writes echoing the famous utterance of Paul, "about the absolute, about the ultimate reality, but does so 'darkly,' reflecting it, as it were, in the mirror of the world."[7]

Not only is ethics to be understood in terms of "this side of good and evil" and symbolism, but also as a philosophy of freedom. It has been previously observed that Berdyaev envisages freedom not as free will but rather as creative activity. The former, as he sees it, is linked with the normative, legalistic morality of traditional scholasticism. It implies that man is perpetually confronted with the choice between good and evil. The choice involves his responsibility in both this life and the life beyond. He will be rewarded if he chooses the good, and punished if he chooses evil. In either case, Berdyaev observes, the free will becomes a source of enslavement since it compels man to the necessity of choice. Only the latter is true freedom—a positive, creative energy which infinitely more than seeking for justification by good works and fulfillment of the norm, actually results in the production of values.

Freedom understood as creativity predicates freedom in evil as well as in good. "There can be no moral life," in Berdyaev's words, "without freedom in evil." For this reason "moral life is a tragedy and makes ethics a philosophy of tragedy."[8] The tragic character of ethics develops not from the opposition between good and evil—an opposition, it was noted, all too relative and symbolic—

but out of human-divine relationship based on freedom. This also gives birth to the paradox.

> Ethics has to deal both with the tragic and the paradoxical. Moral life is made up of paradoxes in which good and evil are intertwined. They cannot be solved rationally, but have to be lived through to the end. The tragic and paradoxical character of ethics is due to the fact that its fundamental problem is not that of the moral norm or of the good, but of the relation between the Divine and the human freedom.[9]

The meaning of this, according to Berdyaev, is that although moral life has always been dominated by social norms and barriers, yet essentially the moral is independent of the social. "Moral life is rooted in the spiritual world, and social relations are merely a projection of it." [10] Society is not the source of moral valuations as Karl Marx, Auguste Comte and Emile Durkheim[11] erroneously taught. Berdyaev goes on to say that even if it were possible to prove the social origin of the distinction between good and evil, this would not help the understanding of the nature of moral valuation. "The object of philosophical ethics," he argues, "is to know not the origin and development of ideas about good and evil, but good and evil as such."[12] Certainly, the ideas about good and evil as they are exemplified in the mores and institutions of an epoch depend upon society; but good and evil in themselves are not conditioned by society: the moral valuations derive from the spiritual, and not social, world. Spirit alone can serve as a standard of moral judgment; from it also the meaning of moral values is derived. Only spirit rises above that which is valued and thus, on the one hand, conveys significance to it and, on the other, points beyond it to a higher plane of existence— that of God. In the ultimate analysis ethics confronts infinity.

In the light of this introductory background we shall now look more closely at Berdyaev's understanding of Christian morality. The life of the Christian, as he sees it, is subject to three types of ethics. We shall examine them in the following order: (1) ethics of law; (2) ethics of redemption; and (3) ethics of creativity.

223

1. ETHICS OF LAW

The ethics of law, according to Berdyaev, is embodied in pre-Christian morality. It is to be found not only in the communities of primitive pagan civilization, but also in the refined philosophical systems of Aristotle and the Stoics. It is likewise the ethics of the Old Testament and, within the limits of Christianity, that of Pelagius and Thomas Aquinas. The ethics of law cannot be interpreted chronologically only, for it exists alongside the ethics of redemption, which is the Christian ethics of grace. But historic Christianity, Berdyaev says, was pervaded with extraneous elements stemming from Greek speculative thought and the Roman legalistic mind. For this reason Roman Catholic theology is so largely normative. Profane abuses of the medieval papacy and the moral corruption brought about by the sale of indulgences were the direct results of this spirit of legalism. It was against this feature of the contemporary Roman Catholic system that Luther protested. He envisioned it as the Babylonian captivity of the Church. In the treatise bearing this title, the German Reformer vehemently denounced this state of affairs. To him indulgences were a "knavish trick of the Roman sycophants," and the papacy "the mighty hunting of the Roman bishop." [13] But Luther's own disciples after him once more introduced legalism into ethics and religion.

Legalistic morality, Berdyaev observes, is deeply rooted in mankind and can be traced back to the primitive clans with their totems and taboos. It is essentially social, and thus distinct from the ethics of redemption and creativity. In his words, "the ethics of law means . . . that the subject of moral valuation is society and not the individual, that society lays down moral prohibitions, taboos, laws and norms to which the individual must submit under penalty of moral excommunication and retribution." [14] The ethics of law, therefore, belongs to the "fallen" world for it was the Fall that subordinated human conscience to society. As long as the human aggregate remains in an unredeemed state, that is, lacking in cohesion and fellowship which are born out of a free, reciprocal love, it must necessarily be held together by compulsory laws lest it should morally degenerate and perish.

Primitive morality was to a considerable extent determined

by the terror and awe inspired by the souls of the departed. The dead exercised a dreadful power over the living. Murder demanded vengeance. The shade of the victim would haunt his kinsmen until they avenged his death. The avenger was at the same time the punisher. As in all early activities, vengeance was not connected with personal guilt; punishment for offenses against life or person was a group matter. The reason for this is to be sought in the keen sense of organic togetherness or kinship which characterized human society during the first stages of its social progress. This kinship meant more than social cohesion. It was also primarily expressive of a psychic unity of all its members, that is a corporate personality. The individual was conceived exclusively in terms of group relations and functions. His rights and duties, thoughts and conduct were conditioned and directed by his social group. He thought of himself as representing the group *in toto* and, conversely, being wholly represented by it.

In the Old Testament the phenomenon of corporate personality is strikingly exemplified in the practice of collective responsibility. In virtue of it the individual bore the penalties of the group, even as the group was punished for the wrong-doing of any of its members.[15] Thus Achan, the only one guilty of a grave offense, was stoned to death together with "his sons and daughters, his oxen, his asses, his sheep, his household, and all that belonged to him."[16] Likewise, the crime of a few "base fellows" of Gibeah was avenged in the slaughter of twenty-five thousand Benjamites.[17]

With Jeremiah and Ezekiel, Berdyaev observes, Hebrew individualism finally came into its own. The two prophets, and especially Ezekiel, "brought out," in the words of an Old Testament scholar, "as had not been done before, the necessary antithesis between a consistent individualism and the traditional ideas of group solidarity."[18] Indeed, Jeremiah's personal religious experience of a new covenant written within men's hearts was erected as an objective principle by Ezekiel. He denounced the practice of collective responsibility, and posited as a universal rule one's nonresponsibility for the acts of another whether individual or group.[19] But this was only a different application of the ethics of law. Ezekiel tried to organize the life of the individual in general. He dealt with personality in the abstract. He showed no interest in

225

the concrete, personal conscience, but only in the objective observance of religious and social norm. Moreover, Ezekiel's stress on ritualism—the attainment of a righteous life through a strict respect of the law—opened wide the career of subsequent Jewish legalism.

The fatal consequence of the new emphasis was portrayed in the haughty form of Judaism represented by the Pharisees. They were the men of law *par excellence*. Their aim was to make of social relations a sheer legalistic network. They knew nothing of the inner man, with his joys and sufferings, his hopes and frustrations. They strove to apply law—the abstract form of the good—to all of life, Jesus' hostile attitude toward them actually meant the rejection of legalistic morality. The Pharisees desperately clung to a way which they thought was leading to salvation—the way of justification by the law. This way, as Jesus saw it, was a false one. Therein lies the tragedy of pharisaism, and not, as some maintain, in its pride and self-righteousness. As Berdyaev puts it,

> The Pharisees stood on the confines of two worlds, at the dividing line between the ethics of law and the ethics of grace and redemption. The impotence of the ethics of law to save from sin and evil had to be manifest to them. The difficulty of the problem lies in the fact that the precepts of legalistic ethics are fully practicable. One can fulfill the law down to the smallest detail and become pure according to the law. This was precisely what the Pharisees did. And then it appeared that the perfect fulfillment of the law and perfect purity do not save. . . . It is powerless to conquer sin. . . . Pharisaism, i.e. the ethics of law . . . is practicable, but it does not help in the struggle against evil thoughts and it is powerless to change one's inner spiritual condition. According to the ethics of law a man becomes good because he does good works. But in truth a man does good works because he is good. . . . Pharisaism is mercilessly condemned in the Gospel because its adherents do not need the Savior and salvation as sinners and publicans need it, because if the final religious and moral truth were on the side of the Pharisees redemption would be unnecessary. Pharisaism means rejection of the Redeemer and redemption and the belief that salvation is to be found by fulfilling the moral law. But in truth salvation means rising above the distinction between good and evil which is the result of the Fall, i.e. rising above the law en-

gendered by that distinction. It means entering the Kingdom of Heaven, which is certainly not the Kingdom of the law or of the good as it exists on this side of the distinction.[20]

A similar interpretation of pharisaism is advanced by Reinhold Niebuhr. He observes also that the conflict in the gospels is between Jesus' prophetic-Messianic interpretation of life and the official legalism of his day. Of course, the endless reinterpretations of the Torah by the Pharisees sincerely tended to do justice to newly rising problems and occasions for which the original law embodied no provision. "But the policy of adding law to law," writes Niebuhr, "cannot solve the essential weakness of law as the disclosure of the divine purpose in history."[21] Then he sums up the criticisms of legalism in the New Testament under three forms. First, "no law can do justice to the freedom of man in history."[22] Since man is both self- and nature-transcendent nothing in the realm of history and nature can finally submit his life to a pre-determined rule or norm. For all laws are relative and temporal in the face of the ultimate law of God. Only the latter is normative for man. Second, "no law can do justice to the complexities of motive which express themselves in the labyrinthine depths of man's interior life."[23] This is exemplified in the Sermon on the Mount in which the moral demands greatly exceed anything which could be legally enforced upon the individual. Law becomes man's inner attitude in his relation to God. And finally, "law cannot restrain evil; for the freedom of man is such that he can make the keeping of the law the instrument of evil."[24] Indeed, law might be made into a vehicle of the sin of pride and self-righteousness. Was it not precisely the case with the Pharisees? At this point Niebuhr is at one with Berdyaev when he writes, "these criticisms, whether indicating the law's ability to define the ultimate good or to restrain the ultimate evil, namely, man's use of virtue as the vehicle of pride, all *reveal Christ's understanding of life and history in terms of the heights of freedom.*"[25]

This was also the experience of Luther. In quest for assurance of God's favor, the young Roman Catholic from Eisleben embarked on a monastic career in the rigorous order of Augustine. But the monastery did not bring him the assurance for which he

227

longed. He sought by the means set forth by the Church to make himself acceptable to God and to earn forgiveness of sins and the salvation of his soul. Yet inward peace seemed to elude him altogether and his periods of depression were dreadful. When eventually the light broke, Luther emerged a new creature with a revolutionary approach to the understanding of the Christian life.

Luther's failure to achieve salvation through monastic perfectionism awakened him, as Niebuhr points out, to two revolutionary convictions: first, that no effort after righteousness can yield final peace, and second, that the Church's pretension at finality and perfection is the root of sinful pride and pharisaic self-righteousness. "The assurance of the Pauline word," in Niebuhr's words, "that 'the just shall live by faith,' . . . came to him as a happy release from the bondage of the 'law,' from the intolerable tension of an uneasy conscience which came the nearer to despair, the more imperious the demand for perfection appeared to it." [26]

As a result, Luther became electrified by the message of men of faith in the Old and New Testaments. He felt life's pulsation throbbing through the texts he was commenting on. He saw the God of the prophets, psalmists, and apostles to be a God "in Christ" and not "in Law." To him faith appeared above all as submission to the Word. We have, first, to receive the Word, then, to submit ourselves to it in all humility. This is the way of salvation. One must resign in favor of God when He judges him, give up to Him when He offers His help, yield to His challenge, respond to His call for action. By faith man opens himself to the bountiful presence of God as the Father, Son, and Holy Spirit. By faith "a Christian man is perfectly free lord of all, subject to none." And by love which flows from faith, he "is a perfectly dutiful servant of all, subject to all." [27] Faith, therefore, is communion with God; and this communion means freedom from all necessity, whether legal or natural, even that of death.

This is, evidently, the thesis of Paul. The Apostle imperatively states that the Christian, by faith, is no longer "under Law." [28] Indeed, to him "no human being will be justified in [God's] sight by works of the Law." [29] Paul reminds the Romans that justification by works of the law and justification by faith exclude each other. The life in Christ is a life of grace and not of norm: "for

228

Christ is the end of the law, that everyone who has faith may be justified." [30] But Paul goes further still; he says not only that the way of works of the law and the way of faith are mutually exclusive, but also that man's efforts to achieve his salvation by keeping the law is sin. The reason for this identification lay in Paul's insight into the nature of both law and sin. The law allures man into the false assurance of achieving salvation by his own strength. It separates him from God in Christ whereby alone salvation is obtainable. And this is sin. Those "who would be justified by the law," writes Paul to the Galatians, "are severed from Christ," and "fallen away from grace." [31] Consequently, the pharisaic promise that observance of the law—good works—can procure righteousness is more than false: it leads man to death. In Paul's words, "the letter kills." [32] To the letter, i.e. the pharisaic law itself, Paul opposes another law, that of the eternal will of God, the "spiritual law" [33] which is the "law of Christ." [34] This law means life and salvation. It is kept by those who have faith, "who walk not according to the flesh but according to the Spirit." [35]

However, Berdyaev remarks, Paul does not completely reject the law. He is aware of its paradoxical ethical status in the world of sin. Despite its insufficiency "law has a positive mission in the world, and for that reason the ethics of law cannot be simply rejected." [36] Law is necessary for human society as long as its "fallen" condition persists. Social life is not possible without law. Peace, order, and justice must be protected, not through grace, but by the law. Individual life and freedom cannot be made to depend wholly upon the spiritual and moral condition of other men, collectivity and its rulers. The rights of the individual must be safeguarded, and this is done by means of government and law. The State, therefore, is necessary for it embodies the principle of justice. It is its duty to have recourse to force and regulations in preserving social welfare and order.

For this reason, according to Berdyaev, the State is not to be confused with the Church. The Kingdom of Ceasar is not identical with the Kingdom of God. Their realms are distinct from each other. The latter is founded on love; the former on justice. A Christian State is a "monstrous impossibility." [37] In other words, the Church and the State have different functions and purposes:

229

one cannot do the work of another. Berdyaev reminds the Christians that they do not have a city here. No Christian city has ever appeared on earth. The city of God is still to come. Accordingly, the Christian is bound to recognize both the legal and the redemptive levels of his life. He is the citizen of two worlds— of grace and of law. Where man's spiritual condition is not sufficiently enlightened by grace, it must be determined by law. In Berdyaev's words,

> We are thus faced with the following paradox: the law does not know the concrete, unique, living personality or penetrate into its inner life, but it preserves that personality from interference and violence on the part of others, whatever their spiritual condition may be. Therein lies the great and eternal value of law and justice. . . . It is impossible to wait for a gracious regeneration of society to make human life tolerable. Such is the correlation of law and grace. I must love my neighbor in Christ, this is the way to the Kingdom of Heaven. But if I have no love for my neighbor I must in any case fulfill the law in relation to him and treat him justly and honorably. It is impossible to cancel the law and wait for the realization of love. That, too, would be sheer hypocrisy. Even if I have no love I must not steal, must not commit murder, must not be a bully.[38]

Because man is destined to live both under the moral law and under the law of the State, there inevitably occur instances of conflict between law and conscience. When such is the case, what should be done? Berdyaev's answer is not a blunt: "We must obey God rather than men." [39] He recognizes that life situations generally involve too many facets to be met with an Aye or Nay. "Absolutely uncompromising moral actions and valuations are mistaken," he declares, "if only because they ignore the existence of the world in which we live and recognize nothing but the moral law and norm." [40] Take for instance the problem of war. It has always been the source of painful moral conflicts. It creates and places above the traditionally accepted individual morality —"Thou shalt not kill"—a new standard of State morality which permits and justifies murder. Yet, Berdyaev argues, to condemn war from the point of view of absolute morality does not solve the problem. For one thing, war may be a lesser evil and eventually

230

even a good: war is preferable to the loss of freedom. For another, a man's acceptance of social sin as manifested in war may raise him to a morally higher level than a sturdy conscientious objection. The Christian must recognize that in our fallen and sinful world the good is never found without some evil in it. The perfect good can only be manifested in the Kingdom of God which is above the good-evil entity. Hence uncompromising ethics is out of place on this side of good and evil. At all events, the Christian should come nearer to the fulfillment of his role in history if he takes his share of the common responsibility. He must do everything to prevent evil from gaining hold on life—whether individual or social; but once the tragedy of evil has begun and can no longer be stopped, the Christian should accept it in the light of the Cross and with spiritual humility, as all other trials of life.

2. ETHICS OF REDEMPTION

It should be clear from the foregoing discussion that the problem of good and evil cannot be solved by law. Normative ethics is powerless to master the irrational forces within human nature. Man needs God Himself to overcome sin and suffering. For this reason, according to Berdyaev, the Christian's adequate ethical standard is determined not by the ethics of law, but by the ethics of redemption. In the act of redemption the suffering God is meeting the suffering man and shares with him the bitter destiny of the world. Redemption conquers fear and sets the person free from sin and evil. It brings about a revaluation of all values. The redeemed man is a being regenerated in and through Christ. In opposition to the ethics of law, the gospel morality sets no idea of good as the aim of human achievement: it is man himself illuminated by divine grace that it regards as the supreme principle of life. The ethics of redemption is a specifically Christian revelation. Other ethical traditions have based their systems not upon the concrete, living being, but upon the idea of an abstract supreme good. But then too they have turned into legalism and become normative.

Such has been the case with the four great Western ethical

231

traditions, namely, of Wisdom, Duty, Pleasure, and Power. The tradition of wisdom which can be traced back to Socrates stresses knowledge as man's supreme goal. Thus for Socrates knowledge alone is the way of virtue. But why? Because, he insists, what every man seeks for in life is his own good. No man can choose what is essentially evil and therefore hurtful to himself. If then what he obtains in exchange of his deeds turns out to be evil, it must be because he did not know all the facts or understand the situation, in other words, because of ignorance. It follows, that knowing what is good and right inevitably leads to seeking them. No conduct informed by reason and based on knowledge can possibly be evil. Indeed, knowledge is virtue.[41]

To Plato likewise all cardinal virtues are subordinated to reason; they can be realized by means of knowledge. Thus wisdom is the knowledge of what is good; courage, of what to fear and not to fear; temperance, of mastery over one's self; and justice, the knowledge of personal and social harmony and stability.[42] Hence Plato's contention that it is possible for the individual to become virtuous through a process of education. For once the good is perceived and recognized, each man, in order to attain it, "would act rationally either in public or private life."[43]

Aristotle's ethical teaching is equally based on the supremacy of reason. Contrary to Socrates and Plato, however, he accepts no identification of knowledge with virtue. He was aware that virtue does not lie in the act itself but in a settled, highly moral character —and this might be achieved only through long and patient practice. Consequently, virtue implies an activity of the soul in accordance with reason. A virtuous man is the one who acts rationally and purposively. To reach one's purpose according to reason, one must avoid both excess and defect; in other words, follow the mean between the two. The mean is determined by reason and is relative to each individual person. To the lofty, somehow vague ethical idealism of Plato, Aristotle opposes the ethical flexibility informed by the common sense of every day experience. In this respect, his definition of virtue has a classical savor. "Virtue," he says, "is a state of character . . . lying in a mean, i.e., the mean relative to us, this being determined by a rational principle, and

232

by that principle by which the man of practical wisdom would determine it." [44]

Despite this improvement over his predecessors, Aristotle still remains a staunch believer in the omnipotence of reason. Indeed, he considers it not only as the highest activity in man, but also as the divine part in human nature. Through reason, he asserts, men are akin to the gods. And though he did not believe in personal immortality, he held reason to be the only immortal feature in the human being.

Berdyaev rejects altogether the theory that reason is the final value of human life. He reproaches Aristotle for identifying a limited area of consciousness with the whole of being. Reason's proper field of application, he maintains, is the world of nature. And even there its value is purely instrumental: it is the tool, not the goal, of man's activity. Furthermore "it is a prejudice to believe that knowledge is always rational, that there is no such thing as irrational knowledge. Actually, we apprehend a great deal more through feeling than by intellection." [45] Both our positive and negative sentiments—love and sympathy, hate and hostility—may help to extend our knowledge. "The heart [rather than reason] is the centre of the entire man." [46] Accordingly, reason cannot serve as a criterion for morality. Contrary to Socrates and Plato's belief, knowing the right thing does not necessarily imply doing the right thing. How much deeper is Paul's insight into human nature when he professes doing "not the good I want, but the evil I do not want." [47] The example of Bolshevik rulers, on the other hand, illustrates the fact that one may be a reasonable being and yet, as Shakespeare's Iago, find a diabolic satisfaction in the suffering and calamity of others.

Christianity, according to Berdyaev, puts its main emphasis not upon knowledge, but rather upon love. It is love, and not reason, that has the power of "illumining and transfiguring reality." [48] Far from being the saving redeemer, as Aristotle and also Spinoza hold, reason may turn into the very source of evil and damnation. The bitter experiences of contemporary man have proved beyond doubt the fallacy of the rationalistic hopes of past centuries. Despite the long lasting intellectual sway of Descartes, Voltaire, Diderot and the Encyclopedists, Isaak Newton and John Dewey, to name a few only, the hope that reason would create harmony out of social chaos and solve all human problems collapsed at the outbreak of World War I. "Since 1914 one tragic experience has followed another," as Niebuhr observes in the vein of Berdyaev's thought, "as if history had been designed to refute the vain delusions of modern man."[49] It took him nearly two thousand years of trial and error to acquire—yet not altogether—the penetrating insight of Paul that salvation is brought about not by reason, but by faith. The apostle, therefore, speaks not of "fruits of reason," but of "fruits of love" and "fruits of spirit." And that is ethics of redemption.

Berdyaev is particularly critical of Kant, the illustrious representative of the second major ethical tradition in the West—the tradition of holiness or harmony with the law of duty—for his failure to grasp the spiritual meaning of Christian ethics. This tradition which has its philosophical origins in the teachings of Epictetus and Marcus Aurelius envisions the supreme good not in terms of man's rational faculty, but rather as conformity to an absolute moral law. Whether the law is to be found objectively in nature (Holbach) or in God (Spinoza) or yet in both (the Stoics), or subjectively in the inner depths of human being (Kant), in either case it is formulated as a categorical imperative.

Kant's ethics, like that of the Stoics, is based upon the assumption that obedience to the law is the sum and substance of the moral life. What law? The law of man's being as it is recognized by reason and experienced as the sense of duty. This is the universal law of right. The whole of morality hinges upon obedience or disobedience to it. There is only one thing that can fundamentally be called good, and that is a good will—loyalty to right itself. A man is not of good will because he succeeded in securing what he sought for; but he is such, on the contrary, if under all circumstances he asks himself the question, What is my duty? and then acts accordingly, whatever the results may be. But how do I know what is my duty? Kant's categorical imperative attempts to solve the problem as follows: "Act only on a maxim by which you can will that it, at the same time, should become a general law."[50] In other words, act only in that way which might, without absurdity, be required of all men in similar circumstance. The application of the principle seems to be chiefly of a negative sort. What I cannot universalize is probably wrong to do. Does this inply that everything that can be universalized is thereby right? What about universalized communism or antisemitism which are not unthinkable possibilities? Moreover there may be many things that are right which cannot be universalized as, for instance, Rockefeller Foundation's allocation for the extension of Protestant seminaries.

Perhaps to stave off some such objections to his categorical imperative, and at the same time stress his argument for an autonomous will which he equates with practical reason, Kant formulates a second maxim, which is, "Act so as to treat man, in your own person as well as in that of any one else, always as an end, never merely as a means." [51] This means that man, as a rational being, possesses an absolute value, and therefore is entitled to respect and consideration everywhere and at all times. Furthermore, since the categorical imperative is derived not from the individual, but from the general practical reason which includes all men, it follows that each individual embodies law not partially, but in its entirety. He becomes a law to himself. He may act as if other men were the legislators of his actions and, conversely, as if he were in the position of a legislator making laws for the universe. Hence Kant's third maxim: "The will of every rational being is a will giving general laws." [52]

All this is well said, argues Berdyaev, but it is meaningless. In the first place Kant's ethics displays no motivation. Why should I comply with duty? While in some respects his theory bears a close resemblance to Stoicism, it contains no reference to the higher order and purpose of the unseen world wherein that ancient morality found both meaning and value for human behavior. Furthermore, Kant seems to pay no heed to the consequences of an action. He fails to recognize that the choice of concrete ends alone, and not the obedience to an abstract moral law, supplies the measure of right and wrong. It is probable that Kant's second maxim was meant to meet this objection. But the rather vague conception of human worth is hardly a substitute for the understanding of moral problems which every man's ethical conduct

235

requires. In Berdyaev's words, "Kant's moral maxim that every man must be regarded not only as a means but an end in himself is undermined by the legalistic character of his ethics, because every man proves to be a means and an instrument for the realization of an abstract, impersonal, universally binding law."[53]

Berdyaev indicates also that, in the rigor of his legalism, Kant "completely denied the emotional side of the moral life."[54] The German philosopher's view of personality is "purely abstract and normative, and has no relation to the concrete and irreplaceable human individuality in which Kant never took any interest."[55] Like the Stoics, Kant was attracted by an abstract mankind, and not by the living persons. But how is such an interest possible at all? What is mankind apart from specific individuals? Berdyaev dismisses Kant's categorical imperative, and by the same token, the whole Western ethical tradition of duty as a "legalistic distortion of Christianity." Indeed, "they preach righteousness achieved through fulfilling the law"[56] only to achieve a dry moralism instead which has no need of grace. He opposes to it the positive Christian values of brotherhood and charity, not toward an abstract humanity, but in regard to concrete individuals. Christianity considers each person as an end worth loving because he is a child of God for whom Christ died on the Cross. The Gospel morality, Berdyaev points out, exhorts man to keep high the quality of his heart, for on its purity depends the fulfillment of the greatest commandment—the love of God and of one's neighbor.

No less severe is Berdyaev's criticism of the third time-honored ethical system, namely, hedonism. The pleasure theory holds that the chief end and motivation of human action or conduct should be the greatest possible amount of pleasure. The experience of pleasure or pain is claimed to be the only criterion of moral valuation: good is what gives pleasure; evil is what generates pain. Hedonism was propounded by Aristippus of Cyrene, a disciple of Socrates and founder of the Cyrenaic School, and later on by Epicurus, the head in Athens of the so-called "Philosophers of the Garden." In the 17th century, hedonism was revived by Thomas Hobbes followed respectively in the 18th and 19th centuries by the hedonist teachings of Jeremy Bentham and John Stuart Mill.

It should be noted, however, that pleasure is not conceived in the same manner by each one of the above mentioned thinkers. Aristippus, for example, understands hedonism quite simply and literally. To him pleasure, whatever its nature, is always the highest good, and therefore it should be sought for and secured at every moment as much as possible. With Epicurus, on the other hand, the word pleasure acquires a different meaning. He declares that the pleasure of the mind is greater and of more value than bodily pleasure. And since the former is more likely to be obtained through the mastery of the passions rather than by a ceaseless pursuit of the latter, Epicurus insisted upon achieving a state of inner tranquillity—freedom from pain and care (*ataraxia*)—as the supreme source of happiness.[57]

Bentham likewise conceives the whole of moral life in terms of pleasure and pain. Pleasure, he believes, is the symbol of health and right; pain, of sickness and wrong. Discarding all theological references, he declares these two sensations the only criteria of moral choices. They were meant by nature to guide and determine man's behavior. He denies, however, all qualitative differences in pleasure, and insists that pleasures and pains could be measured quantitatively. Happiness is a matter of hedonistic quantity: the greater number of pleasures, the happier one is. Bentham even goes so far as to compile mathematically a list of fourteen separate pleasures to be achieved and twelve pains to be avoided. Moreover, social happiness, he thinks, is gauged by private happiness. Therefore, if each individual takes care of his own happiness, the social life as a whole should automatically become better and happier.[58]

Pleasure and pain are to Mill also the foundation of ethics. The facts of everyday experience, he maintains, prove that there is no other motivation behind human conduct. And since all men desire pleasure, as they actually do, this is obviously the most desirable thing that exists. Accordingly, pleasure and happiness are identical. In his words, "by happiness is intended pleasure, and the absence of pain; by unhappiness, pain, and the privation of pleasure."[59] Therefore, he declares, "actions are right in proportion as they tend to promote happiness, wrong as they tend to produce the reverse of happiness."[60]

Contrary to Bentham, however, Mill asserts that pleasure may differ not only in number, but also in quality. To him some pleasures are more desirable and more valuable than others. He distinguishes between higher and lower pleasures, and appeals to the sense of human conscience and dignity to determine the difference. Generally speaking, he offers preference to the mental over the physical pleasures. In his words, "it is better to be a human being dissatisfied than a pig satisfied; better to be Socrates dissatisfied than a fool satisfied." [61] Unlike Epicurus, Mill emphasizes the primacy not of individual, but of social happiness. He also admits the importance for ethics to invoke some sort of religious sanction.

Whatever the variety in meaning of the concept of pleasure from Aristippus to John Stuart Mill, Berdyaev rejects hedonism *in toto* both as false in its understanding of human nature and as contrary to Christianity. It is not true, he affirms that pleasure, i.e., hedonist happiness is the supreme value of man's life. First of all, satisfaction lies not in the object alone; it lies equally in the personality of the man himself. The same object, e.g., a trip to Europe, is apt to yield pleasure to some, while leaving others altogether indifferent. On the other hand, the means of choosing between pleasures requires that they must be quantitatively measured. But this is a factual impossibility. By what standard shall we ascertain, let us say, a senior's comparative pleasure content of a winter vacation in Hawaii with that afforded in anticipation by his graduation if he stays at home and completes his assignments? For this one reason Bentham's calculus is an absurdity. Furthermore, the experience of life proves that an exclusive pursuit of pleasure inevitably works its own defeat. This is true by virtue of a mysterious moral law according to which any single value, if posited as an absolute, will eventually annihilate itself.

From the Christian point of view also hedonism incurs condemnation. Pleasure stands entirely outside the Biblical tradition. The Cross symbolizes not pleasure but suffering. Christianity, Berdyaev maintains, accepts suffering as an inherent element of human destiny. But in the light of the Cross suffering appears not all sin and evil. It "is also redemption and has a positive value." [62] Christianity "teaches us not to fear suffering, for God Himself, the Son of God, has suffered." [63] Indeed, Christ withstood the

238

temptations of happiness in the wilderness, as Dostoyevsky points out in the *Legend of the Grand Inquisitor,* and chose suffering and unhappiness for the sake of remaining free. On Berdyaev's terms, "the idea that happiness is the supreme good and the final end has been instilled into man in order to keep him in slavery. Human freedom and dignity forbid us to regard happiness and satisfaction in this light. There is an irreconcilable conflict between freedom and happiness." [64] Christian grace knows nothing of happiness, but speaks of blessedness and joy—"it gives us only moments of joy and bliss." [65]

Very much the same thing might be said of voluntarism—the fourth great ethical tradition in the West. Its philosophical formulation is supplied by Plato's Thrasymachus in the first book of the *Republic.* According to him, might is right. Therefore, life's supreme goal and value, and also the ultimate motive of every action, consists in the ceaseless acquisition of power. The outstanding representatives of this tradition, besides Thrasymachus, are Machiavelli, Hobbes, Schopenhauer, Nietzsche, and in part, Spinoza.

Voluntarism holds the will as the primary reality prior to both intellect (idealism) and matter (materialism). The will is held by some to be the source of good, by others the root of evil. The former conception is shared by Machiavelli, Hobbes, Nietzsche, and Spinoza. The latter, by Schopenhauer and some Christian mystics.[66] Like Thrasymachus, Machiavelli declares that power is the foundation of ethics. But he goes further in justifying all means in order to obtain and retain power. He advocates the use of hypocrisy, force, and deceit in social relations. "It is necessary," he writes, "to be a fox to discover the snares and a lion to terrify the wolves."[67] Snares and wolves, of course, are simply human beings: Machiavelli in effect believes that human nature is almost completely depraved. Men, he thinks, "are ungrateful, fickle, false, cowardly, covetous, and as long as you succeed they are yours entirely." [68] Consequently, in order to achieve success, "be a great pretender and dissembler." Men are simple, they will take it: "He who seeks to deceive will always find someone who will allow himself to be deceived." [69] As to Machiavelli's opinion on the Church, he denounced it as pernicious because it conceals vice, makes claim to a higher loyalty than that of the state, and because Christians as a rule are bad soldiers.

Thomas Hobbes likewise maintains that man's supreme good is power. For it is by means of power that he is capable both of obtaining those things which he desires and assuring the way of his future desires. Life, therefore, is nothing else but a ceaseless search for more power. He expresses it most emphatically in these words:

> In the first place, I put for a general inclination of all mankind, a perpetual and restless desire of power after power, that ceaseth only in death. And the cause of this is not always that a man hopes for a more intensive delight, than he has already attained to; or that he cannot be content with a moderate power: but because he cannot assure the power and means to live well, which he hath present, without the acquisition of more.[70]

In other words men are moved by sheer self-interest—the desire for individual advantage. Naturally, they seek to harm one another. Many desire the same things, and if they are sufficiently strong, they seize by force the object of their desire; if weak, they are worsted in the struggle and consequently display nothing but hatred toward those who gained the upper hand. The natural condition of mankind is one of war of all against all. Like Machiavelli, Hobbes believes that by nature men are vile and corrupt. To express the idea, he quotes Plautus' famous statement that man is a wolf to man—*homo homini lupus*.[71] Such being the case, man's rights are measured and determined not by any natural standard of right and wrong, of justice and injustice, but only by his power to secure what he desires.

To avoid mutual extermination, and insure safety for life and property even to the weak, Hobbes urges men to agree to transfer all their individual power to the State. The existence of the State implies absolute sovereignty which, in the view of what men naturally are, needs to be supported by force. Thus the State becomes the basis of all morality, individual and social alike. It is to be noted, further, that, contrary to Machiavelli, Hobbes retains a place for the Church in the State. The concession, however,

240

is by no means theologically grounded. The Church is permitted to function on the condition of serving the State. To stress that the latter is supreme in all matters which affect the mutual relations of men, Hobbes deprives Christianity of all social connotations. To him the gospel assumes exclusively an other-worldly, pietistic character. As he puts it, "the Scripture was written to show unto men the kingdom of God and to prepare their minds to become his obedient subjects; leaving the world and the philosophy thereof to the disputations of men for the exercising of their natural reason." [72]

Of all the representatives of voluntarism, Schopenhauer is the first to elaborate a voluntaristic theory of the whole universe. He held that the ultimate reality is will—a blind will to live—which developed itself into the objective world. The development took place by gradual stages from the inorganic to vegetable to animal to man. Every phenomenon, whether in the realm of nature or spirit, is but a particular expression of the will. Especially sex, Schopenhauer thinks, is its imperative manifestation; but such are also all human wants, desires, drives, impulses, and needs. The will is really at the basis of all human life, and the intellect but an instrument of it. Hence, the will is also the underlying ground of all ethical conduct. In his words,

> although every particular action, under the presupposition of the definite character, necessarily follows from the given motive, and although growth, the process of nourishment, and all the changes of the animal body take place according to necessarily acting causes (stimuli), yet the whole series of actions, and consequently every individual act, and also its condition, the whole body itself which accomplishes it, and therefore also the process through which and in which it exists, are nothing but the manifestations of the will, the becoming visible, *the objectification of the will.* [73]

Schopenhauer finds no ground for happiness in the blind struggle of the will for self-assertion in existence. On the contrary, the will's perennial objectivation is to him the source of a perennial pessimism. For the will remains forever unfulfilled. All achievements are but illusions. Life is a pendulum between unsatisfied desire, i.e., pain, and the lure of satisfaction which inevitably

241

brings about boredom. Frustration and ennui are the only permanent content of human workaday experience.

There is nothing for Schopenhauer, then, but to seek for some escape from the misery of the world. He points out two as the most effective. The first is aesthetic experience. Disinterested contemplation of art—architecture, sculpture, painting, poetry, and music—grants relief from the thralldom of desire, but it is not of a permanent effect. The second, a more radical one, is provided by the example of the ascetic. If a man wishes to reach a state of rest, he must deny the world and renounce the will to live. He may, if he persists, attain to Nirvana which for Schopenhauer, under the influence of Buddhism, means a state of non-being characterized by a total absence of will. The way of asceticism, he goes on to say, involves naturally a feeling of sympathy and compassion for the suffering world. The virtuous man, therefore, shares in the common distress and suffers with others. And beyond the wretchedness of existence, he hopefully gazes to blissful nonexistence.

The last notable exponent of voluntarism to be mentioned here is Friedrich Nietzsche. He too assumes power to be the end and goal for life. He accepts Schopenhauer's doctrine of the will to live, but does not follow its ascetic gospel of salvation. He advocates not the denial but the bold affirmation of the will. With him the will to live becomes the will to power. The basis for such an all-embracing conception, he observes, is to be found in the visible struggle of life—from atom to man—for self-realization. Everything in the individual and social make-up—man's beliefs, reasoning, ideas, even the moral law—is both a result and an instrument of the will to power. Accordingly, an ethics rightly construed must always serve the interest of the strong against the weak. This is the law of nature.

Unfortunately, Nietzsche remarks, the weak have in the course of history displaced the natural master morality with a slave morality—that of the feeble, of the herd. By identifying violence and godlessness with wickedness, and humility and poverty with sainthood, the Jews were the first to perform "the miracle of the inversion of valuations, by means of which life on earth obtained a new and dangerous charm for a couple of millenniums. . . . It is with *them* that the *slave-insurrection in morals commences."* [74] **The** Christians, Nietzsche goes on to say, have followed the Jewish example, and reduced ethics to a set of precepts established forever, which condemn the most natural and necessary drives of life; for them the truth is given once and for all in the teachings of the Church with the assurance of happiness and salvation in this life and in the next.

Nietzsche arrives at the conclusion that Christianity has contributed more than anything else to the development of mankind's misery. It is in his opinion the most "contemptible" and "venomous" legacy of the past because its traditional morality justifies the domestication of men, and thus promotes against nature the triumph of the weak over the strong.[75] But the aim of civilization, Nietzsche insists, is not the raising of the weak and the emancipation of the masses, and public education of the population is no sign of progress. The modern veneration of the State and the standing armies is the result of this insane delusion. Contrary to Hobbes and Machiavelli, Nietzsche loathes the State for being the source of corruption, and for taking the weak under its protection. Real progress will be achieved when the only aim of humanity becomes the cultivation of a superior race. Strength and power, ruthless courage and brutal action must be restored to their status of virtue. Christianity with its effeminate morality of pity and cowardice must be done away with forever. Let all essential aspirations of life be brought into the open! Let all the natural instincts, passions, and impulses be satisfied! Let the strong trample under foot and exterminate the weak from the face of the world! Let man surpass himself and give birth to the superman! Thus spake Zarathustra.[76]

Berdyaev regards the ethical tradition of voluntarism under its various aspects, if unreservedly accepted, as unwarranted by human experience and dangerous in practice. Are individual men really actuated so completely by evil desires and self-interest as Machiavelli and Hobbes maintain? Far from it! There is much that should be said in favor of human sympathy, social interest, and self-sacrifice. Man bears within him not only the image of the world, he is also the image of God. True, man lives in a servile dependence upon his own instincts, upon society and the State. The reason for this lies in the fact that man is alienated from himself; he is no longer aware of himself as a free and spiritual being. In Berd-yaev's words, "if . . . man remains a material and economic being and his spiritual nature is regarded as an illusion of consciousness, . . . then man remains a slave." [77] In that state the consciousness of his weakness and insignificance arouses his thirst for power and greatness. But the fruits of the will to power yield no salvation: on the contrary, they bring man into further bondage—bondage to the Prince, the State, the Church, or the Race. Unqualified will to power inevitably leads to unqualified authority, that is, tyranny.

Berdyaev is an uncompromising opponent of all forms of authoritarianism, political, economic, or religious. Authority, he affirms, can never pretend to a primacy over the freedom of the spirit. This is especially true of the State. In agreement with Hobbes, Berdyaev fully recognizes the necessity of the State "in view of the flood of evil which arises from the aggressive will of man." [78] But its function and justification must be carefully defined.

> The state ought to defend freedom and right. That is the justification of its existence. But every process by which the state is made absolute is a great evil. The power of the state possesses no sovereignty of any kind. The state should be limited, it should be brought within bounds which it ought not to go beyond. It is impossible to admit that final objectivization of human existence which the state demands, possessed as it is by the will to power. A totalitarian state is the kingdom of Satan. . . .
> Great kingdoms and mighty empires are nothing in comparison with a man. The state exists for man and not man for the state. . . . Power, government, is only the servant, simply the defender and the guarantor of the rights of man and nothing more. And only those states are to be tolerated which take as their symbol the value of man, and not the majesty of the state. [79]

Berdyaev thinks that Nietzsche's criticism of the Church is in many cases justified. The historical Church has only too often failed in the task of realizing God's will on earth, and not infrequently has been used as a means of screening hypocrisy, corruption, and lack of creativity. But Nietzsche's criticism of Christian morality is altogether untrue, Berdyaev declares. He interprets

Christianity in terms of his own valuation of strength and weakness; but this valuation is much too superficial. The lofty potency of the Roman patrician captivates him by its impression of nobility and vigor, but he seems unable to distinguish between ostensible strength—external, normative, and real strength—inner, spiritual. Because of this confusion of ideas, Nietzsche considers morality affected with weakness and invalidism, and opposes Christianity with hatred and contempt. But, Berdyaev writes,

> The religion of Christ is not at all what Nietzsche took it for. Christian morality is not slavishly-plebeian but rather aristocratically-noble, the morality of the sons of God, with their primogeniture, their high birth and their high calling. Christianity is the religion of the strong in spirit, not the weak. . . . The Christian ethic is an ethic of spiritual victory. . . . Those who have overcome the world, sacrificing this world's goods, are always the strongest, the victors in the truest sense. And in comparison with the power and the victory of the spirit of Christ, every power and victory in this world is illusory and insignificant. . . . True Christian morality lays on man, who has become a son of God, free responsibility for his own fate and for the fate of the world, makes it impossible for the sons of God to feel slavish, plebeian, ignoble resentment against fate, against life and against other people. . . .
> The religion of Christ is the religion of man's highest powers—it is the very opposite of all weakness or depression in man.[80]

In other words, Christian morality is a source of spiritual power which not only enables man to face courageously the problems of life and death, but also overcome the weakness and darkness of the world. And this is made possible on account of the main motivating force of Christianity, namely, love. Of the four ethical traditions discussed above, none deems love important, and some think it quite irrelevant, even pernicious. Yet, Berdyaev says, "love is a force, a radiation of beneficent, life-giving energy."[81] Now love can only be directed upon a living, concrete human being and not upon the abstract good. For this reason Christianity posits as the supreme principle of life neither reason, nor duty, nor pleasure, nor power—mere abstractions; but man himself. This sums up, in Berdyaev's belief, the ethics of redemption. He writes,

Christianity is founded not upon the abstract and impotent idea of the good which, in relation to man, inevitably appears as a norm and a law, but upon a living Being, a Personality, and man's personal relation to God and to his neighbors. Christianity has placed man above the idea of the good and thereby made the greatest revolution in history. . . .

The ethics of the Gospel is based upon existence and not upon norm, it prefers life to law. A concrete existent, a living being, is higher than any abstract idea of the good. The good of the Gospel consists in regarding not the good but man as the supreme principle of life.[82]

It follows from this that moral problems cannot be solved by means of universal norms; each of them demands an individual solution. Therefore,

every moral act must be based upon the greatest possible consideration for the man from whom it proceeds and for the man upon whom it is directed. The gospel morality of grace and redemption is the direct opposite of Kant's formula: you must not act so that the principle of your action could become a universal law; you must always act individually, and everyone must act differently.[83]

In order to become realistic, however, and not remain merely another abstraction, the ethics of redemption requires, again, the practice of Christian love, that is, "seeing the other [person] in God and affirming him in eternal life."[84]

3. ETHICS OF CREATIVITY

Is there any concrete way of putting Christian love into practice? Berdyaev affirms that there is—the way of a creative act. "Man made by God in His own image and likeness, is also a creator and is called to creative work.[85] This is man's sacred vocation. "God calls man to perform the creative act and realize his vocation, and He is expecting an answer to His call."[86] Thus the ethics of redemption finds its ultimate accomplishment in the ethics of creativity. The passage from one to another characterizes man's continuous response to God's perennial challenge.

246

In and through Christ man acquires a power which truly performs a spiritual regeneration of his whole being. He is actuated thereby into accepting love as the ethical standard of conduct. Regeneration alone, however, does not supply the answer to the vital questions of life. It is incumbent on each person to arrive, by a creative act, at a solution of his particular problems. This is the only way leading to spiritual maturity. And what is more important than inner growth? God's purpose for His children, according to Berdyaev, is that they should individually attain the fullest realization of personality. In this task man is obligated to exercise his creative powers. "Creativeness and a creative attitude to life as a whole is not man's right, it is his duty. It is a moral imperative that applies in every department of life. . . . The path of creativeness is also a path to moral and religious perfection, a way of realizing the fulness of life." [87]

Berdyaev finds the scriptural basis for his ethics of creativity in the parable of the talents and the Paulinian doctrine of the variety of gifts. The New Testament implicitly assumes that each person is the possessor of at least one gift of God. Every man has a minimum of one talent. Some have two talents and some have five, but all men are equal in one thing—the power to multiply what they have. Burying one's talents in the ground—absence of creative activity—is condemned by Jesus. Making waste of one's gifts is sinful and self-destructive. Is it not written that men shall be known after their fruits? The very fact that talents and gifts come from God indicate man's creative vocation.

Creativeness, however, implies more than a reference to human personality; it also assumes significance for the entire cosmos. In the creative act of man, Berdyaev sees a step forward toward the achievement of the creation of the world. Creation is not complete; it is still continuing. At it God and man work together. Man's part in the process is that he create new values out of God-given gifts and dedicate them to the common good. In that way a twofold end is achieved concomitantly: on the one hand, the growth of personality, and on the other, the enrichment of the Kingdom. An accomplished scientist is at the same time often a wholesome personality, and the results of his creative work belong to the world as a whole.

Creation, Berdyaev observes, means the making of something distinctly new; something that has never existed before. It is therefore neither emanation, which presupposes a radiation from a present source; nor is it generation, which involves mere redistribution of the given elements of matter, force, and energy. Creation cannot be deduced from, or generated by, anything. But then how is it possible at all? Creativity, Berdyaev states, finds its explanation in the primeval meonic freedom. This is the fathomless, uncreated freedom of the *Ungrund*—the mysterious no-thing which possesses the avidity of becoming all-things. "Such freedom alone," Berdyaev writes, "can give rise to the new, to what had never existed before. Out of being, out of something that exists, it is impossible to create that which is completely new."[88] In other words it is the meonic freedom that makes creativeness possible; but it is man's response to the call of God that makes creativeness actual.

The ethics of creativity differs from that of laws because it recognizes no universally binding rules. On the contrary, it stresses the fact that each man has a unique task to perform, and this can be done on the condition of one's remaining free to create individual, unrepeatable values. To the static nature of ethics of law, the ethics of creativity opposes a dynamic and energetic character. And whereas the former is concerned with the finite, self-contained system of normative pharisaism, the latter stretches out toward the infinite of the ever expanding possibilities and achievements.

Creativity, according to Berdyaev, by its very nature implies *geniality*,[89] that is, creative potentiality inherited in man. *Geniality* is not to be identified with genius. The term does not mean that every man is a born Shakespeare or Rembrandt. It expresses rather man's total relation to life. "It is a characteristic of human personality as a whole and not a specific gift."[90] *Geniality* may be found in the ordinary relations of every day life—in a man's love for a woman, in a mother's love for her child, in a laborer's love for service, in a social worker's love for other people's welfare. *Geniality* is connected much more with the creative attitude of the whole being than with the external realization of creativity.

Creativity, however, naturally bids for outer manifestation. Love

248

seeks expression in fruits of love. Artistic inspiration finds embodiment in works of art. But this propensity is at the same time the source of a twofold conflict. First, the formal realization of creativity never corresponds to "the burning heat of the creative fire."[91] To Berdyaev every expression of creativity—book, picture, statue, social institution, good works—"is an instance of this cooling down of the original flame."[92] Second, creativity fulfilled is not correlative with the moral perfection of its author. A great artist may be morally a worthless man. *Geniality* does not imply sainthood. Indeed, the two may even mutually exclude each other; yet both are necessary for the building of the Kingdom of God.

In order to avoid this duality ethics must formulate a double question: what is the moral significance of the creative act outside the moral life? and what is the creative significance of the moral act? The first question is answered by Berdyaev to the effect that all creative effort is *ipso facto* a moral act. Why is this so? Because "human creativity is not a claim or a right on the part of man, but God's claim on and call to man."[93] Creative achievement constitutes man's relation and response to God. Therefore, it includes its own justification. Conversely—and this is Berdyaev's answer to the second question—every moral act is also a creative valuation. "Moral life itself, moral actions and valuations have a creative activity."[94] This is true, Berdyaev says, in the sense that the ethics of creativity does not consist merely in a negative struggle against evil; its goal, on the contrary, is to transform evil into good. In a word, it is creative energy—the possibility of bringing into being new realities. Hence, its positive value. "The ethics of creativeness overcomes the negative fixation of the spirit upon struggle with sin and evil and replaces it by positive, i.e. by the creation of the valuable contents of life."[95] Indeed, it overcomes not only earthly selfishness but that which is ascribed to the spheres of heaven as well. True creativity spells breaking through the consciousness of sin into the realm of grace and freedom wherein the moral motives are acknowledged as a disinterested love of God, Truth, Perfection, and all higher and positive values of life. For this reason, "fear of punishments in hell can play no part in the ethics of creativity."[96]

It should also be remembered that the moral act always proceeds from a concrete personality. This is not individualism, but personalism—the belief that reality is in the highest sense personal; that there are alongside a personal, creative God only creative persons; that each human being is an idea of God, and therefore "to be oneself means to realize God's idea of one's self." [97] Personality, it was observed, is a spiritual category connected with the divine; it is the image of God in man. It must be distinguished from the individual which is a biological category submitted to nature. The person is neither a biological nor a psychological entity; nor is he a social one. The person is the ultimate ethical and spiritual value. "For God the human personality is an end in itself, a friend from whom He expects responsive love and creative achievement. For man God is the final end, the object of his love, the One for Whose sake he performs creative acts." [98]

For this reason ethics should overcome "symbolic morality"— the morality of ritual and convention—and pass on into "real morality," that of actually transfiguring life into love, goodness, righteousness, and beauty,—above all beauty. In Berdyaev's words,

> The real transfiguration and enlightenment of human nature means the attainment of beauty. The good realized actually, and not formally and symbolically, is beauty. The highest end is beauty. . . . Beauty will save the world, i.e. beauty *is* the salvation of the world. The transfiguration of the world is the attainment of beauty. The Kingdom of God is beauty.[99]

Of course, creativity is not always put into the service of the good and beautiful; it may also be evil and ugly. It may be entirely anti-Christ. Actually, it is degenerate to such a degree in the modern world that it calls forth a revolutionary moral reaction. Art and literature, science, politics, and even religion display ghastly signs of degeneration "in which the spirit of eternity is finally surrendered to the polluted spirit of the time." [100] Indeed, "in every sphere the lust of life damps the creative burning of the spirit." [101] Yet, creativity must overcome the lust of life. For hereon hangs man's ultimate salvation.

With such a lofty goal, the ethics of creativity, according to

Berdyaev, must strive "for the victory of eternity over time." [102]
Creativity is ultimately informed by eternity:

> All the products of man's *geniality* may be temporal and
> corruptible, but the creative fire itself is eternal, and every-
> thing temporal ought to be consumed in it. . . . Creativity
> wants eternity and the eternal, but produces the temporal and
> builds up culture which is in time and a part of history. The
> creative act is an escape from the power of time and ascent to
> the divine.[103]

The ethics of creativity thus passes into eschatology and is
resolved therein. For the ascension to the divine means, on Berdyaev's terms, death and immortality. Man is urged by his destiny
to create eternal values, and at the same time prepare for death.
But the crux of the reference is this: the Kingdom will not come
unless man, by his creative activity, has laid down the highway
for its advent. This means the freeing of life from the dominance
of evil and gaining of paradise.

Evil, it has been said, originates in the unfathomable irrational-
ity of meonic freedom. It is, therefore, by nature spiritual, not
material. The Religious traditions of the Hindus and Greeks are
inclined to identify evil with matter. In Buddhism being and life
are evil: they ought to be renounced for the sake of final salvation
in nirvana. The Stoics, who also place evil in nature, do not for
that renounce the world. They advocate deliverance from its
sufferings and evil through an attitude of indifference and contempt to everything external. Orphism, Platonism, Neo-Platonism,
and Gnosticism likewise conceive of the soul as immured in matter
(the body). Salvation means to be set free and to return to the
realm of the spirit.

The Christian understanding of evil, Berdyaev asserts, is different. Matter is not the source of evil. Matter may serve both
evil and good purposes; but as such it is neutral. Nor is God
responsible for evil. He causes no evil, for there is no evil in Him.
He is the perfect good. Nor yet is there any other ontological
principle or being that could explain evil. Evil is irrational and,
therefore, it cannot be grasped by reason; it has no logical ex-

planation. It belongs not to being, but to non-being. "Evil," Berdyaev writes, "is non-being and has its roots in non-existence. But non-being can have no meaning, for meaning is always ontological. Therefore that evil to which a meaning can be assigned is thereby transformed into a good."[104]

This does not mean that evil is unreal or mere absence of good. The suffering of the world attests to the reality of evil. But it is not real in the sense in which good is real, for it has no ultimate duration. "No evil . . . pursued to the end has any positive content. All evil consumes itself. Its nothingness is laid bare by its own course of development."[105] In the Kingdom of God there is not a trace of evil. For this reason, Berdyaev denies and denounces the idea of hell as it is commonly held by normative ethics.

> Hell as a place of retribution for the wicked, which is a comfort to the good, is a fairy tale; there is not a shadow of reality about it; it is borrowed from our everyday existence with its rewards and punishments. The idea of an external hell as a rightful retribution . . . is one of the most hideous and contemptible products of the triumphant herd-mind. . . . From the point of view of God, there cannot be any hell. To admit hell would be to deny God.[106]

Hell exists, however, but it is neither objective nor eternal. It is experienced in the subject; it is felt in the depth of one's own life. Man, and not God, is the cause of his own hell. The torments of hell, Berdyaev says, are inflicted on man by his self-affirmation and spiritual pride. By taking as the center of his life not the divine but his own self, man is not only alienated from God, but he is also separated from the very source of his own being. But outside God, there is only non-being, the realm of illusion, dividedness, and pain. "Paradoxically it might be said that the horror of hell possesses man when he submits his final destiny to his own judgment and not to that of God. The most pitiless tribunal is that of one's own conscience."[107]

Since hell is not the result of a transcendental punishment, but that of the soul's absorption in its own pride and selfishness, it follows that it is not eternal. "Hell will not come in eternity, it will remain in time."[108] But time is not to remain forever. The ultimate victory of eternity over time marks the end of time; it also indicates the end of hell. The far-reaching implication of this idea is that salvation is universal. The last demand of ethics, according to Berdyaev, is that all must be saved and released from hell. "The moral will must be directed in the first place towards universal salvation." [109] Consequently, men must apply the power of their spirit to destroy the nightmare of sin and pride. They must not create hell either for themselves or for others. They must help to liberate everyone from hell. For the Kingdom of God will not come as long as one single sheep remains lost in the agony of hell.[110]

This means that human beings must affirm the principle of eternal life in their mutual relations. They must live on the highest moral and creative level. They must strive for eternal and immortal life. This is extremely important to realize, because man, Berdyaev teaches, is not naturally immortal. "Death is not only a biological and psychological fact but a spiritual fact as well." [111] Immortality is not given; it must be won, and this involves the struggle of man's spirit for possession of the natural elements. On Berdyaev's terms, the ultimate alternatives confronting every man are not eternal heaven vs. eternal hell, but eternal life vs. eternal death.

Death, he says, may have a double significance: either as the most terrible evil should it reduce the creature to non-being; or as the most valuable fact of life should it lead into immortal and eternal life. Christianity holds that death is the wage of sin and its last enemy which must be conquered and destroyed. If it is not, then death is a denial of eternity—the last moment of life followed by non-being; if it is, then death is an affirmation of eternity—the last moment of life followed by existence in the world beyond. The second alternative is realized only by the spirit that consciously and freely chooses to be born again in Christ. This calls for an intense creativity on man's part to struggle with the deadly forces of evil and to prepare for the coming of the Kingdom of God.

To Berdyaev creativity is not limited to our earthly life; it is also the characteristic feature of eternity. True, eternity cannot be construed in terms of interminable duration, but rather as a blissful quality of life. That quality, however, is an active one. In his words,

Eternity is not a cessation of movement and of creative life; it is creative life of a different order, it is movement which is not spatial and temporal but inward. . . . We must think of paradise as containing not less but more life than our sinful world, not less but more movement—though it is movement of the spirit and not of nature and is not based upon the continuity of time.[112]

Paradise is the supreme goal of human personality. Indeed, it is the highest aim of the entire cosmic process. It is the Kingdom of God revealed in Christianity. Man assumes a great part of the responsibility for its ultimate realization. Paradise, therefore, is man's creative vocation. In order to fulfill it, Berdyaev suggests the following practical rule of moral conduct which is, at the same time, the quintessence of his ethics of creativity:

Act as though you could hear the Divine call to participate through free and creative activity in the Divine work; cultivate in yourself a pure and original conscience, discipline your personality, struggle with the evil in yourself and around you—not in order to relegate the wicked to hell and create a kingdom of evil, but to conquer evil and to further a creative regeneration of the wicked.[113]

Act so that eternal life might be revealed to you and that the energy of eternal life should radiate from you to all creation.[114]

To sum up, then, Berdyaev envisions ethics in reference to the spiritual, not the natural, world. Moral valuations are independent from social and material surroundings; they are derived from the realm of spirit. However, since this world is "fallen" ethics must of necessity pay heed to the social aspect of life. Accordingly, the life of the Christian is subject to three types of ethics. First, the ethics of law. It stresses the priority of social categorical imperatives over individual moral valuations. It also maintains that salvation might be obtained by means of fulfilling the law. Although basically the assumptions of the ethics of law are untrue and insufficient, it cannot be simply rejected. For it has a positive mission in the world, that of maintaining social peace, order, and justice. Second, the ethics of redemption which is wrought in the coming upon earth of a suffering God in the person of Christ to redeem the world and set it free from sin and evil. This is the ethics of divine grace. Its main stress is not upon any abstract, normative good, whether wisdom, or will, or pleasure, or duty, but upon man himself—his personal relation to God and to his neighbor. Love alone is the motivating force of the ethics of redemption. Lastly, the ethics of creativity posits that man made after the image of God the Creator is a creator in his own right. His sacred vocation is to produce new values, and thus contribute to the achievement of the creation of the world. Furthermore, creativity is the condition *sine qua non* of both personal growth and the coming of the Kingdom. Only through positive creativity, that is, the transforming of evil into good, can be secured the victory of eternity over time. For this reason, man stands in the obligation of struggling against his own hell and that of others, and of ceaselessly aspiring toward attaining paradise. On his creative endeavors hinges his *post mortem* destiny: either life eternal or death eternal. The latter spells annihilation. The former signifies active blessedness in God.

CHAPTER V

THE MEANING OF HISTORY:
"AND OF HIS KINGDOM THERE SHALL BE NO END"

> Lord Jesus Christ, the only-begotten
> Son of God, Begotten of the Father be-
> fore all ages, Light of Light . . . who for
> us men and for our salvation came down
> from the heavens, and was made flesh
> . . . and became man, and was crucified
> for us . . . and suffered and was buried,
> and rose again . . . and ascended into the
> heavens . . . and cometh again with glory
> to judge living and dead, of whose king-
> dom there shall be no end.
> —The Nicene Creed

Man is a historic being. His existence in this world is a historic existence. Indeed, "existence," in Berdyaev's thought, "is
history."[1] Man cannot be separated from historic reality, nor can
he be absolved from responsibility for it. It is he who makes history.
And since human personality is the highest value in the world,
history must have both worth and significance. A philosophy of
history is therefore possible.

This is Berdyaev's presupposition concerning the meaning of
history. We shall now proceed to its analysis under the following
three headings: 1) types of historic interpretation; 2) the nature
of history and of time; and 3) the Christian philosophy of history.

1. TYPES OF HISTORIC INTERPRETATION

The many forms of interpretation of history can be, in Berdyaev's view, reduced to three main types: the first type in which history is interpreted through organic participation in historic order, the second in which history is interpreted through divorce from historic order, and the third in which history is interpreted through awareness of the mysteries of the "historical."

A. *History interpreted through organic participation in historic order.* The first type of interpretation equates history with the life of the cosmos. It regards man as a part of nature submitted to its course and destiny, and both man and nature as sharing in the greater historic order which comprehends all there is in heaven and on earth. The main characteristic of this type of interpretation is the view that the temporal world is subject to endlessly recurring cycles. Such was, for example, the Greek understanding of history.

Berdyaev pictures the historic continuity in Hellenic culture as an infinitely recurrent cyclic motion. To illustrate the point we may note that, according to Anaximander (6th century B.C.), the world rises out of chaos, reaches a point of balance or harmony, and then returns into chaos only to rise out of it again, and so on without end. The whole process is the result of the struggle between primeval opposite elements such as dark and light, cold and hot, wet and dry. Achieving the balance is the effect of justice; disrupting the harmony is the work of injustice, that is, the attempt of each element to enlarge its domain to the prejudice of the other. This is the necessary law controlling the universe. "Into that from which things take their rise they pass away once more, as is ordained, for they make reparation and satisfaction to one another for their injustice according to the ordering of time." [2]

Heraclitus (5th century B.C.) also believed that the opposites, which issued from one basic ground—fire, made for life and its perpetual flux and change. But he described these opposites as essentially identical. "Good and ill are one. The way up and the way down is one and the same." [3] Nevertheless, the opposites combine to produce a motion which is rhythm and harmony. The world is without beginning and without end—only a ceaseless passage of things and events, "with measures kindling and measures going out." [4]

To Empedocles (5th century B.C.), basic reality is represented by four elements: earth, air, fire, and water. Their constant mixing in different proportions offers the explanation for the changing complex of the world. They are combined by Eros or Love, and separated by Eris or Strife. Love and Strife are the principles which govern the whole of existence. Empedocles held that there are periods when Love has the upper hand, and others when Strife is stronger. There are four stages in the eternal reiteration: first, Eros is in control—the elements are in perfect harmony; next, Eris gradually penetrates the harmony and separates the elements; eventually Strife is in control—chaos and disharmony reign everywhere; finally, love ascends once more and step by step regains direction over the world. There is no purpose in these cycles. They are governed only by Chance and Necessity.

Anaximander, Heraclitus, and Empedocles reduced history to the proportion of nature. Consequently, they emptied it of all meaning. Even more, they had no sense of history whatsoever. Theirs is a rather static world wherein no radical, permanent change actually takes place. Things just come back again. Life is interpreted from the standpoint of yearly seasons which are going round and round forever. Time has no reality. There is no freedom, purpose, or fulfillment for man and the world. A blind Fate rules the cosmos. Under such circumstances the only possible soteriology is that of escapism. This is exactly what Plato propounds: emancipation from, and not fulfillment in, history. History, to him, is but a mirage. The only reality, the supreme good, is the invisible world of changeless essence underlying the changing world of phenomena. Man must tend by the power of his reason to transcend the appearance of becoming and unite himself with the reality of being. Thus Plato's understanding of history finally culminates in mysticism. [5]

For all his pragmatic approach to the study of human life and institutions, even Aristotle construed the universe in terms of infinite recurrence against a background of metaphysical order and permanence. Time for him is motion that endlessly repeats itself. [6] The future will be what the past was. Aristotle, too, reached the conclusion that man's final attainment is to be found in a passive, impersonal sharing in God's immortality.[7]

The Stoics did not depart from the general classical pattern. They believed that originally there was only fire; then the other elements—air, water, earth, in that sequence—gradually emerged. The world however, is not eternal. Sooner or later, following a cosmic conflagration, it will return to fire. Then it will merge into life again—only to await destruction in a new cosmic catastrophe. The whole process will be repeated endlessly. "The rational soul," wrote Marcus Aurelius, "traverses the whole universe, and the surrounding vacuum . . . and it extends itself into the infinity of time, and embraces and comprehends that those who come after us will see nothing new, nor have those before us seen anything more."[8] Lucretius pictured a similar cyclical rhythm of the world in these words: "Since I see that the chiefest members and parts of the world are destroyed and begotten anew, I may be sure that for heaven and earth as well there has been a time of beginning and there will be a time of destruction."[9]

In Berdyaev's judgment the whole of classical thought did not understand history. The Greek thinkers, he asserts, were unaware of history and "could grasp neither the historical process nor that of historical fulfillment."[10] They were unconcerned with the future, and therefore regarded history as having no issue, no purpose, not even a beginning, subject only to an eternal, futile repetition. The reason for this, Berdyaev believes, lies in the fact that the Greeks acquired no real conception of freedom. "Neither Greek religion nor Greek philosophy evinced any real sense of freedom. Submission to fate is the most characteristic feature of the Hellenic spirit."[11] Their almost exclusive preoccupation with formal perfection in every sphere of life left no room for the irrational content involving human beings. Hence the lack of historic perspective of the ancient Greeks and the limitation of their world outlook.

2. *History interpreted through divorce from historic order.* The second type of interpretation, according to Berdyaev, originated in the Age of Enlightenment. The eighteenth century in the history of Western Europe witnessed the absolute triumph of reason. The unparalleled progress of physics and mathematics in the previous century radically transformed the generally accepted

view of the world. The application of mathematical techniques and formulae to the study of life as a whole, became the sole true method of discovery and exposition. This frame of mind persisted and grew even stronger in the eighteenth century. Newton's mechanical and deterministic explanation of the universe was but the logical culmination of the entire trend of thought which regarded reason as the unique key to the problems of body and soul alike.

The remarkable result of the Age of Enlightenment from the historic point of view lies in the fact, as Berdyaev puts it, "that the knowing subject no longer feels himself directly and wholly a part of the historical object; and this gives birth to the speculations of historical science." [12] But the new outlook did not, in spite of appearances, favor a genuine comprehension of history. The divorce between subject and object, carried too far, actually disclosed a separation of the human being from his innermost life—that of spirit. Reason enthroned as a queen over the world reduced everything to its own limitations. The mysteries of being and of life were denied. Spiritual experience was ignored. Religious faith was branded as a degrading superstition and summarily dismissed.

To Berdyaev the eighteenth century was not an age of enlightenment and history (despite Voltaire's use of the term "philosophy of history" and his many historical works), but rather one of blindness and an anti-historic view of history. This eventuality, he believes, was fatal: it befell reason as a judgment for its extravagant claim of a monopoly on life. "The blindness of the 'enlightened' reason," Berdyaev writes, "was the inner penalty it paid for its self-assertiveness and for the egoism with which it enslaved both the human and the superhuman." [13]

Voltaire is a remarkable case in point of the blindness of reason Berdyaev is talking about. Like Gibbon, his British counterpart and disciple, Voltaire construed history to a large extent in terms of denouncing the evils that beset the world. Two underlying causes, in his conviction, accounted for them: governmental corruption and ecclesiastical clericalism. Accordingly, he undertook a bitter campaign of criticism of the great lords and rulers, on the one hand; and on the other, he scornfully exposed the abuses, intolerance, and persecution concealed under the veil of religion.

Along with this rather negative attitude to history, Voltaire also

260

developed a more constructive approach which imparts the tone to his entire historical outlook. In his vast scientific inquiry about countries and people, he showed no interest for individuals, events, or actions; he focused his inquisitiveness primarily on culture and the spirit of a given epoch. Thus in the introduction to *The Age of Louis XIV,* he made the following statement: "It is not solely the life of Louis XIV that is here to be depicted. A greater object is in view, which is to depict for posterity, not the actions of a single man, but the minds of men in the most enlightened century that there was." [14] The results of Voltaire's historical method are eloquently displayed in his *Essay on the Manners and Customs of Nations.*[15] The Essay constitutes a complete antithesis to Bossuet's *Discourse on Universal History* and Augustine's *The City of God.* For the two Roman Catholic bishops the central matter of their historical narratives was to demonstrate the unity of history, the solidarity of the present with the past rendered by the progressive unfolding of the divine plan. Voltaire, on the contrary, refused to recognize in history anything else except a play of human passions endlessly renewed. Each of his depicted epochs form an almost isolated whole with no relation to the past; to him history's task was preventing the past from weighing on the present. He advised against the study of ancient history as being useless, and emphasized the importance of modern history on account of its rediscovery of reason—"a revolution which changed everything." [16]

To discontinuity in time Voltaire joined a discontinuity in space. Universal history, he pointed out, is something different from the story of Christianity and of the Jews: Asia, and America too, possess independent civilizations which ought to be placed with those of the West. He spoke of Persia, India, and particularly China which in his eyes represented the oldest culture in the world. But here again Voltaire exerted no effort to establish any connection between peoples and cultures whose social life and institutions he was describing.

Whether as a historian or as a critic Voltaire always applied the criterion of reason with decisive rigor. He ordered everything in stable and fixed parcels. To him history had no other sense and direction than those which were determined by human feelings and wills according to their state of being more or less enlightened by reason. He did not admit of unseen realities or secret purposes in history. Denying the presence of a divine intelligence in the fabric of human events, explaining fact and events by necessary mechanical connections, setting reason as the only source of universal redemption—this was Voltaire's controlling design. In turn, he harvested the crop of rationalism—a shallow understanding of human beings and no insight into divine truths. He felt no sympathy for the men he approached. He mocked their errors, stupidities, and miseries; he did not see their efforts toward truth and good. He did not comprehend them, because they were different from himself. Voltaire was unable to get out of his own shell and century: reason which was supposed to enlarge his vision till the confines of the universe, blurred it instead and deprived him of the sense of history.[17] As Berdyaev puts it, "that 'enlightened' reason which celebrates its classical triumphs in the eighteenth century knew comparatively little; its sympathies were few, its intelligence limited, and it had lost all inner contact with the mysteries of historical life."[18] Reason to be redemptive must reestablish contact with the spiritual ground of history, for only then it becomes "the true and enlightened reason."[19]

The ultimate consequence of Voltairian rationalism, in Berdyaev's judgment, is portrayed in Marxian thought. By positing the process of materialistic production as the only reality of the historic process Marx reduced life to economic ontology and human consciousness to an adjunct of economic activity. Here, in Berdyaev's words, "religion, spirituality, culture, art, human life itself, are all presented as the merest accidents of matter in movement and devoid of substantial reality."[20]

The fundamental tenet of Marxism, in effect, is its interpretation of history according to which ideas, beliefs, and institutions of a given time are the end result of, and depend on, the contemporary means of production and exchange. "In every historical epoch," Marx writes, "the prevailing mode of economic production and exchange, and the social organization necessarily following from it, form the basis upon which is built up, and from which alone can be explained the political and intellectual history of that epoch."[21] Every society, as Marx sees it, is made of two morphological levels: (1) infrastructure, which is constituted by the forces of production; and (2) superstructure to which pertain the departments of literature, art, jurisprudence, and religion. The former gives content to the latter. It follows that,

> The production of ideas and conceptions, of consciousness, is . . . directly interwoven with the material activity and the material intercourse of men, language of real life. Men's conceptions, thoughts, spiritual intercourse, here still appear as the direct emanation of their material conduct. The same holds for spiritual production, as represented in the languages of the politics, laws, morality, religion, metaphysics, etc., of a people. . . . In the social production of their subsistence men enter into *determined and necessary relations* with each other which are independent of their wills—production-relations which correspond to a definite state of development of their material productive forces. The sum of these production-relations forms the economic structure of society, the real basis upon which a juridical and political super-structure arises, and to which definite social forms of consciousness correspond. The mode of production of the material subsistence conditions the social, political and spiritual life-process in general. *It is not the consciousness of men which determines their existence, but on the contrary it is their social existence which determines their consciousness.* . . . As little as one thinks of himself, so little can one judge such an epoch of transformation by its consciousness; one must rather explain this consciousness by the *contradictions of the material life*, the conflict at hand between the social forces of production and the relations in which production is carried on. No social formation ever disappears before all the productive forces are developed for which it has room, and new higher relations of production never appear before the material conditions of their existence are matured in the womb of the old society.[22]

This, then, is historic materialism, the end product of Voltaire's "enlightened" reason. It is historic because confined to historic processes alone; it is materialism because based on matter only as the final reality. Moreover, it is dialectic, that is, bearer of a special understanding of life, "the understanding," as Lenin puts it, "of evolution in its fullest, deepest and most universal aspect, the understanding of the relativity of human knowledge, which gives us a reflection of eternally evolving matter." [23]

The inference to which all of history leads is, in Marx' belief, the class struggle. The modes of production in past history have always divided society into two antagonistic classes, the one exploiting the other. "The history of all hitherto existing society," he declares, "is the history of class struggle." [24] In modern times the two classes are respectively the capitalists (the "exploiters"), that is, the owners of the productive forces, and the proletariat (the "exploited") or the working class. How does exploitation take place? To secure their sustenance, Marx answers, labor is compelled to perform extra hours of work which are not paid for by the capitalists. This is possible, Marx explains, on account of the fact that labor power can be compared to a merchandise sold by the worker to the capitalist contractor. Of course, the payment (or wages) the worker receives for it should be equal to the exact value of working hours necessary to the production of that merchandise, that is, the number of hours necessary to the achievement of the worker's means of subsistence. Let us assume, for example, that eight hours of labor are necessary to keep up the man's ability of producing; normally the capitalist should make him work eight hours and pay him for as many. Actually he does pay him for eight hours of work, but at the same time makes him work longer, for instance, ten hours. Thus, the value created by the worker, the value of manufactured products is superior to the wages received by the worker. The difference constitutes the surplus-value, that is, the capitalist's unwarranted profit. Hence the struggle between the two classes. This is a growing struggle, Marx says, because, on the one hand, it is gradually attaining international proportions, and on the other, the proletariat is being more and more aware of its exploited status.

It follows that capitalism is preparing the scourge of its own perdition. Internal contradictions undermine the economic structure of bourgeoisie. The most grave of these lies in the tension between the collective means of production and individual appropriation. In the Middle Ages the forces of production were relatively feeble so that the instruments of production naturally belonged to the producer. With the spread of mechanization, however, the great industry superseded the small enterprise, and production became collective since the modern plant demands the

264

cooperation of a great number of hands. Meanwhile, the owner-ship of the means of production still remains under the control of a few individual capitalists. "In one word," Marx writes, "for exploitations veiled by religious and political illusions, [the bourgeoisie] has substituted naked, shameless, direct, brutal exploitation."[25]

Fortunately, the predicament of labor is not final. There are norms in history which slowly but ineluctably work out the vindication of the proletariat. Marx construes them in terms of three successively developing economic laws. The first he calls the law of capitalistic accumulation. In virtue of this law, there is in the capitalist-workman relationship a straight connection between the paid and the unpaid labor: surplus-value increases in direct proportion to the increase in number of workers. In other words, the greater the capital, the greater the surplus-value; conversely, the greater the surplus-value the greater the capital.

Accumulation of capital results in a greater productivity. The working class, however, is in no positon to buy all the goods it has produced because wages are inferior to the actual value of its work. The visible consequence of this difference issues in the rupture of the equilibrium between production and consumption. Economic crises follow necessarily from it and, in turn, further the absorption of small enterprises by powerful capitalist consortia. Thus the law of capitalist accumulation gives way to the second economic law which Marx terms the law of capitalistic concentration. In his words,

> With the increasing mass of wealth which functions as capital, accumulation increases the concentration of that wealth in the hands of individual capitalists. . . . This means concentration of capitals already formed, destruction of their individual independence, expropriation of capitalist by capitalist, transformation of many small into few large capitals. . . . Capital grows in one place to a huge mass in a single hand, because it has in another place been lost by many.[26] . . . [But] the laboring class, under the domination of capitalism, receives only a part of the values which the former produces; the difference, therefore, between what the laborers are able to consume, and what they should consume in order that all commodities produced be disposed of, constantly

265

increases owing to the continuation of the developmental process in question, which is continually augmenting the production.[27]

Production, however, cannot be stopped: it must continue, Marx says, whether a market be available or not, in order to prevent the depreciation of the value of the vast network of productive plants. This inevitably leads to the irremediable upset of the balance between production and consumption. Eventually, economic crises will end in the liberation of the working class and its triumph over the capitalist exploiters. Marx' third law reads precisely in this sense: the inevitable victory of the proletariat. He expresses it as follows,

> The development of Modern Industry . . . cuts from under its feet the very foundation on which the bourgeoisie produces and appropriates products. What the bourgeoisie therefore produces, above all, are its own grave diggers. Its fall and the victory of the proletariat are equally inevitable.[28]

The banner of the new society, according to Marx' illusory dream, will be: "From each according to his abilities, to each according to his needs." Conclusion: "Working men of all counttries, unite! The proletarians have nothing to lose but their chains. They have a world to win." [29] At this point Voltairianism has turned irrational, and philosophy of history taken the shape of a dangerous utopia.

3. *History interpreted through the awareness of the "historical."* The interpretation through direct participation in a historic order and through divorce from it are alike unfavorable to the elaboration of a true philosophy of history. Neither the static historic thought of Greece nor Voltaire's critical history, nor yet historic criticism that developed after him, have been able to explain the mystery of the religious phenomenon. The latter two did not understand or solve the problem of Christianity. They rendered a real service in gathering all sorts of material and expanding historical information, but, in Berdyaev's judgment, there seemed to be no understanding or vision of the essentials. Only an interpretation of history through the awareness of the "historical" is auspicious to the consideration of the problems of the phi-

266

losophy of history. The third type alone has the grasp of the "historical" and the mysteries of being and life. But what is the "historical"?

To comprehend the meaning of the "historical" as well as Berdyaev's entire philosophy of history, it should be constantly kept in mind that for him reality is not phenomenal but noumenal. History is connected with the realm of spirit not with the sphere of natural and social life—the latter being merely a reflection of the former. Of course, material forces and economic factors do play an important part in human history, yet these forces and factors are themselves based upon a deeper spiritual foundation. The "historical," therefore, is the spiritual reality behind the phenomena—the "historical reality," as Berdyaev terms it, of the spirit in a particular period of existence. In his words,

> It is . . . impossible to regard the 'historical' as a reality of a material, psychological or geographical order. It is likewise unthinkable to consider historical reality in terms of any psychic reality. The 'historical' has its peculiar and specific nature; it is a reality of a particular kind.[30]

> I believe that history and the 'historical' are not merely phenomena, that they are . . . noumena. The historical in the real sense of the word brings with it the revelation of essential being, of the inner spiritual nature of the world and of the inner spiritual essence of man, and not merely of the external phenomena. . . . The 'historical' is a sort of revelation of the deepest essence of universal reality, of the destiny of the world focused in that of man. It is a revelation of noumenal reality.[31]

Accordingly, the philosophy of history is "one of the ways to the knowledge of spiritual reality."[32] This knowledge, however, cannot be acquired by means of historic criticism or the study of historic sources such as monuments, scriptures, and archeological data. These only serve to divorce man from history, making the two mutually exclusive and incomprehensible. History regarded as sheer phenomena, is a history imposed from outside, it is hostile and alien to the human being. Berdyaev suggests a different way to the understanding of the historic process—the way of integration of personal destiny with the history of mankind. He writes,

In the destiny of mankind I must recognize my own destiny, and in the latter that of history. This is the only way in which we can commune with the mystery of the "historical" and discover in it the great spiritual destinies of mankind. And, inversely, this is the only way in which we can realize all the riches and values of our possession and unite our own individual destiny with that of universal history instead of merely discovering the void of our isolation in opposition to all the riches of universal historical life. Thus the real goal of the philosophy of history is to establish a bond between man and history, between man's destiny and the metaphysics of history.[33]

I must have a sense of . . . history as something that is deeply *mine,* that is deeply *my* history, that is deeply *my* destiny. I must situate myself within historical destiny and it within my own human destiny. The presence of the historical destiny then becomes revealed in the very depths of the human spirit. All historical epochs, from the very earliest to that at the topmost peak of modern history, represent my historical destiny; they are all mine.[34]

But how is this possible? How is such total integration realizable? How is the historical reality behind the phenomena to be attained? To grasp the inner life of history, Berdyaev proposes the following five procedures: development of self-consciousness, inner remembrance, prophecy, tradition and myth. We shall now offer a short explanation for each of them.

a) *Development of Self-Consciousness.* Each man, Berdyaev says, is not a minute and separate fragment of the universe, but a world in his own right—a microcosm—in which the whole of reality and of history combine and co-exist. He must discover within himself the deep strata of the historic process by a continuous development in depth of self-consciousness. Only deep down in his own self can man really discover the existence of all the great historic epochs and absorb their meaning. A historian should be able to apprehend within himself the level, for example, of Greek or Jewish history before attempting to interpret its essential nature.

b) *Inner Remembrance.* The apprehension of history within one's self thus made possible by the development of self-consciousness is further realized by a particular kind of awareness which

Berdyaev calls inner remembrance. This is not to be equated with the memory of events. The knowledge of historic events is not sufficient for the comprehension of history. Inner remembrance must be understood in the Platonic sense. Plato's souls "remembered" the ideas they had known prior to their earthly birth. Inner remembrance has the qualitative value of the essential union of the knowing subject with the historic object. It is the intuitive knowledge of man's prehistoric spiritual existence whereby the past becomes an integral constituent of the present. It is the link that existentially connects the present with the past—the existential present of the self with the existential past of the world.

c) *Prophecy.* The present is related not only to the past: it is also linked to the future. But how? By means of prophecy. Prophecy, on Berdyaev's terms, is not foretelling the future. Rather, it is the vision which apprehends things present in the light of their eternal issues. It is dynamic, not static; unconditioned, not determined. As he writes,

> Prophecy . . . interpreted in the widest sense, represents the mystery of transcendent time, the mystery of man's emancipation from its yoke, the mystery of his conquest of the eternal present and of his communion with it. It reveals the mystery of existence, that of the future as an integral part of this existence. The eternal present thus revealed is not a static present, but one in the process of incessant creation outside the frontiers of disintegrated time.[35]

> History is in truth the path to another world. It is in this sense that its content is religious. . . . In its perpetual transition from one epoch to another, mankind struggles in vain to resolve its destiny within history. Disappointed in its expectations, feeling itself imprisoned within the circle of history, it realizes that its problem cannot be solved within the process of history itself, but only on a transcendental plane.[36]

d) *Tradition.* The existential experiences both of the past and of the future within the everlasting present fathers the formation of tradition. Historic tradition, according to Berdyaev, is precisely the embodiment of the intuitive apprehension of the inner mysterious life of the spirit beyond time and space. This does not mean to imply that all historic traditions are equally genuine and acceptable in regard to their content. Historic criticism is right in questioning their pretensions and not taking for granted their own valuations. Berdyaev's argument is that the inner value of historic tradition does not depend upon fables such as that, for example, of Romulus and Remus. "The tradition of a people is valuable in so far as it symbolizes the historic destiny of that people."[37] Real historic tradition reflects the historic undercurrent of mankind whose flow no external course of events can intercept. "Tradition is synonymous with the knowledge of historic life; for its symbolism reveals the inner life and the profound organic union of historical reality with that which man discovers through his own spiritual self-knowledge."[38]

e) *Myth*. The historic tradition usually assumes the form of a myth. "A myth," Berdyaev writes, "contains the story that is preserved in popular memory and that helps to bring to life some deep stratum buried in the depths of the human spirit."[39] Myth, it was previously noted, is no fiction, but a reality. It expresses, however, a different type of reality from that of the fact objectively perceived. Rather it is the disclosure of the significance of facts. Significance alone is important; facts as such are relatively irrelevant. From this point of view, Berdyaev says, myths offer a more truthful presentation of reality than objective statements. Indeed, myth allows the break through the surface of events into the depth of ultimate "historical reality."

Assuming the above mentioned five mutually related procedures of inducing the penetration of the "historical" are valid, the question still remains whether a philosophy of history is actually possible on those presuppositions. Berdyaev's answer is in the affirmative. Ancient Israel, he points out, conceived history in precisely such terms. "It was the Jews," he writes, "who contributed the concept of the 'historical' to world history, thereby discharging, in my opinion, the essence of their specific mission."[40] Old Testament prophetism developed the idea of the progressive unfolding of history from the beginning of the world situated in time and space to a purposive end beyond temporal and spatial dimensions. The call of Abraham as the founder of a chosen nation; the Exodus from Egypt; the covenant between Yahweh and his people; Israel's disobedience and punishment; the Babylon captivity; the

270

promise that a remnant shall return from the Exile from whom a messianic king will arise; that in the last day, the day of judgment, all Yahweh's enemies will be destroyed and his house established on Zion forever with peace and justice for all nations. To ancient Israel, obviously, God reveals himself not only in nature but also, and more fundamentally, in history and through history as a whole.

The Book of Daniel in particular, Berdyaev observes, represents an interpretation of history through the awareness of the mysteries of the "historical." In it the writer conceives history not so much in terms of Palestine, but rather as a whole. The history of Israel is not fully significant in itself but finds its true meaning in relation to the great neighboring empires. Yet even the latter gain significance only when seen in connection with the history of the peoples who preceded them and who will come after them. The unfolding of history is not fortuitous. As empire succeeds empire on the stage of time, each fulfills a God-given mission thus concurring to the final realization of the divine purpose. Daniel's apprehension of history, according to Berdyaev, intimates that he discovered the sense of the "historical" first within the depths of his own self-consciousness through inner remembrance which furnished him with insight into the past, and through prophecy which **revealed to him the vision** of the future. Moreover, he embodied his intuition in the form of a historic tradition which attributed a design to events and a meaning to their occurrences; and he used the language of myth to depict the dramatic process of "historical reality." The Book of Daniel summed up and brought to a climax the historic conception of ancient Israel. The Hebrews, in Berdyaev's words,

> were the first to conceive the world as historical fulfillment in contradistinction to the cyclic process of the Greeks. For the ancient Hebrews the idea of fulfillment was always closely allied to that of Messianism. The Jewish consciousness, unlike that of the Greeks, always aspired towards the future; it lived in the intense expectation of some great decisive event in the destinies of Israel and of other peoples. . . . For the Jews the idea of history turns upon the expectation of some future event which will bring with it a solution of history. . . . [They conceive] history as tragedy.[41]

271

Dynamic, tragic, prophetic, messianic, and eschatological—such is the Old Testament philosophy of history. Christianity will develop its own understanding of history along similar trends of thought.[42]

Berdyaev's first two types of historic interpretation and the third might respectively be compared with Reinhold Niebuhr's understanding of history. The American theologian construes the history of mankind in terms of the presence or absence within it of messianic expectation. Where Christ is not expected, history, according to him, is either "reduced to nature" as with the Stoics, or "swallowed up in eternity" as with Plato and Plotinus. In both cases there is "no expectation of a Christ, no Messianic hope. . . . There is no necessity or possibility . . . of a fuller revelation of the ultimate sovereignty of life in history and therefore of a fuller disclosure of the meaning of life." [43] Where Christ is expected, history is envisaged in the perspective either of a false messianism, "the egoistic-nationalistic" or "the ethical-universalistic," or of a true, that is, prophetic messianism which apprehends history "as a universal whole," and God "as the sovereign of all peoples." [44] Only the latter, Niebuhr affirms, represents the Christian point of view.

2. THE NATURE OF HISTORY AND OF TIME

Berdyaev stresses the point that it was Christianity which actually formulated a real philosophy of history by ripening the insights gained in the Old Testament and blending them with the New Testament apprehension of history. Christianity, in his view, envisages history under three main aspects. Those are the following:

a) *History is dynamic.* It is the scene of growth and development. It is movement and progression. It has a moment of departure and a point of arrival. History is concerned not with a static, abstract being, but rather with a living, dynamic becoming. The Bible finds in the world no rigidity or immutability; it regards it as a plastic world of action and change. Historic dynamism is connected with the idea of immediacy and uniqueness of events. History is the course of the spontaneous, unusual and non-recurrent.

272

It admits of the impossible and unpredictable. A miracle is precisely the Biblical category for the extraordinary event. Such an understanding of history ranks at the opposite pole from that of the Greek philosophers who conceived the world as a finite and harmonious cosmos ruled by law and order. The Hellenic world acknowledged only the usual, the possible, and the predictable. Aristotle's aesthetical and indifferent "unmoved mover," standing aloof from human concerns, had absolutely nothing in common with the mighty and energetic "Lord of hosts" who is so intimately involved in the affairs of men. While the Greeks lived in a world of the ordinary, Christianity placed an unusual event in the very center of history—the revelation of Christ. History, in Berdyaev's words, "both ends and begins with the fact of Christ's Revelation. This fact determines both the profound dynamism of history and its movement towards and away from the heart of universal history." [45]

b) *History is tragic.* Christianity conceives the world process in terms of crisis and catastrophe. It is a perennial tragedy. History is dramatic. It is not a slow, gradual continuity after a Darwinian pattern; it proceeds rather by mutations, bounds, and unpredictable upsets. The tragic interpretation of history postulates a central fact—that of freedom. As Berdyaev writes,

> Christianity first introduced that conception of freedom which had been ignored by the Hellenic world but which was essential to the building up of the idea of history and of its philosophy. It is impossible to conceive history without such an understanding of freedom, which centers on history its dramatic and tragic character, the tragedy of free action, evil and darkness. This fact determines the dramatic conflict and movement of history, unsuspected by the Hellenic mind with its view of good, beauty and truth as divinely essential. But because it first acknowledged that the eternal can have a temporal fulfillment, Christianity brought us the contribution of both history and its idea.[46]

The temporal fulfillment of the eternal is to Berdyaev the revelation wrought in Christ—the revelation of a suffering God who yearns for the return of His fallen children and whose outpouring love, forever frustrated, awaits always with hope; but it is also the revelation of man who longs for communion with his Creator, but whose meonic freedom—the irrational principle in him—always present, unfailingly prevents the ultimate human-divine encounter. Without the uncreated freedom, independent of both natural and divine necessity, there would be no drama of history, no tragic development of events expressing the tension and strife between God and man. "There would be no universal history without the freedom of the human spirit conceived as an autonomous principle . . . and one that is both irrational and unfathomable." [47] But the fact that history is grounded in freedom makes it an arena of trial, crisis, and catastrophe.

c) *History is eschatological.* History moves toward a final goal. Historic progression is not endless; it issues in fulfillment and termination. "No conception of history is feasible without the idea of fulfillment because history is essentially eschatological." [48] The meaning of history is bound up with the end. If there were no end, no conclusion to the historic matter, that is, if life in our world continued forever, history would have no meaning. It would appear only as an endless, and therefore senseless, flux of occurrences in time. Meaning lies beyond the confines of time, and its discovery presupposes an end of time. "Without this sense of an end, the process cannot be conceived as historical movement. Without this eschatological perspective progression cannot be considered as history for it lacks inner purpose, significance and fulfillment." [49] Eschatology is the revelation of the purpose and significance of history.

History is related to time. To speak of history is to visualize events evolving in a stream of time—decades, centuries, millennia, eras. The philosophy of history, according to Berdyaev, is to a large extent the philosophy of time. Indeed, the one defines the nature of the other. For history which is essentially change indicates that time also is the effect of change and *vice versa.* In his words,

> Time exists because there is activity. . . . But this activity . . . is discontinuous and disintegrated; it has no roots in eternity. Time is the product of *changing* realities, beings, existences. Time can therefore be transcended. The degraded time of our world is the outcome of the Fall that occurred in

the depths of existence. It is the product of objective processes, of an objective, disintegrated and determined world.[50]

Activity and disintegration, then, are the two polar causes of time. For this reason Berdyaev's interest in time is neither metaphysical nor mathematical; he envisages it exclusively in relation to the problem of human destiny. The important question, on his terms, is not to know what time is, but how it should be construed in regard to history. Berdyaev comprehends the relation between the two as threefold. Accordingly, he distinguishes three forms of time: cosmic, historical, and existential. History presupposes all three.

a) *Cosmic time.* This is symbolized by the circle. The motion of the earth on its axis; the revolution of the planets about the sun; the succession of the seasons through the year and of hours round the clock: all these represent a circular movement constantly repeated. This is nature's time, subject to measurements and division. Hellenic philosophic speculation was primarily concerned with the apprehension of cosmic time. To Plato time is created by God after the pattern of motionless eternity. It is the "moving image of eternity," and is closely connected with the circular motions of the heavens. Eternity "rests in unity," but the image "revolves according to a law of number."[51] Aristotle defines time as "number of movement in respect of the before and after."[52] The boundary separating the past movement from the future is made up of endlessly moving nows. Contrary to Plato who seems to identify time with the astral revolutions, Aristotle apparently interprets it as different from, but not independent of, movement. He describes the one as the attribute of the other. But since "we perceive movement and time together"[53] Aristotle's time is barely anything else than the recurrent cosmic time.

Both the objectivized world and man as natural being are subject to the rhythm of cosmic time—past, present, and future; and also to its law of final alternative—birth and death. Cosmic time, as Berdyaev puts it,

> inevitably leads on to death. . . .Natural life, cosmic life in natural cosmic time rests upon the alternating change of birth

and death. It knows a periodic spring of the revival of life, but the revival takes place not for those whom death has carried away, but for others. Victory over death is impossible in cosmic time. The present, which cannot be seized because it falls between the past and the future, annihilates the past in order to be itself annihilated by the future. In cosmic time, the realm of life is subject to death, although the engendering power of life is inexhaustible. Cosmic time is death-dealing not for the race but for personality; it desires no knowledge of personality and takes no interest in its fate.[54]

Spengler's historical thought moves precisely on this cosmic plane. To him history is a cyclic movement of various cultures construed as distinct organisms independent from each other. As any living organism, "every culture," in his words, "passes through the age-phases of the individual man. Each has its childhood, youth, manhood, and old age." [55] After all the inner potentialities of a culture have been developed, it becomes a *gestalt*—a closed organic unity which is understandable to none but itself. There are no eternal historic truths. Knowledge is relative to the given culture. History is not one linear continuity but "the drama of a number of mighty cultures . . . each stamping its material, its mankind, in its own image; each having its own idea, its own passions, its own life, will and feeling, its own death." [56]

Regarding in particular the Western or, as he calls it, the Faustian culture, Spengler distinguishes four stages in its cyclical development.[57] The first, which he calls spring, dates from the tenth to fourteenth century. Here belong Bernard of Clairvaux, Joachim of Floris, Francis of Assisi, the legends of Siegfried, the theology of Thomas Aquinas, and the poetry of Dante. This is the period of great intellectual and artistic creativity of the newly awakened Faustian soul, that of Giotto, Gothic cathedral, and mysticism. Next follows summer from the fifteenth to seventeenth century. This is the age of the Reformation, that is, the age of Huss, Luther, and Calvin; of Savonarola, French Jansenists, and English Puritans. This is also the age of philosophy and science dotted with such brilliant minds as those of Galileo, Bacon, Descartes, Bruno, Leibnitz, and Pascal. In architecture this is the reign of the baroque; in sculpture and painting—of Leonardo,

Raphael, Michelangelo, Titian, and Rembrandt. In music—of Orlando Lasso and *tutti quanti* to Heinrich Schütz. The cultural summer is generally characterized by the ripening of human consciousness.

Then comes autumn which is the season of great philosophical systems. Spengler identifies it with the eighteenth century Age of Enlightenment represented by such thinkers as Locke, Voltaire, and Rousseau; Schelling, Hegel, and Fichte; and such artists as Goethe, Bach, and Mozart. It is the season of prolific city creativity. But soon arrives winter—the last stage of Western culture. The nineteenth and twentieth century mark the decline of the West. In it spiritual creative forces decay into extinction. The touch with the primary realities of life is being lost. There is no more sense of blood, or race, or soil. Religious depth-experience as manifested in Gothic cathedrals is now superseded by a mock-religiosity exemplified by occultism, theosophy, and Christian Science. Eventually every trace of form and style will disappear. A new primitivism will gradually pervade the whole of human life and activity. Superstition and penchant for the mysterious and the supernatural will take over true religion and science. A rhythmic period of the cosmic time will come to completion. And this will be the end of the West.

b) *Historical time.* This is symbolized by a straight horizontal line stretching out forward into the future. Inasmuch as it can be reckoned in months, years, and centuries, historical time is subject to cosmic time, but because its onward movement is directed by human activity it escapes to a certain extent the determinism of circular recurrence. Historical time is linked with the past thanks to memory. Its distinctive characteristic, however, is looking forward into what is coming. "It waits for the disclosure of a meaning" [58] in the perspective of the future. Unlike cosmic time, historical time is irreversible. For this reason, it admits of newness and uniqueness. "Every event in historical time is individually particular, every decade and century introduces new life." [59] But historical time also enslaves man, although in a different way. It constantly lures him to escape from an intolerable present either into complacency of the past or the utopia of the future. In Berdyaev's words,

Historical time gives birth to illusions; the search in the past for what is better, truer, more beautiful, more perfect (the illusion of the conservative) or the search in the future for the fulness of achievement and the perfection of meaning (the illusion of progress). Historical time is time which is torn to pieces. It does not find completeness in any kind of present (the past and the future are always a kind of present at the same time). In the present man does not feel the fullness of time, and he seeks it in the past or in the future, especially in periods of history which are transitional and full of suffering. This is the seductive illusion of history. The present in which there is fullness and perfection is not a part of time, but an emergence from time, not an atom of time, but an atom of eternity.[60]

To historical time belong the utopias of a terrestrial paradise, characteristic of the Age of Enlightenment and Marxism with their beliefs that history progressively moves from evil toward good, and from suffering toward happiness. But, Berdyaev says, "there is no such thing in history as simple progress in human happiness. There is only progress in the tragic sense of the inner principles of being . . . of good and evil in collaboration. The fundamental significance of mankind's historical destiny resides in this antithesis and in its manifestation." [61]

Hegel's interpretation of history is, according to Berdyaev, a classical illustration of historical time. He sees history as "a continuous disclosure of spirit." [62] The Hegelian universe, in effect, is pictured as a dynamic manifestation of the Absolute Idea or Ultimate Reality, in the process of self-realization from a state of unconscious potentiality to a state of conscious actuality. The Absolute Idea, in Hegel's thought, is the sum of all reality without qualification, finitude, or partiality. It is simply that which *is*, Being, moving along a straight line through finite phenomena toward its fulfillment—its self-consciousness and freedom. History is the embodiment in time of the timeless Idea. The whole process is developing after a threefold dialectical pattern: thesis, antithesis, and synthesis. Hegel describes it as follows. Everything existent (reality, idea, situation) is thesis. But in virtue of its existence it necessarily presupposes a contrary thing (reality, idea, situation), that is, an antithesis; hence a painful contradiction. In order to escape from it, there must be assumed a third and higher thing (reality, idea, situation) in which thesis and antithesis are unified in a conciliatory synthesis. The new synthesis, however, is also a new thesis: it elicits therefore another antithesis and, consequently, a fresh effort toward the next synthesis. The process repeats itself endlessly until the Absolute Reality achieves complete realization.

The tragic irony of historical time, Berdyaev points out, is exhibited in the pitiful end-product of Hegel's idealism. To him the perfect way leading to spiritual self-consciousness and freedom is none other than the State. Individuals are nothing, the State is everything. Men cannot even exist without it. The State, in Hegel's words, "constitutes their existence, their being." [63] The German thinker shows no interest in common people. His enthusiasm is aroused exclusively by the great heroes of history, the "world historic individuals" such as Alexander, Caesar, and Napoleon because they are the embodiment of the Absolute marching forward into a victorious future. But ultimately, Berdyaev observes, both heroes and ordinary folk are "but a means to the triumph of the common and the universal." [64]

To avoid the deadly consequences of cosmic and historical times, Berdyaev suggests a re-orientation of thought toward the third form of time.

c) *Existential time.* This is symbolized by the point, which implies movement in depth. It cannot be measured or extended or divided. It is not susceptible to exteriorization or objectivation. It is wholly inward and subjective. It is qualitative not quantitative. However, it must not be understood as completely isolated either from cosmic or from historical time. Existential time is "the irruption of eternity into . . . cosmic and historical time." [65] It is also the fulfillment of the eternal in the framework of the temporal. As Berdyaev explains,

> It would be untrue to say that existential time is identical with eternity, but it may be said that it is a participant in several moments of eternity. Every man knows from his own inward experience that he is a participant in several of his own moments of eternity. The protraction of existential time has nothing in common with the protraction of objectivized

279

time, cosmic or historical. This protraction depends upon the intensity of experience within human existence. Minutes which are short from the objective point of view may be lived through as an infinity, and an infinity in opposite directions, in the direction of suffering and in the direction of joy and triumphant rapture. Every state of ecstasy leads out from the computation of objectivized mathematical time and leads into existential qualitative infinity. One moment may be eternity, another moment may be an evil and repellent endlessness. . . . The greater part of men's life is unhappy and is, therefore, chained to mathematical time. Suffering is a phenomenon of the existential order, but it is objectivized in mathematical time and appears to be infinite in the quantitative sense of the word.[66]

It is within this time that the exalting creative impulse takes place and ecstasy is achieved. "Every creative act is performed in existential time and is merely projected in historical time." [67] Within it also flourishes the messianic prophetic consciousness which "out of the depth of existential time speaks about historical time." [68] The revelation of God in history belongs to it. Indeed, the redemption wrought in Christ moves in existential time. This is Scriptural. Referring to the God-chosen time in offering salvation to mankind through the instrumentality of His Son, the New Testament uses a special term for it —kairos which conveys a distinct meaning from that of aion, another expression for time employed by the apostolic writers. Commenting on the semantic difference between the two, Oscar Cullman writes: "The characteristic thing about kairos is that it has to do with a definite point of time which has a fixed content, while aion designates a duration of time, a defined or undefined extent of time." [69] Tillich likewise voices the opinion that the use of the word kairos—the right time— "makes it a main category of the New Testament interpretation of history. Time has a direction, periodization, qualitative differences, by the very fact of having a kairos." [70]

Man's life, Berdyaev observes, is connected with all three forms of time—cosmic, historical, and existential. But it is only in proportion as he plows the way, through his creativity, for the establishment of the Kingdom, that the final victory of existential time over the cosmic and historical will be accomplished. This also will signify the end of time and the passage of history "into the realm of the freedom of the spirit." [71]

The Christian philosophy of history, he believes, moves precisely on such a plane.

3. THE CHRISTIAN PHILOSOPHY OF HISTORY

Basic to the Christian conception of history, according to Berdyaev, is the hypothesis that history is bound up not only with earth, but also with heaven; not only with man, but also with God. History is both terrestrial and celestial; human and divine; phenomenal and noumenal. Cosmic and historical times manifest the former; existential time discloses the latter. Christian revelation bridges the two, and at the same time points to the end of history.

Accordingly, we shall consider Berdyaev's view on history in the following order: (1) Celestial History; (2) Terrestrial History; (3) History Liberated; and (4) The End of History.

1. *Celestial History.* Berdyaev teaches that history begins with a prologue in heaven which "predetermines the terrestrial destiny of mankind." [72] The prologue sets forth the theme for the entire subsequent process of history, namely, that of the relationship between God and man as it is revealed simultaneously both in man's spiritual experience and the world's historic events. The relationship discloses a mutual longing for each other. "The inner tragedy," Berdyaev writes, "of the love felt by God for His other self [that is, man] and its longing for reciprocal love constitutes that very mystery of the divine life which is associated with the creation of the world and of man." [73]

The drama of history is not only the drama of man but also that of God according to Berdyaev's mystical conception of a dynamic and suffering God, which we have already described in chapter one of the second part of the present work. It may be summarized as follows: both the divine Trinity and meonic freedom are realized in the *Ungrund*; thereupon God creates the world and man out of meonic freedom. Creation occurs within the realm of spirit not in the order of nature. The world of nature is the consequence of the Fall—of man's rebellion and hostility toward God. After the Fall, which likewise happened in the spiritual world, began man's destiny in nature. This is the subject-matter of study of such disciplines as biology, sociology, and psychology. The fallen man, however, is not solely the product of nature as is claimed by the evolutionary point of view. The theory of evolution, in Berdyaev's judgment, contains a great deal that is true in regard to man's origin and destiny in the world. But its main concern is with secondary, not primary processes. It throws no light on the primeval sources, which preceded the birth of our world of space and time, and on those processes of which sacred traditions of all great religions speak, and which only metaphysical knowledge can apprehend. Despite the Fall, man still remains the child of God. He belongs simultaneously to the world of nature and to the world of spirit. The Fall marked the passage of celestial history into terrestrial, and of spiritual man into natural. This passage is not easy to determine. One can notice such uneasiness in the world mythology and especially in the myths of the Bible, where the line of demarcation between the temporal and the eternal is not clearly drawn.

2. *Terrestrial History*. The philosophy of man's terrestrial destiny, Berdyaev declares, originates with the Jewish people. To him they represent the axis about which rotates the whole of world history. The destiny of the Jews, he maintains, has played the most significant role in the history of mankind. It was their religious consciousness, as noted above, which first grasped the reality of the "historical," and disclosed the work of God in history. No other contemporary people possessed a similar religious vision and foundation. In Berdyaev's words,

> The religious nature of the Jewish spirit contained a principle which was to determine its intensely historical character and destiny. A comparison between the Jewish religion and that of other pre-Christian pagan peoples confirms the contention that Jewish history represented the revelation of God in the historical destiny of humanity, while that of other pagan peoples represented the revelation of God in nature. This distinction between the foundation of the Jewish and pagan Aryan religions helps us to establish the historical character of the Jewish people.[74]

282

The pivot of Jewish religion is the messianic idea. Israel lived in expectation both of the Day of Judgment and of the Advent of the Messiah. But, Berdyaev remarks, the messianic expectation gave rise to a dualism in the Jewish religious consciousness: it looked forward not only to the coming of a heavenly Messiah, but also to the arrival of a terrestrial Messiah. In other words, its messianism was oriented, on the one hand, toward Christ, and on the other, toward Antichrist. As Berdyaev puts it,

> The dualism inherent in the Jewish messianic consciousness determined the fateful destiny of the Jews in so far as it combined the expectation of the true Messiah, the Son of God, Who was to appear among the Jews, and that of the false Messiah or Antichrist. As a result of this dualism the Jewish people, with the exception of a chosen few made up of the Apostles and a few early Christians, did not recognize the true Messiah. They failed to recognize and repudiated the Messiah in Christ.[75]

The rejection of Christ implies the negation of spiritual freedom and an attempt at establishing the Kingdom of God on earth. This falls back upon the idea that the problems of individual and social life must, at any cost, find their solution and fulfillment within the framework of terrestrial history. The attempt, however, inevitably resolves in compulsion. The inability of Israel to situate man's destiny in the perspective of eternal life, but only in that of its historic process on earth, has proved tragic both for the Jews and the rest of mankind. For earthly messianism always ends in political tyranny either of the "right" or of the "left." Marxism, Berdyaev notes, is the end product of the expectation of the false Messiah after the repudiation of the true one. And so are all other social and political utopias which expect to build an earthly paradise around a Caesar instead of founding it on God. Jewish dualistic messianic expectation is the source, Berdyaev writes,

> of the tragedy that was to oppose Judaism and Christianity: the Messiah was destined to come among the Jewish people and the Jewish people could not accept a crucified Messiah. The Jewish people had longed for the Messiah and prophesied concerning Him: but it finally repudiated Him because it could not accept Him in the role of a servant. Its expectation

had been of a king who would realize the kingdom of Israel on earth.[76]

The tragedy, however, is not of the Jewish people only; it is also that of the Christian world and, by repercussion, of the whole planet. The French writer Léon Bloy, whom Berdyaev quotes, summed up in his *Le salut par les Juifs* the universal predicament as follows: "The Jews will be transformed only when Christ descends from the Cross, and Christ can descend from the Cross only when the Jews are transformed."[77] Christ was repudiated because he died on the Cross instead of destroying the evil and inaugurating an age of justice and blessedness in history. The same tragedy, Berdyaev observes, distorts Christianity itself. The main objection raised against Christianity is that it has not yet, after two thousand years of existence, abolished suffering or established justice on earth. This objection is related to the false messianism which does not see the impossibility of redeeming evil within the narrow limits of a single life-time, but tries to achieve fulfillment exactly in so many years. This can be done only in another life.

Berdyaev's judgment on the Jews in no wise spells anti-semitism. Without the Jews, he remarks, there would have been no Golgotha, and therefore no Christianity. "Hatred of the Jews is a non-Christian feeling."[78] Moreover, anti-semitism has not yet grasped the religious essence of the Jewish problem: its solution depends not on history, but solely on eschatology, on the final struggle between Christ and Antichrist.

Berdyaev's placing the beginning of history in a heavenly prologue and his insistence upon the axiological significance of the Jews in the history of the world are in many respects similar to the views of Augustine, though the two thinkers travel quite different roads. For the Bishop of Hippo history also originates in heaven. It begins on the first day of creation, before firmament and earth come into being: celestial history precedes the terrestrial. In the light of the first day Augustine sees the creation of angels by whom the foundations of the City of God are laid. This is the spiritual city of blessedness and felicity. Some among the angels, however, "having turned away from this light, have not won this wise and blessed life."[79] This resulted in the celestial Fall of bad

284

angels which later was followed by the terrestrial Fall of Adam.

The two cities, that of the first day of creation and that of the Fall—the heavenly and the earthly—have been, in Augustine's words, "formed by two loves: the earthly by the love of self, even to the contempt of God; the heavenly by the love of God, even to the contempt of self." [80] Both cities are coexisting within the limits of terrestrial history. They grow and progress together until the last judgment when the earthly city, the city of wickedness, will be sent to its eternal doom, and the City of God, the city of the saints, to its eternal beatitude. The City of God is represented, before Christ, by the Jews; after Christ, by the Church. Thus Augustine traces the progress of the City of God from Abel to Abraham to David and Jesus in a straight-forward line of Israel's history comprising Moses, Solomon, Amos, Hosea, Micah, Isaiah, Jeremiah, Ezekiel, the post-exilic prophets, and Joseph the father of Jesus. For Augustine, as for Berdyaev, the Old Testament is an unfolding revelation of the City of God which culminates in the coming of Christ. For both authors it occupies a central position in regard to other nations and bears a universal significance for the life of the world. [81]

3. *History Liberated.* With the revelation of Christ something new and revolutionary conclusively entered history for the first time and forever affected it: the principle of freedom. Both the Greek and the Hebrew world ignored it. Hellenic thought stressed the primacy of reason, while Judaism worshiped the law. Both ended under the sway of historic necessity. Christianity alone, according to Berdyaev, postulated "the fulfillment of history through the agency of a free subject and spirit." [82] Such a fulfillment constitutes the essential nature of the Christian understanding of history and the greatest contribution of Christianity to the liberation of mankind from the domination of nature. As he puts it,

> The greatest contribution of Christianity, although it is not fully recognized by the Christian world, consisted in that it liberated man from the power of the baser elemental nature and demons. It did so through the agency of Christ and the mystery of Redemption. It rescued man forcibly from his immersion in elemental nature and revived his spirituality. It distinguished him from baser nature and set him up as an

independent spiritual being, freeing him from submission to the natural world and exalting him to the heavens. Christianity alone restored the spiritual freedom of which man had been deprived by the power of demons, the natural spirits and elemental forces in the pre-Christian world. The essential contribution of Christianity therefore lay in that it liberated man and offered a free solution for human destiny.[83]

The consequences of the liberation, Berdyaev observes, are at first sight paradoxical. The repudiation by Christianity of the power of nature brought about its mechanization and stimulated the development of positive science and technique. "It is impossible," Berdyaev says, "to build railways, invent the telegraph or telephone, while living in fear of the demons."[84] It is true that the mechanical conception of the world launched a revolt against Christianity, but it is itself the result of the new religion which set man free from nature.

The main effect, however, of the historic rise and expansion of Christianity was the recognition of the "infinite value of the human soul, which is set above all the kingdoms of the world."[85] Man, no longer a part of nature, was lifted above it and enthroned as its lord and master. The "collective" man of the Old Testament was replaced by the "personal" man of the New Testament; the Old Adam was superseded by the New Adam. Christianity wakened mankind to the consciousness of the human personality and thus posed the problem of man's eternal destiny. "The development of the human personality," Berdyaev asserts, "constitutes the peculiar achievement of the Christian period of history."[86]

The change, according to him, was facilitated by two essential factors of the ancient world. First, the gradual spiritual and material unification of the pagan East and West on the basis of religious syncretism. The universalism of the Roman Empire paved the way for the spread of Christianity. Second, the fall of Rome which established the proof of the Christian doctrine of the original Fall. The decline and collapse of the ancient world was no accident, but the consequence of an inner disease. It was the visible manifestation of fallen human nature; and it brought out the profound truth of "the instability and fragility of all terrestrial things and cultural achievements."[87] It taught the lesson that each culture, each achievement contains the seed of its own destruction.

Following Spengler, Berdyaev draws a distinction between culture and civilization. He construes culture as the matrix of new spiritual values. It is a living process, he says, an active organism, a principle of life. Civilization is the material fulfillment of culture, its objectivation. But it is also its petrification tolling the approaching end. Berdyaev subscribes to Spengler's judgment that civilization is "the inevitable *destiny* of the Culture,"[88] its conclusion and death. Civilization necessarily follows culture; it is a phase of historic existence. "Culture," he writes, "having lost its soul, becomes civilization. Spiritual matters are discounted; quantity displaces quality."[89]

Berdyaev likewise discards the doctrine of progress in a direct line, and holds that every culture has its stages of birth, flowering, and decay. Unlike the German philosopher, however, he does not believe that cultures are independent organic wholes without inner continuity of correspondence. On the contrary, he maintains that all cultures possess an eternal principle which they successively transmit one to another. Thus Roman law and Greek art and philosophy are still alive in the Western civilization. Moreover, Berdyaev does not think that the end of a culture should be equated with its death; nor that it should inescapably assume the form of a catastrophe. The close of a culture, he feels, might also culminate in a religious transfiguration, that is, the passage to a higher plane of life—a spiritual plane where truth is realized in the experience of human-divine encounter. Berdyaev expects of Christianity the ushering into the world to come of precisely such a religious transfiguration.

Accordingly, he substitutes his own pluralistic and optimistic view on the historic destiny of the West for Spengler's seasonal and gloomy interpretation of the modern time. There are, Berdyaev declares, four stages in man's historic destiny after Christ: barbarism, culture, civilization, and religious transfiguration. Having discussed Berdyaev's classification in chapter six of the first part of the present work, we shall outline it here only by way of a reminder:

i) *Barbarism* (A.D. 7th to 9th century). This is the period of the Dark Ages in which the classical civilization was overcome and apparently annihilated by the barbarian invaders. The faith in God almost disappeared. Moreover, there occurred a rupture between the East and the West.

ii) *Culture* (A.D. 10th to 15th century). It was during this period that the new spiritual forces took shape and grew in potency. In the Middle Ages man's image was chiefly defined in terms of the monk and of the knight. Monachism and chivalry strengthened human personality, while Christian asceticism concentrated the spiritual forces and precluded their dispersion. The acme of Western Culture was expressed in the *Trecento*, the age of Francis of Assisi, Dante, and Giotto. Human freedom, however, was at the same time too bridled. Besides, the Church was imposing a theocratic ideal without realizing it. As to man, he did not know how to make use of freedom in order to assert his autonomy and attain the experience of his power and weakness alike.

iii) *Civilization* (A.D. 16th to 20th century). The Renaissance meant the bursting of a dam. Man's creative forces swept far and wide, and only in our own day did we comprehend the importance of the movement. Man desired to exercise his newly acquired freedom by setting himself free from God; what he achieved instead was the loss of freedom and, consequently, dehumanization. The process of secularization has passed through four stages: a) Sixteenth century Humanism and Reformation; b) Eighteenth century Enlightenment and French Revolution; c) Nineteenth century Positivism, Socialism, Marxism, and Anarchism; and d) Twentieth century Communism. The whole process has been activated by the introduction of the machine. Although the latter has, on the one hand, incontestably enriched man's life, yet, on the other, it has enslaved him as well. The West, Berdyaev affirms, is now entering the night of a New Middle Ages which will mark the end of both Capitalism and Communism.

iv) *Religious Transformation.* At the end of the secular and atheistic civilization, the World will experience a revival of religious faith so profound and soul-searching that it will bring about a radical change of the individual and social life. The new period will witness the establishment of the Church Ecumenical, Social Organic Fellowship, and International Universalism.

It should be noted that Berdyaev's historic progression has nothing of Spengler's organic determinism. The above four stages are not the product of necessity, but rather the outcome of man's inner dialectic freedom. A redirection of human freedom and creativity may, at any time, according to Berdyaev, alter the course of events and assign an unsuspected significance to history. Whether history be fulfillment or catastrophe is always determined by the kind of use man is making of his freedom.

Toynbee's thought is similar to that of Berdyaev in regard to human freedom. He, too, points out that the decline of civilizations always involves some mistake into which they are lured by their freedom, and not because of any principle of necessity. As his commentator puts it, "a society does not ever die 'from natural causes,' but always dies from suicide or murder—and nearly always from the former." [90] Sometimes societies perish because the leaders may become infected with the "mechanicalness of mimesis," that is, the passive imitation of the great and inspired originals, permissible only to the uncreative majority, and turn either truant or dominant. Sometimes the new social forces released by the creative minority find no adequate outlets. The old institutions prove unsuitable and intractable. One of two results may follow: either a revolutionary break-up of the institutions, or their survival and the consequent perversion of creativity working through them. The sins of omission—the "mechanicalness of mimesis" and the intractability of institutions—are not, however, the only reason of the breakdown of civilizations. The sins of commission—"the nemesis of creativity" —are, in Toynbee's belief, equally as dangerous for social survival. He equates them with idolatry of which, in his view, history shows three kinds: first, the idolatry of "an ephemeral self," that is, "an intellectually and morally blind worship of the creature instead of the Creator;" [91] second, the idolatry of "an ephemeral institution" as that of states, kings, parliaments, and ruling castes, whether bureaucracy or priesthood; and finally, the idolatry of "an ephemeral technique," an excessive concentration of a given society's faculties upon its characteristic specialization.

No civilization comes to an end, however, without some previous attempt at salvaging it. There are, according to Toynbee, two types of saviors: "of" and "from" a disintegrating society. In the former case, the would-be savior is a man of dominant minority—"the savior with the sword"—who, if successful, will become the founder of a transitory historic situation. In the latter, the would-be savior seeks salvation either in reconstructing the past (archaists), or in escaping into an imaginary future (futurists), or again in making speculative thought the ally of the throne after the Platonic pattern of the philosopher-king. Neither of them is a real savior. Only he, Toynbee concludes, who points the way to spiritual transfiguration can be hailed as the true savior. But this is no other than the Lord Jesus Christ. Quoting John 3:16,[92] Toynbee writes,

> This is in truth the final result of our survey of saviors. When we set out on this quest we found ourselves moving in the midst of a mighty host, but, as we have pressed forward, the marchers, company by company, have fallen out of the race. The first to fail were the swordsmen, the next the archaists and futurists, the next the philosophers, until only gods were left in the running. At the ordeal of death, few, even of these would-be savior gods, have dared to put their title to the test by plunging into the icy river. And now, as we stand and gaze with our eyes fixed upon the farther shore, a single figure rises from the flood and straightway fills the whole horizon. There is the Savior; 'and the pleasure of the Lord shall prosper in his hand; he shall see of the travail of his soul and shall be satisfied' (Isaiah 53:10-11).[93]

This is also Berdyaev's conclusion. He, too, looks forward into the future and sees the Savior amidst darkness as the only source of transfiguration of man and nature alike. "The light which shines from the Crucified is a light shining in the darkness. It is this light which both illuminates the obscurity of being and overcomes the darkness of non-being."[94]

3. THE END OF HISTORY

It was noted that Berdyaev holds history as having an end. And endless history would be meaningless. "History is in truth the path to another world."[95] The problem of individual destiny cannot be solved within the process of history itself: it requires a transcendental plane. Indeed, "man's historical experience has been one of steady failure and there are no grounds for supposing that it will ever be anything else. Not one single project elaborated within the historical process has ever proved successful."[96] French Revolution, Positivism, Socialism, Marxism, Anarchism, Capitalism, to name only a few modern political, scientific, and philosophic movements have fallen short of their goals and ideals. Even Christianity, Berdyaev says, is a failure in that for two thousand years it has not fulfilled the ideals of Christian faith. The failure of history and of Christianity, however, does not constitute an indictment against their validity and truth. Success and achievement in time cannot be taken as criteria of the true. Man's failure within the framework of historic process simply means that he "is destined to realize his potentialities in eternity, in conditions far more real than those which have so far hemmed in his efforts."[97]

The kingdom of God indicates not only redemption from sin and return to original purity, but the creation of a new world—a world where all man's creative possibilities will achieve their full expression. But this means that man must freely choose to respond creatively to the call of God. He must through his creative activity overcome the Fall in order to enter the new heaven. In Berdyaev's words,

> The slavery of man is his Fall, his sin. This Fall has its own structure of consciousness, it is conquered not only by repentance and redemption from sin, but by the activity of all the creative powers of man. When man does that to which he is called, then only will the Second Coming of Christ take place, and then there will be a new heaven and a new earth and the kingdom of freedom will come.[98]

Then terrestrial history once again will be integrated in the celestial thus bringing the prologue in heaven to its blissful angelic finale:

> New Strength have angels at the sight,
> Amazed at thy infinitude,
> And splendid as in primal light
> Are all thy mighty works renewed.[99]

And of this—God's—Kingdom there shall be no end.

CHAPTER VI

AN EVALUATION:
"MY WAYS ARE NOT YOUR WAYS"

> It is no longer I who live, but Christ
> who lives in me; and the life I now live
> in the flesh I live by faith in the Son
> of God.
>
> —Galatians 2:20

Berdyaev described his philosophy as "existential"[1] to indicate that his thought was rooted not in discursive reason, but in life experience. He never related himself, however, to any of the existential schools, and least of all to the atheistic variety represented by Jean-Paul Sartre which often is erroneously identified with existentialism *par excellence.* He shares in the basic conviction of all existentialists, namely, that existence precedes essence, but he differs from most of them in that he derives his primary insights into philosophy and religion mainly from Boehme, Khomyakov, and Dostoyevsky instead of Kierkegaard.

Existential philosophy permeates the whole of Berdyaev's thinking. Its starting point is not an abstract concept, but the concrete person. Without keeping this in mind one cannot undersand his teaching at all. To help, therefore, in performing an evaluation of his philosophical and theological work we shall turn briefly to the chief characteristics of his existentialism. Berdyaev affirms the primacy of subject in opposition to the object and the objective world. The subject alone exists and is truly real. The object is secondary, not real, but a mere symbol of reality. Subject is connected with the noumenal realm of spirit and freedom; object is related to the world of nature and determinism. Berdyaev, therefore, places personality, the existent subject, in extreme contrast to being which he regards as a product of thought. Being has no existence; only personality exists. Spirit can be experienced only in personality, in subject, not in being, in object. It follows that the former alone, not the latter, represents the criterion of truth.

Berdyaev's existentialism should in no way be confused with egocentricity. It is personalism, not individualism. "Personalism does not mean, as individualism does, an egocentric isolation." [2] Egocentricity and egoism are the product not of the personality, but of the Ego." [3] Ego is the enemy of personality. Indeed, the realization of personality necessarily involves the destruction of Ego. "Personality presupposes a going out from self to another and to others, it lacks air and is suffocated when left shut up in itself." [4] "The personal needs another. . . . Communion belongs to the realm of freedom and means liberation from slavery," [5] both to himself and the world.

Neither should Berdyaev's understanding of spirit be mistaken for subjectivism. It is not a state of individual consciousness, nor is it consciousness itself. Spirit is not subjective, although it exists in subject. Spirit is rather a reality transcending subject and independent from it; but at the same time it is immanent in subject whereby alone it can be apprehended. Spirit is freedom, and activity. It is opposed not to matter which, according to Berdyaev, possesses no "autonomous reality," [6] but to necessity of the objectified world which it attempts to set free by a process of transfiguration.

Since the world of objects is deprived of reality, the identification of the "objective" with the "real" as recognized in positivist world outlooks, is unwarranted and erroneous. It is, Berdyaev observes, precisely the result of objectivisation, namely, the substitution of symbols for the realities they are supposed to represent. In the process the world of natural objects, social institutions, and intellectual conceptions tend to become accepted as realities while true primal reality, that of spirit, is lost. For this reason scientific knowledge cannot discover the ultimate truth. Science deals exclusively with objects. In this respect it is justified and useful. But science has nothing to say about their meaning; this is imparted by the existential subject alone. Science is descriptive, not explanatory. It describes the order of becoming, not the source of being. It indicates means, not ends. It depicts the "how," not the "why" of things. The latter is found only by personality in a creative act. It is the true knowledge.

Berdyaev's epistemology, then, is anthropocentric, active, and existential. It is rooted in the concrete reality of life—spiritual not natural. This is so, in his judgment, because man, a spiritual being, is not alien to noumenal reality; on the contrary, he is wholly immersed in it. "I, the knower, abide in reality from the very first and am an inalienable part of it. I know reality in and through myself, as man. Only an existent can know existence."[7] Knowledge, therefore, is not merely a passive intellectual information "about something," but an intuitive dynamic "something,"[8] a creative spiritual experience involving man's whole self. It is an event within the existential subject revealing the reality of the spirit. It is a communion between the knower and the known. "Knowledge of truth is communion with truth and life in it."[9]

Such are, then, the distinctive characteristics of Berdyaev's thought. It is existential, personalistic, and intuitive. It presupposes activity and freedom. But first and foremost, it postulates the spirit as the alpha and omega of all that exists. We shall now, against the above outlined background, proceed to a critical appraisal of Berdyaev's teaching. We shall follow the pattern established in the second part of the present work, namely, 1) God; 2) man; 3) God-Man; 4) Ethics; and 5) Philosophy of History. We shall conclude by singling out Berdyaev's perennial contribution to Western and Christian thought.

1) *God.* We have seen that at the foundation of Berdyaev's world-view lay not an intellectual concept but a mystical intuition —the intuition of the unfathomable *Ungrund.* The term designates the Godhead, the *Mysterium Magnum* from which are realized both the triune God and Freedom. The creation of the world by God-the-Creator is a secondary act. In this regard three questions might be raised. First, is the mystical apprehension valid?

Second, what is the nature of creation? And third, is the idea of "uncreated freedom" Christian?

The first question apparently calls for an affirmative answer. Mysticism is too old and too common an experience to be dismissed as merely a psychological aberration or as the fruit of unbridled imagination. "Mysticism," writes Rufus M. Jones, "is as old as humanity, is not confined to any one racial stock, is undoubtedly one of the original grounds of personal religion."[10] As to the character of mysticism, the same writer defines it as an "immediate experience of a divine-human intercourse and relationship."[11] William James also believes that "personal religious experience has its root and centre in mystical states of consciousness."[12] In other words, "to be a mystic is simply to participate here and now in that real and eternal life."[13]

Two facts in connection with mysticism are undeniable, whatever it may be, and whatever part it is destined to play in the unveiling of truth and reality. On the one hand, it is the leading characteristic of some of the greatest religious personalities of the world—the founders of the Eastern Religions; Plotinus and Francis of Assisi; Eckhart and Bruno; Catherine of Siena and John of the Cross; Jacob Boehme and George Fox; Brother Lawrence, William Blake, and William Wordsworth. On the other, all the mystics, whatever their time, or personal, mental, and physical constitution, alike strongly declare that in their experiences they transcend the created world and attain direct knowledge of ultimate reality —namely, God.[14] Moreover, they all predicate God as the unity underlying diversity, as the *coincidentia oppositorum* in whom antitheses co-exist in a harmonious synthesis. This knowledge, they maintain, is based not on revelation, logic or reason, or demonstrated facts, but on intuitive, immediate apprehension of the divine in an I-Thou encounter.[15]

Berdyaev's religious existentialism is obviously mystical. To him, too, mysticism is the source of true religious knowledge. "Mysticism," he writes, "understood as a mode of knowledge rather than a finished product, has always exercised my imagination. I believe in the existence of a universal mystical experience."[16] This means "a penetration into the innermost recesses of the spiritual world, where . . . nothing is external to me, everything is in me and with me, within the depths of myself." [17] This knowledge is possible, he believes, because human nature is endowed with a godlike quality, namely, the spirit. As the intellect is given man to perceive natural things, so the spirit is given him to apprehend spiritual things. It is in and through the spirit that the human-divine encounter is made possible.

Berdyaev's attitude, I think, is both correct and Christian. Christianity has always been an inexhaustible source of mystical experience. The vast and uninterrupted flow of Christian mystics, and the compelling earnestness of their messages, bear witness to the authenticity of their basic ecstasies and visions. It might also be noted that Jesus' own psychology, as illustrated in the Gospels, is analogous to that of the mystics. "In its pains and splendors," writes Underhill, "its dual character of action and fruition, it reflects their experience upon the supernatural plane of more abundant life." [18]

Furthermore, is not the main point of Christian epistemology as a whole that we know incomparably more and better through faith, hope, and love than by means of intellect? And what else are the three New Testament virtues if not precisely the channels of intuitive cognition? Such cognition, or rather the possibility of it, is by no means the exclusive appanage of the mystics. I am inclined to think that each human being carries within himself the seed of mysticism. Of course, few undertake the continuous, painstaking training of will and spiritual concentration requisite in achieving an insight which could be identified as mystical. But the fact that all through the ages the rank-and-file of Christians have faithfully and repeatedly responded to the message of the mystics seems to prove the existence of an intimate kinship between the two groups.

Berdyaev, then, may definitely be placed in the category of the Christian mystics. He regarded himself primarily as a *homo mysticus* rather than a *homo religiosus*.[19] His awareness of God is founded on spiritual revelation first, and only then confirmed by the revelation in the Scriptures. It should be noted, however, that Berdyaev's mysticism is not of the monistic type so current both in Eastern and Western Christianity. He rejected the neoplatonic mysticism of the One which from Plotinus was carried over into

Christian life by Pseudo-Dionysius the Areopagite. Monistic mysticism is necessarily hostile toward man, his freedom and personality. It obliterates all distinction between the divine and the human and postulates the final absorption of the latter by the former. Berdyaev is, of course, on solid ground when he argues from Boehme's point of view that, for Christian metaphysics, the relation between the Creator and the creature is one of partnership, and not absorption. Christian revelation recognizes and maintains the distinction between God and man. Christ the Crucified Lord constitutes the meeting, not a blending, ground of the divine and human personalities. He symbolizes the dialectic of freedom and love between God and man. Christian mysticism, then, is dualistic, not monistic.

Berdyaev's religious experience lends itself to an interesting comparison with Martin Buber's theological thought. The Jewish philosopher likewise is the representative and one of the main sources of religious existentialism. The core of his teaching is that "all real living is meeting." [20] The meeting, according to Buber, is based on two types of relations expressed in "primary words" I-Thou and I-It. These refer not to the object of the relation, but to the nature of the relation itself. The I-Thou locution indicates a relation of person to person, of subject to subject, and implies the commitment of one's whole being. The term I-It, on the other hand, designates a relation of a person to a thing, of subject to object, and involves not a total, but only a partial commitment of one's being. Naturally the I-Thou relation takes priority over the subject-object relation. Indeed, it is only within the I-Thou relation that personality is realized: "Through the *Thou* a man becomes *I*." [21] The I-Thou relation introduces man in dialogue mainly, though not exclusively, with other men and with God. Now God is the eternal Thou in whom "the extended lines of relations meet." Thus, "every particular Thou is a glimpse through to the eternal Thou; by means of every particular Thou the primary word addresses the eternal Thou." [22] God is the true Thou of a man's life, "which cannot be limited by another Thou, and to which he stands in a relation that gathers up and includes all others." [23]

The human-divine encounter, Buber insists, does not annihilate the I. Man before God remains forever a "Single One,"—a distinctive, independent personality—"praying and serving and loving, such as is possible only by an I to a Thou." [24] Like Berdyaev, Buber rejects the monistic, absorptionist type of mysticism. "All doctrine of absorption," he writes, "is based on the colossal illusion of the human spirit that is bent back on himself," [25] while actually the Ego has no real existence outside of its relationship with the Thou. Buber's conclusion on the subject is of a piece with that of Berdyaev. "Not before a man can say I," he declares, "in perfect reality —that is, finding himself—can he in perfect reality say Thou—that is, to God." [26]

To ascertain the validity of Berdyaev's existential mysticism is no problem when attempted in the light both of the time-honored tradition of Christian mysticism and the modern religious existentialism. But when we become concerned with the content of his mystical experience, then difficulties begin to arise in the shape of striking antinomies. Thus in regard to the question of the nature of creation, Berdyaev's answer reveals vagueness and contradiction. Granted that God-the-Creator and the meonic freedom proceed from the transcending divine Ungrund; granted again that the former creates out of the latter a spiritual world and man;[27] yet nothing is said which clarifies the nature of that creation. Was it similar to the Platonic pattern of the world of Ideas? At first view such an approximation might seem plausible. Berdyaev, it has been noted, declares that man is capable of "remembering" things he had seen in the lost paradise, prior to his earthly life. But a closer examination proves the comparison preposterous. Plato's noumenal world represents a static, ontological scheme of things. Not so Berdyaev's. To him the world of spirit denotes a voluntaristic character; it is dynamic. The one spells immutability, the other involves changeableness.

Further, was it the abode of one or many spirits? Every man's spiritual pre-existence should support the second supposition. Berdyaev's continuous stress on the One who consents to creation, however, would rather suggest the existence in the spiritual world of only one human spirit, the archetype and the source of all other individual souls. If it be so, how does the passage from the one to the many take place? Moreover, Berdyaev says that God-the-

Creator made the world out of meonic stuff. But at the same time he affirms that the Other is none else than the Second Person of the Trinity—the divine manhood. If the Other's response to God requires the use of meonic freedom, as Berdyaev suggests, then the world would be the result of no creation at all, for a "response" evidently cannot be identified with "creation." And even if, contrary to elementary coherence, such identification were forcibly assumed, the initiative for creation should be ascribed not to God but to the Other. In case, however, God did create the world out of the meonic stuff, it still remains to explain what relation the "response" of the Other bears to creation. If none, as might be advanced, then the creation of the world would appear not as a free response of "no-thingness" to the call of God, but a deliberate manifestation of God's incentive and omnipotence—a thesis diametrically opposed to Berdyaev's understanding of God's nature and character. Finally, it might be observed, in spite of all Berdyaev's reservations and qualifications, the meonic freedom conveys much more the idea of "somethingness" rather than "no-thingness."

The main criticism, however, has been voiced not against Berdyaev's confused picture of creation, but against his conception of "uncreated freedom." It is argued that if man's freedom is not created and given to him by God, but proceeds from another non-divine source, then ontological dualism becomes inescapable. The theory might, so the commentators contend, indicate Zoroastrianism or Manicheism, but assuredly it does not express the Christian point of view. Evgeny Lampert, for example, calls it "the most disastrous conclusion in his [Berdyaev's] whole philosophy; and one which seems in fact in no way warranted by his own fundamental presuppositions."[28] Matthew Spinka also agrees with this judgment. The reasons for his dissent from Berdyaev on the subject are, in his enumeration, the following: first, God's endowment of man with freedom does not make Him "responsible for man's abuse of that freedom"; second, the "'uncreated freedom' . . . does not free God from responsibility for at least consenting to use the 'meonic' stuff in creation, although he knew it contained freedom,"[29] that is, the possibility of evil; and finally, the whole idea, Spinka believes, is gnostic not Christian.

Lampert and Spinka's remarks are quite typical of the common criticism formulated against Berdyaev's view. We shall, therefore, dwell shortly upon them. Proceeding with the above mentioned argument, only in reverse order, we may first underscore that, with regard to the subject under discussion, Berdyaev can scarcely pass for a gnostic. Of course, his teaching on the pre-existence of souls and man's falling away from a higher realm of goodness and freedom into a lower world of phenomena and necessity is related to gnosticism. But his representation of God-the-Creator has nothing in common with the gnostic Demiurge fashioning the world in subordination to the Supreme Being. Berdyaev's theogony—the realization of the divine Trinity in the *Ungrund*—does not mean that God has a beginning: the theogenoic process is eternal; and so is God.

The next objection concerning God's responsibility for using the meonic stuff in engendering the world is met by Berdyaev with the assumption that God, as it were, could not help it. Since the very essence of His nature is creativity, He must create whatever way there is in the unfathomable mystery of primeval spiritual reality. But God is not only the creator, He is also the Redeemer. If He cannot help creating, He does redeem the creation. The Incarnation is precisely an act of divine redemption whereby men are called to become the partners of God in gaining victory over meonic evil, nay, in realizing the transformation of evil into good.

The third objection apparently presents a real difficulty. Evidently God cannot be held responsible for man's abuse of freedom. Berdyaev was well aware of that. In fact, his whole philosophy, in accord with the Christian tradition, hinges on man's direct responsibility for his own destiny. Although his explanation of that responsibility is, as we have seen, at variance with the one commonly held by the Christian churches. He contends, in effect, that man is responsible for himself because he stands absolutely free in relation to God. A freedom created and given by God should, in Berdyaev's belief, signify only one thing, to wit, that God is the Lord and Controller of Freedom. The doctrine inevitably leads to metaphysical monism, on the one hand, and predestinarianism, on the other. It also eliminates the insight of divine tragedy, and imposes instead the idea of a farce God is playing to Himself

Lampert's argument to the effect that the theory of "uncreated freedom" is both a "disastrous conclusion" of Berdyaev's philosophy and "unwarranted by his own fundamental presuppositions" is the least acceptable of all four. Fielding Clarke rightly questions its validity when he declares that Berdyaev's idea of "uncreated freedom" is "the very reverse of a conclusion. How can it be unwarranted by Berdyaev's 'fundamental presuppositions' when it is quite obviously itself one of those very same 'fundamental presuppositions'?" [30] It must be reiterated that without grasping Berdyaev's fundamental metaphysical presuppositions no understanding of his thought can ever be achieved. God and "uncreated freedom" do not constitute an ontological dualism. Berdyaev admitted himself that the manner of his thinking may have contributed to the misunderstanding of his philosophy. But then he ceaselessly insisted that terms such as "Ungrund," "God-the-Creator," and "Uncreated Freedom" are not rational concepts but descriptive symbols. They are not susceptible to rationalization. All one can do, in his view, is to interpret them in the light of one's experience. Berdyaev's own interpretation might be formulated as follows: I apprehend the ultimate reality neither in terms of monism nor of dualism but *as if* there were at the root of existence a basic antithesis, to wit, between God and uncreated freedom both of which, however, are transcended in the final mystery of the divine Godhead.[31] He who will adapt this approach to Berdyaev's thought will alone gain access to its depth and significance.

2) *Man.* Next to "uncreated freedom" Berdyaev's passionate emphasis on the supreme value of man is the most characteristic feature of his philosophy. He regards the human person primarily as the bearer of the image of God and eternity, and not of time and the world. Each man is an absolute end in himself. Each human being is rooted in God. Each individual shares with God a part of divine nature. Berdyaev's staunch belief in man drew upon him much criticism from the Orthodox, Catholics, and Protestants alike. Yet he never abated an inch. He summed up his position in the following words: "It is not possible for my faith to be shaken by man, however low he may sink; for this faith is grounded not on what man thinks about man, but on what God thinks about him." [32]

Accordingly, Berdyaev predicated man not so much as a sinful creature, as one who is destined to creativity and transformation.

The final truth about man is not his sin, but a creative ascent. He declared that,

> Religious meaning of life and being is not wholly a matter of redemption from sin, but that life and being have positive, creative purposes. . . . Salvation from sin, from perdition, is not the final purpose of religious life: salvation is always *from* something and life should be *for* something. Many things unnecessary for salvation are needed for the very purpose for which salvation is necessary—for the creative upsurge of being. Man's chief end is not to be saved but to mount up, creatively. For this creative upsurge salvation from sin and evil is necessary. From the religious viewpoint the epoch of redemption is subordinated to the epoch of creativeness.[33]

Berdyaev's understanding of human nature at this point may appear both dangerously individualistic and biblically unwarranted. However, it is neither. It has already been pointed out that Berdyaev professed personalism not individualism. Indeed, he drew a sharp distinction between the two. Individuality is of nature; personality, of the spirit. The one belongs to the world of phenomena; the other is related to the noumenal order. Nevertheless, they are not alien to each other. A realized personality is the harmonious integration of both with the spiritual principle "having the mastery over all the powers of man's soul and body."[34] The accent on spiritual supremacy should necessarily absolve Berdyaev of all suspicion of individualism.

Further, his teaching finds justification also in the Scripture. Of course, the Old and New Testaments alike repeatedly insist on the idea that man is a sinner. And so he is. But then he equally reflects the image of God. Of the two terms determining the source of human inner polarity, namely, "the Image of God" and "the Fall," the living reality and final truth can be attributed to the former alone. John's story of Jesus and the adulteress affords an excellent illustration of the case in point. The Master is depicted as facing a woman taken in adultery, dragged before him as a guilty sinner, indicted by the law of Moses, and condemned to death by stoning. But when her accusers dissolved and left Christ alone with her, he directed his appeal not to her sinfulness, but to something deeper, something the crowd of Pharisees, blinded by the jurisprudential

302

awareness of sin, could not see—the image of God in her. "Jesus looked up and said to her, 'Woman, where are they? Has no one condemned you?' She said, 'No one, Lord.' And Jesus said, 'Neither do I condemn you; go, and do not sin again.' " [35]

This particular instance is in no way exceptional. The New Testament repeatedly indicates a high estimate of man. Certainly, men are foolish and wicked. And yet, the ultimate truth about man penetrates deeper than his sinfulness: he is first of all a son of God; fallen, but not rejected; wounded by the fall, but not depraved. Paul wrote to the Thessalonians: "You are all sons of light" [36]; to the Galatians: "Because you are sons, God has sent the Spirit of his Son into our hearts"; [37] to the Corinthians: "We are the temple of the living God"; [38] to the Romans: "It is the Spirit himself bearing witness with our spirit that we are children of God" [39]. To Paul's insight into human nature the writer of the First Letter of John adds his own testimony: "We are God's children now; it does not yet appear what we shall be." [40]

It should be noted, however, that the evangelical stress on God-like dignity and worth of man is not laid upon him as an independent creature. He is of a supreme value only when viewed in the light of Christ. Such is also Berdyaev's anthropology. It is in Christ and through Christ, he affirms, that the wound caused by the Fall is healed, that the sins are forgiven, and redemption achieved. "Man cannot forgive himself his sins," he writes, "he is unable to forget his evil past. But Christ has taken upon Himself the sins of the world, and He can take away our sin and forgive it. It is only in and through Christ that the past can be forgiven and forgotten." [41] The redeemed man is a free and transformed man whom God illuminates from within and inducts into the divine life. Whereupon man achieves his creative ascent. [42] The conclusion of the matter is that Berdyaev's emphatic anthropodicy or defence of the infinite value of man is both scriptural and Christian.

3) *God-Man.* We have seen that the concept God-Manhood, as incarnated in Jesus Christ, the Son of God and the Son of Man, summarizes the quintessence of Berdyaev's thought. Berdyaev is incontestably one of the most Christ-centered philosophers. Indeed, his very emphasis on man's freedom points inescapably in the direction of Christ. "Freedom has brought me to Christ," he writes,

"and I know of no other path leading to Him." [43] What has been said about Spinoza may *mutatis mutandis* be equally applied to Berdyaev: he was a Christ intoxicated Christian. His too loudly heralded anthropomorphism is actually a Christomorphism. Indeed, Christ, as Fielding Clarke rightly observes, constitutes the "inner consistency" of Berdyaev's thought. In the British commentator's words,

> Of Berdyaev it may be said that he is the most literally Christian of all Christian thinkers, for Christianity did not start as a philosophy but as the 'Way.' It begins in a meeting with Christ, the God-Man, and everything—theology, prayer, sacraments, the Church, the life and witness of Christians in the world spring out of this meeting. [44]

It has already been noted that to Berdyaev Christ is the fullest and most concrete expression of the fundamental and dramatic mutual relatedness of God and man. He is the fulfillment of the I-Thou human-divine encounter. In Christ not only God reveals Himself to man, but man also is revealed to God. Through Christ man is recognized as divine, and God as human. The presence of the divine in man is disclosed in God's image in him and in his capacity for love and creativity. The appearance of the human in God is displayed in His need for man, for man's love and response.

Compared with traditional Christologies of rational theology Berdyaev's comprehension of Christ might seem exceedingly bold and almost irreverent. Does it not obliterate the distinction between the creature and the Creator? Does it not place both of them on the same level of necessity and impotence? Do not they emerge as eternal victims of the meonic freedom? There is some confusion here, so much so that, as was previously noted, Berdyaev makes a double assertion which is logically contradictory. On the one hand, he construes mankind in terms of the Second Person of the Trinity, and on the other, he affirms that God created man out of the meonic stuff. Accordingly, it is not clear whether, besides God-the-Creator, Christ reveals God-the-Son or the fallen meonic humanity, or both. If the first is true, then how is it possible for Christ to reveal the fallen nature of man, since obviously the Second Person of the Trinity cannot be conceived in terms of the

Fall. If the second is correct, then again it is not easy to see the sinless Christ (and Berdyaev accepts Him as such) disclosing the sinfulness of human nature. Finally, if the third supposition is true, the question still remains unanswered concerning the reciprocal relation within Christ of the two natures, not human and divine, but fallen and unfallen.

The above mentioned objections, correct as they may be from the logical standpoint, are, however, scarcely applicable to Berdyaev's picture of Christ. In fact, he would reject them as just so many instances of rational objectification incapable of seizing the truth of a religious experience. To him the term God-man does not at all designate an intellectual concept. It is a myth, that is, a verbal description, necessarily inadequate, of the primordial divine-human mystery as he apprehends it in the depth of his spirit. Berdyaev's idea of God-manhood stands closer to the Eastern Orthodox than to Roman Catholic and Protestant traditions, although it is not alien to the West. Eckhart, Tauler, and Silesius commonly expressed it. But it was Vladimir Solovyev who, the first, developed it systematically.[45] Difficult as it may appear to the rank-and-file of Christians, the whole idea affords, however, spiritual justification. The Bible continuously discloses God's need of man. God needs man for the realization of His purposes. If He is active in nature, yet more so is He within human souls and hearts.

Berdyaev's doctrine of God-Man actually drives home the simple and fundamental truth of the centrality of Christ—the God-Man —in history and the personal destiny of man. He is the great Liberator. He Himself threw light upon the nature of His earthly mission by deliberately quoting Isaiah at the threshold of His ministry: "The Spirit of the Lord is upon me," Christ declared in His first recorded sermon, "because he has anointed me. . . . He has sent me to proclaim *release* to the captives . . . to set at *liberty* those who are oppressed." [46] At the close of His ministry the message was the same: "So if the Son makes you *free*, you will be *free* indeed." [47]

Christ sets man free from the slavery of sin; and there is no sin which He cannot wipe out and forgive. He liberates the human being from slavery to himself—to his passions, pride, and egotism; from slavery to nature, its necessity and determinism; from slavery to society, its pretense for primacy and dominion; and from slavery to life's evils, suffering, and futility. But most of all, Christ's freedom raises man to the glory of inner rebirth and spiritual transformation. This represents the highest human-divine achievement in man whereby, in Paul's words, "it is no longer I who live, but Christ who lives in me." [48]

It is in the light of man transformed through Christ into a new creature that Berdyaev's view on the Church should also be considered. He is right in affirming that the Kingdom of God is not, and never can be, associated with the existence of any particular church, not even with all the churches combined. The true Christian Church is the invisible *koinonia* of those who live in Christ and in whom Christ lives. Her scope is ecumenical for she cuts across all national and racial barriers to reach with her saving touch of grace every human being under the sun. Her purpose is cosmic for, beyond the salvation of the individual believer, she tends to the transformation of society and the world as a whole. Her distinctive quality, when fully manifested, is *sobornost,* that is, a divinely enlightened spiritual communion wherein the entire creation—animate and inanimate—is brought under the light of Christ "in whom all things hold together." [49]

4) *Ethics.* Berdyaev's moral teaching stems directly from the substance of his existential philosophy: Man, God, and Freedom. It is, in my estimation, the finest attainment of his thought. Moreover, it is rooted in the Christian experience and justified by the Holy Writ. The ethics of law is directed toward the dualism between good and evil and the moral destitution of the sinful state of man. In the fallen world of vindictiveness, tyranny, greed, lust, and envy; of interminable conflicts between values and tragic contradictions in life, the law is necessary. Although it is oppressive, it is also protective. It restrains unruly instincts, controls offensive behavior, and creates social order. Without external compulsion and legalistic norms no social life could be possible. Lawlessness would inevitably spell license and anarchy. It was with this insight in mind that Paul admonished the Christians in Rome to make certain each of them remains a loyal "subject to the governing authorities. . . . For rulers are not a terror to good conduct, but to bad." [50] The Christians, therefore, are not despisers of law, but its

306

respecters. They realize the importance of the normative function of the state and act in accordance with the rules and regulations of their respective lawful government.

It is obvious, however, that large areas of human experience in virtue of their very nature are amenable to no juridical compulsion. Intellectual and emotional life, for instance, are barely affected by law. The fear of prison can prevent me from stealing or murdering, but not from brooding over ill thoughts. No law is ever capable of wiping out my past, forgiving my sins, or making me good and just. Law is powerless to change my inner mental and spiritual condition. Moreover, the ethics of Law, as Berdyaev accurately underlines, assumes rather a negative character. The "do not" provides no automatic clue to what I positively should do. Life issues are far from being always as clear and defined as black versus white. My moral problems are not necessarily confined to the telling of right from wrong. There are circumstances in life far more complex and troublesome which involve my choice, not between an act distinctly good and one manifestly bad, but between two acts each of which is either bad or good.

In other words, to achieve insight, wisdom, and purity which make for a wholesome personality; to convert pride and egocentricity into humility and theocentricity which alone characterize the unfallen state of man; and finally to receive the forgiveness of my sins and a spiritual rebirth I need not the law, but a redeemer. Berdyaev's ethics of redemption comes straight from the pages of the Gospel. In a language burning with faith in Christ, the great Orthodox Christian preaches the reconciliation of man to God wrought in the Revelation, the liberation from sin, the acquisition of new power through the Redeemer, the victory of hope, faith, and love over despair, darkness, and pain. Time and again he directs our attention to the abiding truth that we are the Sons of God, not of Satan; of spirit, not of matter, meant for fellowship and life with our Creator. Accordingly, he invites us to affirm each man in God and focus our love, not on an abstract, non-existent humanity, but on each concrete, living human being. In the light of Christ all men are brothers; toward that light they are all called. In it also is disclosed the infinite love of God for His estranged children, and His suffering awaiting of their return. "For God so loved the world that he gave his only Son, that whoever believes in him should not perish but have eternal life." [51]

Redemption, however, is not God's final end for man. Its positive significance consists in creativity. Man is redeemed from sin and the law in order to create. It has already been noted that the New Testament repeatedly insists on man's creative vocation. Berdyaev's summoning the world to creativity, particularly in the moral sphere, is moving and inspiring. Creativity, he rightly reminds us, penetrates deeper than the distinction between evil and good; even deeper than the obligation to struggle against evil and promote the good; actually it signifies the transformation of evil into good. Is not this the idea Paul wanted to convey when he wrote: "Do not be overcome by evil, but overcome evil with good"?[52] The Kingdom of God is precisely life regenerated in which there is left no trace of evil, because, through man's moral creativity, and with the grace of Christ, it was overcome and turned into good.

Berdyaev's teaching of universal salvation is the logical development of the doctrine of cosmic transfiguration. It admits of Christ's final victory over all aspects of Antichrist. It testifies that the Kingdom of God—the realm of love, goodness, and righteousness—will eventually be established. Hence, naturally, Berdyaev repudiates the concept of eternal hell. "If hell is eternal," he exclaims, "then I am an atheist." [53] This viewpoint stands in rather sharp contrast to the one traditionally held by the majority of the Christian divines whether Catholic, Orthodox, or Protestant. All three denominations admit the existence of eternal torments of hell along with eternal bliss of heaven. On whose side is the truth?

The point in question, of course, is to know which of the two sides is actually borne out by scriptural justification. A critical examination of the New Testament seems at first to indicate that Christ believed and taught that the doom of the finally impenitent will be eternal. In effect, He frequently warned His hearers against the danger of incurring final reprobation. He also spoke of the "eternal fire" [54] into which the hardened sinners will be thrown.[55] Yet a closer scrutiny of Jesus' figurative sayings discloses no sufficient evidence to support the belief in eternal damnation. Many of these passages, if not arbitrarily taken out of context, must as

308

Schleiermacher justly suggests, "allude to some earlier event." [56] Others are couched in the conditional tense which seems to cast doubt as to the eventual realization of the possibility of irremediable doom.[57] Others again, intimate universalism. Consider the following: "[God] desires all men to be saved and to come to the knowledge of truth." [58] "[God] is the Savior of all men, especially of those who believe." [59] "For the Son of man came to save the lost." [60] He is "indeed the Savior of the world." [61] He was sent by the Father "not to condemn the world, but that the world might be saved through him." [62] Thus the scriptural conclusion on the matter appears more likely on the side of Berdyaev than on that of Augustine, Luther, and Calvin. "The New Testament references," writes Schleiermacher in the vein of Berdyaev's thought, "forbid us to think of the definitive victory of evil over one part of the human race, and from which we must rather infer that before the general resurrection evil will have been completely overcome." [63] In the end, then, all creation will be gathered with its creator, and God will be "everything to every one." [64]

Not only Scripture, but human consciousness at is best also seems to issue no warrant for the doctrine of everlasting hell-fire: an endless suffering is deeply felt as unjust whatever men may have done. Even the human law punishes the offender, primarily not from the motive of retribution or self-protection, but with a view toward his reformation. There is hope of making him again a useful member of society such as he was before the offense. An endless punishment in hell would defeat its own purpose. It would rob the sinner from benefiting by the punishment and turning his evil ways into steps leading to God. But the truth is different. The Shepherd never abandons his flock. On the contrary, he is always out in the search for the lost sheep, and when he finds it, "he rejoices over it more than over the ninety-nine that never went astray." [65]

Berdyaev's radiant vision of universal salvation is unfortunately blurred with vexatious inconsistencies. His affirmation that man does not possess immortality as an endowment, but that he must win it appears to contradict his idea of the pre-existence of the spirit. On the other hand, the annihilation of the self which he conceives to be the alternative to salvation is both opposed to universality and scarcely more ethical than eternal hell. In the first case, salvation precludes all concept of universality as long as there are spirits who disintegrate into nothingness; in the second, the final determination either of eternal life or of eternal death, within the framework of a man's three score and ten odd years of blunders and mistakes, without any chance for a new start, looms as fantastic and immoral as the idea of the everlasting punishment itself. Finally, Berdyaev seems to speak of resurrection as well as immortality. Although he formulates the former in terms of Paul's spiritual, not fleshly, body, yet it does not appear wholly consistent with the latter. Is the spiritual body formed immediately after death? If so what happens to it before the resurrection? Is it raised on the eve of the judgment day? But then its status meanwhile is likely to resemble one of total annihilation. Can anything be resurrected out of nothing? Despite the above mentioned discrepancies one is left, after a long and assiduous study of Berdyaev's thought, with the impression of his believing that negative assumptions will never reach fulfillment. He remains to the last confident in the destiny of man and in the final human-divine encounter. Indeed, Berdyaev is a metaphysical optimist.

5) *Philosophy of History*. Berdyaev's understanding of history preserves to a striking degree a biblical flavor, though not quite as it is commonly accepted. His basic conviction that "nothing seems to succeed in history and yet all things are significant in it," [66] is strongly supported by scriptural references. History acquires significance on account of God's active presence within it. He created the world, in the first place, which also means that history was intended by Him for a purpose; He must therefore attach a deep interest to the historical happenings whereby the destiny of the world is carried out. Hence "all things are significant in it." The Hebrew Psalmist expressed the same conviction when he uttered that "the earth is the Lord's and the fullness thereof, the world and those who dwell therein." [67] But the world is also a fallen world. Within the framework of its objectified, unredeemed state it has no permanent stability. Everything in it is of necessity inconstant, fleeting, forever unachieved. It is, as the same Psalmist noted, "founded upon the seas, and established upon the rivers." [68] Such

310

a floating world cannot have solid foundations in time. For this reason "nothing seems to succeed in history."

No wonder, then, that Berdyaev's sense of history should engender a twofold experience: "the experience of history's hostile and alien character and of my implication in it." [69] The early Christians felt very much in like manner. They were, in John's words, "not of the world," but only "out of the world." [70] Yet they were also aware of their high calling as "ambassadors for Christ" [71] appointed to go into the world "and make disciples of all nations." [72] What resolves the tragic polarity of history is, as Berdyaev saw it in the light of the Gospel, that history has an end. This is also what imparts the supreme meaning to the historical process. The Kingdom of God, then, cannot be attained in the world of time and history. It can be realized only beyond time in the eternal order of the spirit.

Berdyaev's eschatology, however, has no relation with any sort of apocalypticism. The establishment of the Kingdom is not a unilateral proposition—from God to man—but rather a human-divine achievement. As Spinka justly comments, "this is the creative, dynamic understanding of Christian eschatology. A passive expectation of the end is more likely to bring about God's terrible judgment than the Kingdom of God." [73] Actually, according to Berdyaev, there is a foretaste of the Kingdom in every present creative act. "Every moral act of love, of mercy, and of sacrifice brings to pass the end of the world where hatred, cruelty, and selfishness reign supreme. Every creative act entails . . . the promise of a new, an 'other' world, where God's power is revealed in freedom and in love."[74] This is the language of the Christian faith.

Nobody more than Berdyaev himself was conscious of the logical inconsistencies of his thought. To explain these he pointed out that,

> The inconsistencies and contradictions which are to be found in my thought are expressions of spiritual conflict, of contradictions which lie at the very heart of existence itself, and are not to be disguised by a façade of logical unity. True integrality of thought, which is bound up with integrality of personality, is an existential, not a logical, unity. . . . The philosopher is guilty of treason if the basic themes of his phil-

osophical thinking are altered, the fundamental *motifs* of his thought, the groundwork of his scale of values. One can change one's view about where and how freedom of the spirit is realized. But if love of freedom is replaced by love of servitude and violence, then treason is the result.[75]

Berdyaev preferred to remain faithful to his intuitions rather than to logical coherence. He made no attempt to formulate a system of philosophy. In fact, he was just the opposite of a systematic philosopher. "My vocation," he acknowledged, "is to proclaim not a doctrine but a vision." [76] Yet this vision in its entirety is less affected with logical error than many another systematic exposition. His philosophy is all of one piece. Its main themes— God, man, Christ, objectification, freedom, creativity, eschatological solution of the dualism of the noumenal and phenomenal worlds —preserve a remarkable internal coherence. Each of these themes postulates the next one and, in turn, can be deduced from it. Put together they form a harmonious whole—a whole which gives expression to one of the deepest and most majestic spiritual experiences of the divine, and in which faith borrows the language of philosophy, and philosophy becomes an act of faith.

We have now come to the end of our study of Berdyaev's life and teaching. From the early years of his childhood to the last hour of his earthly pilgrimage we have beheld him evolving through storm and struggle, seldom amidst calm waters, in search for the meaning of life. We have followed him moving on from his exclusive native environment to Marxism, then to "Idealism," finally to Christianity. Along the way we have been inspired by his visions, stirred by his speech, instructed by his wisdom, and humbled by his faith. At times we felt him near like a brother; at others he appeared aloof and withdrawn, almost an alien. But we have never stopped marveling at the prophet, admiring the orator, respecting the teacher, and loving the Christian. As the curtain goes down and the lights are put out, and we bid farewell to our fiery, yet so gentle, so human master and friend, it behooves us to answer one more question. What, if any, is Berdyaev's perennial contribution to Western and Christian thought?

Berdyaev will always mean many things to many people. Never will he mean all things even to a faithful disciple. No philosopher could, or indeed should, expect an unreserved recognition. One thing, however, will rally over his name more and more thoughtful minds, whether Christian or not. This is his impassionate DEFENSE OF HUMAN PERSONALITY. To an age gradually surfeited with religious paganism, ethical indifferentism, and political tyranny; in which man is treated as an economic tool and his soul accounted for nothing; in which the processes of mechanization are threatening to erect a social structure after the pattern of Huxley's *Brave New World*—the voice of Berdyaev resounds as an eloquent declaration of faith in man. With splendid courage and invincible constancy he reminds mankind that man is never a means, always an end in himself; his nature is spiritual, not material; his destiny is eternal, not temporal; and that for these reasons his personality is the highest value in the world. The supreme command, therefore —and this is Berdyaev's final philosophical and religious bequest— is "to be human in this most unhuman of ages, to guard the image of man, for it is the image of God." [77]

PART I

INTRODUCTION

1 Quoted by Nicolas Berdyaev, *The Russian Idea* (New York: The Macmillan Company, 1948), p. 1.

2 John Donne, *The Complete Poetry and Selected Prose* (New York: The Modern Library, 1952), p. 441.

3 Nicolas Berdyaev, *Freedom and the Spirit* (London: The Centenary Press, 1935), p. viii.

4 *Time,* The Weekly Newsmagazine (Chicago), June 18, 1956, p. 90.

5 George Vernadsky, *A History of Russia* (New Haven: Yale University Press, 1951), p. 1.

6 *Ibid.,* p. 5.

7 Quoted by C. Stählin, *La Russie des origines à la naissance de Pierre le Grand* (Paris: Payot, 1946), p. 9.

8 S. Platonov, *Histoire de Russie* (Paris: Payot, 1929), p. 9.

9 See S. Platonov, *op. cit.,* p. 16.

10 See George Vernadsky, *op. cit.,* p. 16.

11 See Kenneth Scott Latourette, *A History of the Expansion of Christianity* (New York: Harper & Bros., 1938), Vol. II, p. 253.

12 *Ibid.,* p. 255.

13 *Ibid.,* p. 403.

14 *Ibid.,* p. 402.

15 See S. Platonov, *op. cit.,* p. 60.

16 *Ibid.,* p. 61.

17 *Ibid.,* p. 64.

18 See Nicolas Zernov, *The Church of the Eastern Christians* (London: Society for Promoting Christian Knowledge, 1944), p. 52.

19 Sergius Bulgakov, *The Orthodox Church* (London: The Centenary Press), p. 99.

20 *Ibid.*, p. 9.
21 Nicolas Zernov, *op. cit.*, p. 63.
22 Sergius Bulgakov, *op. cit.*, p. 14.
23 *Ibid.*, p. 15.
24 Nicolas Zernov, *op. cit.*, p. 54.
25 Sergius Bulgakov, *op. cit.*, p. 121.
26 *Ibid.*, p. 123.
27 *Ibid.*, p. 124.
28 *Ibid.*
29 *Ibid.*, p. 120.
30 *Ibid.*, pp. 126f.
31 *Ibid.*, p. 129.
32 John Donne, *op. cit.*, p. 441.
33 Sergius Bulgakov, *op. cit.*, p. 150.
34 *Ibid.*, p. 151.
35 *Ibid.*, p. 158.
36 See Walter Schubart, *L'Europe et l'âme de l'Orient* (Paris. Albin Michel, 1949), p. 75.
37 See George Vernadsky, *op. cit.*, p. 56.
38 See Walter Schubart, *op. cit.*, p. 75.
39 See Kenneth S. Latourette, *op. cit.*, p. 257.
40 See George Vernadsky, *op. cit.*, p. 51.
41 See Kenneth S. Latourette, *op. cit.*, p. 258.
42 *Ibid.*
43 See George Vernadsky, *op. cit.*, p. 59.
44 See Kenneth S. Latourette, *op. cit.*, p. 259.
45 Pierre Kovalevsky, *Manuel d'Histoire Russe* (Paris: Payot, 1948), p. 81.
46 See C. Stählin, *op. cit.*, p. 149.
47 See George Vernadsky, *op. cit.*, p. 71.
48 Quoted by Nicolas Berdyaev, *The Russian Idea*, p. 8.
49 Quoted by S. Platonov, *op. cit.*, p. 194.
50 *Ibid.*
51 Nicolas Berdyaev, *op cit.*, p. 9.
52 See Nicolas Zernov, *Three Russian Prophets: Khomiakov, Dostoyevsky, Soloviev* (London: S.C.M. Press, Ltd, 1944), p. 48.
53 See N. O. Lossky, *History of Russian Philosophy* (New York: International Universities Press, Inc., 1951), p. 31.
54 *Ibid.*
55 Nicolas Zernov, *op. cit.*, p. 51.
56 Aleksei Khomyakov, *Sotchineniya* (Moscow: J. N. Kooshnerev and Company, 1911), Vol. I, p. 161.
57 Quoted by Zernov, *op. cit.*, p. 58.
58 *Ibid.*, p. 59.
59 *Ibid.*
60 Khomyakov, *op. cit.*, Vol. II, p. 216.

61 *Ibid.*, Vol. I, p. 327.

62 *Ibid.*, pp. 278f.

63 V. V. Zenkovsky, *A History of Russian Philosophy* (New York: Columbia University Press, 1953), p. 195.

64 *Ibid.*

65 Khomyakov, *op. cit.*, Vol. I, 281f.

66 Quoted by Nicolas Zernov, *op. cit.*, p. 60.

67 See A. Gratieux, *A. S. Khomiakov* (Paris: Les éditions du cerf, 1939), Vol. II, pp. 108 ff.

68 Quoted, *Ibid.*, p. 109.

69 Quoted by Nicolas Zernov, *op. cit.*, p. 58.

70 Quoted by V. V. Zenkovsky, *op. cit.*, p. 188.

71 *Ibid.*

72 *Ibid.*

73 *Ibid.*, p. 189.

74 See Sergius Bulgakov, *op. cit.*, p. 75.

75 Quoted by Nicolas Zernov, *op. cit.*, p. 61. Cf. Khomyakov, *op. cit.*, Vol. II, pp. 3ff.

76 *Ibid.*

77 See N. O. Lossky, *op. cit.*, p. 37.

78 Khomyakov, *op. cit.*, Vol. II, p. 220.

79 See Walter Schubart, *op. cit.*, p. 221.

80 Nicolas Berdiaeff, *L'Esprit de Dostoievski* (Paris: Editions Stock, 1946), p. 39.

81 *Ibid.*, pp. 67ff.

82 Personage in *Crime and Punishment.*

83 Personages in *The Possessed.*

84 Quoted by Nicolas Berdyaev, *The Russian Idea*, p. 90.

85 Fyodor Dostoyevsky, *The Brothers Karamazov*, translated by Constance Garnett (New York: The Modern Library, 1950), pp. 298ff.

86 *The Russian Idea*, p. 180.

87 *Ibid.*, p. 168.

88 Quoted by Nicolas Zernov, *Three Russian Prophets*, p. 133.

89 Quoted by V. V. Zenkovsky, *op. cit.*, pp. 494f.

90 *Ibid.*, p. 506.

91 *Ibid.*, p. 498.

92 *Ibid.*

93 Quoted by N. O. Lossky, *op. cit.*, p. 105.

94 *Ibid.*

95 Quoted by N. O. Lossky, *op. cit.*, pp. 106f.

96 See V. V. Zenkovsky, *op. cit.*, p. 508.

97 *Ibid.*, p. 500.

98 *Ibid.*, p. 511.

99 *Ibid.*

100 *Ibid.*

101 Quoted by Berdyaev, *The Russian Idea,* p. 171.
102 *Ibid.,* p. 172.
103 *Ibid.,* p. 173.
104 Zenkovsky, *op. cit.,* p. 513.
105 *Ibid.*
106 Quoted by Nicolas Zernov, *Ibid.,* pp. 137ff.
107 *The Russian Idea,* p. 176.
108 Quoted by V. V. Zenkovsky, *op. cit.,* p. 517.
109 Quoted by N. O. Lossky, *op. cit.,* p. 122.
110 *Ibid.*
111 See Nicolas Zernov, *op. cit.,* pp. 140f.

CHAPTER I

1 Quoted by Edouard Schuré, *Les Grands Initiés* (Paris: Librairie Académique Perrin, 1939) , p. 465.

2 Although at variance in other respects, Orphism and Pythagoreanism shared in common the belief in (1) the divine origin of souls and their pre-existence in the realm of spirit; (2) their fall into the world of matter and subsequent corruption and depravity which were rendered inheritable by innate wickedness; (3) their condemnation to a necessary and endless cycle of births and deaths; and (4) the possibility of release to return into the heavenly fellowship of the gods and communion with them through personal purification and initiation into the secret rites of the mysteries. The two schools held the body to be the prison of the soul. (See P. Gardner, "Mysteries," *Encyclopedia of Religion and Ethics,* edited by James Hastings, New York: Charles Scribner's Sons, 1955, Vol. 9, p. 78; and John Burnet, "Pythagoras and Pythagoreanism," *ibid.,* Vol. 10, pp. 523ff. Cf. Plato, *Cratylus,* 400 C, *Phaedo,* 61D-62B, and *Theaetetus,* 176B-D) .

3 The Gnostic systems likewise turned around two basic ideas—fall and redemption. Accordingly they taught: (1) the world of matter is intrinsically evil and stands in opposition to the world of spirit; (2) the latter is the native region of the soul, from which, as the result of some cosmic disaster, it had fallen prior to its conscious life, and forever seeks to escape back to its original source; and (3) the process of deliverance involves the voluntary descent from the higher world into the world of matter of a *Soter* or savior whose purpose is to communicate the hidden *gnosis* or knowledge by means of which the elect souls are freed from their earthly bondage of darkness and restored to the kingdom of light. (See E. F. Scott, "Gnosticism," in Hastings, *op. cit.,* Vol. 6, pp. 235f.) .

An interesting *rapprochement* may be made with the doctrine of the Essenians to whom Jesus has sometimes been related: "For it is their firm opinion that, while the body is corruption, and its substance transient, the soul is permanent and immortal; that the soul comes from the thinnest air by a sort of natural spell to be imprisoned, as it were, within the body; and that, on being released from the fetters of the flesh, it joyfully soars away into freedom from the long bondage." (James Moffat quoting Josephus in "Essenes," Hastings, *op. cit.*, Vol. 5, p. 398. Cf. Millar Burrows, *The Dead Sea Scrolls* [New York: The Viking Press, 1955] pp. 273ff.).

4 Nicolas Berdyaev, *Dream and Reality, An Essay in Autobiography* (New York: The Macmillan Co., 1951), p. 1. This posthumously published work is the best source of biographical material concerning Berdyaev.

5 *Ibid.*, p. 50.

6 *Ibid.*, p. 33.

7 *Ibid.*, p. 4.

8 Nurse.

9 Chief.

10 An office created by Catherine the Great in order to draw more of the provincial nobility into public affairs.

11 In Russian Orthodoxy one could undertake "secretly" monastic vows, and live an ordinary life.

12 Berdyaev, *Dream and Reality*, p. 17.

13 *Ibid.*, p. 6.

14 *Ibid.*

15 Kiev was the celebrated "Holy City" of Orthodox Russia and the main rallying point of Western and Byzantine civilizations in the East. It was in Kiev that the first Russian Christian Prince, St. Vladimir (980-1015), ordered the pagan idols cast into the River Dnieper and, after the fashion of Charlemagne, imposed mass-baptism on the inhabitants (c. A.D. 989). He also engaged in intensive intercourse with the courts of foreign sovereigns. These outstanding events marked the beginning of both Russian Christianity and her political and cultural relations with Western Europe (Cf. S. Platonov, *op. cit.*, pp. 50ff.).

16 Berdyaev, *Dream and Reality*, p. 13.

17 *Ibid.*, p. 83f. Cf. Berdyaev, *Slavery and Freedom* (New York: Charles Scribner's Sons, 1944), p. 8.

18 Berdyaev, *Dream and Reality*, p. 83.

19 *Ibid.*, p. 37.

20 Berdiaeff, *L'Esprit de Dostoievski*, p. 7.

21 Quoted by Eugene Porret, *Berdiaeff, Prophète des Temps Nouveaux* (Neuchatel: Delachaux & Niestlé, 1951), p. 36.

22 Berdyaev, *Dream and Reality*, p. 13.

23 *Ibid.*, p. 17.

24 *Ibid.*, p. 12.

25 *Ibid.,* p. 33f.
26 *Ibid.,* p. 20.
27 *Ibid.,* p. 34.
28 *Ibid.,* p. 37.
29 *Ibid.,* p. 54f.
30 *Ibid.,* pp. 78f.

CHAPTER   II

1 Quoted by Berdyaev, *The Russian Idea,* p. 28.
2 Berdyaev, *Dream and Reality,* p. 118.
3 *Ibid.,* p. 118.
4 *Ibid.,* p. 18.
5 Peasant.
6 The Russian word *"Pravda"* designates, in its wider meaning, both truth and justice.
7 *Ibid.,* pp. 108ff.
8 *Ibid.,* pp. 117f.
9 *Ibid.,* pp. 110f.
10 It was they who eventually succeeded in achieving the communist revolution.
11 Berdyaev, *The Origin of Russian Communism,* (New York: Charles Scribner's Sons, 1937), pp. 123ff.
12 Berdyaev, *Slavery and Freedom,* pp. 13f.
13 Berdyaev, *Dream and Reality,* pp. 91f.
14 The political police of the Tsar.
15 *Ibid.,* p. 120.
16 The book, with a foreword by Peter Struve, took for its theme the critique of Mikhailovsky's excessive subjectivism which placed truth in the moral consciousness of the individual and thus led to an extreme relativism and the denial of the objectivity of truth.
17 *Ibid.,* pp. 122ff.
18 *Ibid.,* p. 125.
19 *Ibid.,* p. 128.
20 Berdyaev, *Slavery and Freedom,* p. 15.
21 Berdyaev, *Dream and Reality,* p. 126.
22 *Ibid.,* pp. 113ff.
23 Nicolas Berdyaev, *Christianity and Class War* (New York: Sheed and Ward, 1935), pp. 22f.

CHAPTER III

1 Quoted by V. V. Zenkovsky, *op. cit.,* p. 364.
2 *Ibid.,* p. 891.

3 Cf. David Shub, *Lenin* (New York: The New American Library, 1951), pp. 34ff.

4 Berdyaev, *Dream and Reality*, p. 135.

5 Platonov, *op. cit.*, p. 960.

6 Berdyaev, *Dream and Reality*, p. 136.

7 *Ibid.*, p. 139.

8 Berdyaev, *The Russian Idea*, p. 219.

9 Berdyaev, *Dream and Reality*, p. 155.

10 Berdyaev, *The Origin of Russian Communism*, p. 127.

11 Zenkovsky, *op. cit.*, p. 458.

12 Berdyaev, *The Russian Idea*, pp. 229ff.

13 Zenkovsky, *op. cit.*, p. 772.

14 Berdyaev, *Dream and Reality*, p. 161.

15 Zenkovsky, *op. cit.*, p. 760.

16 Berdyaev, *Dream and Reality*, p. 137.

CHAPTER IV

1 Quoted by Zenkovsky, *op. cit.*, p. 395.

2 Berdyaev, *Dream and Reality*, p. 172.

3 *Ibid.*, p. 172.

4 *Ibid.*, p. 170.

5 *Ibid.*, p. 174.

6 *Ibid.*, p. 185.

7 *Ibid.*, p. 146.

8 Quoted by Zenkovsky, *op. cit.*, p. 460.

9 *Ibid.*, p. 461.

10 *Ibid.*, p. 461.

11 Berdyaev, *Dream and Reality*, p. 150.

12 Zenkovsky, *op. cit.*, p. 758.

13 *Ibid.*

14 *Ibid.*, p. 759.

15 *Ibid.*, p. 460.

16 Berdyaev, *Dream and Reality*, pp. 149f.

17 Quoted by Matthew Spinka, *Nicolas Berdyaev: Captive of Freedom*, (Philadelphia: The Westminster Press, 1950), p. 22.

18 Ternavtsev as quoted by Zenkovsky, *op. cit.*, p. 758.

19 Quoted by Spinka, *op. cit.*, p. 22.

20 Berdyaev, *Dream and Reality*, p. 163.

21 Berdyaev, *The Russian Idea*, p. 189.

22 Berdyaev, *Dream and Reality*, p. 176.

23 *Ibid.*, p. 185.

24 Platonov, *op. cit.*, p. 646.

25 Kenneth Scott Latourette, *A History of Christianity* (New York: Harper and Brothers, 1953), p. 920.

26 Berdyaev, *Slavery and Freedom,* p. 16.

27 Berdyaev, *Dream and Reality,* p. 202.

28 Quoted by Spinka, *op. cit.,* pp. 34f.

29 Quoted by Eugene Porret, *op. cit.,* p. 69.

30 Quoted by Spinka, *op. cit.,* pp. 40f.

31 *Ibid.,* p. 38.

32 *Ibid.,* p. 43.

33 Monastic elders believed to be great experts in the art of spiritual guidance.

34 Berdyaev, *Dream and Reality,* p. 212.

35 Quoted by Porret, *op. cit.,* p. 78.

36 Berdyaev, *Dream and Reality,* p. 213.

CHAPTER V

1 Quoted by M. Hofman, *Histoire de la littérature russe* (Paris: Payot, 1934), p. 578.

2 Quoted by David Shub, *op. cit.,* p. 76.

3 During the first year of the war, the German-sounding name of the Russian capital, St. Petersburg, was changed into the corresponding native form, Petrograd.

4 Bernard Pares, *Russia, Its Past and Present* (New York: The New American Library, 1953), pp. 47f.

5 Berdyaev, *Dream and Reality,* p. 137.

6 Quoted by Spinka, *op. cit.,* p. 52.

7 Quoted by Porret, *op. cit.,* p. 97.

8 Quoted by Spinka, *op. cit.,* p. 53.

9 *Ibid.,* p. 54.

10 *Ibid.,* pp. 57-59.

11 Berdyaev, *The Origin of Russian Communism,* p. 145.

12 Nicolas Berdyaev, *The End of Our Time* (New York: Sheed & Ward, Inc., 1933), p. 125.

13. *Ibid.,* p. 134.

14 *Ibid.,* p. 135.

15 *Ibid.,* p. 131.

16 *Ibid.,* pp. 140f.

17 Berdyaev, *The Origin of Russian Communism,* pp. 207f.

18 Nicolas Berdyaev, *Un Nouveau Moyen Age* (Paris: Librairie Plon, 1927), p. 237.

19 Berdyaev, *Dream and Reality,* p. 230.

20 Quoted by Porret, *op. cit.,* p. 106.

21 Berdyaev, *Dream and Reality,* p. 237.

22 *Ibid.,* p. 239.

23 *Ibid.,* p. 240.

24 *Ibid.,* pp. 242f.

CHAPTER VI

1 Quoted by Berdyaev, *The End of Our Time,* p. 120.

2 Berdyaev, *Dream and Reality,* p. 245.

3 *Ibid.,* p. 250.

4 Nicolas Berdyaev, *The Meaning of History* (New York: Charles Scribner's Sons, 1936), p. 128.

5 *Ibid.,* p. 131.

6 *Ibid.,* pp. 140f.

7 *Ibid.,* pp. 144f.

8 *Ibid.,* p. 162.

9 *Ibid.,* pp. 146f.

10 Berdyaev, *The End of Our Time,* p. 29.

11 Friedrich Nietzsche, "Zarathustra's Prologue, II," in *The Philosophy of Nietzsche* (New York: The Modern Library, 1927), p. 6.

12 *Ibid.,* IV, p. 8.

13 Nicolas Berdyaev, *The Divine and the Human* (London: Geoffrey Bles, 1949), p. 37.

14 Nicolas Berdyaev, *The Fate of Man in the Modern World* (New York: Morehouse Publishing Co., 1935), p. 18.

15 Berdyaev, *The Meaning of History,* p. 217.

16 *Ibid.,* p. 218.

17 *Ibid.*

18 Berdyaev, *The Fate of Man in the Modern World,* p. 88.

19 *Ibid.,* p. 54.

20 *Ibid.,* pp. 25f.

21 Berdyaev, *The End of Our Time,* p. 44.

22 *Ibid.,* p. 41.

23 *Ibid.,* p. 42.

24 *Ibid.,* p. 50. (This was writen in 1919, a quarter of a century before the invention of the atomic bomb!)

25 Berdyaev, *The Fate of Man in the Modern World,* p. 19.

26 Berdyaev, *The End of Our Time,* p. 80.

27 Berdyaev, *The Fate of Man in the Modern World,* p. 31.

28 *Ibid.,* p. 32.

29 Berdyaev, *The End of Our Time,* p. 25.

30 *Ibid.,* p. 34.

31 *Ibid.,* p. 70. (Italics mine.)

32 *Ibid.,* pp. 25f.

33 *Ibid.,* pp. 103f.

34 *Ibid.,* p. 82.

35 *Ibid.,* p. 106.

36 *Ibid.,* p. 108.

37 *Ibid.*

38 *Ibid.,* pp. 119f.

39 Berdyaev, *Dream and Reality,* p. 254.

40 *Ibid.,* p. 255.
41 *Ibid.,* pp. 258f.
42 See Sergius Bulgakov, *op. cit.,* p. 119.
42ª See Porret, *op. cit.,* p. 143.
43 Berdyaev, *Freedom and the Spirit,* p. xix.
44 *Ibid.,* p. xviii.
45 Nicolas Berdyaev, *The Destiny of Man* (London: The Centenary Press, 1937) , p. 26.
46 Quoted by Spinka, *op. cit.,* p. 88.
47 See Porret, *op. cit.,* p. 162.
48 *Ibid.,* pp. 167f.
49 Berdyaev, *Dream and Reality,* p. 323.
50 *Ibid.,* p. 324.
51 *Ibid.,* p. 325.
52 From the Latin text sent to the writer by Professor W. K. C. Guthrie, the Public Orator at the University of Cambridge, Great Britain.

PART II

CHAPTER I

1 John Milton, *Paradise Lost* (New York: Walter J. Black, 1943), pp. 139f.
2 Nicolas Berdyaev, *Spirit and Reality* (New York: Charles Scribner's Sons, 1946), p. 129. Cf. *Dream and Reality,* p. 179.
3 Quoted by Berdyaev in *Spirit and Reality,* p. 130. Cf. Nicolas Berdyaev, *The Beginning and the End* (London: Geoffrey Bles, 1952), pp. 105ff.
4 Cf. Howard H. Brinton, *The Mystic Will* (New York: The Macmillan Co., 1930), pp. 95ff; Charles A. Muses, *Illumination on Jacob Boehme* (New York: King's Crown Press, 1951), pp. 77ff; Caroline F. E. Spurgeon, *Mysticism in English Literature* (Cambridge: The University Press, 1913), pp. 94ff.
5 *The Destiny of Man,* p. 33; Cf. *Spirit and Reality,* pp. 127ff.
6 *Freedom and the Spirit,* p. 194.
7 *Dream and Reality,* p. 179.
8 *The Destiny of Man,* pp. 33ff.
9 *Freedom and the Spirit,* p. 195.
10 *Ibid.,* p. 11.
11 *Ibid.*
12 *Ibid.,* p. 24.
13 *Ibid.,* p. 71.

14 Paul Tillich, "Theology and Symbolism," in *Religious Symbolism* edited by F. Ernest Johnson (New York: Harper and Brothers, 1955), p. 108.

15 *Freedom and the Spirit*, p. 81.

16 Paul Tillich, *Systematic Theology* (Chicago: The University of Chicago Press, 1951), Vol. I, p. 240.

17 Reinhold Niebuhr, *Faith and History* (New York: Charles Scribner's Sons, 1951), p. 33.

18 *Freedom and the Spirit*, p. 9.

19 *Ibid.*, p. 11.

20 *The Beginning and the End*, pp. 102f.

21 *Freedom and the Spirit*, p. 13. Cf. *Spirit and Reality*, p. 10f.

22 *Freedom and the Spirit*, p. 13. With this compare C. G. Jung: "At first the materialistic error seems to be inevitable. Since the throne of God could not be discovered among the galactic systems, the inference was that God had never existed. The second inevitable mistake is psychologism: If God is anything, He must be an illusion derived from certain motives, from fear, for instance, from will to power, or from repressed sexuality. . . . I have constantly to repeat that neither the moral law nor the concept of God nor any religion has ever fallen down from outside, so to speak from heaven, upon mankind, but man has all this within him from the beginning and therefore he creates it out of himself. Hence it is just an idle thought that only enlightenment is required to drive out these ghosts." From *Psychological Reflections*, an anthology from the writings of C. G. Jung selected and edited by Jolande Jacobi, (New York: Pantheon Books, Inc., 1953), pp. 300f., 302.

23 *Freedom and the Spirit*, p. 13.

24 *Dream and Reality*, pp. 98f.

25 *The Divine and the Human*, p. 15.

26 See G. W. F. Hegel, *The Philosophy of History* (New York: Willey Book Co., 1944), pp. 9f.

27 *The Beginning and the End*, p. 95.

28 Sören Kierkegaard, *The Journals of Sören Kierkegaard*, (New York: Oxford University Press, 1938), pp. 357f.

29 *The Beginning and the End*, p. 95. Cf. *Slavery and Freedom*, pp. 73ff.

30 Quoted by John Wild, *The Challenge of Existentialism* (Bloomington: Indiana University Press, 1955), pp. 65f.

31 Quoted by Joseph de Tonquédec, *L'Existence d'après Karl Jaspers* (Paris: Beauchesne et ses Fils, 1945), p. 18.

32 Quoted by L. Harold DeWolf, *A Theology of the Living Church* (New York: Harper & Brothers, 1953), p. 97.

33 Exodus 3:14, margin.

34 *Slavery and Freedom*, pp. 82f.

35 *Ibid.*, p. 83.

36 Matthew 12:26.

37 John Calvin, *Institutes of the Christian Religion* (Philadelphia: Presbyterian Board of Christian Education), Vol. I, p. 220.

38 *Ibid.*, Vol. II, p. 181.

39 Romans 9:20.

40 Calvin, *op. cit.*, Vol. II, p. 175.

41 *The Destiny of Man*, p. 33.

42 *Ibid.*, p. 32.

43 Calvin, *op. cit.*, Vol. II, p. 199.

44 Pascal, *op. cit.*, p. 576.

45 *Slavery and Freedom*, pp 85f. Cf. *The Destiny of Man* pp. 36ff.

46 Reinhold Niebuhr, *The Nature and Destiny of Man* (New York, Charles Scribner's Sons, 1951), Vol. II, p. 46.

47 *Freedom and the Spirit*, p. 34.

48 *The Destiny of Man*, p .34.

49 *Freedom and the Spirit*, p. 192.

50 *Ibid.*, p. 191.

51 *The Divine and the Human*, p. 43.

52 *Freedom and the Spirit*, p. 200.

53 *Slavery and Freedom*, p. 76.

54 *The Destiny of Man*, p. 163.

55 See Spinka, *op. cit.*, p. 121.

56 Nicolas Berdyaev, *The Realm of Spirit and the Realm of Caesar* (New York: Harper and Brothers, 1952), pp. 105, 109.

57 *Freedom and the Spirit*, p. 121.

58 Henri Bergson, *Essai sur les données immédiates de la conscience* (Genève: Editions Albert Skira, 1945), pp. 131ff.

59 *The Realm of Spirit and the Realm of Caesar*, p. 103.

60 *Freedom and the Spirit*, p. 127. Cf. *The Destiny of Man*, p. 45.

61 *Ibid.*, p. 125.

62 *Ibid.*, p. 121f.

63 John 8:36.

64 *Freedom and the Spirit*, p. 132.

65 *Ibid.*, pp. 133f.

66 *Ibid.*, p. 135.

67 *Ibid.*, p. 139.

68 *Ibid.*, p. 135.

69 To avoid a possible confusion it ought to be noted that Berdyaev uses the term creation not in any of the usual senses. In his view God's "creation" is the outcome of the response of His "Other" to the Father's call.

70 *The Destiny of Man*, p. 34.

71 *Freedom and the Spirit*, p. 21. Cf. *The Destiny of Man*, p. 34.

72 *Ibid.*, p. 22.

73 *Ibid.*

74 *Ibid.,* p. 54. Cf. *The Beginning and the End,* p. 59.
75 The second Adam is Christ.
76 *The Destiny of Man,* p. 47.
77 See *Freedom and the Spirit,* p. 162.
78 *The Destiny of Man,* p. 48.
79 See *Freedom and the Spirit,* pp. 31, 199.
80 Hegel, *op. cit.,* pp. 321f.
81 *The Destiny of Man,* p. 50.
82 *Ibid.,* p. 48.
83 *Ibid.,* p. 49.
84 *Ibid.*
85 *The Beginning and the End,* pp. 56f.
86 *Ibid.,* p. 59.
87 *Ibid.,* p. 66.
88 *The Destiny of Man,* p. 51.

CHAPTER II

1 Reinhold Niebuhr, *The Nature and Destiny of Man,* p. 1.
2 H. L. Mencken, ed., *A New Dictionary of Quotations* (New York: Alfred A. Knopf, 1952), pp. 737ff.
3 *The Oxford Dictionary of Quotations* (London: Oxford University Press, 1955), pp. 102, 211.
4 Reinhold Niebuhr, *Ibid.*
5 *The Destiny of Man,* p. 60.
6 *Slavery and Freedom,* p. 20.
7 *The Nature and Destiny of Man,* p. 3.
8 Quoted by Niebuhr, *op. cit.,* p. 9.
9 *Ibid.,* pp. 8f.
10 *The Destiny of Man,* p. 61. Cf. B. Hansoul, o.p., *Esquisse d'une théologie de l'homme* in *Initation Théologique* par un groupe de théologiens (Paris: les éditions du Cerf, 1955) Vol. II, pp. 350ff.
11 *Ibid.,* p. 61. Cf. John Calvin, *op. cit.,* Vol. I, p. 270.
12 *Ibid.*
13 *Ibid.,* p. 68.
14 *Ibid.,* p. 69.
15 See Alfred Stern, *Sartre, His Philosophy and Psychoanalysis* (New York: The Liberal Arts Press, 1953), p. 174.
16 *The Destiny of Man,* p. 69.
17 *Freedom and the Spirit,* pp. 7f.
18 Cf. Ex. 30:32; Lev. 6:10; Num. 8:7; Job 14:22; Ps. 16:19.
19 See Gustav Friedrich Oehler, *Theology of the Old Testament* (New York: Funk & Wagnalls, 1883), pp. 149f.

20 Isa. 40:6; Job 34:15; Deut. 5:26.

21 Albert C. Knudson, *The Religious Teaching of the Old Testament* (New York: The Abington Press, 1918), p. 220.

22 Gen. 2:7.

23 Johs. Pederson, *Israel, Its Life and Culture* (London: Oxford University Press, 1946), Vol. I, p. 178.

24 Gen. 7:4, 23; cf. 6:17.

25 Otto J. Baab, *The Theology of the Old Testament* (New York: Abington-Cokesbury Press, 1949), p. 136.

26 Oehler, *op. cit.,* p. 149.

27 *Ibid.,* p. 153.

28 Cf. Ecc. 5:6; 11:2; Ps. 16:9; 84:2; 131:1; Eccl. 1:8; Prov. 23:6.

29 Pedersen, *op. cit.,* p. 176.

30 *Ibid.*

31 *Ibid.,* p. 146.

32 Knudson, *op. cit.,* pp. 221f.

33 Pedersen, *op. cit.,* p. 100.

35 Knudson, *op. cit.,* p. 223.

36 Gen. 35:18; I Kings 19:4; Jonah 4:3.

37 I Kings 17:23.

38 Oehler, *op. cit.,* p. 150.

39 Gen. 12:5.

40 Gen. 46:27.

41 Joshua 10:28.

42 Gen. 46:18.

43 Gen. 27:25, Cf. the French word *âme.*

44 Knudson, *op. cit.,* p. 224.

45 Pedersen, *op. cit.,* p. 103.

46 *Ibid.,* p. 171.

47 Knudson, *op. cit.,* p. 225.

48 Pedersen, *op. cit.,* p. 130.

49 Knudson, *op. cit.,* p. 230.

50 *Spirit and Reality,* p. 19.

51 Knudson, *op. cit.,* p. 231.

52 See Morton Scott Enslin, *Christian Beginnings* (New York: Harper & Brothers, 1938), pp. 154ff.

53 Mark 2:23-28.

54 Matt. 5:12.

55 Luke 17:21.

56 Matt. 5:21-30.

57 Matt. 5:44, 45.

58 Matt. 23:23.

59 Matt. 5:16, 45, 48.

60 Matt. 6:33.

61 Mark 2:17.

62 Matt. 18:21-35.

63 Luke 10:33-35.
64 Matt. 18:2.
65 Matt. 18:20-35.
66 Matt. 5:21-37.
67 Matt. 7:23.
68 Matt. 15:19, 20.
69 Matt. 7:16.
70 Luke 15:11-32.
71 Matt. 11:27.
72 *Spirit and Reality*, p. 20. Cf. Rudolf Bultmann, *Theology of the New Testament* (New York: Charles Scribner's Sons, 1951), Vol. I, p. 209.
73 Rom. 8:7.
74 I Cor. 1:16.
75 Rom. 7:9.
76 Rom. 8:13.
77 Rom. 5:12.
78 Gal. 3:22.
79 Rom. 3:23; cf. 3:9, 19.
80 Rom. 5:21.
81 Rom. 6:23.
82 I Cor. 15:56.
83 *Freedom and the Spirit*, p. 11.
84 I Cor. 15:42, 44.
85 Oehler, *op. cit.*, p. 146.
86 *Ibid.*
87 Hermann Schultz, *Old Testament Theology* (Edinburgh: T. and T. Clark, 1892), Vol. II, p. 258.
88 Charles Piepenbring, *Theology of the Old Testament* (New York: Thomas Y. Crowell & Co., 1893), pp. 171f.
89 Paul Heinisch, *Theology of the Old Testament* (Collegeville: The Liturgical Press, 1950), p. 156.
90 Knudson, *op. cit.*, p. 235.
91 Walther Eichrodt, *Man in the Old Testament* (London: SCM Press, Ltd., 1951), p. 30.
92 Reinhold Niebuhr, *The Nature and Destiny of Man,* pp. 153f.
93 Quoted by Niebuhr, *Ibid.*, p. 154.
94 Whitney J. Oates, Ed., *Basic Writings of Saint Augustine* (New York: Random House, 1948), Vol. I, pp. 153f.
95 *Ibid.*
96 *Ibid.*, p. 152.
97 Quoted by Niebuhr, *op. cit.*, p. 157.
98 Calvin, *op. cit.*, Vol. I, pp. 206, 208.
99 *Ibid.*, p. 214.
100 *Ibid.*, pp. 214f.
101 *Ibid.*, p. 210.

102 Quoted by Niebuhr, *The Nature and Destiny of Man*, Vol. I, p. 160.

103 *Ibid.*

104 *The Destiny of Man*, p. 70.

105 *Ibid.*, p. 69.

106 *The Destiny of Man*, pp. 69f.

107 *Freedom and the Spirit*, p. 212.

108 *Slavery and Freedom*, pp. 20f.

109 *Ibid.*, p. 22.

110 *Ibid.*, p. 10. Cf. *Freedom and the Spirit*, p. 25.

111 Emmanuel Mounier, *Le Personnalisme* (Paris: Presses Universitaires de France, 1950), pp. 10f.

112 Harry Emerson Fosdick, *A Guide to Understanding the Bible* (New York: Harper & Brothers, 1938), p. 94.

113 *Slavery and Freedom*, pp. 27f.

114 *Ibid.*, p. 28. Cf. *Solitude and Society*, pp. 106ff.

115 *Ibid.*, p. 29.

116 *Ibid.*, Cf. *Solitude and Society*, pp. 131f.

117 *Ibid.*, p. 30.

118 *Ibid.*, p. 38.

119 *Ibid.* Cf. *The Destiny of Man*, p. 74.

120 *Ibid.*

121 *Ibid.*, p. 42. Cf. *The Destiny of Man*, p. 75.

122 *Ibid.*, p. 47.

123 *Ibid.*

124 *Ibid.*, p. 48.

125 *Ibid.*, p. 55. Cf. *Solitude and Society*, p. 147.

126 Plato, *Symposium* pp. 200, 206; *Phaedrus* pp. 237ff., 242ff.

127 Quoted in Gehard Kittel, *Bible Key Words* (New York: Harper and Brothers, 1951), p. 27.

128 *Slavery and Freedom*, p. 56.

129 *Freedom and the Spirit*, p. 20.

130 *Ibid.*

CHAPTER III

1 *Freedom and the Spirit*, p. 189.

2 *Ibid.*

3 *Ibid.*, p. 195.

4 *Ibid.*, p. 196.

5 *Ibid.*, p. 189.

6 *The Realm of Spirit and the Realm of Caesar*, p. 37. Cf. *The Divine and the Human*, p. 111.

7 *Freedom and the Spirit*, p. 189.
8 *The Divine and the Human*, p. 110.
9 *Ibid.*
10 *Ibid.*, p. 110f.
11 *Slavery and Freedom*, p. 45.
12 Nicolas Berdyaev, *The Meaning of the Creative Act* (London: Victor Gollancz Ltd., 1955), p. 81.
13 Cf. George Seaver, *Nicolas Berdyaev, An Introduction to His Thought* (New York: Harper and Bros., 1950), p. 18.
14 Romans 8:16-17.
15 *Freedom and the Spirit*, pp. 50f.
16 *Ibid.*, p. 60.
17 *Ibid.*
18 *Ibid.*, p. 34.
19 William Temple, *Christus Veritas* (London: Macmillan & Co., 1924), p. 147.
20 Nicolas Berdyaev, *Truth and Revelation* (New York: Harper & Brothers, 1953), p. 97.
21 *Ibid.*, p. 98.
22 Emil Brunner, *The Mediator* (Philadelphia: The Westminster Press), p. 159 note.
23 *Ibid.*, p. 172.
24 Quoted by D. M. Baillie, *God Was in Christ* (New York: Charles Scribner's Sons, 1948), p. 36. Cf. Otto Weber, *Karl Barth's Church Dogmatics* (Philadelphia: The Westminster Press, 1953), pp. 41ff.
25 Bultmann, *op. cit.*, p. 188.
26 Rudolf Bultmann, *Jesus and The Word* (New York: Charles Scribner's Sons, 1934), pp. 8f. Cf. *Theology of the New Testament*, Vol. I, pp. 33ff.
27 Tillich, *Systematic Theology*, Vol. I, p. 136.
28 *Freedom and the Spirit*, pp. 90f.
29 *Ibid.*, p. 96.
30 *Ibid.*, p. 94.
31 *Ibid.*, p. 88.
32 *Slavery and Freedom*, p. 55.
33 William Temple, *Nature, Man and God* (London: Macmillan and Co., 1951), p. 306.
34 Quoted by Arthur Cushman McGiffert, *A History of Christian Thought* (New York: Charles Scribner's Sons, 1950), Vol. I, p. 218.
35 *Slavery and Freedom*, pp. 198f.
36 *Ibid.*, p. 138.
37 *Ibid.*
38 *Ibid.*, p. 140.

39 *Ibid.*

40 *Ibid.*

41 Matt. 16:16.

42 I Corinthians 1:23.

43 *Slavery and Freedom*, p. 141.

44 Cf. I Cor. 12:14, 27: "For the body does not consist of one member but of many. . . . Now you are the body of Christ and individually members of it." Col. 1:18: "He is the head of the body, the church."

45 *Freedom and the Spirit*, p. 330.

46 *Ibid.*, p. 329.

47 *Ibid.*, p. 333.

48 *Ibid.*, p. 328.

49 *Ibid.*, p. 334.

50 *Ibid.*, p. 336.

51 Bulgakov, *op. cit.*, p. 138.

52 *Ibid.*, p. 329.

53 Nels F. S. Ferré, *The Christian Faith* (New York: Harper and Brothers, 1942), pp. 166f.

54 Gustaf Aulén, *The Faith of the Christian Church* (Philadelphia: The Muhlenberg Press, 1948), p. 335.

55 *Ibid.*, p. 331.

56 *Freedom and the Spirit*, p. 330.

57 I Peter 2:9.

58 *Freedom and the Spirit*, p. 331.

59 *Ibid.*

60 Paul Tillich, *The Interpretation of History* (New York: Charles Scribner's Sons, 1936), p. 345.

61 *Freedom and the Spirit*, p. 339.

62 Reinhold Niebuhr, *Faith and History*, p. 238.

63 Reinhold Niebuhr, *Does Civilization Need Religion?* (New York: The Macmillan Co., 1929), p. 2.

64 *Freedom and the Spirit*, p. 347.

65 *Ibid.*, p. 348.

66 *Ibid.*, p. 355.

67 *Ibid.*

68 *Ibid.*, p. 356.

69 *Ibid.*

70 *Ibid.*

71 *Ibid.*, p. 356f.

72 *Ibid.*, p. 330.

73 Nels F. S. Ferré, *The Christian Fellowship* (New York: Harper & Brothers, 1940), p. 134.

74 Nels F. S. Ferré, *The Christian Understanding of God* (New York: Harper & Brothers, 1951), pp. 15f.

75 *Freedom and the Spirit*, p. 189.

1 Robert Elliot Fitch, *The Kingdom Without End* (New York: Charles Scribner's Sons, 1950), p. 2.

2 *The Destiny of Man*, p. 21.

3 *Ibid.*, p. 22.

4 *Ibid.*, p. 23.

5 *Ibid.*

6 *Ibid.*, pp. 24f.

7 *Ibid.*, p. 25. Cf. I Cor. 13:12: "For now we see in a mirror dimly, but then face to face. Now I know in part; then I shall understand fully."

8 *Ibid.*, p. 26.

9 *Ibid.*

10 *Ibid.*, p. 27.

11 Cf. Durkheim's declaration: "La morale n'est pas seulement faite pour la société, on peut dire qu'elle est faite par la société." From Emile Durkheim, *Sociologie et Philosophie* (Paris: Alcan, 1924), p. 77.

12 *Destiny of Man*, p. 27.

13 Martin Luther, *Three Treatises* (Philadelphia: The Muhlenberg Press, 1947), p. 128.

14 *The Destiny of Man*, p. 112.

15 Cf. Pedersen, *op. cit.,* Vol. I, pp. 376ff.

16 Exodus 20:5.

17 Judges 19-20.

18 Knudson, *op. cit.*, p. 341.

19 Ezekiel 18.

20 *The Destiny of Man*, pp. 127f.

21 Niebuhr, *The Nature and Destiny of Man,* Vol. II, p. 39.

22 *Ibid.*, p. 40.

23 *Ibid.*

24 *Ibid.*

25 *Ibid.*, pp. 40f. (Italics mine.)

26 *Ibid.*, p. 185.

27 Luther, *op. cit.*, p. 251.

28 Gal. 5:18; Rom. 6:14.

29 Rom. 3:20.

30 Rom. 10:4.

31 Gal. 5:4.

32 II Cor. 3:6.

33 Rom. 7:14.

34 Gal. 3:21.

35 Rom. 8:4.

36 *The Destiny of Man*, p. 111.

37 *The Meaning of the Creative Act*, p. 278.

38 *The Destiny of Man*, pp. 130f.

39 Acts 5:29.

40 *The Destiny of Man*, p. 253.

41 The subject is treated in *Meno*.

42 This is the theme of the fourth book of *Republic*.

43 *Republic*, VII, 517.

44 *Nichomachean Ethics*, 1106b36-1107a2.

45 Nicolas Berdyaev, *Solitude and Society* (London: The Centenary Press, 1947), p. 11.

46 *Ibid.*, p. 12.

47 Rom. 7:19.

48 *The Destiny of Man*, p. 138.

49 Niebuhr, *Faith and History*, pp. 6f.

50 Immanuel Kant, *Metaphysical Foundations of Morals* in *The Philosophy of Kant* ed. by Carl J. Friedrich (New York: The Modern Library, 1949), p. 170.

51 *Ibid.*, p. 178.

52 *Ibid.*, p. 180.

53 *The Destiny of Man*, p. 125.

54 *Ibid.*

55 *Ibid.*, pp. 122f.

56 *Ibid.*, p. 126.

57 Cf. Whitney J. Oates, ed. *The Stoic and Epicurean Philosophers* (New York: Random House, 1940), pp. 35ff.

58 Cf. Jeremy Bentham, *The Principles of Morals and Legislation* (New York: Hafner Publishing Company, 1948), pp. 24-42.

59 John Stuart Mill, *Utilitarianism, Liberty, and Representative Government* (London: J. M. Dent & Sons, Ltd., 1948), p. 6.

60 *Ibid.*

61 *Ibid.*, p. 9.

62 *The Destiny of Man*, p. 151.

63 *Ibid.*

64 *Ibid.*, p. 132.

65 *Ibid.*

66 Also, in Asia, by Buddhism.

67 Nicolo Machiavelli, *The Prince* (London: J. M. Dent & Sons, Ltd., 1948), p. 138.

68 *Ibid.*, p. 130.

69 *Ibid.*, pp. 138f.

70 Thomas Hobbes, *Leviathan* (London: George Routledge & Sons, Ltd., n.d.), p. 61.

71 *Ibid.*, p. 81.

72 *Ibid.*, p. 48.

73 Irwin Edman, ed., *The Philosophy of Schopenhauer* (New York: The Modern Library, 1928), pp. 70f.

74 Nietzsche, *op. cit.*, pp. 485f.

75 Friedrich W. Nietzsche, *The Antichrist* (New York: Alfred A. Knopf, 1918), pp. 108ff.

76 The first approximation of what is the most important in Nietzsche's philosophy is to be found in Plato's *Gorgias*. There a certain Callicles expounds his own views according to which mankind consists of two types of men: the weak and the strong. Natural justice demands that the strong should have everything for the sole reason of their being strong; the weak should have nothing on account of their weakness. But what happened? The weak understood how much this law was contrary to their interest. Thereupon they agreed to reverse in their favor the whole proposition. For justice according to nature, they substituted justice according to the civil law. As a result, the strong have to respect the weak, help and protect them even at their own expense. Callicles comes to the conclusion that the strong should set themselves free from the injustice of the civil law and bring back the rule of natural justice.

77 *Slavery and Freedom*, p. 60.

78 *Ibid.*, p. 148.

79 *Ibid.*, pp. 149-150.

80 *The Meaning of the Creative Act*, p. 260.

81 *The Destiny of Man*, p. 150.

82 *Ibid.*, p. 136.

83 *Ibid.*, p. 137.

84 *Ibid.*, p. 139.

85 *Ibid.*, p. 163.

86 *Ibid.*, p. 164.

87 *Ibid.*, p. 169.

88 *Ibid.*, p. 163. Cf. *Dream and Reality*, pp. 212ff.

89 For the Russian abstract noun *genialnost* which is derived from *genii*—genius. This is the best English approximation. The italics indicate, however, that it is not used in its ordinary sense.

90 *Ibid.*, p. 166.

91 *Ibid.*

92 *Ibid.*

93 *Dream and Reality*, p. 208.

94 *The Destiny of Man*, p. 169.

95 *Ibid.*, p. 171.

96 *Ibid.*

97 *Ibid.*, p. 172.

98 *Ibid.*, p. 314.

99 *Ibid.*, p. 313.

100 *Ibid.*, p. 175.

101 *Ibid.*

102 *Ibid.*, p. 174.

103 *Ibid.*

104 *Freedom and the Spirit*, p. 163.

105 *Ibid.*, p. 183.

106 *The Destiny of Man*, p. 341. Cf. *The Divine and the Human*, pp. 163f.

107 *Ibid.*, p. 353.

108 *Ibid.*

109 *Ibid.*, p. 357.

110 Ferré expresses a similar universalism when he writes: "There are no incorrigible sinners; God has no permanent problem children. Heaven, to those who truly love all, can be heaven only when it has emptied hell. . . . Each one in hell is also completely important to God, and without the salvation 'unto the last' God cannot be sovereign love. . . . Hell is not heaven unattained, but heaven rejected." (*The Christian Understanding of God*, p. 229.)

111 *The Destiny of Man*, p. 319. Cf. *The Divine and the Human*, pp. 149ff.

112 *Ibid.*, p. 366.

113 *Ibid.*, p. 377.

114 *Ibid.*, p. 334.

CHAPTER V

1 *The Fate of Man in the Modern World*, p. 2.

2 Quoted by Bertrand Russell, *History of Western Philosophy* (London: George Allen and Unwin, 1947), p. 45.

3 *Ibid.*, p. 63.

4 *Ibid.*, p. 62.

5 Cf. Niebuhr, *The Nature and Destiny of Man*, Vol II, pp. 11ff.

6 Cf. Paul Tillich, *The Protestant Era* (Chicago: The University Press, 1948), p. 19.

7 Cf. Emile Bréhier, *Histoire de la Philosophie* (Paris Félix Alcan, 1946), Vol. I, pp. 223ff.

8 Oates, *op. cit.*, p. 571.

9 *Ibid.*, p. 167.

It should be noted that the cyclical theories of history were not exhausted with the passing of the Greek classical period. They have, under various versions, continued a fruitful career down to our own time. Thus Plotinus, the last of the great thinkers of antiquity, took the philosophy of Plato and worked it out into a cyclical theory of the entire universe. From the ineffable One, according to Plotinus, the world emanates as light from the sun; this occurs in three stages—*nous* or spirit-reason, *psyche* or soul, and finally matter. The return to the One is secured also in three phases —*catharsis* or moral and aesthetic purification, *theoria* or contemplation of the One, and ultimately ecstasy, that is, reunion with the One. The vertical two way process is endless. John Scotus

Erigena (9th century A.D.), following Plotinus, maintained that there are two movements in the world process: one from God to the sensible world (devolution); another from the world back to God (involution). The movements are eternal and made possible by Christ.

In the 19th century the cyclical theory reappeared with Herbert Spencer's *First Principles*. To him everything passes from diffusion to integration, and from simplicity to complexity (evolution), and back again from integration to diffusion, and from complexity to simplicity (dissolution). The cycle of evolution and dissolution will be repeated endless times again. Nietzsche also made an attempt at binding history to the endless recurrences of nature whence everything comes and whither everything returns. Oswald Spengler likewise construed history in terms of closed cultural cycles; every culture is a closed period of time—it has a moment of beginning and a point of termination. Recently Arnold Toynbee expounded a new interpretation of history which in some of its aspects approximates the classical pattern. He contemplates history as an indefinite series of the rise and fall of civilizations.

The West has no monopoly on the cyclical understanding of history. Indeed, before Anaximander's time the Chinese, perhaps even as early as 1000 B.C., evolved a theory according to which the world and every phenomenon within it are the results of two interacting forces, the *Yang* (masculine in character—active, light, and positive) and the *Ying* (feminine in character—passive, dark, and negative). The two principles are accountable for success and failure, rise and fall, ascendance and decay in all things. The alternates are forever recurrent. The Hindu approach to history betokens a similar trend of thought. The world originates in, and returns to, Brahma—endlessly.

10 *The Meaning of History,* p. 27.

11 *Ibid.,* p. 29.

12 *Ibid.,* p. 3.

13 *Ibid.,* p. 7.

14 Quoted by Fritz Stern, ed. *The Varieties of History* (New York: Meridian Books, 1956), p. 40.

15 Cf. Voltaire, *Essai sur les moeurs et l'esprit des nations* (Stoutgart: Expédition de l'histoire de notre temps, 1829), 4 vol.

16 Quoted by Fritz Stern, *op. cit.,* p. 37.

17 It should be pointed out to Voltaire's credit, however, that if he lacked the sense of history, he possessed to a high degree that of the historian's craftsmanship. He persistently studied the original sources pertaining to his subject, inquired of survivors of famous events, and accepted nothing as true before a critical scrutiny of evidences. For these reasons he might be rightly called the founder of the modern concept of history.

18 *The Meaning of History*, p. 7.
19 *Ibid.*
20 *Ibid.*, p. 10.
21 Max Eastman, ed. *Capital, The Communist Manifesto and Other Writings by Karl Marx* (New York: The Modern Library, 1932), p. 318.
22 *Ibid.*, pp. 9-11. (Italics mine.)
23 Quoted, *Ibid.*, p. xxii.
24 *Ibid.*, p. 321.
25 *Ibid.*, p. 324.
26 *Ibid.*, pp. 167f.
27 *Ibid.*, p. 309.
28 *Ibid.*, p. 334.
29 *Ibid.*, p. 355.
30 *The Meaning of History*, p.12.
31 *Ibid.*, p. 16.
32 *Ibid.*, p. 14.
33 *Ibid.*, p. 17.
34 *Ibid.*, p. 16.
35 *Solitude and Society*, p. 107.
36 *The Meaning of History*, p. 197.
37 *Ibid.*, p. 24.
38 *Ibid.*, pp. 24f.
39 *Ibid.*, p. 23f.
40 *Ibid.*, p. 28.
41 *Ibid.*
42 Tillich and Niebuhr agree with Berdyaev in their respective interpretation of the Old Testament philosophy of history. To Tillich Jewish prophetism "must be considered as the real birthplace of a universal historical consciousness in world history." (*The Protestant Era*, p. 22). Niebuhr likewise holds that "Old Testament messianism . . . lays the foundation for the Christian, rather than the modern, attitude toward history by the fact that the expected messianic reign is always conceived as in some sense the end, as well as the fulfillment, of historic meanings." (*Faith and History*, p. 134.).
43 *The Nature and Destiny of Man*, Vol. II, p. 15.
44 *Ibid.*, p. 23.
45 *The Meaning of History*, p. 34.
46 *Ibid.*, pp. 34f.
47 *Ibid.*, p. 37.
48 *Ibid.*, p. 32.
49 *Ibid.*
50 *Solitude and Society*, p. 97.
51 *Timaeus*, 37-39.
52 *Physics*, 220a, 25.

53 *Ibid.*, 219a, 5.
54 *Slavery and Freedom*, pp. 258f.
55 Oswald Spengler, *The Decline of the West* (New York: Alfred A. Knopf, 2 vols., 1950), Vol. I, p. 107.
56 *Ibid.*, p. 21.
57 This holds equally true of the rest of the cultures in Spengler's classification, namely, Apollonian or Greco-Roman, Magian or Irano-Hebrew-Arabian, Egyptian, Chinese, Indian, Mexican, Babylonian, and, marginally, Russian.
58 *Slavery and Freedom*, p. 259.
59 *Ibid.*
60 *Ibid.*, p. 260.
61 *The Meaning of History*, pp. 192f.
62 *Truth and Revelation*, p. 78.
63 Hegel, *op. cit.*, p. 52.
64 *Truth and Revelation*, p. 79.
65 *Slavery and Freedom*, p. 260.
66 *Ibid.*, p. 261.
67 *Ibid.*, p. 262.
68 *Ibid.*, p. 260.
69 Oscar Cullmann, *Christ and Time* (Philadelphia: The Westminster Press, 1950), p. 39.
70 Paul Tillich, *The Protestant Era*, p. 28.
71 *Slavery and Freedom*, p. 263.
72 *The Meaning of History*, p. 40.
73 *Ibid.*, p. 49. Cf. *The Destiny of Man*, p. 34.
74 *Ibid.*, p. 88.
75 *Ibid.*, p. 92.
76 *Ibid.*, p. 104.
77 *Ibid.*, p. 105. Cf. Léon Bloy, *Le salut par les Juifs* (Paris: éditions Crès, 1928), p. 70.
78 *Ibid.*, p. 106. Cf. Nicolas Berdyaev, *Christianity and Anti-Semitism* (New York: Philosophical Library, 1954), p. 8.
79 Saint Augustine, *The City of God* (New York: The Modern Library, 1950), p. 356.
80 *Ibid.*, p. 477.
81 In his *Discours sur l'Histoire Universelle,* Bossuet likewise accords to the Chosen People the central position in the history of mankind. To him the history of all other nations in the world is to be viewed in the light of Hebrew history. However, he seems to relegate all the Jews into one camp, that of the deicide—the murderers of God—who were punished by the diaspora and have no longer any part in the progressive course of human history.
82 *The Meaning of History*, p. 110.
83 *Ibid.*, pp. 113f.
84 *Ibid.*, p. 117.

85 *Ibid.*, p. 118.
86 *Ibid.*, p. 125.
87 *Ibid.*, p. 121.
88 Spengler, *op. cit.*, p. 31.
89 *The Meaning of History*, p. 216.
90 Arnold J. Toynbee, *A Study of History*, abridgement by D. C. Somerwell (New York: Oxford University Press, 1950), p. 273, foot-note 1.
91 *Ibid.*, p. 309.
92 "For God so loved the world that he gave his only Son, that whoever believes in him should not perish but have eternal life."
93 Toynbee, *op. cit.*, p. 547. *Note*: Toynbee's recent apparent religious syncretism is incomparably below his magnificent spiritual insight as it is expressed in the above quoted passage.
94 *Freedom and the Spirit*, p. 188.
95 *The Meaning of History*, p. 197.
96 *Ibid.*, p. 198.
97 *Ibid.*, p. 201.
98 *Slavery and Freedom*, p. 268.
99 Goethe, *Faust* (London: The Penguin Books, 1954), p. 39.

CHAPTER VI

1 *Slavery and Freedom*, p. 8. Cf. *Dream and Reality*, p. 96.
2 *Slavery and Freedom*, p. 36.
3 *Solitude and Society*, p. 32.
4 *Slavery and Freedom*, p. 42.
5 *Ibid.*, p. 43.
6 Nicolas Berdyaev, *Towards A New Epoch* (London: Geoffrey Bles, 1949), p. 11, footnote.
7 *The Destiny of Man*, p. 16.
8 *Ibid.*, p. 17.
9 *Ibid.*, p. 18.
10 Rufus M. Jones, *Mysticism* in Hastings Encyclopedia, Vol. 9, p. 83.
11 *Ibid.* Cf. Rufus M. Jones, *Pathways to the Reality of God*, (New York: The Macmillan Company, 1931), pp. 21ff.
12 William James, *Varieties of Religious Experience* (New York: The Modern Library, 1902), p. 370. He goes on to say that "mystical states offer us *hypotheses*, hypotheses which we may voluntarily ignore, but which as thinkers we cannot possibly upset. The super-naturalism and optimism to which they would persuade us may, interpreted in one way or another, be after all the truest of insights into the meaning of this life" (*Ibid.*, pp. 419f.).

13 Evelyn Underhill, *Mysticism* (New York: E. P. Dutton and Company, 1912), p. 534.

14 Cf. Rudolf Otto, *Mysticism East and West* (New York: The Macmillan Company, 1932), p. 141: "Mysticism enters into the religious experience in the measure that religious feeling surpasses its rational content . . . to the extent to which its hidden, non-rational, numinous elements predominate and determine the emotional life."

15 It should be noted, however, that there exists within Christianity another major tradition going through Jeremiah, Paul, Augustine, etc., and which is at odds with the mystical heritage.

16 *Dream and Reality*, p. 83.

17 *Freedom and the Spirit*, p. 267. Cf. *The Meaning of the Creative Act*, pp. 296ff.

18 Underhill, *op. cit.*, p. 535.

19 *Dream and Reality*, p. 83.

20 Martin Buber, *I and Thou* (New York: Charles Scribner's Sons, 1955), p. 11.

21 *Ibid.*, p. 28.

22 *Ibid.*, p. 75.

23 *Ibid.*, p. 76.

24 Martin Buber, *Between Man and Man* (Boston: Beacon Press, 1947), p. 43.

25 Buber, *I and Thou*, p. 93.

26 Buber, *Between Man and Man*, p. 43.

27 Cf. *The Destiny of Man*, p. 34.

28 Evgeny Lampert, "Nicolas Berdyaev" in Donald Attwater, ed., *Modern Christian Revolutionaries* (New York: The Devin-Adair Company, 1947), p. 346, footnote 4.

29 Spinka, *op. cit.*, pp. 121f.

30 Oliver Fielding Clarke, *Introduction to Berdyaev* (London: Geoffrey Bles, 1950), p. 87.

31 Compare this with Brightman's statement concerning "The Given." He writes: "All experience testifies [that] the eternal nature of God contains a principle of delay and suffering within itself. Every choice of God is limited not merely by the eternal necessities of reason (which prohibit contradictions), but also by the eternal and *uncreated nature of divine experience*. . . . We may say that the content of this experience is such that it both renders necessary eternal pain in God and also renders possible the kind of triumph over pain that the inexhaustible good will of God achieves." Edgar Sheffield Brightman, *The Finding of God* (New York: The Abingdon Press, 1931), p. 119. (Italics mine).

32 *Dream and Reality*, p. 180.

33 *The Meaning of the Creative Act*, p. 105.

34 *Slavery and Freedom*, p. 31.

35 John 8:10-11.

36 I Thes. 5:5.

37 Gal. 4:6.

38 II Cor. 6:16.

39 Rom. 8:16.

40 I John 3:2.

41 *The Destiny of Man*, p. 140.

42 It should be understood that Berdyaev's idea of creativity is not to be equated with the modern activism which, in most cases, threatens to exclude man's spiritual life and cut him off from religious sources of his life. Berdyaev's idea of the creative act is related to the spiritual, not material, significance.

43 *Freedom and the Spirit*, p. x.

44 Fielding Clarke, *op. cit.*, p. 175.

45 Cf. Solovyev, *Lectures on Godmanhood.*

46 John 4:18. Cf. Isaiah 61:1.

47 John 8:36.

48 Gal. 2:20.

49 Col. 1:17.

50 Romans 13:1, 3.

51 John 3:16.

52 Romans 12:21.

53 *Dream and Reality*, p. 293.

54 Matt. 18:8. Cf. Matt. 25:41, 46; Mark 3:29; 9:43-48; II Tim. 1:9; Jude 7.

55 Cf. Matt. 5:22, 29; 8:12; 10:15; 11:22; 12:32; 25:41-46. Cf. Mark 3:29.

56 Friedrich Schleiermacher, *The Christian Faith* (Edinburgh: T. & T. Clark, 1956), p. 720. Cf. Matt. 24:30-34; John 5:24-25.

57 Cf. Mark 3:29; Matt. 18:8, 9.

58 I Tim. 2:4.

59 I Tim. 4:10.

60 Matt. 18:11.

61 John 4:22. Cf. I John 4:14.

62 John 3:17.

63 Schleiermacher, *op. cit.*, p. 720.

64 I Cor. 15:28.

65 Matt. 18:13.

66 *Dream and Reality*, p. 294.

67 Psalm 24:1. Cf. Exodus 9:29; 19:; Deut. 10:14; Job 41:11; Psalm 50:12; I Cor. 10:26, 28.

68 Psalm 24:2. Cf. Genesis 1:9; Job 38:6; Psalm 104:5; II Peter 3:5. *Note*: The Psalmist's obvious reference to the story of creation does not preclude a symbolic, to wit, deeper and truer comprehension of his realism.

69 *Dream and Reality*, p. 295.

70 John 15:19.

71 II Cor. 5:20.
72 Matt. 28:19.
73 Spinka, *op. cit.*, p. 195.
74 *Dream and Reality*, pp. 297f.
75 *Slavery and Freedom*, p. 8.
76 *Dream and Reality*, p. 289.
77 *Ibid.*, p. 302.

BIBLIOGRAPHY

Note: An effort has been made to give the original Russian title whenever possible and its corresponding title in English. All known French, German, and Spanish translations of Berdyaev's books have been listed under the Russian titles.

I. Berdyaev's Own Writings

1. Books

Subyektivism i individualism v obshchestvennoi filosofii (Subjectivism and Individualism in Social Philosophy). St. Petersburg: Electritcheskaya Tipografia, 1901.

Sub specie aeternitatis: Opyty filosofskiye, sotsialniye i literaturniye (In the Light of Eternity: Philosophical, Social and Literary Essays). St. Petersburg, 1907.

Novoye religiosznoye soznaniye i obshchestvennost (New Religious Consciousness and the Social Problem). St. Petersburg: M. V. Piroshkov, 1907.

Filosofiya svobody (Philosophy of Freedom). Moscow, 1911.

Dukhovny krizis inteligentsii (Spiritual Crisis of the Intelligentsia). St. Petersburg, 1911.

Dusha Rosii (The Soul of Russia). Moscow, 1911.
   Translation:
      L'âme russe. Paris: Bloud et Gay, 1927.

Aleksei Stepanovich Khomyakov (Alexis Stepanovich Khomyakov). Moscow, 1912.

Smysl tvorchestva (The Meaning of Creativity). Moscow: G. A. Lemana and S. I. Sakharov, 1915.
   Translations:
      Der Sinn des Schaffens. Translated by Reinhold von Walter.

Tubingen: Mohr, 1927.
The Meaning of the Creative Act. Translated by Donald A. Lowrie. London: Victor Gollancz Ltd., 1955.
Sudba Rossii (The Fate of Russia) Moscow, 1918.
Smysl istorii (The Meaning of History). Berlin: Obelisk, 1923,
Translations:
Der Sinn der Geschichte. Darmstadt: O. Reichl, 1925.
Le sens de l'histoire. Translated by S. Jankélévitch. Paris: Aubier, 1948.
The Meaning of History. Translated by George Reavey. New York: Charles Scribner's Sons, 1936.
El sentido de la historia. Barcelona: Araluce, 1943.
Mirosozertsanie Dostoyevskago (Dostoyevsky's World-view). Prague: Y.M.C.A. Press, 1923.
Translations:
Die Weltanschauung Dostojewskiis. Translated by Wolfgang E. Groeger. Munich: C. H. Becksche Verlh, 1925.
L'esprit de Dostoievski. Translated by Alexis Nerville. Paris: Stock, 1946.
Dostoyevsky. Translated by Donald Attwater. New York: Sheed and Ward, 1934.
El Credo de Dostoyevsky. Translated by Alexis Markoff, Barcelona: Apolo, 1935.
Flisofiya neravenstva: Pisma k nedrugam po sotsialnoi filosofii (Philosophy of Inequality: Letters to Enemies on Social Philosophy). Berlin: Obelisk, 1923.
Translation:
Philosophie der Ungleichheit. Darmstadt, 1923.
Russkaya religioznaya idea (The Russian Religious Idea). Berlin: Obelisk, 1924.
Translations:
Die russische religiöse Idee. Darmstadt: Otto Reichl, 1926.
L'idée religieuse russe. Paris: Cahiers de la nouvelle journée, 1927.
Novoye srednevyekovie (The New Middle Ages). Berlin: Obelisk, 1924.
Translations:
Das Neue Mittelalter. Translated by Alexander Kresling. Darmstadt: Otto Reichl, 1927.
Un nouveau moyen âge. Translated by A. M. F. Paris: Plon, 1927.

The End of Our Time. Translated by Donald Attwater. New York: Sheed and Ward, 1933.

Problemy russkago religioznago soznaniya (Problems of Russian Religious Consciousness). Paris Y.M.C.A. Press, 1924.

Konstantin Leontyev (Constantin Leontiev) Paris: Y.M.C.A. Press, 1926.

Translations:

Constantin Leontieff. Translated by Hélène Iswolsky. Paris: Desclee de Brouwer, 1936.

Leontiev. Translated by George Reavey. Toronto: S. J. R. Saunders, 1940.

Filosofiya svobodnago dukha (Philosophy of the Free Spirit). 2 vols., Paris: Y.M.C.A. Press, 1927.

Translations:

Die Philosophie des freien Geistes. Translated by Reinhold von Walter. Tubingen: Mohr, 1930.

Esprit et liberté. Translated by I. P. and H. M. Paris: Editions "Je sers," 1933.

Freedom and the Spirit. Translated by Oliver Fielding Clarke. New York: Charles Scribner's Sons, 1935.

O dostoinstvye Khristianstva i nedostoinstvye Khristian. (The Worth of Christianity and the Unworthiness of Christians). Warsaw, 1928.

Translations:

De la dignité du christianisme et de l'indignité des chrétiens. Translated by I. P. and H. M. Paris: Editions "Je sers," 1931.

"The Worth of Christianity and the Unworthiness of Christians," in *The Bourgeois Mind and Other Essays.* Translated by Countess Bennigsen and Donald Attwater. New York: Sheed and Ward, 1933.

El Cristianismo y la Lucha de Clases; Dignidad del Cristianismo e Indignidad de los Cristianos. Translated by Maria de Cordona. Madrid: Espasa-Calpe, 1935.

Von der Würde des Christentums und der Unwürde der Christen. Translated by I Schor. Lucerne: Vita Nova Verlag, 1936.

Marksizm i religiya (Marxism and Religion). Warsaw, 1929.

Translation:

Le Marxisme et la religion. Paris: Edition "Je sers," 1929.

Khristianstvo i aktivnost chelovieka (Christianity and the Activity of Man). Paris: Y.M.C.A. Press, 1929.

Translation:
"Christianity and Human Activity" in *The Bourgeois Mind.*
Translated by Countess Benningsen and Donald Attwater.
New York: Sheed and Ward, 1933.
O naznachenii chelovyeka: Opyt paradoksalnoi etiki (On the Destiny of Man: Essay in Paradoxical Ethics). Paris: Y.M.C.A. Press, 1931.
Translations:
De la destination de l'homme: essai d'éthique paradoxale.
Translated by I. P. and H. M. Paris: Editions "Je sers," 1934.
Von der Bestimmung des Menschen. Translated by J. Schor.
Bern: Gotthelf-Verl., 1935.
The Destiny of Man. Translated by Natalie Duddington.
New York: Charles Scribner's Sons, 1937.
O samoubiitstvie (On Suicide). Paris: Y. M. C. A. Press, 1931.
Russkaya religioznaya psikhologiya i kommunisticheskii ateizm (Russian Religious Psychology and Communistic Atheism). Paris: Y.M.C.A. Press, 1931.
Translations:
The Russian Revolution: Two Essays in its Implications in Religion and Psychology. Translated by Donald Attwater in *Essays* in Order, No. 6. New York: The Macmillan Company, 1932.
Problèmes du communisme. Paris. Desclée de Brouwer, 1933.
Wahrheit und Lüge des Kommunismus mit einem Anhang: Der Mensch und die Technik. Translated by J. Schor. Lucerne: Vita Nova Verlag, 1934.
El cristianismo y el problema del communismo. Translated by Maria de Cardona. Madrid: Espasa-Calpe, 1936.
Khristianstvo i klassovaya borba (Christianity and the Class War). Paris: Y.M.C.A. Press, 1931.
Translations:
Le Christianisme et la lutte des classes. Translated by I. P. and H. M. Paris: Demain, 1932.
Christianity and the Class War. Translated by Donald Attwater. New York: Sheed and Ward, 1933.
El cristianismo y la Lucha de Clases; Dignidad del cristianismo e indignidad de los cristianos. Translated by Maria de Cardona. Madrid: Espasa-Calpe, 1934.

Khristianstvo pered sovremennoi deistvitelsnostyu (Christiani. and Modern Reality). Paris: Y.M.C.A. Press, 1932.

Cheloviek i mashina. Paris: Y.M.C.A. Press, 1933.

Translations:

L'homme et la machine. Paris: Editions "Je sers," 1933.

Man and The Machine. Translated by Countess Benningsen and Donald Attwater. New York: Sheed and Ward, 1933.

El Hombre y la Máquina. Translated by Paul Silva Castro. Santiago de Chile: Editiones Ercilla. 1933.

Sudba chelovyeka v sovremennom mire (Fate of Man in the Modern World). Paris: Y.M.C.A. Press, 1934.

Translations:

The Fate of Man in the Modern World. Translated by Donald Lowrie. Milwaukee: Morehouse Gorham Company, 1935.

Das Schicksal des Menschen in unserer Zeit. Translated by J. Schor. Lucerne: Vita Nova Verlag, 1935.

Destin de l'homme dans le monde actual. Paris: Stock, 1936.

Ya i mir obyektov (I and the World of Objects). Paris: Y.M.C.A. Press, 1934.

Translations:

Cinq méditations sur l'existence. Translated by Irène Vilde-Lot. Paris: Fernand Aubier, 1936.

Solitude and Society. Translated by George Reavey. London: Geoffrey Bles, 1947.

Dukh i realnost (Spirit and Reality). Paris: Y.M.C.A. Press, 1937.

Translations:

Spirit and Reality. Translated by George Reavey, New York: Charles Scribner's Sons, 1939.

Esprit et réalité. Paris: Aubier, 1943.

O rabstvie i svobodie chelovieka (On Man's Slavery and Freedom). Paris: Y.M.C.A. Press, 1939.

Translations:

Slavery and Freedom. Translated by R. M. French. New York: Charles Scribner's Sons, 1944.

De l'esclavage et de la liberté de l'homme. Translated by S. Jankelevitch. Paris: Montaigne, 1946.

Khristianstvo i antisemitizm (Christianity and Anti-Semitism). Paris: Editeurs réunis, 1939.

349

Translations:
Le Christianisme et l'antisémitisme. Translated by Princess Théodore. Paris: Editeurs réunis, 1940.
Christianity and Anti-Semitism. Translated by Alan A. Spears and Victor B. Kanter. New York: Philosophical Library, 1954.
Russkaya ideya (The Russian Idea) Paris. Y.M.C.A. Press, 1946.
Translation:
The Russian Idea. Translated by R. M. French. New York: The Macmillan Co., 1948.
Opyt eskatologicheskoi metafiziki (Essay on Eschatological Metaphysics). Paris: Y.M.C.A. Press 1947.
Translations:
Essai de métaphysique eschatologique. Translated by Maxime Herman. Paris: Fernand Aubier, 1947.
The Beginning and the End. Translated by R. M. French. London: Geoffrey Bles, 1952.
Samopoznanie (Self-Knowledge) Paris: Y.M.C.A. Press, 1949.
Translations:
Dream and Reality. Translated by Katherine Lampert. New York: The Macmillan Co., 1951.

Additional English Titles
The Russian Revolution. London: Sheed & Ward, 1934.
The Origin of Russian Communism. Translated by R. M. French. New York: Charles Scribner's Sons, 1937.
War and the Christian Conscience. London: James Clarke and Company, 1938.
The Divine and the Human. Translated by R. M. French. London: Geoffrey Bles, 1949.
Toward a New Epoch. Translated by Oliver Fielding Clarke. London: Geoffrey Bles, 1949.
The Realm of Spirit and the Realm of Caesar. Translated by Donald Lowrie. New York: Harper and Brothers, 1952.

Additional French Titles
Pensée Russe sur l'Eglise. Paris: L'institut Oriental, 1926.
Christianisme et réalité sociale. Paris: Editions "Je sers," 1933.
Le communisme et les Chrétiens. "Personne Humaine et Marxisme," pp. 178-201. Paris: Plon, 1937.

350

Les sources et le sense du communisme russe. Translated by Alexis Nerville. Paris: Gallimard, 1938.
L'Orient et l'Occident. Paris: Edition "Je sers," n. d.
Dialectique existentielle du divin et de l'humain. Paris: Janin, 1947.
Au Seuil de la nouvelle époque. Translated by Doria Olivier. Neuchatel-Paris: Delachaux et Niestlé, 1947.
Royaume de l'esprit et royaume de César. Translated by Philippe Sabant. Paris: Delachaux et Nietlé, 1951.
Die menschliche Persönlichkeit und die überpersönlichen Werte. Vienna: Bermann-Fischer, 1937.
Sinn und Schicksal des russischen Kommunismus. Translated by J. Schor. Lucerne: Vita Nova Verlag, 1937.

Additional Spanish Titles
Las Fuentes y el Sentido del Communismo Ruso. Translated by Vincente Mendivil. Buenos Aires: Editorial Losada, 1939.

2. Articles

"A. Lange i kriticheskaya filosofiya" (A. Lange and Critical Philosophy), in *Mir Bozhii* (July, 1900).

"O novom religioznom soznanii" (On the New Religious Consciousness), in *Voprosy zhizni* (St. Petersburg, 1905).

"Russkii soblazn" Po povodu Serebryanogo Golubya A. Belago ("The Russian Temptation," Concerning A. Beloy's Silver Dove), in *Russkaya Mysl* (1910).

"A. S. Khomyakov" (A. S. Khomyakov), in *Put'* (1911).

"Stilizovannoe pravoslavie" (Conventional Orthodoxy), in *Russkaya Mysl* (1914).

"Religiya Monisma" (Monist Religion), in *Voprosy Filisofii i Psikhologii* (1914).

"Stavrogin" (Stavrogin), in *Russkaya Mysl* (1914).

"Religiya voskresseniya. Filosofiya obshchago dyela N. F. Fedorova" (The Religion of Resurrection. N. F. Fedorov's Philosophy of the Common Deed), in *Russkaya Mysl* (1915).

"Tipy religioznoi mysli v Rossii; Novoe Khristianstvo" (Types of Religious Thought in Russia; the New Christianity), in *Russkaya Mysl* (1916).

"Dva tipa mirosozertsaniya" (Two types of World-views) in *Voprosy Filosofii i Psikhologii* (1916).

"Povest o nebesnom rodye" (The Tale of the Heavenly Origin),
in *Russkaya Mysl* (1916).

"Khomyakov i svyashchennik P. A. Florensky" (Khomyakov
and the Priest Florensky), in *Russkaya Mysl* (1917).

"Dusha Rossii" (The Soul of Russia), reprinted in *Sudba Rossii*
(Moscow, 1918).

"Konetz Renessansa" (The End of Renaissance), in *Sofiya* (Berlin, 1923). Also in *The End of Our Time* (New York: Sheed &
Ward Inc., 1933).

"Zhivaya Tserkov' i religioznoe vozrozhdenie v Rossii" (The
Living Church and the Religious Revival in Russia), in *Sofiya*
(Berlin, 1923).

"Tsarstvo Bozhie i tsarstvo kesaria" (The Kingdom of God and
the Kingdom of Caesar), in *Put'*. Vol. I (September, 1925), pp.
31-52.

"Evraziytsy" (Eurasians), in *Put'*, Vol. I (November, 1925), pp.
134-139.

"Neotomism" (Neo-Tomism), in *Put'*, Vol. I (December, 1925),
pp. 169-171.

"Spasenie i tvorchestvo (Salvation and Creativity), in *Put'*, Vol.
II (January, 1926), pp. 26-46.

"O dukhovnoi burzhuaznosti" (On the Spiritual Bourgeoisie),
in *Put'*, Vol. III (March-April, 1926), pp. 3-13.

"Otvet na pismo monarkhista" (The Answer to a Monarchist's
Letter), in *Put'*, Vol. III (November, 1926), pp. 140-144.

"D'Erbini o religioznom obraze Moskvy v oktyabre 1925"
(d'Herbigny and the Religious Aspect of Moscow in October,
1925), in *Put'*, Vol. III (November, 1926), pp. 145-147.

"Koshmar zlogo dobra" (Nightmare of the Evil Good), in *Put'*,
Vol. IV (June-July, 1926), pp. 103-116.

"Dnevnik filosofa" (The Diary of a Philosopher), in *Put'*, Vol.
IV (June-July, 1926), pp. 176-182.

"Die Krisis der Kultur" in *Europäische Revue,* Vol. II (March,
1926), pp. 6-12.

"Josef de Mestr i masonstvo" (Joseph de Maistre and Free-
masonry), in *Put'*, Vol. IV (September, 1926). pp. 183-187.

"Tserkovnaya smuta is svoboda sovyesti" (Church Troubles and
the Freedom of Conscience), in *Put'*, Vol. V (October-November,
1926), pp. 42-54.

"Novaya kniga o Jakovie Beme" (A New Book on Jakob Boehme), in *Put'*, Vol. V (December, 1926), pp. 119-122.

"Nauka o religii i khristianskaya apologetika," (Science of Religion and Christian Apologetics), in *Put'*, Vol. VI (January, 1927), pp. 50-68.

"N. Losskiy. Svoboda voli" (N. Lossky. The Freedom of the Will), in *Put'*, Vol. VI (March, 1927), pp. 130-131.

"Iz razmyshlenii o teoditseye" (Reflections on Theodicy), in *Put'*, Vol. VII (April, 1927), pp. 50-62.

"Syezd v Avstrii" (The Meeting in Austria), in *Put'*, Vol. VIII (September, 1927), pp. 131-133.

"Problema khristianskago gosudarstva" (The Problem of the Christian State), in *Sovremenniya zapiski*. Vol. XXXI September, 1927), pp. 280-305.

"Utopicheskiy statizm evraziytsev" (The Utopian Statism of the Eurasians), in *Put'*, Vol. VIII (October, 1927), pp. 141-144.

"Obvineniye Zapada" (Accusation of the West), in *Put'*, Vol. VIII (October, 1927), pp. 145-148.

"Die Läuterung des Russischen Nationalismus" in *Preussische Jahrbücher*, Vol. CCX (November, 1927), pp. 198-202.

"Metafizicheskaya problema svobody" (The Metaphysical Problem of Freedom), in *Put'*, Vol. IX (February, 1928), pp. 41-53.

"Katolichestvo i Action Française" (Catholicism and Action Française), in *Put'*, Vol. X (April, 1928), pp. 115-123.

"Jean Izoulet. Paris, capitale des religions ou la mission d'Israel," in *Put'*, Vol. X (May, 1928), pp. 130-132.

"Try Yubileya: L. Tolstoy, G. Ibsen, N. Fedorov" (Three Jubilees: L. Tolstoy, G. Ibsen, N. Fedorov), in *Put'*, Vol. XI (June, 1928), pp. 76-94.

"Augustin Jakubisiak: Essai sur les limites de l'espace et du temps," in *Put'*, Vol. XI (September, 1928), pp. 127-129.

"Der neue Typus des Russischen Jungen," in *Europäische Revue*, Vol. III (October, 1928), pp. 811-817.

"Obskurantizm" (Obscurantism), in *Put'*, Vol. XIII (October, 1928), pp. 19-36.

"Svoboda i tvorchestvo" (Freedom and Creativity), in *Put'*, Vol. XIII (November, 1928), pp. 78-86.

"Pravoslaviye i svobodomyslie" (Orthodoxy and Free thinking), in *Sovremenniya Zapiski*, Vol. XXXII (November, 1928), pp. 245-260.

"Illyuzii i realnosti v psikhologii emigrantskoi molodyozhi" (Illusions and Realities in the Psychology of the Emigrant Youth), in *Put'*, Vol. XIV (December, 1928), pp. 3-30.

"Dnevnik filosofa" (A Philosopher's Diary), in *Put'*, Vol. XVI (April, 1929), pp. 82-94.

"O Sofiologii" (On Sophiology), in *Put'*, Vol. XVI (May, 1929), pp. 95-99.

"Jean Wahl. Le Malheur de la conscience dans la philosophie de Hegel," in *Put'*, Vol. XVIII (June, 1929), pp. 104-107.

"Drevo zhizni i drevo poznaniya" (The Tree of Life and the Tree of Knowledge), in *Put'*, Vol. XVII (September, 1929), pp. 88-106.

"Novaya kniga o Yakove Beme" (A New Book on Jakob Boehme), in *Put'*, Vol. XVIII (October, 1929), pp. 116-122.

"A. K. Gornostaev. Rai na zemle" (A. K. Gornostaev. Paradise on Earth), in *Put'*, Vol. XIX (December, 1929), pp. 114-116.

"Iz etyudov o Ya. Beme. Etyud I. Uchenie ob ungrunde i svobode" (From the Sketches on J. Boehme. Sketch I. Teaching on Ungrund and Freedom), in *Put'*, Vol. XX (Febuary, 1930), pp. 47-49.

"Friedrich Karl Schuman. Der Gottesgedanke und der Zerfall der Moderne," in *Put'*, Vol. XX (March, 1930), pp. 113-116.

"Iz etyudov o Ya. Beme. Etyud II. Uchenie o sofii i androgine. Ya. Beme i russkiya sofiologicheskiya techeniya (From the Sketches on J. Boehme, Sketch II. Teachings on Sophia and Androgynous. J. Boehme and Russian Sophiological Currents), in *Put','* Vol. XXI (April, 1930), pp. 34-62.

"Pamyati Kn. G. N. Trubetskogo" (In Memoriam, Prince G. N. Trubetskoy), in *Put'*, Vol. XXI (May, 1930), pp. 94-96.

"Vostok i Zapad" (The East and the West), in *Put'*, Vol. XXIII (September, 1930), pp. 97-109.

"E. Brunner, Gott und Mensch," in *Put'*, Vol. XXIV (September, 1930), pp. 122-124.

"Spor ob antroposifii" (The Controversy on Anthroposophy), in *Put'*, Vol. XXV (December, 1930), pp. 105-114.

"Paradoksy svobody v sotsialnoi zhizni" (The Paradox of Freedom in Social Life), in *Novy Grad*, Vol. I (January, 1931), pp. 3-15.

"V zashchitu A. Bloka" (In Defense of A. Blok), in *Put'*, Vol. XXVI (February, 1931), pp. 109-113.

"Asmus. Otcherki istorii dialektiki v novoi filosofii" (Asmus.

Sketches on the History of Dialectics in the New Philosophy), in *Put'*, Vol. XVII (May, 1931), pp. 108-112.

"Emanuel Berl. Mort de la morale bourgeoise," in *Put'*, Vol. XXVIII (June, 1931), pp. 80-92.

"Literaturnoie napravlenie i 'sotsialnyi zakaz'" (The Literary Trends and the "Social Requirement"), in *Put'*, Vol. XXIX (September, 1931), pp. 80-92.

"Pravda i lozh kommunizma" (The Truth and Lie of Communism), in *Put'*, Vol. XXX (October, 1931), pp. 3-34.

"Utopia Come True," in *Living Age*, Vol. CCCXLI (October, 1931), pp. 155-158.

"O gordosti smirennykh" (On the Pride of the Humble), in *Put'*, Vol. XXXI (December, 1931), pp. 70-75.

"Psychology der Russischen Gottlosigkeit," in *Hochland*, Vol. XXIX (May, 1932), pp. 440-444.

"Khristianstvo pered sovremennoi sotsialnoi deistvitelnosti" (Christianity and Contemporary Social Reality), in *Put'*, Vol. XXXI (February, 1932), pp. 45-55.

"Pages choisies du P. Laberthonnière," in *Put'*, Vol. XXXII (March, 1932), pp. 103-105.

"General'naya liniya sovyetskoy filosofii i voinstvuyushchii ateism" (The General Line of the Soviet Philosophy and the Militant Atheism) in *Put'*, Vol. XXXIV (July, 1932), pp. 1-28 (supplement). Translated "The General Line of Soviet Philosophy," in *The End of Our Time* (London: Sheed and Ward, Inc., 1933).

"Dukhovnoie sostoyanie sovremennago mira" (The Spiritual State of the Modern World), in *Put'*, Vol. XXXV (September, 1932), pp. 65-68.

"Garrigou-Lagrange. La Providence," in *Put'*, Vol. XXXV (October, 1932), pp. 97-99.

"Dva ponimaniya Khristianstva" (Two Understandings of Christianity), in *Put'*, Vol. XXXVI (November, 1932), pp. 17-43.

"Comte Hermann de Keyserling. Meditation Sud-Américaines," in *Put'*, Vol. XXXVI (December, 1932), pp. 89-93.

"N. A. Setnitskiy. O poslednem ideale" (N. A. Setnitsky. On the Ultimate Ideal), in *Put'*, Vol. XXXVI (December, 1932), pp. 93-95.

"Chelovyek i mashina. Problema sotsiologii i metafisziki tekniki" (Man and Machine. The Problems of Sociology and Metaphysics of Technique), in *Put'*, Vol. XXXVIII (January, 1933), pp. 3-37.

"Martin Buber" (Martin Buber), in *Put'*, Vol. XXXIX (February, 1933), pp. 87-91.

Zhurnal "Esprit" i dukhovno-sotsialnia iskaniya frantsuzkoy molodeji (The magazine "Esprit" and the Spiritual and Social Search of the French Youth), in *Put'*, Vol. XXXIX (March, 1933), pp. 78-82.

"Schmidhauser. Der Kampf um das geistige Reich," in *Put'*, Vol. XL (April, 1933), pp. 66-70.

"Herring. Dieu et César," in *Put'*, Vol XL (May, 1933), pp. 7-72.

"Christianity and Communism," in *Commonweal*, Vol. XVIII (September, 1933), pp. 440-442.

"The Bourgeois Spirit," in *Dublin Review*, Vol. CXCIII (October, 1933), pp. 169-180.

"General Line of Soviet Philosophy," in *American Review*, Vol. I (October, 1933), pp. 536-559.

"Mnogobozhie i natsionalizm" (Polytheism and Nationalism), in *Put'*, Vol. XLIII (January, 1934), pp. 3-16.

"Poznanie i obshchenie" (Knowledge and Communication), in *Put'*, Vol. XLIV (April, 1934), pp. 44-49.

"Komediia pervorodnago griekha" (The Comedy of the Original Sin), in *Put'*, Vol. XLIV (June, 1934), pp. 68-72.

"Metamorphosis of Marxism," in *American Review*, Vol. III (September, 1934), pp. 401-515.

"Man, the Machine, and the New Heroism," in *Hibbert Journal*, Vol. XXXIII (October, 1934), pp. 76-89.

"O Khristianskom pessimizme i optimizme" (On Christian Pessimism and Optimism), in *Put'*, Vol. XLVI (January, 1935), pp. 31-36.

"Young France and Social Justice," in *Dublin Review*. Vol. CXCVI (January, 1935), pp. 37-46.

"Can Man Survive? I. The Breakdown of the Humanistic Theory of Progress," in *The Living Church*, Vol. XCII (January, 1935), pp. 97-99.

"Can Man Survive? II. The Decadence of Liberty," in *The Living Church*, Vol. XCII (February, 1935), pp. 133-135.

"Kto takoe cheloviek?" (What is Man?), in *Put'*, Vol. LXVII (April, 1935), pp. 86-89.

"Personalizm i Marksizm" (Personalism and Marxism), in *Put'*, Vol. XLVIII (June, 1935), pp. 3-19.

"Russkiy dukhovny renessans nachala XX vyeka i zhurnal 'Put'"

(Russian Spiritual Renaissance of the beginning of the 20th Century and the Magazine 'Put'), in *Put'*, Vol. XLIX (September, 1935), pp. 3-22.

"Dukh velikago inkvizitora" (The Spirit of the Great Inquisitor), in *Put'*, Vol. XLIX (October, 1935), pp. 72-82.

"Uchenie o perevoploshchenii i problema chelovyeka" (The Teaching on Incarnation and the Problem of Man), in *Pereselenie dush* (October, 1935), pp. 9-15.

"O religioznom sotsializme" (Religious Socialism), in *Put'*, Vol. XLIX (November, 1935), pp. 86-91.

"Destin de l'homme dans le monde actuel," in *Revue Politique et Littéraire*, Vol. LXXIV (January, 1936), pp. 73-78.

"Lev Shestov" (Leo Shestov), in *Put'*, Vol. L (April, 1936), pp. 50-52.

"Pamyati Georgiya Ivanovicha Chelpanova" (To the memory of George Ivanovich Chelpanov), in *Put'*, Vol L (April, 1936), pp. 56-57.

"I. N. Danzas. L'itinéraire religieux de la conscience russe," in *Put'*, Vol. LI (May, 1936), pp. 53-65.

"War and the Christian Conscience," in *The Living Church*, Vol. CXIV (May, 1936), pp. 621-623.

"Christian Optimism and Pessimism," in *Christendom* (Spring, 1936), pp. 417-427.

"Neogumanism, Marksizm, i dukhovniya tsennosti" (Neo-Humanism, Marxism, and Spiritual Values), in *Sovremenniya Zapiski* (September, 1936), pp. 7-16.

"Is Russia Going Fascist?" in *Christian Science Monitor* (February 17, 1937), pp. 1-2.

"Ortodoksiya is chelovyechnost" (Orthodoxy and Humanity), in *Put'*, Vol. LIII (April, 1937), pp. 53-65.

"Pamyati Andreya Fedorovicha Karpova" (To the Memory of Andrew F. Karpov), in *Put'*, Vol. LIV (May, 1937), pp. 72-73.

"Kirche, Volk und Staat. Stimmen aus der Deutschen Evangelischen Kirche zur Oxforder Weltkirchenkonferenz," in *Put'*, Vol. LIC (May, 1937), pp. 74-76.

"Chelovyecheskaya lichnost i sverkhlichnya tsennosti" (Human Personality and Supra-Human Values), in *Personalism* (May, 1937), pp. 27-35.

"The Crisis of Christianity," in *Christendom*, Vol. II (Spring, 1937), pp. 228-240.

"O fanatizme, ortodoksii i istine" (On Fanaticism, Orthodoxy

357

and Truth), in *Russkiya Zapiski* (September, 1937), pp. 12-23.

"Khristianstvo i antisemitizm" (Christianity and Anti-Semitism), in *Put'*, Vol. LVII (April, 1938), pp. 3-25.

"Spiritual Dualism and Daily Bread," in *American Scholar*, Vol. VII (April, 1938), pp. 223-229.

"Crime of Anti-Semitism," in *Commonweal*, Vol. XXIX (April, 1938), pp. 706-709.

"J. Grenier. Essai sur l'esprit d'orthodoxie," in *Put'*, Vol. LVII (May, 1938), pp. 84-86.

"Fatality and Faith," in *Christian Century*, Vol. 56 (May 10, 1939), pp. 603-604.

"O sovremennom natsionalizme" (On the Contemporary Nationalism), in *Russkiya Zapiski* (September, 1938), pp. 23-31.

"Marx Versus Man," in *Religion in Life*, Vol. VII (Autumn, 1938), pp. 483-496.

"Pravomyslie i svobodomyslie" (The Right Thinking and the Free Thinking), in *Russkiya Zapiski* (November, 1938), pp. 17-23.

"Osnovnaya ideya filosofii L. Shestova" (The Basic Idea of the Philosophy of L. Shestov), in *Put'*, Vol. LVIII (January, 1939), pp. 44-48.

"Pamyati papy Piya XI" (In Memoriam, Pope Pius XI), in *Put'*, Vol. LIX (March, 1938), pp. 55-56.

"Kristianstvo i sotsialnyi stroy" (Christianity and the Social Order), in *Put'*, Vol. LX (September, 1939), pp. 33-36.

"The Paradox of Falsehood," in *Christendom* (Autumn, 1939), pp. 494-501.

"S. Frank. Nepostizhimoye" (S. Frank. The Inconceivable), in *Put'*, Vol. LX (October, 1939), pp. 65-67.

"Voyna i eskhatologiya" (War and Eschatology), in *Put'*, (December, 1939), pp. 3-14.

"Attitudes Toward the Revolution," in *Commonweal*, Vol. XLII (September, 1945), pp. 570-572.

"The Crisis of European Consciousness," in *The Living Church*,

"Le sens de l'act créateur," in *Esprit* (August, 1948), pp. 179-194.

"La transformation du Marxisme en Russie," in *Esprit* (August, 1948), pp. 195-206.

"The Spiritual State of the World Today," in *Religion in Life*, Vol. XVII (Autumn, 1948), pp. 503-516.

"N. F. Fedorov," in *Russian Review*, Vol. IX (April, 1950), pp. 123-130.

II. Works about Berdyaev

Allen, E. *Freedom in God: A Guide to the Thought of Nicolas Berdyaev* (London: Hodder & Stoughton, n. d.).

————. "Nicolas Berdyaev," in *Contemporary Review,* Vol. CLXXXVI (August, 1954), pp. 94-97.

Anonymous. "Berdyaev, Orthodox Religious Philosopher, Dies in Paris," in *The Living Church,* Vol. CXVI (April 4, 1948), p. 8.

Archambault, P. "Le drame de la liberté dans la philosophie de Berdiaeff," in *Politique,* Vol. XI (February, 1937), pp. 123-143.

Aubrey, E. "The Philosophy of Nicolai Berdyaev," in *Theology Today,* Vol. IV (January, 1948), pp. 522-533.

Braybrooke, N. "Significance of Berdyaev," in *Catholic World,* Vol. CLXXIV (October, 1951), pp. 47-51.

————. "Berdyaev, Christianity, and Anti-Semitism," in *Catholic World,* Vol. 179 (April, 1954), pp. 12-15.

Bourke, V. "The Gnosticism of N. Berdyaev," in *Thought,* Vol. XI (December, 1936), pp. 409-422.

Clarke, O. F. "Nicolai Berdyaev 1874-1948," in *Current Religious Thought,* Vol. VII (April, 1948), pp. 7-10.

————. *Introduction to Berdyaev* (London: Geoffrey Bles, 1950).

Coates, J. "Nicolas Berdyaev," in *The Congregational Quarterly,* Vol. XXIX (July, 1951), pp. 21-223.

Coleman, A. "Berdyaev on Human Destiny," in *Queen's Quarterly,* Vol. LII (August, 1945), pp. 299-310.

Davy, M. M. "Nicolas Berdiaeff," in *Esprit,* No. 147 (August, 1948), pp. 162-177.

Dalton, W. *The Doctrine of Man as Interpreted by Reinhold Niebuhr, Jacques Maritain, and Nicolas Berdyaev* (Th. D. Dissertation, Pacific School of Religion, 1954).

Delasalle, J. "Cinq méditations sur l'existence," in *Revue de Philosophie,* Vol. VII (1937), pp. 56-68.

Fedotov, G. "Nicolas Berdyaev as Thinker," in *The Living Church,* Vol. CXVII (September, 1948), pp. 15-24.

Fenn, E. "Nicolas Berdyaev—Lover of Wisdom," in *The Frontier,* Vol. II (April, 1952), pp. 148-160.

Heinemann, F. *Existentialism and the Modern Predicament* (New York: Harper and Brothers, 1953).

Hoffman, R. "Nicholas Berdyaev's Philosophy of History," in *American Review,* Vol. VIII (December, 1936), pp. 151-163.

Inge, W. B. "The Philosophy of Berdiaeff," in *Philosophy,* Vol. XXI (November, 1946), pp. 195-204.

———. "Russian Theology," in *Hibbert Journal,* Vol. LI (January, 1953), pp. 107-122.

Kennedy, P. *A Philosophical Appraisal of the Modernist Gnosticism of Nicholas Berdyaev,* (Ph.D. Dissertation, St. Louis University, 1936).

Lampert, E. "Nicolas Berdyaev," in *Modern Christian Revolutionaries,* Donald Attwater, ed. (New York: The Devin-Adair Company, 1947), pp. 309-390.

Munzer, E. "Nicolas Berdyaev," in *The University of Toronto Quarterly,* Vol. XIV (Spring, 1945).

Phytian-Adams, W. "Thought and Significance of N. Berdyaev" in *Church Quarterly Review,* Vol. CXXVI (July, 1938), pp. 245-268.

Porret, E. *Nicolas Berdiaeff et la philosophie religieuse Russe du XIXe siècle* (Neuchatel, 1936).

———. "La philosophie sociale de Nicolas Berdiaeff," in *Christianisme social,* Vol. LI (July, 1938), pp. 16-30.

———. *La philosophie chrétienne en Russie: Nicolas Berdiaeff* (Neuchatel: Editions de la Baconnière, 1944).

———. *Berdiaeff, prophète des temps nouveaux* (Neuchatel: Delachaux & Niestlé S. A., 1951).

Pouch, E. "Un gnostique moderne: Nicolas Berdiaeff," in *Foi et Vie,* n. 99-100 (1938), pp. 184-199.

Prunet, O. "Les grands thèmes de l'éthique de Berdiaeff," in *Revue d'Histoire et de Philosophie Religieuses,* Vol. 32 (1952), pp. 266-281.

Reymond, A. "Les caractères de la philosophie russe d'après Nicolas Berdiaeff," in *Revue de Théologie et de Philosophie,* Vol. XXXIV (April-June, 1946), pp. 89-90.

Rowell, E. "Meditation on Berdyaev's Three Times," in *Hibbert Journal,* Vol. XLVIII (April, 1950), pp. 252-256.

Schimanski, S. "Nicolas Berdyaev," in *Hibbert Journal,* Vol. XLVI (July, 1948), pp. 312-314.

Seaver, G. *Nicolas Berdyaev, An Introduction To His Thought* (New York: Harper & Brothers, 1950).

Shestov, L. "Nikolai Berdyaev" (Nicolas Berdyaev), in *Sovremenniya Zapiski* (1938).

Spinka, M. "Oirigen and Berdyaev: a Comparison," in *Church History,* Vol. 16 (March, 1947), pp. 3-21.

———. "Berdyaev's Critique of Communism," in *International Review of Missions,* Vol. 37 (July, 1948), pp. 264-272.

———. *Nicolas Berdyaev: Captive of Freedom* (Philadelphia: The Westminster Press, 1950).

———. "Nicholas Berdyaev," in *Christianity and the Existentialists,* Carl Michalson, ed. (New York: Charles Scribner's Sons, 1956).

Tillich, P. "Nicholas Berdyaev," in *Religion in Life,* Vol. VII (Summer, 1938), pp. 407-15.

Warren, A. "A Note on Nicholas Berdyaev," in *American Review,* Vol. V (1935), pp. 322-328.

Wieman, H. "Two Ways of Salvation: Berdyaev and Macmurray," in *Journal of Social Philosophy,* Vol. IV (1939), pp. 341-351.

Williams, B. *Berdyaev's Philosophy of History* (Ph.D. Dissertation, Boston University Graduate School, 1949).

Acknowledgment. For the order and classification of the four Western ethical traditions, Part II, Chapter IV, I am indebted to my teacher and friend, Professor Robert Elliot Fitch, Dean of the Pacific School of Religion, Berkeley, California.

INDEX

Abel, 285
Abraham, 285
Alexander, 44, 111, 279
Amos, 285
Anaximander, 188, 257, 258
Anderson, Paul, 123
Apollinarius, 196
Aquinas, Thomas, 156, 163-4, 172, 224, 276
Aristippus, 236, 237, 238
Aristotle, 156, 164, 171-2, 177, 186, 188-9, 224, 232-3, 258-9, 273, 275
Augustine, Saint, 12, 46, 157, 163, 182-3, 184, 185, 186, 284-5, 309
Aulén, Gustaf, 213

Bach, 277
Bacon, 276
Bakunin, 46
Balzac, 46
Barth, Karl, 135, 141, 156, 193
Batu, 16
Baudelaire, 80
Bebel, August, 69
Belinsky, 22
Bely, Andrey, 80f.
Bentham, Jeremy, 236, 237
Berdyaev, Alexander, 43
Berdyaev, Lydia, 144
Berdyaev, Mikhail N., 42
Bergson, 23
Bernard of Clairvaux, 276
Blake, William, 295
Blok, Alexander, 80
Bloy, Leon, 284

Heroclitus, 188, 257-8
Herren, 46
Hesiod, 188
Hobbes, Thomas, 236, 239, 240, 241, 244
Hoffmann, 46
Homer, 188
Hosea, 285
Huss, 276
Huxley, 313

Ibsen, 46, 61, 79
Igor, 10
Isaac the Syrian, 92
Isaiah, 285
Ivan, III, 18, 19
Ivan the Terrible, 19, 20
Ivanov Vyacheslav, 75, 80, 81, 82, 92, 116

James, William, 295
Jaspers, 157
Jeremiah, 285
Jesus Christ, 69, 195ff, 285, 290, 296, 297, 302, 304, 305, 306, 308
Joachim of Floris, 276
Job, 46
John of the Cross, 295
Jones, Rufus M., 295
Joseph, father of Jesus, 285

Kamenev, 118
Kant, 46, 51, 58, 69, 80, 128, 168, 220, 234, 235-36
Kartashov, Anton, 81
Katamenkov, 42
Kautsky, Karl, 61, 69
Kerensky, 105, 117
Keyserling, Count Hermann, 123
Khomyakov, 22, 23, 24, 25, 26, 76, 79, 92, 292
Kierkegaard, 95, 157, 186, 292
Kireyevsky, Ivan, 22, 79
Klyutchevsky, 3
Knudson, 182

Kudoshev, Princess, 43, 44
Kullman, 123

Laberthonniere, Abbé, 141
Lampert, Evgeny, 299-301
Lange, F. A., 60, 61
Lasso, Orlando, 277
Lawrence, Brother, 89, 295
Lecerf, Auguste, 141
Leibnitz, 187, 276
Lelbknecht, Wilhelm, 69
Lenin, 71, 72, 102
Leonardo, 276
Leontyev, 46, 76
Lincoln, Abraham, 1
Lormontov, 21, 46
Locke, 277
Logvinsky, David, 53, 54
Lomonosov, Michael, 21
Lowry, Donald, 123
Lucretius, 259
Lunstcharsky, 54, 58f., 59, 63, 116
Lvov, Prince, 105
Luther, 163, 185, 186, 224, 227-8, 276, 309

Machiavelli, 239
Malroux, André, 141
Marcel, Gabriel, 141, 157
Marcion, 93
Marcus Aurelius, 234, 259
Maritain, Jacques, 141, 156
Martov, 71, 72
Massignon, 141
Marx, Karl, 46, 53, 55, 65, 69-72, 86, 107-108, 130, 131, 174, 223,
    262-3, 264-7
Menzhinsky, 118
Merezhkovsky, 79, 81, 88, 89-90, 91, 92
Micah, 285
Michelangelo, 277
Mikhailovsky, 22, 54
Miliukov, Paul, 72